The Chicano/Latino Literary Prize

An Anthology of Prize-Winning Fiction, Poetry, and Drama

EDITED, WITH AN INTRODUCTION,
BY STEPHANIE FETTA

Arte Público Press
Houston, Texas

RCV

181730641

The Chicano/Latino Literary Prize. An Anthology of Prize-Winning Fiction, Poetry, and Drama is made possible in part from grants from the city of Houston through the Houston Arts Alliance, the University of California at Irvine Chicano/Latino Literary Prize, and by the Exemplar Program, a program of Americans for the Arts in Collaboration with the LarsonAllen Public Services Group, funded by the Ford Foundation.

Recovering the past, creating the future

Arte Público Press
University of Houston
452 Cullen Performance Hall
Houston, Texas 77204-2004

Cover art by Alfredo Arreguín, "Los muertitos, 2004"
Cover design by Exact Type

The Chicano/Latino Literary Prize: An Anthology of Prize-Winning Fiction, Poetry, and Drama / Edited, with an introduction, by Stephanie Fetta.
    p. cm.
Includes bibliographical references and index
ISBN: 978-155885-511-3 (alk. paper)
    1. American literature—Hispanic American authors. 2. American literature—Mexican American authors. 3. American literature—20th century. 4. Hispanic Americans—Literary collections. 5. Mexican Americans—Literary collections. I. Fetta, Stephanie.

PS508.H57C47 2008
810.8'0868—dc22

                      2007047389
                      CIP

8 9 0 1 2 3 4 5 6 7   10 9 8 7 6 5 4 3 2 1

This book is dedicated to Juan Villegas,
founder and consistent supporter of the Chicano/Latino Literary Prize.

TABLE OF CONTENTS

PREFACE

The problem with being given a project like this one is no one is quite sure what to expect really. It took me a while to figure out how I was going to edit an anthology with an incomplete set of winning entries. And how to navigate without access to full texts. Or that I'd play sleuth to hunt down texts and authors, some of whom were never to be found, and others who sadly decided not to include their important works in the anthology after all. Then the technical challenges emerged. There was the scanning mess, yellowed texts filled with difficult-to-identify computer language garble that had to be standardized, letter by letter, space by space. By necessity, this project taught me a bit about the work of literary historians, and gave me a new level of appreciation for the tedious technical work of producing a book. The anthology turned into an enterprise, but was well worth the effort.

The experience as a literary critic was different than I had imagined. Once I amassed the texts that I was to evaluate, initially some of the texts seemed somewhat dated to me. At times I found it challenging to work through my own biases in order to identify and appreciate the cultural work done by each piece in this book. Later, I realized I had underestimated the complexity of these works, and many times became inspired by them. I began to understand my field much more deeply and I grew humbled. For this too, I am grateful. During this period, I bore two children in addition to the wonderful son I already had. My family grew. What a long road. The events of my life gave me time to think the texts through, and to make more thoughtful decisions. It became important to me to rethink standard editing criteria. As a result, I chose selections that would showcase the author's talent, or I selected the passage from which I gained insight into the real work of the piece, rather than follow convention. What I realized in the process is that each text of the anthology contributed to the bigger project of founding of an ethnic literature —a fascinating process to discern. Through all the twists and turns, I really appreciate how the project unfolded.

I would like to thank all those authors who were kind enough to allow their work to be reprinted here without economic compensation. In funding this project, the Department of Spanish and Portuguese of the University of California, Irvine, continues to demonstrate its commitment to the Chicana/o Latina/o community and I thank the department for this commitment and for entrusting me with this project. Likewise, the commitment of Nicolás Kanellos and Arte Público Press to these literatures goes without saying. Arte Público Press is a critical arm of dissemination of Chicana/o and Latina/o letters, but their work also gives our cultures a very rich and beautiful national face. I thank Arte Público's Marina Tristán for her vision of the anthology, and Gabriela Baeza Ventura for her work to make this into a book. My friends and colleagues have also been generous with their time and attention to this project. I received the extensive assistance of Fabio Chee who helped locate, copy, and scan most of the documents included. Saúl Jiménez who was originally appointed co-editor was really helpful in selecting many of the early entries. I appreciate the help of Ignacio López Calvo, José Guillermo Pastrano, Michelle Conboy, Lisa Pizula, and Xóchitl Morales, all of whom proofread parts of the manuscript. I thank all of them for their friendship and collegiality. I thank Fortunato Strumbo for his efforts, time, and spirit on this project which has redefined my definition of friendship. I thank the Chicano/Latino Literary Prize's founder Juan Villegas for commenting on the manuscript, and Jacobo Sefamí and María Herrera Sobek, for their support and long-standing belief in me. Alejandro Morales is the person to whom I am most grateful for recognizing what I have to offer and accepting my self-styled career. My love goes out to my three elf-size sages, my children, Max Emiliano, Leonardo, and Helena Rose, and to Farrokh, for loving me no matter what.

INTRODUCTION

FROM A POETICS OF CONTESTATION TO AN AESTHETIC OF AGENCY

The early Chicano Movement produced literary texts that tended to respond to issues of social and political oppression, of the reality of poverty, and of the desire to assert the paradigm of Chicano as a modality of social rehabilitation. Over the twenty-five years included in the anthology, we read of these concerns that have come to characterize what is thought of as Chicana/o and Latina/o (hereafter C/L) literatures, but we will also read something more. The texts anthologized here will show the reader that the scope of C/L literatures has always been broader, deeper, richer than what is often thought. The politicism of early works becomes more nuanced over time evolving from a "poetics of contestation" to an "aesthetic of agency." Nuanced, but not necessarily more subtle or effaced. The expression of contestation was often emphatically critical in tone and a declarative style fueled by outrage molded a poetics that characterized this type of writing. The move from a poetics to an aesthetic becomes evident when contrasting poetry like 1974-75 winner Rita Mendoza's "Ahí venimos"[1] with Alma Luz Villanueva's poetry of 1976-77, where political concerns move from the declarative form of indictment to an aesthetic that explores the political through the interior state of the Chicana subject. Mendoza's poem expresses clear political concerns of the movement era that become a call to action:

> Hey Chicano, ¿qué no miran que tienen que trabajar?
> A unirnos en el pleito para el saco no arrastrar.
> A juntarnos todo el bonche y peliar con el patrón.
> Sean trucha, no pendejos, no les den ya su pulmón!
> A enseñarle, que cabeza también nosotros tenemos.
> Hey, patrón, mucho cuidado, los Chicanos—ahí venimos. (1-6)

In contrast, the speaking voice's will to agency in Villanueva's poetry no longer bases itself in power relations between institutions and the community. Here, Villanueva develops an aesthetic that situates the poetic voice through its relation to the universe and simultaneously, through its earthy

---

[1] Mendoza was not located to secure permission to include her poems in the anthology.

feminine body, uncovers political agency from within itself. Both poets respond to the real constraints of their historical moment but respond with a different literary approach. The anthology provides a good diachronic data set to witness how the literatures move from a political poetic to an agential aesthetic. However, a diachronic analysis will resist facile conclusions as the work of Mendoza and Villanueva evidence. Those social and political issues that motivated the Chicano Movement and its letters are still with us, and therefore consistently present in the writings over the twenty-five year span of the anthology.

The project of this anthology was to collect and present the winning entries of the Chicano/Latino Literary Prize (hereafter CLLP) from the year of its inception, 1974, to its twenty-fifth anniversary, 1999. While the first-prize winners were to be the foundation of the anthology, the second- and third-prize winners as well as those texts that won honorable mention were also considered for inclusion. Selections were based on the aesthetic merit of the entry, and/or the history of the writer in question. The remarks below are written as a critical introduction to this anthology. For each text, the reader is given a synthesis, rather than a summary, of the complete text of which s/he will find an excerpt in the anthology. A critical perspective is also proposed as a way to understand how deeper arguments emerge of significant social and political significance through each text.

The beginnings of the anthology show an aesthetic and range of thematic concerns as evidenced by its first winner, Ron Arias's "The Wetback," and again, in the fifth year, with Helena María Viramontes's "Birthday." The variety of themes engaged challenges the assumption of C/L letters as simply a minor literature bound to political aims. Its aesthetic breadth trumps the position of literary critics who minimize, if not infantilize, Chicana/o and Latina/o writing as unsophisticated.[2] A picture forms from the anthology of a more complex and dynamic literature than the one sometimes thought of.

The anthology presents a diverse and thoughtful literature, a compendium of texts written by novices as well as some of the best-known Chicana/o and Latina/o writers. In fact, many of the pieces included here have been published as books, becoming foundational texts of the Chicana/o Latina/o canon, reprinted many times in as many venues. The contest has drawn texts what have become instant classics like Manuel Ramos's *The Ballad of Rocky Ruíz*, and the late Andrés Montoya's *The Iceworker Sings and Other Poems*. The anthology also presents texts of lesser-known authors that merit scholarly study. In this introduction, the texts are presented in chronological order and, where appropriate, are contextualized within the body of the author's

---

[2]Literary critics like Harold Bloom have criticized C/L literatures as too contingent on their historical condition, rather than writing their experience into more "universal" themes that make literary oeuvres. "If Chicano poetry is to survive its own Mexican heritage, then the poets will have to go beyond the constraints and repetitions of politics. Ideology at best can produce period-pieces, not poems" (2, *Hispanic-American Writers*, Philadelphia: Chelsea House, 1998).

work. The introduction gives particular critical attention to those texts that may only appear here,[3] and so their corresponding analyses are deliberately more extensive than those better-known texts that already enjoy significant bodies of critical study. It should be noted that most, but not all, of the winning entries are included in this anthology. Certain authors did not grant permission to reprint their entries or could not be located[4] which has sadly resulted in no entries for 1992-93.

GENRES

The selection chosen from each work depended upon the availability of original manuscripts. In the case of poetry, few complete manuscripts were available. Where collections were complete, a limit of four to five pages of poetry was put in place as a measure of consistency. In some instances, the type of poetry, like Juan Felipe Herrera's poems of 1978-79, where the rant stylizes the form, or in the case of Andrés Montoya's work that, to adequately convey its essence as a collection, the editor felt compelled to break the previously imposed limit and to extend the number of poems or pages included. In many cases, poems previously selected and printed in the contest's yearly publication were the only poems available for consideration, so they, by default, are again printed here. As an editor, this is not to suggest any disappointment. On the contrary, their original selection infers their merit. Collections of poetry are indicated by title whereas untitled poetry collections are simply referred to as "Poems."

The case of selecting excerpts from dramatic work was more strategic. Often in anthologies, the first act of a play is selected as standard to anthologize. Rather than take the conventional route of a comfortable read of introducing the plot and characters provided by the first scene or act while the brilliance of the writing goes un- or under-noted, here, I choose an excerpt that best demonstrates the author's talent.[5] The reader should therefore allow a moment to orient his/herself as the excerpt sometimes begins *in medias res*.

Short stories presented their own challenge given the condensed nature of the genre and the difficulty of extracting a section from a work that tends to explore a single aspect of the human condition in just a few pages. Among them, "shorter" short stories are printed in full while an excerpt from longer short stories was sufficient to demonstrate the writer's ability. For novels, this intention was easily achieved with the selection of a single chapter.

LANGUAGE

As the following will show, the CLLP has drawn writings that run the linguistic gamut. A critical study could be done on the range of multilingual

---

[3] Individual contest publications were difficult and sometimes were not located.
[4] An appendix of all winning entries between 1974 to 1999 is included to appreciate the scope of writers represented over the twenty-five years covered.
[5] Except in the case of Angelo Parra's *Song of the Coquí*, who selected his own excerpt.

expression alone found in the anthology. Most entries are written primarily in English, some exclusively in Spanish. Others code-switch between English and Spanish, while others insert sporadic Spanish phrases in an English text, and still others use some English phrases in a Spanish text. These works demonstrate multilingualism as a valuable aesthetic tool for these writers and shows the richness of our lived experience from which writers draw their literary sensibility. I object to graphically separating Spanish and Chicano words from English by conventions that would suggest a foreign quality to the experience expressed by these writers. As such, monolingual readers should expect to elaborate a context for themselves from which to gloss the meaning of certains words. It should be noted that those texts written exclusively in English or Spanish most likely will not be accessible to monolingual readers.

THE IMPORTANCE OF LITERARY CONTESTS

Even though some of the prominent C/L writers chose not to include their work in this anthology, the CLLP has helped promote a significant percentage of writers whose work has become part of the C/L canon. That is to say, the anthology demonstrates the importance of prizes and university backing in the authorization of marginalized voices. The Quinto Sol prize has proven this point well but the contests at the University of California, University of Notre Dame, University of New Mexico, and others have also laid significant groundwork in creating literary and intellectual space for these writings to develop into literatures. An appendix of all the CLLP's winners shows the extent of well-known C/L writers recognized by the University of California's contest.

LESSONS FROM THE ANTHOLOGY: THE INTRODUCTION

The anthology shows that, over time, a pact forms among and between C/L writers and their audiences. Writers begin to demonstrate a basis of mutual cultural intelligibility with their audiences. The case of theater demonstrates this point clearly. If we consider the actos of Teatro Campesino, it is important to recognize how much dramatic time was spent on instructing its audience on how to cognitively understand it; that it was a political theater hoping to inspire social action from its viewers, that the social problems that it sought to dramatize were to be type-cast as recognizable stock characters.[6] Teatro Campesino worked to create a cognitive register for what it was presenting as Chicano theater to its audiences. In the anthology, we see an evolution of this pact between drama and audience when we consider Josefina López's play, *Simply María or America's Dream*. Winner of the 1988-89 contest, López writes in set descriptions and dialogue that are impressionistic rather than realistic. The work of Teatro Campesino,

---

[6] As in the character of Miss JIM-in-ez, or the Latina who plays white in the play "Los vendidos," published by Teatro Campesino in 1971, and again in 1990 and 1994 by Arte Público P, Houston, TX.

that of many playwrights in between, and in fact, the totality of the cultural production of Chicana/o and Latina/o cultures from the 1960s through the cusp of the 1990s, allows López to write of random shouts of Los Angeles-street characters and know that her audience will understand that the shouts signify the shock of immigration and the deception with the American Dream. This impressionistic approach builds its communicability upon the didacticism of the work by Teatro Campesino and others, demonstrating the strengthening of a system of referenciality of C/L literatures within themselves and their audiences over time. López writes on the assumption that audiences—Chicana/o, Latina/o, and hegemonic alike—already understand the basic tenets of the enterprise of C/L literatures.

Over the course of the years, the reader will notice that certain symbols recur with enough frequency that a system of ethnic signs develops. Thinkers like William Boelhower (*Through a Glass Darkly: Ethnic Semiosis in American Literature*, New York: Oxford UP, 1986), describe such a system as an "ethnic encyclopedia" where this coding and auto-referentiality creates the parameters of how a particular ethnic population will articulate itself. Far from static, these signs are represented and renegociated as a dynamic of the individual writer, and his/her moment and place, in relation to the development of this canon. Angelo Parra's *Song of the Coquí* is a great example of this dynamic. Parra presents the coquí, the native Puerto Rican frog whose song typifies life on the island. When taken off the island, the coquí will not or cannot sing much like the protagonist in the play "Ray," a Latino in New York. Ray's internal dilemma of living between two cultures and not feeling really a part of either leads him to an uneasy, unsettled, indeterminate existence. The motif of the coquí is readily understood by the Puerto Rican community and probably by most of the Latino community in New York. Parra explains the motif for other audiences who are perhaps more familiar with Chicano nomenclature and less so with Puerto Rican or Nuyorican. This theme and its representation in the symbol of the coquí exemplifies the process of codification of how C/L writers construct their sensibility of ethnicity through symbols and figures to be understood by their readers as commonalities of their collective ethnic experience.

Another example of this production of signs is found in the figure of the loving, yet resentful, daughter who serves the male members in her family. Deborah Fernández Badillo's poems and Patricia Santana's *Motorcycle Ride on the Sea of Tranquility* show sexism, gender performance, and subordination as prevalent themes of C/L literatures. That these themes are constructed around the figure of a woman doing domestic work for the men of her family engages a bigger social issue of gender oppression, a definitive theme of Chicana and Latina literatures. The figure of the daughter depicted in this way also works to become a sign of the literatures themselves, as literatures with a primary feminist concern.

This system of signs broadens with time, and simply as a consequence of the amount of texts that will be written. But who is writing, or rather, whose writing will be allowed to be inscribed as C/L, will broaden too. The CLLP has sought to include a variety of voices within the Chicana/o and Latina/o communities—those who have been typically denied access and authority as writers, or those whose writing has been considered marginal within a "minor" literature. Here, I refer to lesbian and gay C/L writers, women writers who portray forbidden themes of feminine sexual desire and deviance, abusive mothering, as well as pinto poets, biracial themes, and themes and concerns of the Chicana/o and Latina/o middle-class. The anthology shows the expansion of what is to be considered thematically legitimate to the canon of C/L literatures by recognizing and thereby validating writing like Cherríe Moraga's[7] lesbian biracial poetry, Ana Castillo's[8] sensibility that may fall in the face of traditional notions of how a "Mexican" woman should be, Jack López's middle-class youth in Orange County, California, and Andrés Montoya's treatment of God and gang-banging. The anthology privies the reader to the appearance, validation, and incorporation of these voices that has opened up the thematic specificity of C/L letters as literatures.

In this anthology, we are presented with an opportunity to understand this group of writings in the process of forming literatures and literary canons, observing how they specify who, what, and how they will be. The perspective provided by the anthology is unique in that the reader is able to discern particular dynamics of canon formation as an outcome of the concerns of the literatures, but the reader can also witness this formation in relation and response to postmodernism and postcolonial theory; they too impel their implications into the processes of C/L canon formation. The observation that the thematic concerns and aesthetic treatment of these writings does not follow some kind of narrow linear development but seems to weave through and within demonstrates the literatures' postmodern reality. An example in the recurring image of the uneasy Chicano or Latino male in the writings from the 1970s through the 1990s responds to a contingent postcolonial reality that challenged many C/L males in the 1970s as it does today.

What is notable through reading the anthology is the professionalization of the writing, or the maturation of Chicana/o Latina/o letters, more than the expression of any particular writer. The texts begin to show an auto-referentiality to earlier texts and/or aesthetics that show these "minor" literatures taking on a life of their own with an organic logic and parameters of interest and intelligibility, an aesthetic sensibility in the process of establishing itself.

---

[7] The reader should note that Cherríe Moraga chose not to include her work in the anthology. Moraga won third place for poetry in 1987-88.

[8] Likewise, Ana Castillo declined to authorize the inclusion of her work in the anthology. Castillo won Honorable Mention for her poetry in 1976-77.

THE ENTRIES

"The Wetback," the first winning entry of the first contest of 1974-75, became part of Ron Arias's highly acclaimed novel *The Road to Tamazunchale* (1975). Influenced perhaps by Gabriel García Márquez's story, "El ahogado más bello del mundo," "The Wetback" both appropriates and parodies Latin American Magical Realism. In this Chicano tale, David, the beautiful corpse discovered by an urban Chicano community in a dry riverbed in a Los Angeles barrio, serves a similar role as Esteban does in Márquez's story. The fact that the body is brown and dead is oddly common in Chicana/o literature. Part of what is accomplished in the figure of the dead Chicana/o in society is the reduction of the Other as devoid of individuality, of humanity, of dignity, of worth.

Here, Arias co-opt the figure to reinscribe it with just the opposite set of characteristics in the vitality and freedom that David is ascribed with. As an exercise of agency in the ability to resignify its meaning, the community is fascinated with David's beauty and his imperviousness to the physical degradation of death. David conquers death in this manner and so upsets his assignation as a simple border casualty in reawakening a sense of dignity and potentiality in the community. A dead migrant would be considered a border blip from a hegemonic perspective, but for this community, the corpse is the screen onto which the town's people project their individual and collective fantasies.

The dead Chicana/o works at the level of symbol to consolidate the racialized social organization of the US capitalist system that sustains the unethical use of the migrant worker, enforces the worker's complicity with the system, and alienates the humanity of Chicana/o labor as disposable. Arias uses dark humor to criticize and subvert this ultimate idealization of white imperialist and racist fantasies of mastery and domination.

In the 1975-76 contest, well-known Chicana feminist literary critic Rosaura Sánchez fictionally explores a world of working-class Chicanos and Mexicans in unspecified urban and rural environments. Her winning collection of short stories "Transparencias" takes the form of unrelated vignettes that take the reader from an outhouse in a forgotten barrio outside of city limits to a Mexican fast-food production line where we witness the robotization of a Latino worker. Stylistically, Sánchez shows a sensibility to the age and circumstance of the vignette's particular speaker. She also varies the narration from the form of interior monologue to dialogue with equal finesse. Here, Sánchez, like Rolando Hinojosa Smith's Klail City Death Trip Series and others, the vignette is I argue a characteristic form of Chicana/o expression. Playing on Homi K. Bhabha's concept of the western narrative as the privileged literary form that defines and contains its subject within its discourse, the vignette contests the colonizer's demand of the colonized to reproduce her/himself in the narrative which would make her/himself knowable and manageable within the political economy of imperialism. From the kidnapping and death of a Latino baby to the narration of a young person's suicide, Sánchez's texts share underlying circumstances of the internally colonized, illustrating the grip of power of global capitalism on economically impoverished Chicanos and Mexicans in the United States.

Alma Luz Villanueva's collection is a poetic tour de force, garnering first prize in the 1976-77 contest. While many rightly compare her poetry to that of Pablo Neruda and Walt Whitman, Villanueva's Irvine collection later included in her collection *Bloodroot* (1977), should also be considered a treatise on Chicana feminism. The collection takes what heterosexist society might consider dirty little secrets of Chicana womanhood as her poetic *raison d'être*. The power of the female body is explored through various treatments on the menses, pregnancy, and heterosexual pleasure. Villanueva's poetry calls on women to remember their unique physical abilities traditionally revered in Indian societies and to reinscribe them as positive in our contemporary historical moment and place. Her poetry arises from her desire to valorize women in ways that Western society often demeans. The collection begins with an untitled poem which functions as a ritual invocation of a muse. Invoking her grandmother as muse challenges the traditional rhetorical device that bases itself on a heterosexual tension between male poet and female love object. Here, the figure of the grandmother as muse not only motivates the poet's writing, but much of the poetry explores the life the two shared of love and poverty. At the same time, the specificity of their relationship is calibrated by a persistent reference to the universal. Throughout the collection, the poetic I is also deeply embedded in her place within the cosmos. In this way, Villanueva understands women in relation to their particular circumstances within a celestial landscape.

Nedra Ruíz's poetry collection chosen for first prize in the 1977-78 contest takes the reader down a disparate path of poems. These poems create a syntactic and semantic journey that meanders from concrete experience to other realms of existence. The poetry becomes complicated when the ephemeral, the somatic, and the hallucinogenic form a second discursive realm interspersed with the first. Themes of writing, sexual desire, and altered psychological states create an imaginary baseline for the contemplation of landscape, everyday interactions, lost love, and human relations with inanimate objects. Ruíz's poetry boldly asserts an autonomous C/L feminine subject freeing herself from gendered social constraints. The social space into which she enters recognizes her fragmented self that she expresses as a dispersed subjectivity. Ruíz's poems rework the subject position of the Lacanian gaze where disjointed, incongruous objects of contemplation shatter into numerous subject positions of observation.

Juan Felipe Herrera's 1978-79 collection *Antiteatro y poemas* plays upon his experience in theater to put forth a unique theatrical poetry. Herrera's *antiteatro* erodes the barrier between written word and individual reception in a poetic discourse best described as a collaborative performance of "authors and creators" (25). His intention as prefaced in "Direction Notes" is to meld object with subject, the individual with the collective, not necessarily to eradicate their autonomy, but to unveil their continuity. Blue is the color that will visually stimulate this connectivity, and ultimately, blue will reveal the futility of the same in a depressive image that ends "La carta," an invisible jail cell of the mind too accustomed to its sociological incarceration to contemplate an escape. Technically, Herrera experiments with the theatrical in the future and imperative tenses, with verses directed to "tú" or "you," which work in "launching a vascular electricity" in order to "decipher the impossible" (25). In Brechtian fashion, Herrera highlights the formulaic devices of Western poetry when he includes the citational norm of the backslash to indicate verse in his drama and in some of his poems. Many of Herrera's poems such as "B Street Second Floor Mural / 14x14," "5x25 Mundo Mexicano Mural," and "Portrait of Woman in Long Black Dress/Aurelia" of which the first is included here, are ekphrastic, using paintings as the subject matter of poetry. These poems create an intense yet scant narrative line to the paintings Herrera contemplates, and, like his antitheater, the poems tend to view humans as solitary units compelled by the power of nature to commune. Yet, the subject and object are not able to recognize or find solace in their connection. They remain immune. Other poems like "Green," "Dudo las luces," and "La furia de las abejas" (the first included), combine dissonant images of the pressures of contemporary life. Here, people of color punctuate the cityscape as a bodily site of the grossest objectification while, ironically, colored people come to represent the possibility of salvation. In Herrera's poetry, the reader perceives the influence in style and intent of Federico García Lorca and Antonin Artaud. Like Lorca's *Poeta en Nueva York* in Herrera's poetry there is a surreal dynamic that removes the Western subject from its central position to focus on its tangential relation to others. Influenced by Artaud's "Theater of Cruelty," Herrera reveals global capitalism as a myopic form of oppression that mutates the cosmic order of things into a chaos of isolation and perversion.

The acclaimed writer Helena María Viramontes won first prize in 1978-79 for "Birthday," the short story of Alice, a young woman undergoing an abortion. Her mental anguish is lyrically presented as the story explores the social inscription of maternity on women as vessels of reproduction in opposition to the sentient, sexual woman that Alice knows herself to be. Ultimately, "Birthday" makes abortion the ironic process through which Alice rebirths herself. Along with the burden of making such a difficult choice, Alice also enjoys the newly discovered power that comes from determining her life's path. Viramontes presents sections that stylistically follow a stream of consciousness interspersed with third-person omniscient narration without remarking these transitions. These fluctuations become more complex with the temporal changes from past conversations to the present where Alice awaits an abortion in the clinic. Typographically, the story varies between the conventional presentation of text to sections written primarily in lower case with little punctuation, randomly adhering to standard English grammar. The structure of the story graphically manifests the conflict and emotional instability of the protagonist. "Birthday" was later revised and included in Viramontes's well-known short story collection *The Moths and Other Stories* (1985) and demonstrates her early interest in feminist issues as well as her unique ability with language.

Through the figure of the agricultural field worker, the theme of global capitalism is also explored in David Nava Monreal's 1979-80 first-prize novel, "A Pastoral Tale." The story follows the lives of Rosa Ramírez and Raúl Nava, a young couple who begins their courtship in the fields as migrant workers, and then during their married life, ascend to the middle class. While the first half of the story sets the stage for a tale seemingly uncritical of its suppositions, the title is an ironic indication of the adversity to come. The subsequent reversal in the second half of the story is foreshadowed in the opening scene of Raúl and his best friend, Jorge. The pride Raúl feels in owning a humble dwelling foments a desire in Raúl to attain the American Dream of economic prosperity. This desire to climb the social ladder will be Raúl's proverbial Achilles' heel that will find Raúl, Rosa, and their son Miguel, dead at the story's end. Thematically, "A Pastoral Tale" demonstrates how cultural assimilation can exact and deteriorate one's sense of self. Monreal plays with the convention of the pastoral that normally romanticizes the countryside in the eyes of the jaded or cynical, yet sophisticated, urban poet. Here, the countryside and the simple life of migrant laborers ironizes the convention of the locus amoenous characteristic of the pastoral. The fragile life of the undocumented worker finds little respite in arduous manual labor or life in a shanty. Ultimately, the convention of the traditional pastoral is upset and laid bare by the perspective of Chicana/o fieldworkers and the project of assimilation. Monreal's "A Pastoral Tale" denaturalizes and denationalizes the American countryside to expose it as a site of international movement, oppression, and containment of Mexican bodies who perform stoop labor for capitalists.

Rubén Medina's first-prize poetry collection of 1979-80 also concerns the plight of laborers and uses nature to reveal the true state of the human spirit. In "Danzón," Papá's infidelities and Mamá's misery were like those Sundays when Papá would take the kids to play baseball before heading off to meet up with his mistresses. Once the beautiful grass that comforted falls, now has become the visual vantage point of the depressed speaker. In Medina's poetry, nature entices human connection and nurturance, but in the last instance, nature becomes a metaphor for human deception. The second poem

"Lluvia" uses a thunderstorm to express the speaker's tender knowing of his beloved Abuela. Thunderstorms that often disrupt daily life force the child and his grandmother indoors. In images that meld Grandma's power to calm with the sun that will come out (39), Grandma is the figure who is able to manage the disruptive force of nature, the spirit world, and their impact on a vulnerable little boy. The third poem "Day-Off" speaks bitterly of domestic labor and the contrasts in lifestyle that forces a juxtaposition between differing economic classes. Leisure time for the worker is the possibility of being with one's true self outside the system of labor where a graduated depth of color—be it phenotypic or cultural—often influences economic rank. On his day off, the house servant can become the artist or the fisherman, the lover of poetry, the friend, in union with the earthly delight of a cup of coffee, the bird's song, the sweet murmur of the elderly. This weekly refuge of the true self on his day off returns in the penultimate stanza with a pledge to remember that each worker will be redeemed in the many "days off" to come. Stylistically, Medina's poetry is narrative in tone and expressed in free verse with lengthy stanzas where nature is the allegorical prism for human relations.

Juan Manuel Bernal's first-prize winning poetry entry *Confesiones de un seudopoeta: digresiones de un demente* of 1980-81 opens with a self-reflexive piece called "Él y yo" that establishes two competing internal voices of the speaker. The voice addressed as "yo" is an unassuming Chicano youth who suffers from loneliness, while "él" is a sociable college student who enjoys extensive knowledge of language and literature. This duality of the speaker is played out in the body of the work where intermittently "yo" will appear, or "tú" will be addressed. The verses directed to the reader in first-person singular and second-person singular responds to the central concern set up in the first entry—a view of the world where "[a]bsurdo hoy, absurdo ayer, absurdo mañana: absurdo siempre" (41). The thesis of the collection is expressed as the frustrated promise of modernity presented through the episteme of baroque Spanish literature, and contemporary Mexican literature. Supposing these particular genealogies the heritage of the Chicano voice, the voices of the speaker question the viability of the sociological enterprise of literature to represent human experience. Bernal stylizes classical figures and formal poetic registers with humor by interspersing free verse, dialogic form, and neologisms. His point is to juxtapose the modern legacy of history and high art with the social decay of not only today, but also of yesterday. The competing voices mock structures of hegemony such as the language and art, the artificial imposition of nations and nationality, the rigidity of hegemonic language, the hypocrisy of middle-class activists, and the tyrannical nature of many political organizations, including the Chicano Movement. Bernal's work veers on the edge of absurdism, an appropriate aesthetic to communicate the irrationality of modern life as a person of color under late capitalism.

Chicano detective novelist Michael Nava, tied for third prize in the 1980-81 contest, intimates the inner life of homoerotic love in his collection, "Sixteen Poems." The poetic voice emerges during silent moments of erotic tenderness. The poems "Long Distance," "For David," "The Lover," and "For W." demarcate the construction of physical, emotional, and psychological boundaries between the inside and outside. Love and sexual desire become emotive dynamics that challenge the authority of Western concepts of space and time. The poems entitled "Translations from Neruda" and "Translations from Rubén Darío" share the conjunction "from." "Of" would have suggested Nava as linguistic translator or interpreter of the poems whereas "from" proposes something different. Nava's own poetic sensibility concerned with chicanismo and queer loving are developed through his perspective of the work of Darío and Neruda, an interesting intertextual approach. Homoerotic love, time, and being are themes that Nava will explore again at book length such as in his 1992 detective novel, *The Hidden Law*.

Jesús Rosales, short story winner of the 1980-81 contest, divides "Parte del proceso" into three sections: "Tal vez al hablar más con ellos," "Imposible en el extranjero," and "Sin duda aquí." These titles are the first indicator of a narrative construction that challenges the formalistic notions of the genre of short story. Partial sentences that suggest conversational responses begin a dialogical narration of a young adult coming of age during his college years. For Latinos, the coordinates of this process are particular in the requirements of geographical movement, initiation rituals into the subculture as a young adult, the confrontation of the subject as Other, and in the negotiation of subjectivity in multiple spaces and registers. I argue for an understanding of a Latino Bildungsroman with this specificity.

The first part is made up of six stories that tell the tale of Alberto's trip to Mexico. Told in first person, the narrator changes unidentified and without contextualization. The geographical and cultural space of the mother country allows Alberto to ponder border architecture, the social structure of rural Mexico and who/how his father is Mexican. At the trip's end, Alberto returns to the university where he encounters the pressures and pleasures of college life for Chicanos in a Spanish department. The second part "Impossible en el extranjero" traces Alberto's tenure as an exchange student in Spain, an important element of the Latino Bildungsroman—the postcolonial fantasy of the return home. In a somber tone reminiscent of Carmen María Gaite's *El cuarto de atrás*, Alberto's presumed ethnic connection to Spain erodes into vignettes of isolation and disillusionment. The third part "Sin duda aquí" resituates Alberto at his American university, placed in a social milieu in which he is uncomfortable. While in this environment, Rosales's stories highlight ethnic and class differences within drug and music cultures, hallmarks of student life. As the title infers, this maze of events is critical in the trajectory to Latino adulthood as "parte del proceso." Rosales's Bildungsroman shares with many other Latino coming-of-age stories the specificity of this ethnically marked process.

Mary Helen Ponce won honorable mention in 1981-82 for her short story "Recuerdo: When Rito Died," that later became part of her autobiography, *Hoyt Street: An Autobiography* (1993). Melancholy marks the tone of her tale as she recounts the death of her brother, Rito. She describes this pivotal event of her childhood in Pacoima, California, as tender with love and kinship but stark with the silence of mourning. Her memories are rotund in scope. As she allows the reader entrance into the inner perceptions of a Chicana girlhood, the reader becomes privy to the difficulties of living between the interstices of race, gender, and class which are at times tragic, but which occur alongside inspired moments of love, compassion, and sometimes beauty. Ponce's "recuerdo" is almost ethnographic in the way that Pacoima, California, experienced Mexican immigration, and the ways that these immigrants interacted, negotiated and adopted Anglo-Euro culture as well as institutional cultures like the Catholic Church. True to Ponce's aesthetic of her autobiography, "When Rito Died" brings with it pulchritudinous sobriety.

Wilfredo Q. Castaño won first prize for his poetry collection called "Bone Games" in 1982-83. Castaño's poetry explores different vantage points from which to consider the possibility of innocence in modern day America. There is a tension between its minute expressions and an environment of cataclysmic decadence, evil, and decay in which they occur. The first poem "Dedications" exemplifies this dynamic found throughout the collection. It begins by describing a birth, a death, and sexual intercourse as specific on-the-edge-moments of life where the relative inability to control the body implies a moment of innocence. These moments are consecrated in an almost religious sense by a human "I" who is described as an eagle in flight that, as it peers down at the chaotic world, notices horrendous things, nonsensical things, and yet, wonderous things. When read in full, the three poems here elaborate an image of awakening to the reality of our contemporary world described as ". . . innocence / betraying itself and capitulating / to its own suicide, . . . " (63).

Jack López deals with the themes of friendship and recollection in his winning short story of 1982-83, "The Boy Who Swam With Dolphins." In this early work, López writes a fictional account of what he will later address in his autobiography, *Cholos and Surfers: A Latino Family Album* (1988). In "The Boy Who Swam With Dolphins," López looks at a Chicano middle-class adolescence experienced through the surf subculture of Southern California. The protagonist is a young Chicano intrigued by his interethnic experiences of "riding the waves" with Anglo-Euros and African Americans. The story's plot takes the reader on a surfing trip to Mexico with a group of friends, when one of its members becomes lost at sea. Eventually, the narrator sees the character Po Boy riding with dolphins on the Mexican coast. The scene is almost surreal when the narrator believes Po Boy has become a dolphin. López writes a touching and important story in its depiction of the surf sub-culture that allows for a particular intimacy among men and nature. In a broader sense, this story trumps the reductive notion of the inherent dominance of ethnicity in the conceptualization of the self to open up discursive space to explore other foundations of self.

Luis J. Rodríguez, author of the acclaimed *Always Running La Vida Loca: Gang Days in L.A.* (1994), took second place in the 1982-83 contest for his story "Sometimes You Dance With a Watermelon." Rosalba, a Mexican immigrant and mother, tells her story of misery and isolation in a shanty home in Los Angeles which she shares with her current husband, Pete, her twenty-four-year-old daughter, Sybil, Sybil's drug-addicted boyfriend, Stony, and her four children. The story plays upon the contrast between the sunny climate of Southern California—one of the wealthiest regions in the world—and the stark poverty of many of its residents; in this case, Mexicans and Chicanos living in an unincorporated area of Los Angeles County. Rosalba awakens to a glorious sunrise, sensitive to the hunger of Sybil's children. Frustrated, Rosalba thieves Stony's car to go downtown to find some way to earn a few dollars for food. Beaten down by an American life that has fallen short of the American Dream, Rosalba trudges forward, spirit unbroken, when she begins to dance in the middle of the hustle and bustle of downtown LA with a watermelon on her head, as she had done as a young woman in Oaxaca. The dance conjures smiles, applause, curiosity, and indifference, but she is momentarily freed from the juggernaut of racism, sexism, and classism that underlie her life circumstance. This story is a tribute and a celebration of people who refuse to surrender their true selves to a society that denies them their humanity.

The well-known poet Francisco X. Alarcón won the 1983-84 poetry contest for his collection "Tattoos." Alarcón's poetry instructs its reader on social issues and alternate realities manifest in a mostly bilingual format. Alarcón unveils the extent to which what we understand to be common notions are determined by a particular and pervasive viewpoint, or hegemony. He often gives his poems brief titles that evoke specific associations. These associations are then deconstructed and recontextualized in the body of the poem. Alarcón isolates a term and, with his rhythmic yet terse verses, he arrests a hegemonic subjectivity that lies at the base of our cultural cognition of the word, and its reflection of the world. In its place, Alarcón makes lyrical an alternate economy of meaning informed by racialization and oppression. The imagistic cadence of this dynamic is represented as light and shadow, or rather shadow and light. From the socially marked body of the speaker comes the darkness, but only as a shadow made from the light of his inner self. Graphically, Alarcón seldom capitalizes proper nouns which creates fluidity in his poetry, allowing the reader to take in the graphic form.

Through these processes of defamiliarization, Alarcón's "Tattoos" upsets a hegemonic mindset that presumes universal understanding and complicity.

In "Shadows on Ebbing Water," the Chicana detective fiction writer Lucha Corpi presents an interesting story of love, death, and birth that won first prize in the 1983-84 contest. Corpi deploys a double conversation—two voices in conversation unknowingly with one another—to structure her tale. The character Eva authors the first voice in a series of journal entries. Through these entries, Eva tries to piece together three unexpected events that have disrupted her life: the suicide of her beloved cousin Silvia; the riff between her and her husband Laz; and her unexpected pregnancy after fifteen years of marriage. The questions that Eva asks in her diary are inadvertently addressed by the second voice, the voice of Laz. These entries are interspersed without explanation by this second voice written in the form of a stream of consciousness, unconcerned with documenting complete thoughts. Instead, this voice gives the reader scant details that, when taken together, form a second narrative, the story of Laz's secret life. When Eva's long-lost cousin Silvia comes home to California, a type of love triangle is set in motion. Laz, Eva's husband, immediately senses a shared bond with Silvia founded on emotional grief and sorrow. The subtlety with which Corpi writes this story of a moment of re/cognition in a woman's life—of her true nature, of the ways she avoids pain, of her past naïveté—is most delightful for a reader who can savor the balmy, incandescent language and style that create a narrative that reads like "shadows on ebbing water."

Bilingual Review Press editor Gary D. Keller was given honorable mention in 1983-84 for his short story, "The Raza Who Won Big in Anáhuac." "El güero valín" or the "fair preppy" is the protagonist of this story of a Chicano's symbolic return to the country of his ancestors, Mexico. Once again, the theme of the return to origin is an important one for most immigrant populations in the United States, but it is particularly so for Chicana/o(s). Through the form of the Latino Bildungsroman, the acceptance of ethnic ambivalence seems a critical step in the formation of the Chicana/o adult subject. Keller's story is unique in the way he explores how the Chicano becomes a Pocho in a Mexican socioscape, drawing out the types of cultural capital as well as cultural deficit he is seen as possessing. "El güero valín" and his Mexican friend pretend common cultural space of Mexicanness to found a shared understanding that differential poverty will override, but to no avail. Keller, along with several other C/L writers, points to the reality of incommensurable differences that disrupt this postcolonial Chicano idealization. Keller writes with great wit and is especially adept at mixing registers of discourse with bilingualism and code-switching.

Deborah Fernández Badillo's 1984-85 collection of poetry points to her frustration with social roles that women play. In the first poem "Pinched Toes" the poetic voice comically complains about the demands on an exasperated mother, who is also a wife to a dependent husband, and a worker. These roles leave her no space for herself as an autonomous person. The image of the cheap shoes she must wear that painfully pinch her toes represent her frustration. "Soltera" also explores the theme of loss of self as a woman. Cloistered in her room, the voice is physically hemmed in and spiritually frustrated and disappointed. The poem calls out to God to recognize her true self, but this gesture seems doomed by the poem's end when we find the speaker under her bed, pounding her feet in desperation. The third poem "Terror Eye" moves from the collection's present to her girlhood past. In "Terror Eye," a friend and a friendship is torn asunder by domestic abuse, excising her old friend Tina from the power and freedom Tina used to express with the unadulterated laughter of her youth. Read in reverse order, the three poems point to a trajectory of a girl's passage from youth to adulthood. Even when humorous, this passage is pained, devoid of illusions. Badillo's poetry is narrative in tone with a cadence that conjures the poet's presence for the reader, like that of a performative monologue.

Juan Felipe Herrera wrote "Memoir: Checker-Piece," second-prize winner of 1984-85. This short story takes a critical look at the generation of Chicano students at the end of the Chicano Movement. The political battles of the movement are becoming innocuous expressions of "initiation rites" carried out with drugs, tortillas, and in the making of an obscure film. The subtitle "checker-piece" evokes the notion of everyman's game of strategy, but becomes more complicated in this story as a trope to tie architecture with the ultimate stagnation and unexpected gentrification of Chicano students. The narrator fixates on the homogeneity of the endless drone of LA houses that feel to him like a "checkered infinity" as does the endless drive down the highway. The sameness meets the sweltering heat of summer in inland Los Angeles to set the stage for the only element of contrast: a group of four Chicano university students meeting up to make a counter-culture 8mm film. While their presence and aims as Chicano activists of the 1970s could have undercut the pervasive sense of oppression of both the weather and the infrastructure of the city, these students' endeavor feels like more of a pop version of chicanismo made up of gesture and posturing. Herrera writes of the amusing side of chicanismo, but there is also a criticism of the devolution of the movement reaffirmed by the final image of the story: a beige checker-piece looms behind the vato-mobile "la cucaracha" under an oppressive sun, symbolizing the power of hegemony at isolating, and to perhaps a significant degree, domesticating student rebellion.

Margarita Luna Robles won second prize in 1984-85 for her short story, "Urbano: Letters of the Horseshoe Murder." Implicit in the title is the suggestion, if not the normality of, then the routine violence of modern urban life in the United States. The fact that "urbano" is written in Spanish suggests a specific ethnic context to this situation. It is an epistolary story followed by a dialogue. The correspondence suggests a murder and the primary suspect is a young gregarious gang member named Randy. Held in jail, the letters of his sorrowful mother, his girlfriends, and other friends inform the reader of social issues that come to make up the urban environment addressed in the title. Some of the themes treated include brown-on-brown crime, interracial romance, broken families, the situation of the single Latina mother, the problematic relationship between the police and people of color, the prison system, illegal substance abuse, and questions of gender. The text conveys a feeling of immediacy with the reader because of the genres used like the sudden dialogue of a police shooting at a barrio party. The seriousness of the scene trumps the levity of many of the letters communicating ultimately its depressing message of urban strife.

"Sunland" is the ironic title of Gloria Velásquez winning 1984-85 short story that tells multiple histories of a small town in the United States. Perhaps influenced in tone and structure by Gabriel García Márquez's *One Hundred Years of Solitude*, "Sunland" is the name of a village enshrouded in darkness. The obscurity creates an infertile environment, a metaphor for the social alienation and stagnation experienced by the town's people. The story begins with an unnamed female voice recounting the death of her grandmother and her estrangement from her husband. The narration turns to the family drama incited by the impending death of a neighbor, the elderly Doña Soledad. While the death of the narrator's grandmother, la Nana, is expressed with grief, and the intimate hole left by Nana's absence, the reader is brought into the physicality of Doña Soledad's agony. Culpable of neglect, the personal histories of Doña Soledad's trite children confront the emotional and practical difficulties of dealing with death. In contrast with la Nana, Doña Soledad's last days become the stage on which notions of life, family, and love display the disingenuousness of her progeny. The intrigue around Doña Soledad's moribund body plays on a deeper level as an allegory of the dark, barren, and dying town of Sunland. This story briefly mentions the year 1848—the end of the US-Mexican war—as the beginning of the period of physical darkness that slowly envelopes the Southwest and so alludes to the dark history of the conquest and subjugation of indigenous and mestizo peoples from the triumph of US imperialism in the Southwest to modern times. In just a few pages, "Sunland" weaves these themes concisely and dramatically with a kinesthetic language where humor counters the seriousness of the plot.

Gustavo Segade won first prize in 1985-86 for his poetry collection that, in three poems, traces a genealogy of his sense of becoming Chicano. "State of the Art" is the first poem where "Pain walks a long, winding, / bitter path to anger" (123), a physical and emotional condition that leads to social disconnection. The second poem turns the discussion from the path of pain, to pain management through marijuana, political activism—specifically the Chicano Movement—and through the escape of dreams, and insanity. But the experience produces the voice's politicization as a Chicano however little need he has for the term. The third poem "Crossing" analyzes the path back to Mexico, the "home country" where lack of familiarity, particularly in socio-economic forms of slum life and desperate labor, further alienates the poetic I from a sense of belonging. Segade employs Latin phrases and Greek figures to broaden the colloquial language of his poetry. Combining erudite references with Chicano themes seen more often beginning in the 1980s compels a broader level of literary authority and reflects the reach of these poets to scholars across disciplines.

First-prize winner of the 1986-87 contest, David Nava Monreal's play *Cellmates* explores the psychological underpinnings of a sexual oppressor. Set in a jail cell, Ray, an inmate, is confronted by Luke, an unexpected visitor to his cell. Their dialogue uncovers the patriarchal basis of Ray's peculiar nuclear family. Luke, like a Dickensesque ghost of the family's dysfunctional past, coerces Ray to tell his treacherous story of physical and psychological abuse of his lover, Doreen, and their daughter, Lolly. While the play establishes Ray as an exceptional male in a negative sense, this type of cruelty is not uncommon in American heterosexual relations, when ruled by asymmetrical power relations and limited emotional intelligence. *Cellmates* is most successful where it is critical—in the reconstruction of Doreen's suicide and in the homicide of their daughter as consequences of Ray's insecure role in the heterosexual family romance.

Carlos Morton, Professor of Drama and accomplished playwright, shows his predilection for reinterpreting European classics in his 1986-87 play *Johnny Tenorio*, third-prize winner. Here, Morton reinterprets the Don Juan Tenorio legend of the nineteenth century in a twentieth-century Chicano context. The plot consists of the ghost of Johnny who, unaware of his own death, returns to Big Berta's bar to relive his last moments but finds himself forced to confront his many peccadilloes as a philanderer. The play uses dramatic tenets from the traditional Spanish tale within a Chicano cultural frame. The Chicano adaptation of the play can be interpreted from different perspectives: a criticism of Chicano intergenerational heterosexism in the adoption and the perpetuation of the figure of Don Juan; or as an inadvertent capitulation to hegemonic stereotyping of Chicanos in the figure of the Latin lover, or worse, the mongrel. The scene included in the anthology consists of the climatic moment when Berta helps Johnny face his friend Louie, his wife Ana, and his father Don Juan. *Johnny Tenorio* captures the vibrancy of the Chicano community through Morton's wonderful use of language and humor with which important social issues are dramatized.

Well-known as a performance artist Carmen Tafolla shocks her reader into learning different truths to womanhood in her collection of poetry that won her first prize in the 1986-87 contest. In her poem "Hot Line," Tafolla reinterprets stretch marks caused by pregnancy as a physical palimpsest that allows her to remember and communicate with her deceased first-born. The reader's curiosity and pretension to understand such a loss is left hanging by the undisclosed circumstances of the baby's death. The structure of the stanzas imitates the lines on the speaker's body, the first verse being longer than the rest, the subsequent verses taking their own routes, as do stretch marks. And so, the poem twists and pulls at the reader, bringing into poetry the physicality of child-bearing, and the interconnectedness of the processes of giving life, living, and death. "Nine Moons Dark" follows the theme of maternity in a poem that juxtaposes a spiritual exploration of pregnancy in the Native Mexican tradition with the adoption industry, delineating how the forces of capitalism intersect with these processes, rendering the sacredness of maternity into a means of survival, a way to financially profit. The poems "Sweet Remember" and "In Guatemala" interrogate patriarchy's notion of femininity and the sacred notion of justice, respectively. Both poems work within an economy of violence that virulently dismantles the pretense of each. Tafolla's poems remind the reader of the regimes of power that use women's bodies and minds as fodder for political and economic domination. These poems call the reader to replace such demeaning rhetoric with an invocation to personal and collective empowerment.

Alfred Arteaga presents the reader with a counter-nationalist discourse of the female body. His 1986-87 poetry *Cantos* won honorable mention from which his poem "Canto Primero" is reprinted here. The poem traces the cultural legacies of Mexico through its descendents who currently inhabit the United States. In Nahuatl, Arteaga writes of la Malinche, polemic Indian mother and co-originator of the mestizo people in the Mexican national myth. In an onomastic gesture, the voice focuses on geography, and moves from Tenochtitlán to the US/Mexico border and then to US Southwest renaming— no, reconceptualizing—spaces with indigenous and Mexican names. When native, this region is spoken of as sensuous female body, while the border and its man-made structures assault the senses in images like "threading the steel mesh / como nada" (149). He retraces Chicano ancestry in three languages: Nahautl, Spanish, and English. By valorizing the feminine in the concept of the mother country, Arteaga defies national boundaries and reorganizes the Chicano community through the contours of the indigenous female body thus reincorporating California into Mexico, making it a whole contiguous geographical and cultural space. Here, official boundaries are blurred, linguistic registers miscegenated, and the dominant masculine of North American iconography overwhelmed by the supple, warm body of the Indian woman. Arteaga's collection interprets Chicano nationalism in a very sensual, erudite, yet playful way, without losing any of the seriousness of his concerns.

An American meditation on insanity is the theme elaborated in the late Reymundo Gamboa's short story "50/50 Chance" for which he won first prize in the 1986-87 contest. The character Strawman is the purported madman who has escaped from an insane asylum on his way to Santa Barbara where he longs to see the coast. He is caught by hospital authorities and the remainder of the story describes Strawman's struggle to perform sanity as determined by particular social norms. Gamboa explores Strawman's circumstance and condition brilliantly by the way he teases out Strawman's heightened consciousness that understands the game at stake between himself and Mary, his hospital psychotherapist, for his freedom. Strawman's sudden insights into the artificiality of the conditions of sanity deconstruct the binary sane/insane into liminal degrees of moderated yet pervasive insanity demonstrated by all. Gamboa writes a highly sympathetic protagonist in this first-person narrative that compels his reader to reconsider the notion of sanity, and to question the legitimacy of the asylum as a rehabilitative institution.

Demetria Martínez, well-known for her 1991 novel *Mother Tongue*, is also a wonderful poet as her first-prize collection of 1987-88 attests. Included are two of her poems, "Chimayó, New Mexico" and "One Dimensional Man." "Chimayó, New Mexico" situates a landscape as the central character of the poem through which a pair of lovers fails to emotionally and spiritually connect. Here, Martínez contextualizes the architecture, topography, and the flora and fauna of Chimayó, New Mexico, to tell of a spiritual desire for an erotic encounter. Perhaps related to Martínez's interest in the Sanctuary Movement, "One Dimensional Man" speaks in staccato-like spurts of a postcolonial fantasy where an imperialist male's sexual interest in the oppressed Other is energized by his prejudice. The implication is that sexual attraction nor intimacy necessarily compels the racist to challenge his/her beliefs. Rather, the attraction is often rooted in an erotic of oppression. Martínez unfastens the myth of biracial romance through a poetic voice that links the heterosexist and racist desire of Other with the desire to annihilate the Other, themes developed as well in *Mother Tongue*. True in the best of Chicana/o literature, Martínez establishes Chicana/o subjectivities within social, historical, and economical contingencies and sets them to poetry, concise, biting, and lyrical.

Silviana Wood's story "And Where Was Pancho Villa When You Really Needed Him?" won her first prize in 1987-88. Through the genre of the Bildungsroman, Wood's tale conjoins the coming of age of a young girl with her cognition of racism and the subsequent material conditions of poverty. This process begins with the difficult circumstances with which her community lives that become a source of social shame. The story embraces with humor the ingenuity of a group of sixth graders, the young Chicanos of Miss Folsom's class, who protect themselves from being institutionally demeaned. They circumvent their teacher's chastisement when they distract Miss Folsom from recognizing symbols of their poverty like lice and ill-fitted clothing, and from their ethnicity represented by un-American lunches, and their willingness to accept English names. Told in a child's voice, Wood subtly exposes the larger project of education in the United States—to indoctrinate the young in a skewed value of nationalism to distinguish the self-proclaimed real American citizen from the ethnic "imposter."

Silviana Wood in her play *Una vez, en un barrio de sueños . . .* , first-prize winner of the 1988-89 contest brings her reader into a barrio where generations at odds merge together. Don Anselmo, a grouchy old man, leaves the scolding behind when he finds a common bond of intellectual curiosity with a neighborhood boy, Federico. Together, Don Anselmo and Federico grow a tomato plant that embodies their collective dream of renewal and sustenance in the midst of a hardened urban slum. The fact that the tomato is selected ties this spiritual and communal act to the tomato's indigenous roots in America. The poor quality of the earth in which the tomato is planted shows the foolish care shown the earth in modern America, further evidenced in the crop of a few pathetic tomatoes. Perhaps a trademark of Chicana/o and Latina/o literatures, Wood's play evokes a gentleness of spirit that creates a backdrop from which the community draws its strength and determination under grim social circumstances.

Josefina López wrote her highly acclaimed play *Simply María or America's Dream,* second-prize winner of the 1988-89 contest. The play questions the heterosexist romantic fantasy at the heart of both North American and Mexican cultures that often predetermines the lives of many women. María is the daughter of Carmen, herself once a rebellious daughter who, in her youth, had eloped with a still-married man, María's father Ricardo. In pursuit of better economic opportunities, the family ventures pa' el norte, but María follows her own American Dream. In María's version, she wants to pursue an education and wins herself a scholarship to attend university. Pulled by tradition, María's parents forbid her to pursue her dream because they believe an educated María will frustrate her scripted obligations of future wife and mother. The drama that ensues incorporates alter egos in the form of three girls who expose María's inner conflict between becoming American, maintaining her place in Mexican culture, or falling outside both to pursue her own individual calling. Still a significant theme in Chicana/o literature in the late 1980s and early 1990s, *Simply María or America's Dream* is very much a Chicana tale of the difficulties of negotiating gender roles between two cultures. The sets, placards, and the unexpected inclusion of cameo narrators show the legacy of the important techniques pioneered by El Teatro Campesino. López's aesthetic of truncated dialogue in the form of partial conversations, dramatic lines that punctuate the action on stage in a performative way, the dream scene, and the sparse voices of the three girls make evident that this theme only requires an abbreviated treatment to be intelligible to a Latina/o audience of the 1990s, and by this moment in time, to mainstream audiences as well. In addition to the dramatic interrogation of the heterosexist family, *Simply María or America's Dream* illustrates that contemporary Chicano theater had successfully educated its audiences to the epistemology of Chicano cultural production. The scene presented here portrays the social forces that María and Carmen will have to contend with in America forewarned by their first experience of downtown Los Angeles.

From Alberto Ledesma's collection *Poetry for Homeboys on the Foul Line*, first-prize winner of the 1988-89 contest, are three poems: "José," "82nd Avenue," and "Ay-ay-ay!" Each portrays a vision of barrio life from three discrete spaces: the home altar, the family room, and the city street. These three spaces allow for two different selves to be explored. The domestic realm is the space where the poetic voice ethnically circumscribes himself Chicano. The public sphere is where the Chicano self is contested as Other. Racist paradigms are enacted that create an internal and external tension between the self as Subject and the self as Other. The first poem "José" draws out the religious contradiction of these spaces represented in kneeling at the altar in his home while preparing for a drug deal to be enacted on a street corner. The second poem "82nd Avenue" draws this comparison between the life of empowered citizens and the continuity they enjoy with the privacy of the home and the public space of the street. For the economically and ethnically oppressed, the sense of self and safety procured in the home is disrupted by suspicion and surveillance that deterritorializes the self in the street. The poem dramatizes this shift when describing the threshold of the house where "white wood porch steps" are traded for "a trail of asphalt crumbs" (175). The instability of self and community is registered again in the last poem included. Here, watching a televised Mexican movie on a Saturday night, Mamá remembers and reexperiences herself as freely Mexican—a luxury of home that the asphalt of Monday will contest.

In 1988-89, Liliana Valenzuela won first prize for her story, "Zurcidos invisibles," the touching story of the dreary life of Marta, a spinster. Thirty-year old Marta works as a seamstress and is the caretaker of her three relatives and additional boarders in the family home. Her biological age is surprising given the tone of her voice that displays a level of disillusionment usually wrought by older age. The seams of her life begin to unravel while repairing a worn-out elbow of a boarder's coat as Marta compares the life lived through the worn fabric with her pristine life of duty and chastity. She pricks her finger and the globule of blood let symbolizes a longing to live outside of her imposed familial servitude. Dolores, her old abusive aunt, uses social custom to chain Marta to a life of domestic service. The story begins and ends with an earthquake that should leave Marta's family for dead. Still alive, their survival becomes the real tragedy of Marta's life. "Zurcidos invisibiles" is reminiscent of Eduardo Mallea's short stories in its monotonously gray tone that aptly depicts the sadness and tragedy of constraining social arrangements.

Widely published author Benjamín Alire Sáenz won second prize for his short story "Alligator Park" in 1988-89. Jaime is a Chicano living in El Paso,

Texas, who helps political refugees gain legal status in the United States. The story opens with a conversation between Jaime and Franklin, a teenage refugee from El Salvador. Franklin appears at Jaime's door looking for legal help to seek political asylum in the United States. The precarious life Franklin is forced to lead, spending his days hiding out from INS officials in their trademark green vans, is juxtaposed to the story Franklin tells of his life in his home country under siege by political assassinations, massacres of civilians and more. When Franklin asks Jaime what it is like to be an American citizen, Jaime baulks when he utters the adjective "nice" (182), and so subtly complicates the good life supposed of US citizenship. Sáenz's story unveils the reality of life in the proverbial home of the free and the brave that, in fact, looks and feels only somewhat different from the vantage point of an undocumented immigrant, and too often for citizens of color as well. Sáenz deftly imbricates the justice system into the pandemic racism of the United States when Jaime recognizes the futility of his efforts to help Franklin and others like him. In this story, Sáenz also gives voice to the experience of children of war opening a psychological window to consider the complexity of experience for a portion of US Latino communities.

David Meléndez wrote *No Flag* and won first prize for drama in 1989-90. The structure of his play draws the reader into an unexplained situation of imminent violence that is gradually understood to be motivated by ethnic and/or class strife and thus resonates the avant-gardist structure of Samuel Beckett's *Waiting for Godot*. The trope of the play can be described as *in medias res* found in its dialogic tone, plot development, and scene change. This rhetorical strategy opens up the delicate subject of ethnic rage that, in this play, foments in the premeditation of violence against unspecified hegemonic powers. There are suggestions of ethnic discord that give a scant context to understand the motivation behind the terrorist plot. Ultimately, its eventual execution and consequences are left unknown, leaving the reader with unanswered questions. Thus, the play is really about its silences rather than what is staged. The historical links to the Chicano Movement of the 1970s to the drama's late-1980s present, the objective of the terrorist plot, and the mystique of Garathy Hill, all remain unexplained. The play is located in City Terrace, California, an area of heavy gang activity bounded by East Los Angeles at one end, and California State University, Los Angeles, at another. In this sense, the true drama is the intensity of the tension of daily life for people of color that is intimated rather than openly discussed. The reader is given decontextualized indications of the substance of these silences, such as the breakdown of our social pact, pointing specifically to compromised journalism, racist police, the disregard of women's knowledge, the dark side of human beings, the nature of subversive power, and the rational thought of a terrorist's mind.

Carlos Nicolás Flores's short story "Cantina del gusanito" for which he won first prize in the 1989-90 contest tells of an outing to Don Gallardo's bar where two old friends, Américo and Porfirio, meet, get drunk, and converse. The story is almost ethnographical in its depiction of Chicanos and Mexicans. Both intellectuals, the men expound on their frustrations, and the futility of their ability to affect their respective worlds in mid-life. The story captures a snapshot of Mexican friendship, the function of alcohol among men, their values, and their vices. It is a well-written story that on another level explores sociality on the border. The dynamic of the border infuses populations on the two sides with variable Otherness, or conversely, subject-hood. The fact that the cantina scene takes place on the Mexican side of the border is important to consider. The tension in a similar type of bar with a crowd of working-class Mexican migrants, residents, and/or citizens—all of whom are subject to suffer from second-class citizenship, racism, and poverty—would unlikely create a celebratory atmosphere. Yet, similar circumstances on the Mexican side of the border become imbued with a qualitative Mexicanness. Hence the ethnography of place allows a different type of experience for its patrons; namely, a distinct intimacy amongst men. The two characters of the story, Américo and Porfirio, draw life from the opposite side of the border; yet, they allow themselves to befriend each other in particular ways because of the cultural space of the cantina.

Well-known novelist Graciela Limón won third prize in 1989-90 for her short story entitled "Concha's Husband." This is a story of love and deception in a small town in Mexico set sometime in the distant past. The story begins with a wake in the living room of Concha's home that acknowledges, rather than honors, the death of her husband. The writer privileges the voices of the townsmen who murmur condolences to the widow while internally chastising the dead man. The townswomen, on the other hand, lament the loss of their collective lover who had stolen the hearts and bodies of young and old. Limón draws out the distinct perception of each group of the town's lecher who drew hatred, lust, love, and envy. Limón shows the style that will characterize much of her work in which a gentle narrative pace creates a respite from which she explores difficult, and sometimes anti-social, psychologies of her characters. It is with this cadence that Limón turns the narrative focus from the grieving widow and the emotional outpour of the town to the real plot of the story: the act of murder as deliverance from a philandering husband.

Cultural critic, journalist, and essayist Rubén Benjamín Martínez won third prize in 1989-90 for his poetry "Plaza mayor" of which two poems are included: "The Borders" and "Lago de Ilopango, El Salvador, 1971." The first poem takes the motif of borders to explore the dichotomy between two realities of the speaker. US suburbia shows an aegis of a modernist utopia, a fantasy made reality of solid construction, tidy public spaces, and a general air of ironic "frenetic" (190) contentment. Martínez contrasts this reality, or lived experience, with the underbelly that makes such a place possible; namely the sweat of underpaid laborers. As the poetic voice moves along and through suburbia, the speaker is viscerally aware of this underbelly-world that disrupts the pristine landscape in the image of cracked walls, the intrusion of ants, and exploding neon signs (189). Humanity is the other casualty in this poem that capitalism exacts for the benefit of the middle and upper classes. The quality of life that suburbia supposes is shown as hollow and elusive and the "moving border" (189) is the speaker's double-vision where he witnesses the promise and the price of late capitalism, simultaneously. A more fulfilled society is found in Martínez's "Lago de Ilopango, El Salvador, 1971." The concrete path, met with skepticism in the beginning of the first poem, converts into a dusty, rural path made beautiful by a child's "quick / exited steps" (190). Set in a rural setting, the poem elegizes the relationship between grandfather and grandson as they set off before dawn to fish. In contrast with "The Borders," the economic system of the pueblo of Ilopango harmonizes nature and society. Perhaps romanticized by the perspective of youth, nevertheless the rural Salvadoran village is able to connect its inhabitants to a paradigm of emotional, economic, and intergenerational interdependence and well-being, something bereft in US suburbia.

Author Manuel Ramos turns his critical attention to the Chicano Movement in his novel, *The Ballad of Rocky Ruíz* (1993), first-prize winner of the 1990-91 contest. The writing of a crime novel provides Ramos with the opportunity to examine the mythic stature of the Chicano Movement. Under his critical eye, the reader learns of the inner politics of some of its leaders, the role of the FBI in its demise, and the way the movement for some, had become primarily an occasion for fraternizing. This story is fashioned in the aftermath of the Chicano Movement, tracing the lives of college leaders some years after graduating from the University of Colorado, Denver. Rocky Ruíz, one member of their group murdered during college creates the first mystery for the novel to unravel. The remaining members including Luis are being threatened twenty years later by an unidentified man. While Ramos's depiction of heterosexual relations is perhaps realistic for many men, it is also fodder for feminist critics, and in this sense, is problematic. However, the novel accomplishes something very important. *The Ballad of Rocky Ruíz* establishes its fictional reality from within the Chicano Movement. The importance of this gesture is to move the movement from periphery to center in America's historical memory. Ramos accomplishes this point without apology or explanation. He writes comfortably under the assumption that his readership has sufficient acumen of Chicano culture and history. This authorial position marks the impact and dissemination of the movement's cause in the realm of national culture. Ramos's textual assumptions allow a different kind of Chicano protagonist to be developed as well. Luis Montez is Chicano in a very unselfconscious, indeliberate way. His ethnicity and how it plays out in himself and in how he moves through the world is an accepted reality about which there is again, nothing to explain, contest, protest, or affirm. It just is. Based in the 1990s, the story questions the movement's future perfect that seems to be failing in significant ways. The novel in this way criticizes current Chicano activism as apathetic, embittered, or at least distracted. The corrido that ends the book reminds the reader of the importance of oral history and so re/connects contemporary Chicanos with this Mexican way of knowing. Ramos's text has become an instant classic in many circles for the quality of the writing and the way it uses the genre of the crime novel to tell a Chicano story. Ramos joins other contest winners like Lucha Corpi and Michael Nava in this first generation of Chicano detective fiction writers. Their successes highlight the CLLP's importance in acknowledging the unique merit of Chicana/o voices in the genre of detective fiction.

In 1990-91, Graciela Limón won third prize for her novel *A Voice in the Ramah* republished as *In Search of Bernabé* (1993). Located in El Salvador, this story shares a common history of civil war, US involvement, and destroyed families with other war-torn Central American republics. Set in the 1980s, Luz Delcano searches for her son Bernabé, lost in the aftermath of a government attack on civilians and rebels alike during a funeral procession honoring the murdered Archbishop Romero. Tying the fictional story to historical events seeks to ground the reading in reality. This grounding is furthered by the genealogy of two of the main characters, Bernabé and Lucio, but with an ironic intention. Genealogy is the allegorical structure of the novel that exposes the dysfunction and disunity of this nation. Through the characters of Lucio Delcano, Bernabé's unknown half-brother turned military higher-up, who is the progeny of incest between Luz, his biracial mother, and his white aristocratic great-grandfather; and Bernabé himself, the bastard child of Luz and her employer, Don Grijalva. Allegorized, these familial relations provide a critical look at the postcolonial legacies of racism and miscegenation as they play out in contemporary civil strife in this Central American story. The story of Luz Delcano is a Latino story because of what it shares with many Central American immigrants who reside in the United States. It is also the story of a subjugated woman, of her defiant ways of love and desire, her ability to provide succor to others beyond those to whom she shares biological ties, and of her ferocity of spirit to honor her love of her son. Reflecting back on the argument of this introduction, as the political contestation incorporates broader geographic zones, Limón's Chicana sensibility acknowledges the merit and poetry of Salvadoran Luz's life. Limón's prose is diaphanous, providing a thin shield from the horrendous truths of international politics, history, and commerce in human lives in Central America.

Terri de la Peña's short story collection *Ventanas* constructs interesting plots and characters, depicting the joys and struggles of urban Chicana lesbians. The selection included from the first-prize winner of the 1991-92 contest is the title story "Ventanas," a story of two police officers' encounter with homophobia. Set in Los Angeles, partners Ron and Lu face the terror of harassment from the point of view of its victim, Chicana lesbian Pat Ramos. Ron, a Chicano divorcé, and Lu, an African-American widow, are confronted with Gus Becerra, a homophobic vigilante who threatens beautiful Pat and her friends. What becomes perhaps the more interesting problem for the story to examine is the pervasiveness of homophobia, not merely in the fringe figure of Gus Becerra, but in Ron and Lu, the police officers on the case, the police captain McNeill, and nearly every other character in the story. The day-to-day way this homophobia is expressed as well as the degree to which Pat's sexual orientation subtly yet strongly disturbs Ron illustrate the extensive and ingrained nature of homophobia in American society. The emotivity of racialization, sexual orientation, and gender expectations interweave from one character to the next and, in so doing, take these issues out of the particular context of victim/perpetrator, law officer/civilian, or straight/gay to create a worldview where average people are brought to their lowest common denominator by their homophobia, racism, and sexism. De la Peña's characters are written well so that the reader feels them as realistically heroic and flawed.

Prolific playwright Elaine Romero's drama *Walking Home*, first-prize winner of the 1993-94 contest, broadens the concerns of Chicanos to focus on the condition of womanhood in the continent of North America. Predicated on race, the play draws upon historical documents and interviews to portray how African-American, Chicana, Mexican, and Anglo women have lived, suffered, died, and sometimes survived their circumstances. The drama converges on the body of moribund María, a young Chicana who has attempted suicide on a Los Angeles beach. As her body lapses into death, she is visited by her alter ego, Woman in the Sand, who will be her guide through a Dickenesque tale of the ghosts of women past. Woman in the Sand is a haunting figure who delivers María from her reverie of indifference to face her impending death, compelling María to reveal the events that led to María's decision to commit suicide. María's story is intercalated by stories of oppression from women that vary in ethnicity, historical moment, and circumstance over generations. The breadth of characters appreciates the suffering of American women across the continent and across time. Their stories build a common history of racial and sexual oppression that will enable María to come to terms with the source of her misery, her abandonment by her father at a young age. María's ensuing death is interwoven with the physical demise of Woman in the Sand's who languishes alongside María, trying to convince María to surrender to her truth. Woman in the Sand's agony provides María with a corporeal reflection of her dying body and consciousness cannot recognize or accept. Structurally, María's story is knowable only in relation to the suffering of these women; their stories make space for María to tell her story, bit by bit. María's denial of her personal drama is countered by a dramatic insistence on returning the reader to the physicality of María's dying body, reminding the reader of the type of day-to-day suffering that does in fact push many to suicide.

In 1994-95, Evangeline Blanco won first prize for *Caribe*, a historical novel that relays the failed attempts to politically and psychologically free Puerto Rico from its colonial status. The novel opens and nearly ends with the life of Rafael Rodríguez, son of an incestuous union between Mamá Tumbú, voodoo priestess, and her brother, Uncle Moncho. When Rafael becomes Dr. Rodríguez, he defies his cruel upbringing by his white "aunts" that had threatened to crush his sense of self. However, Dr. Rodríguez did not leave his "aunts'" home unscathed. As a professional, Dr. Rodríguez perversely uses his title to exact sexual services for medical ones. He inverts his traumas into a delirious fantasy of creating a great mixed race by taking advantage of white female patients. This abuse is committed in the name of creating a biologically appropriate Puerto Rican race of mulattoes who, under Dr. Rodríguez's tutelage, should become Puerto Rico's liberators. At the heart of the text lies a cultural critique of the nationalist use of mestizaje and the concomitant denial of racism set within the context of Puerto Rico's struggle for liberation. While Blanco may have generalized the particular situation of Puerto Rico by implicating the Caribbean in her title, this fast-paced novel opens up the subject of the particularity of racism and its political implications in a Caribbean context.

Mike Padilla presents a touching collection of short stories called *Hard Language* that won first prize in 1995-96 as well as the Joseph Henry Jackson Award. His stories vary in subject matter as well as geographic space, but offer a notable breadth of perspectives. What unifies his protagonists is their subject position as Chicana/os. Far from a facile understanding of what that implies, Padilla uses the term Chicana/o as a rubric to understand its polyvalency. The situations of the protagonists are so different that what becomes the collection's larger project is how these characters, situations, and spaces can correlate under the auspices of the term Chicana/o. Padilla is adept at focusing in on the mini-dramas of the everyday that present themselves to Chicana/os in specific ways. Padilla's writing tenderly perceives what motivates the human heart in such a way that his stories, grounded in the particular circumstances of members of the Chicano community, effortlessly unravel the politics of race, class, and gender that precipitate such subject positions. The title story "Hard Language" is the story of Pilar and Antonio, a married couple who has recently immigrated to the United States from Mexico, who then decide to learn English in their efforts to economically get ahead. A seemingly innocuous decision, the implications of bilingualism are explored in this subtly gripping story of the effect of the American Dream on marriage, migrancy, and self-construction.

The late Andrés Montoya's *The Iceworker Sings and Other Poems*, the 1996-97 first-prize winner for poetry, is a moving collection of poems taken from the life of a young Chicano in the urban slums of Fresno, California. Winner of the American Book Award, the ice worker of the title is the poetic voice of the collection who counters the monotonous and physically challenging work of stacking blocks of ice by tending to his soul through song and verse. The emotional rigor of his poetry defiantly exposes a barrio's heart of darkness set up by a capitalist system that leaves millions of people undereducated, emotionally broken, and impoverished. Unrelentingly, the voice finds in each poem a moment of beauty, of tenderness, of spirituality in the most decrepit of circumstances. His work does not glamorize or romanticize violence and poverty. Nor should his treatment of religious faith be confused with facile escapism. His Christian images emanate from the street, in the bodies—whether drugged, orgasmic, beaten, or dead—that he encounters. Rather, the work of Andrés Montoya turns violence and poverty into poetry. Montoya's poetry distinguishes itself with his agility of imagery, the determination of tone, and his message of deliverance.

In 1997-98, Angelo Parra's *Song of the Coquí* won first prize for drama. Set in the present, this play dramatizes the American Dream in crisis. Edna and Ramón (now called Raymond) are a couple in their sixties who migrate from Puerto Rico to New York after World War II. Their only son Ray embraces and then dispels the American Dream of his parents. Each family member portrays the hollowness of this dream: Ray is disillusioned with his law career and is stuck in a relationship with a drug-abuser; Edna is a depressed alcoholic, and Raymond, his father, lives his life in front of the television where he argues and criticizes his wife and son, in place of facing his own misery. The American Dream interpolates the intergenerational dynamics of a Nuyorican family in a lively, well-paced drama that more poignantly delineates the fall out racialization on C/L manhood. Hence, the "coquí," as Ray was once known, the small singing frog of Puerto Rico, becomes the metaphor of his fate to survive in the United States, but he "will never sing again."

Combining a sense of humor with the realities of raising a large family on a modest income, Patricia Santana's 1998-99 winning novel *Motorcycle Ride on the Sea of Tranquility* examines a Chicano family and its experience of the Vietnam War. Set in a barrio in San Diego, California, during the late 1960s, Santana frames this discussion with the well-written coming-of-age story of Yolanda Sahagún which is juxtaposed against the trials of her older brother Chuy. Yolanda's childhood of tranquility suggested in the title is disrupted by her experiences of miscegenation, racism, and sexual oppression. Chuy is a Vietnam veteran who escapes his internal horror of war on long motorcycle trips, distraught with Post-Traumatic Stress Disorder. While Yolanda experiments with her budding sexual awakening, she is simultaneously confronted with her gender inscription caring for the Sahagún men. And her beloved Chuy no longer talks. In fact, he has disappeared. *Motorcycle Ride on the Sea of Tranquility* situates the Chicano family not only in relation to global history vis-à-vis the Vietnam War, but it also places the Chicano subject into the socio-economic realm of the middle class where the Sahagún family is embroiled in this historic moment. Santana's novel suggests that this family will retain its sense of Chicanoness, that their ethnicity is a pillar of emotional stability despite the personal catastrophe of war.

Over the twenty-five years compiled here, it is clear how the CLLP has supported Chicana/o and Latina/o writers in many ways. The contest has helped launch careers of writers whose quality and quantity of work have come to form a substantial part of the Chicana/o Latina/o canon. The CLLP has been a community contest, drawing talent from non-professional writers evidenced in their many winning entries. The contest has also provided a space for the fictional writing of a third community of writers, Chicana/o and Latina/o academics. The CLLP's malleability in terms of the types of writing it supports—mixed genres, style, theme, linguistic register, and language—is invaluable in doing the cultural work of authorizing C/L letters in their multiple dimensionality. The winning entries reprinted in this anthology show the intellectual and creative openness of the contest's directors, demonstrating a commitment to follow the artistic pulse of a given historical moment. Now entering its thirty-fourth year, its longevity has created a dependable and accessible base for Chicana/o and Latina/o communities to share our voices both in and outside the academy.

The Chicano/Latino Literary Prize
An Anthology of Prize-Winning Fiction, Poetry, and Drama

1974-75

Ron Arias **First Prize: Short Story**

The Wetback

That afternoon Mrs. Rentería's neighbor's grandchildren discovered David in the dry riverbed. The young man was absolutely dead, the children could see that. For a long time they had watched him from behind the clump of cat-o'-nine-tails. His body lay so still even a mouse, poking into one dead nostril, suspected nothing. The girl approached first, leaving behind her two brothers. David's brow was smooth. His gray-blue eyes were half-closed. His hair was uncombed and mixed with sand. His dark skin glistened clean and wet; and the rest of him, torn shirt and patched trousers, was also wet.

"He drowned," the girl said.

The boys ran over for their first good look at a dead man. David was more or less what they expected, except for the gold tooth in front and a mole beneath one sideburn. His name wasn't David yet. That would come later when the others found out. David was the name of a boy who drowned years ago when Cuca predicted it wouldn't rain and it did and the river overflowed, taking little David to the bottom, or to the sea, no one knew, because all they found was a washtub he used as a boat.

"How could he drown?" one of the boys asked.

"There's no water."

"He did," the girl said. "Look at him."

"I'm telling," the other boy said, backing away.

The boys ran across the dry sand pebbles, up the concrete bank and disappeared behind the levee. Before the crowd of neighbors arrived, the girl wiped the dead face with her skirt hem, straightened his clothes as best she could and tried to remove the sand in his hair. She raised David's head, made a claw with her free hand and raked over the black hair. His skull was smooth on top, with a few bumps above the nape. Finally she made a part on the right side, then lay his head on her lap.

Tiburcio and the boys were the first to reach her, followed by the fisherman Smaldino and the other men. Most of the women waited on the levee until Tiburcio signaled it was okay, the man was dead. Carmela helped Mrs.

1

Rentería first, since it was her neighbor's grandchildren who had discovered David, then she gave a hand to the other older women. Mrs. Rentería, who appeared more excited than the others, later suggested the name David.

For some time they debated the cause of death. No bruises, no bleeding, only a slight puffiness to the skin, especially the hands. Someone said they should remove the shoes and socks. "No," Tiburcio said. "Leave him alone, he's been through enough. Next you'll want to take off his clothes." Tiburcio was overruled; off came the shoes, a little water and sand spilling out. Both socks had holes at the heels and big toes.

"What about the pants?" someone said.

In this way they discovered the man not only lacked a small toe on one foot but also had a large tick burrowed in his right thigh and a long scar running from one hip almost to the navel.

"Are you satisfied?" Tiburcio asked.

Everyone was silent. David was certainly the best looking young man they had ever seen, at least naked as he now lay. No one seemed to have the slightest shame before this perfect shape of a man. It was as if a statue had been placed among them, and they stared freely at whatever they admired most. Some of the men envied the wide chest, the angular jaw and the hair, thick and wavy. The women for the most part gazed at the full, parted lips, the sunbaked arms, the long, strong legs and of course the dark, soft mound with its finger of life flopped over, its head to the sky.

"Too bad about the missing toe," Tiburcio said. "And the tick, what about that?" Mrs. Rentería struck a match and held it close to the whitish sac until the insect withdrew. There were 'oos' and 'ahhs,' and the girl who had combed the dead man's hair began to cry. Carmela glanced at the levee and wondered what was keeping her uncle, Fausto.

They all agreed it was death by drowning. That the river was dry occurred only to the children, but they remained quiet, listening to their parents continue about what should be done with the dead man. Smaldino volunteered his ice locker. No, the women complained, David would lose his suppleness, the smooth, lifelike skin would turn blue and harden. Then someone suggested they call Cuca, perhaps she knew how to preserve the dead. Cuca had cures for everything. Why not David?

"No!" Mrs. Rentería shouted, unable to control herself any longer. "He'll stay with me." Although she had never married, never been loved by a man, everyone called her "Mrs." out of respect, at times even knowing the bite of irony could be felt in this small, squarish woman who surrounded her house with flowers and worked six days a week changing bedpans and sheets at County General. "David is mine!" she shouted for all to hear.

"David?" Tiburcio asked. "Since when is his name David? He looks to me more like a . . . ," Tiburcio glanced at the man's face, ". . . a Luis."

"No, señor!" another voice cried, "Roberto."

"Antonio!"

"Henry."

"¿Qué Henry? ¡Enrique!"

"Alejandro!"

Trini, Ronnie, Miguel, Roy, Rafael . . . the call of names grew, everyone argued their choice.

Meanwhile, Mrs. Rentería left her neighbors, who one by one turned away to debate the issue. After kneeling a moment beside David, she stood and wrung out the sopping, gray shorts, then began slipping his feet through the leg holes, eventually tugging the elastic band past the knees to the thighs. Here she asked for help, but the group didn't seem to hear. So with a determination grown strong by years of spinsterhood, she rolled David onto one side, then the other, at last working the shorts up to his waist. The rest was the same, and she finished dressing him by herself.

When the others returned no one noticed the change, for David appeared as breathtaking dressed as he did naked. "You're right," Tiburcio announced, "his name is David . . . but you still can't have him."

About this time Fausto arrived, helped by Mario, a goateed boy whose weaknesses were stealing cars and befriending old men. The two figures stepped slowly across the broken glass and rocks. Fausto, winking at his niece, immediately grasped the situation. David was a wetback. Yes, there was no mistake. Hadn't he, years ago, brought at least a dozen young men from Tijuana, one, sometimes two at a time, cramped into the trunk of the car? Of course Fausto knew, for even after they found work months later, they would return to the house dressed in new clothes but always the same type of clothes. Fausto wasn't too quick to recognize women illegals, but the men, like young David there, were an easy mark.

"How can you tell?" Smaldino asked.

The old man raised his staff and pointed to the gold tooth, the cut of hair, the collar tag, the narrow trouser cuffs, the thick heeled, pointy shoes. "It's all there. You think I don't know a mojado when I see one?" As a last gesture, he stooped down and closed the dead man's eyes. "Now . . . what will you do with him?"

"No, hijita, he's too old for you."

Mrs. Rentería repeated her claim, placing her body between David and the others. Before they could object, Fausto asked in a loud voice what woman among them needed a man so greatly that she would accept a dead man. "Speak up! Which of you can give this man your entire love, the soul of everything you are? Which of you, if not the señora here who has no one?"

The wives looked at their husbands, and the girls and unmarried women waited in awkward silence.

"Then it's settled," Fausto said with unusual authority. "You, Tiburcio . . . Smaldino, and you, Mario, take this man to her house."

"Hey, I ain't touchin' no dead man," Mario said.

Carmela stepped forward. "Yeah, you'll steal cars, but you won't help your own kind."

"Alright, alright," Mario muttered, "one time and no more."

That evening so many visitors crowded into the small, frame house next to the river that late-comers were forced to wait their turn in the front yard. Even Cuca, her stockings rolled down to her ankles, had to wait in line.

Mrs. Rentería had bathed and shaved David, clipped his hair and lightly powdered his cheeks. He wore new clothes and sat quietly in a waxed and polished leather recliner. The neighbors filed by, each shaking the manicured hand, each with a word of greeting, some of the men with a joking remark about the first night with a woman. And most everyone returned for a second, third and fourth look at this treasure of manhood who might not survive another day of summer heat.

Like all discoveries, it was only a matter of time till David's usefulness for giving pleasure would end, till the colognes and sprays would not mask what was real, till the curious would remain outside, preferring to watch through the window with their noses covered, till the women retreated into the yard, till the men stopped driving by for a glance from the street, till at last only Mrs. Rentería was left to witness the end.

Happily this was a solitary business. For several days she had not gone to the hospital, her work was forgotten, and she passed the daylight hours at David's feet, listening, speaking, giving up her secrets. And not once did he notice her wrinkled, splotchy hands, the graying hair nor the plain, uninspired face. During the warm afternoons David would take her out, arm in arm, strolling idly through the lush gardens of his home, somewhere far away to the south. He gave her candies and flowers, kissed her hands and spoke of eternity, the endless pulse of time, two leaves in the wind. At night she would come to him dressed as some exotic vision, a sprig of jasmine in her hair, and lay by his side till dawn, awake to his every whisper and touch.

On the third day, Fausto knew the honeymoon was over. "Señora," he called at the door, "it is time David left."

Mrs. Rentería hurried out from the kitchen. Her hair was down in a carefree tangle and wore only a bathrobe. "You're too late," she said with a smile. "He died this morning. . . about an hour ago."

Fausto examined her eyes, quite dry and obviously sparkling with something more than grief.

"He died?"

"Yes," she stated proudly. "I think it was too much love."

The odor of death was so strong Fausto had to back down the steps. "Señora, I'd be more than happy to take him away for you. Leave it to me, I'll be right back." He turned quickly and shuffled toward the sidewalk.

"Wait!" she shouted. "David's already gone."

"I know, but I'll take him away."

"That's what I mean. The boy, that greñudo friend of yours, carried him off, just before you came."

"Mario?"

"I think so . . . he's got pelitos on his chin?"

"Está bien, Señora, your David will get the best burial possible."

Mrs. Rentería said she insisted on going with him, but Mario refused.

"Don't worry," Fausto said, "we'll take care of him. The body goes, but the soul . . ."

"I know, his soul is right here . . . in my heart."

"Señora, keep him there, because if you ever lose him, watch out for the other women."

"He'll never leave. You'll see, I have his word." She pulled a folded scrap of paper from between her breasts and studied the scribbled words.

Fausto asked if he should say something special at the burial. "Some prayer. . . a poem?"

Mrs. Rentería answered with a toss of her head, and for a moment the glassy eyes were lost in the distance. Then she closed the heavy wooden door, clicked both locks, dropped the blinds behind the big bay window and drew them shut.

But David was not buried. He left the valley as fresh and appealing as he had arrived. A man so perfect should not be buried, Fausto told Mario, and with the boy's help and using a skill more ancient than the first Tarahumara Indian, the old man painstakingly restored David to his former self. Even the missing toe was replaced.

By late evening the restoration was complete. Only one chore remained. Carmela brought the pitcher of water into the yard and wet the dead man's clothes, the same shabby clothes he wore when he arrived.

"More water," Fausto said. Mario took the pitcher and skipped into the house. David was about his own age, and ever since Mrs. Rentería had taken him home, Mario's admiration for the dead man's quiet sense of confidence had grown. The vato is cool, Mario thought.

After the second pitcher of water was poured, Fausto asked for the egg—a dried quetzal egg Mario had plucked from the Exposition Park Ornithology Hall.

"What's that for?" Carmela asked.

"Oh, Cuca once told me that you do this"—and here Fausto lightly brushed the egg on the dead man's lips—"and it brings him good luck. I don't believe it . . . but just in case . . ."

Mario struggled with the body, lifting it over one shoulder. "Is that it?"

"Follow me," Fausto said.

Carmela opened the picket-fence gate and silently watched the two silhouettes walk into the darkness. "Tío!" she called. "Where you taking him?"

"Further down the river," came the faint reply, ". . . where others can find him."

Mario, Fausto and David—once again the best-looking dead man this side of Mexico—crossed the street and disappeared under the broken street lamp.

1975-76

Transparencias

I

Era un excusado de madera, medía unos 6 pies y medio de alto. El sol y la lluvia habían dejado aquella madera descolorida, casi ploma. Había tres retretes de madera, dos para adultos y uno pequeño para niños. El excusado quedaba retirado de la casa, allá cerca del callejón. A veces había papel higiénico pero si no, nunca faltaban los pedazos de periódico ensartados en un alambre al lado de la puerta. Por dentro se trancaba la puerta con una aldaba y por fuera había una tranca. La puerta tenía varias hendiduras pequeñas que nos permitían sentarnos y observar lo que acontecía en el solar para que nadie pudiera vernos de fuera. Por eso cuando oímos lo de la presa, mi hermano Pepito y yo corrimos al excusado para escondernos y allí nos estuvimos una hora entera, mirando por las hendiduras, esperando que llegara Amá del centro.

La troca del dompe volvió a pasar por la calle Irving. Iban dos gringos en frente y nosotros temblábamos.

"Ya es la segunda vez que pasa".

"A lo mejor les andan echando el ojo a los de doña Huences ¿Y te fijaste? Es de las trocas que usan allá en la presa para acarrear tierra y piedras".

"Sí, dice Apá que ya merito acaban".

"Mira, ahí va otra vez. Es que quieren uno esta misma tarde. Dice Chava que lo ponen en las compuertas".

"Y, ¿pa' qué será?"

"Pos pa' cuando haya creciente".

"¿Creciente?"

"Sí, hombre, entonces dicen que se oye el grito. Así le avisa a la gente pa' que tenga chanza de salir. Si no, se ahoga todo el pueblo".

"Y, ¿tiene que ser mexicano?"

"Pos, dicen".

De repente vimos a Chava que venía corriendo hacia el excusado.

"Chato, Pepe, ¿'on 'tán?"

Pronto desganchamos la puerta y salimos.

"¿Ya se fueron?"

"Sí, y hace rato que no pasan más. Dicen que por la villita se robaron un recién nacido."

"¡Jiiijo! ¿Y la mamá no se dio cuenta?"

"Pos no. Dicen que andaba acá la vecina y se metieron los gringos y lo sacaron".

Al niño lo metieron los gringos en una caja pequeña de madera y ésta la sentaron en el cemento como parte de las compuertas de la represa. Ahora, cada vez que llueve mucho, el agua sube y sube hasta que llega a donde está el cuerpecito del niño. Entonces lanza un llorido agudo y los que viven allá en las afueras de la ciudad, cerca de la presa, salen de sus *country-style homes* a las tierras altas.

Así dicen.

II

Me suicidé esa noche allí en mi taller. Con mi 22. No me salió exactamente como quería. En vez de desplomarme el corazón, me metí los balazos en el pulmón. Bien pude haberme levantado y salido a la calle para pedir auxilio, nomás de pura rabia por no haberlo hecho como era debido, pero decidí esperar. Estaba acostumbrado a esperar, aunque me disgustaba bastante. Pues sí, por fin había decidido quitarme de tanta espera. Quería ser yo el que decidiera y produjera aquella muerte. Quería estar completamente unido a mi tarea. Pero nada. Tuve que esperar hasta que me llenó el pulmón de sangre. Luego me vino el pataleo, esos espasmos musculares sobre los cuales uno no tiene ningún control. Estaba yo allí otra vez, marginal al asunto. Claro que sin mí todo aquello no hubiera sido. Era yo la materia prima, la mano de obra y el explotador. Enajenado de la obra y a la vez, la obra misma. No tuve que esperar mucho. Me compró luego el gran Consumidor.

III

Había trapeado pisos en el hotel, cepillado madera en el taller de muebles, lavado ollas y platos en la cocina del hospital y ahora estaba en la carnicería, cortando y empacando carne. Tenía que jugarse muy águila.

"¡Cuidao con el gancho! Ten cuidao, muchacho, que en vez del pernil te quedas tú encajao allí".

Aquel día estaba pasando los costillares de borrego cuando vio cómo Juan caía contra el serrucho eléctrico.

Tuvieron que llamar una ambulancia.

No aguantaba más. ¿Pero qué se habían creído los jefes? ¿Qué eran? ¿Máquinas programadas para lavar, trapear, cepillar, piscar y cortar carne? No había derecho.

Se fue a la oficina del mayordomo. El mayordomo llamó al gerente. Entonces se desahogó.

El administrador caminó hacia él. Se acercó y con la mano derecha pareció acariciarle el pelo. Con el índice encontró el interruptor, cortó la conexión eléctrica, destapó el cráneo, sacó una pieza pequeñísima e introdujo otra que traía en el bolsillo.

IV

Era una gran pecera rectangular con cinquenta pececillos de distintos tamaños y colores. Los dorados eran los que más abundaban. Entre ellos había uno que nadaba agitadamente de un extremo al otro perseguido por seis o siete pececillos. ¿Le hacían el amor o le daban guerra? Cogió una ramita suavemente y meneó el agua ante los agresores que retrocedieron. Entonces pudo observar cómo el pececillo dorado respiraba exhausto entre el alga marina. De nuevo se reanudó el ataque y el pececillo se deslizó por el agua una vez más tratando de escapar. La pecera ya no parecía tan grande puesto que limitaba la vía de escape. Meneó el agua una, dos, tres, cuatro, cinco, seis veces más, hora tras hora, hasta que comenzó a cansarse. Al anochecer buscó la linterna y siguió meneando el agua.

Cuando despertó se encontró tirado al lado de la pecera. Ya era de día y los pececillos se paseaban de un lado al otro. Buscó al suyo y lo encontró.

Estaba muerto al fondo de la pecera.

Se levantó enfurecido. Pensó volcar la pecera para que murieran todos pero no pudo hacerlo.

Se alejó de allí lentamente, siguiendo la orilla limítrofe de su propia pecera.

V

"A tu tío lo arrastraron por el pueblo, hasta que se le despedazó el cuerpo. Pos, ya debía muchas. Siempre se andaba aprovechando del prójimo. Le achacaban algunas muertes y decían que se había hecho de propiedades con algunas jugadas sucias. Ya se la tenían sentenciada. Ese día que bajó al pueblo, ya lo estaban esperando. Dicen que hasta había una muchacha de por medio. No, sí tu tío era casado y tenía sus hijos pero ya ves como son los hombres. Allí lo lazaron y luego lo arrastraron por las calles empedradas hasta que lo destrozaron todo. Así se lo dejaron a tu tía Eugenia, frente a su casa. No, si no les hicieron nada. Dicen que ya debía muchas por allá por Coahuila".

VI

"¡Juan! ¡Juan!"

"¿Qué pasa, hombre?" Le dijo mientras descansaba recargado sobre el mostrador de la cantina.

"Juan, acaban de matar a tu hermano en la cantina de Rodríguez".

"¿Qué dices, desgraciado? Dime pronto quién fue".

"Lo mató el Serapio".

Salio corriendo del Roxy por la calle Main. Conocían bien el camino. Primero había que llegar a la avenida L y doblar allí a la derecha. Cuatro cuadras más arriba y allí tomaba la calle Oakes. Hasta con los ojos vendados podría haber llegado. En la calle Oakes dobló a la derecha y tomó el bajío. Iba encalmado, lleno de polvo, sudando a chorros.

Entró y lo vió rodeado de policías, cantineras y hombres. Todos eran bultos que identificó intuitivamente. En el suelo vio claramente a su hermano con la sien sangrando.

A Serapio ya lo tenían sujeto con esposas.

Juan se acercó de golpe a Serapio. Allí le dio de puñaladas hasta que cayó muerto. Entonces pudo respirar.

VII

JACINTHE$BAG

Corta, corta, corta, la cebolla, bolla, bolla. Corti, corti, corti. Zas. Sale la bandeja. Echa la cebolla. Corta la cebolla, Corta más. Más. Más. Más. Zas. La bandeja. Ponle más cebolla, ponle más, ponle más. Corta, corta, corta. Corti, corti, corti. La bandeja. El peste. El lagrimeo. Corta, corta, corta. Ya no aguanto. Ya no aguanto. Corta, corta, corta pa' los tacos congelados. Corti, corti, corti pa' poner en la bandeja. Zas. Ponle más. Zas. Ponle más. Ponle más. Ponle más. Ya no aguanto. Ya no aguanto. Me arden mucho los ojos. Corti, corti, corti. Zas. Zas. Zas. Con cuidado. Con cuidado. Corti, corti, corti.

"Ya párale pa' lonchar, Mere".

"Oye, Viken, ya no aguanto, qué dolorón de cabeza tengo con esta peste".

"Mira, creo que te van a mandar a las tortillas, anyway, porque vas muy despacio y ya anda repelando el mayordomo".

". . . Bueno, y aquí, ¿cómo le hago?"

"Verás, van caindo las tortillas y tú las vas doblando y les vas poniendo el relleno que tienes en esa fuente y prontito las vas poniendo en el transportador y sigues lo' lueguito con las otras que van caindo. Nomás no dejes que se te amontonen las tortillas por que si no, se te echan encima los viejos esos. Huy, ya te quemastes. Con la punta de los dedos nomás. Ándale, ándale, así nomás. Así, así. Bueno, te dejo. Tengo que volver a mi rincón".

Dobli, dobli, las tortillas, tillas, tillas. Chingao, que me estoy quemando. Y las tortillas nomás cayendo, nomás cayendo. Doble y llena. Doble y llena. Doblillena. Doblillena. Doblillenidoblillenidoblillenidobillenimequemuime quemuidoblidoblidobli.

"Hey, you're doing okay for a starter. See if you can go a little faster tomorrow, though."

1976-77

Alma Luz Villanueva First Prize: Poetry

Poems

TO JESUS VILLANUEVA, WITH LOVE

my first vivid memory of you
mamacita,
we made tortillas together
yours, perfect and round
mine, irregular and fat
we laughed
and named them: oso, pajarito, gatito.
my last vivid memory of you
       (except for the very last
       sacred memory
       i won't share)
mamacita,
beautiful, thick, long, gray hair
the eyes gone sad
with flashes of fury
when they wouldn't let you
have your chilis, your onions, your peppers
       —what do these damned gringos know of MY stomach?
so when I came to comb
your beautiful, thick, long, gray hair
as we sat for hours
(it soothed you
  my hand
  on your hair)
I brought you your chilis, your onion,
  your peppers.
and they'd always catch you
because you'd forget
and leave it lying open.
they'd scold you like a child
and be embarrassed like a child

silent, repentant, angry
and secretly waiting for my visit, the new
   supplies
we laughed at our secret
we always laughed
               you and I

you never could understand
the rules
at clinics, welfare offices, schools
any of it.
I did.
you lie. you push. you get.
I learned to do all this by
the third clinic day of being persistently
sent to the back of the line by 5 in the
          afternoon
and being so close to done by 8 in the
          morning.
so my lungs grew larger
and my voice got louder
and a doctor consented
to see an old lady,
and the welfare would give you the money
and the landlady would remember to spray for cockroaches
and the store would charge the food till the check came
and the bank might cash the check if I got the nice man this time
and I'd order hot dogs and cokes for us
at the old "Crystal Ice Palace" on Market Street
and we'd sit on the steps
by the rear exit, laughing
               you and I

mamacita,
I remember you proudly at Christmas
time, church at midnight services:
you wear a plain black dress
your hair down, straight and silver
 (you always wore it up
  tied in a kerchief,
  knotted to the side)
your face shining, your eyes clear,
your vision intact.
you play Death.

you are Death.
you quote long stanzas from a poem I've long
        forgotten;
even fitful babies hush
such is the power of your voice,
your presence
fills us all.
the special, pregnant
silence.
eyes and hands lifted up
imploringly and passionately
the vision and power
offered to us,
eyes and hands cast down
it flows through you
to us,
a gift.

your daughter, my mother
told me a story I'd never
heard before:
        you were leaving Mexico
        with your husband and two
        older children, pregnant
        with my mother.
        the U. S. customs officer
        undid everything you so
        preciously packed, you
        took a sack, blew it up
        and when he asked about
        the contents of the sack,
        well, you popped it with
        your hand and shouted
        AIRE MEXICANO

aiiiiiiiii mamacita, Jesus,
I won't forget my visions and reality.
to lie, to push, to get
just isn't
enough.

I WAS A SKINNY TOMBOY KID
    I was a skinny tomboy kid
    who walked down the streets
    with my fists clenched into
                 tight balls.
    I knew all the roofs
    and backyard fences,
        I liked traveling that way
            sometimes
        not touching
            the sidewalks
      for blocks and blocks
          it made
               me feel
      victorious
          somehow
  over the streets.
    I liked to fly
        from roof
          to roof
            the gravel
               falling
                  away
  beneath my feet,
        I liked
                         the edge
        of almost
  not making it.
        and the freedom
        of riding
      my bike
        to the ocean
  and smelling it
        long before
  I could see it,
        and I travelled disguised
          as a boy
      (I thought)
            in an old army jacket
            carrying my
                 fishing tackle
              to the piers, and
            bumming bait
            and a couple of cokes
  and catching crabs

                    sometimes and
            selling them
to some chinese guys
            and i'd give
                    the fish away,
I didn't like fish
            I just liked to fish—
            and I vowed
                    to never
                                grow up
                    to be a woman
            and be helpless
                    like my mother,
but then I didn't realize
            the kind of guts
              it often took
            for her to just keep
              standing
where she was.

I grew like a thin, stubborn weed
watering myself whatever way I could
believing in my own myth
            transforming my reality
                    and creating a
                            legendary/self
every once in a while
            late at night
                    in the deep
            darkness of my sleep
              I wake
                    with a tenseness
in my arms
            and I follow
                    it from my elbow to
                            my wrist
and realize
            my fists are tightly clenched
and the streets come grinning
            and I forget who I'm protecting
and I coil up
            in a self/mothering fashion
                    and tell myself
it's o.k.

THERE WERE TIMES
> there were times
> you and I
> were hungry
> in the middle of a city of
> full bellies
>> and we ate bread with
> syrup on top and we joked
> and said we ate dessert morning
> noon & night, but
> we were hungry—
> so I took some bottles to the
> store and got milk and
> stole deviled ham because
> it had a picture of the devil
> on it and I didn't care—
>> my favorite place
>>> to climb
>>>> and sit was
>>>>> Devil's Rock,
>>>> no one else
>>>>> would sit there, but
>>>>>> it was the
>>>>>>> highest place
>>>>>>>> around—
> taking care
> of each other,
> an old lady and a child
> being careful
> not to need
> more than can be
> given.
>> we sometimes went to the
> place where the nuns lived and
> on certain days they would
> give us a bag of food, you
> and the old Mexican nun talking,
> you were always gracious;
> and yet their smell of dead
> flowers and the rustle of their robes
> always made me feel
> shame: I would rather
> steal.

and when you held my bleeding nose
for hours, when I'd become
afraid, you'd tell me

—Todo se pasa—.

after you died I learned
to ride my bike to the ocean
        I remember the night
            we took the '5 McCallister
                to the ocean and it was
                    storming and frightening
                but we bought frozen chocolate bananas
            on a stick and ate them
            standing, just you and I
            in the warm, wet night—
and sometimes I'd wonder why
things had to pass and I'd
have to run as fast as I could
till my breath wouldn't let me
or climb a building scaffold to the
end of its steel or
climb Rocky Mountain and
sit on Devil's Rock
and dare the devil
to show his face
or ride my bike till the
end of the streets hit
sand and became ocean
and I knew
the answer, mamacita, but
I wouldn't even say it to
myself.

grandmother to mother to
daughter to my daughter,
the only thing that truly
does not pass is
love—
and you
knew it.

1977-78

Poems

EXTRAORDINARY

Chessman is part of my childhood,
rumors of a man saying goodbye;
It is in my head that there was
a bright light on his smiles,
a light like a stroke
of a China brush.
Shadows cluster near the light,
a man with a rat up his sleeve
drops the trick in the bucket
and steps back to see:
The water boils with hair and shit,
spit dots the floor. The eyes turn
white as they look to the brain.
At such and such a time
this man, who wrote his life
on toilet paper, heaves his
guts into his lungs and begins to rot.

LOOKING AT MY LEGS I THINK OF HIM

Mifune monkey young, a samurai,
standing in front of sparrow villagers:
His ass pulls down below his knees,
he jiggles their teeth as his
butt snaps
the white legs.
His cheeks grab the sky: dogs bark,
women hide.

19

Hired to kill, the ass walks the torso,
shoulders, head,
each bone set calmly,
swing of a man with no belly.
The ass spits a sword,
the ground thuds
with separate arms, heads.

His ass does all.

A cop, he wore white linen. Tall
folds of cloth hung from an ice cream butt.
He looked at suspects, his ass shrinking their
balls and sending a panel of sweat through his coat.

He spoke English, made race cars, dressed in a
kimono on an English lawn,
his belly skin tight to keep his butt in back.

Mifune walking the dirt, butt twitching to fleas
and stick drum music.
Women who've said,
"Toshiro. Toshiro."
As they pulled the long strong distance
between their ass and his.

I'd strap my legs around your shoulders,
a cheek in each hand, and whisper,
        cú
            cú
                cú
All night.

OUT OF REACH

I decided to go into the
world on yellow paper.
Dreaming of laughing conversations,
knowing the stopped clock lied,
leaving friends in foul weather,

I sat feeling my finger bones:

Remember when you gripped
the grass to keep from falling
off a spinning earth?

I brace my legs against the stall
        (feet in sandals, patas de india)
On the other side black pumps answer, "I'm fine,"
                    they leave.
Holding the lather off my shirt
I ease to the sink
                breathing my lunch,
those slimy hands slide round the sink.
It is your name that washes me.
green grimy soap / a thick sweet smell

As I laugh sideways the floor jumps Up,
        ready for the filthy whispers
                I would tell myself.

ON THE BREATH

Well, there's some-
one following me,
who
I don't know.
Yeah. Yeah. Yeah.
She's a small dog
and called it Chickee
and every evening
she'd spoon out dog
food: "Here chick chick chick."
Play your cards, write poems
and men will say "Hi"
as you walk
until you think
you're dripping.
I've never seen your belly button,
your cock's always . . .

I close my eyes
and kill a cop
with a shotgun.

There are so many ways
to spend a day.
I can make a day
a heaven
in any combination.
Morning:
        newspaper
        coffee
        sweet stuff.
Wandering past my rooms
        the radio takes me
        to places
        and leaping grace
        in the kitchen.

When I am not writing poetry;
I live in Woolworth's.

Wild as any boy in a cage
he threw his jacket out the window
to get past his mother.
He got in his father's car
and drove through a drugstore window.

Wanting an explosion
he match lit gasoline and paper
and only his sister's hands
saved his eyes.

MY BODY HEEDS ITSELF

The wind at my wet ears.
I've washed my hair.
The rags, the clouds, the sun
all out there.
My body bleeds and bleeds—
The sun out there—
My body heeds itself—
The sun out there—
My body heeds itself.

On some stations
you notice time between songs,
now it's twelve,

now 12:30.
The kitchen light
flattens my eyes.

Walking back
I thought:
We are the budgies;
that noise like tiny sucks.
True enough.
Then I must be grey.
You are green.
I am spiteful,
scare you from the millet,
bite your bill, your neck,
tell you in my cheeky voice:
We are rich.

I said
oh where are you
and she flipped a look at me,
talking to myself.
My God, she thinks I'm nuts.

Everyone kept saying Hi.
Oh honey I did it again,
she must think I'm out to lunch.

I stopped at a window,
let her feel safe.
But up the block
she peeked at me
as I walked by the alley
where she had been waiting.

Juan Felipe Herrera   Second Prize: Poetry

Antiteatro y Poemas

LA CARTA / NOTAS DE DIRECCIÓN

No existen personajes. El grupo acciona colectivamente e individualmente para desanudar la emoción, la imagen y la llama de una cierta esclavitud. Es posible utilizar varias representaciones directas del texto: ramas, M-16, gaviotas, tuberculosis, secretarias, ancianos, abejas, pasto, candados. O se puede intentar algo distinto: ramasgaviotas, ancianospasto, abejascandados. Lo imprescindible es que el grupo se convierta en un líquido metamórfico; pastosecretariacandado.

El vestuario será la estrategia para construir, frente al público, un mural humando de frío. Todos se arroparán en diversos matices de azul. El uniforme: pantalones de talla grande (khaki) y camisetas sin manga. Un tono gris se aplicará alrededor de los ojos.

El texto de La Carta, así como funciona como materia maleable para realizar la obra, simultáneamente sirve como manual de dirección dramática. Estos aspectos forman las dos voces de La Carta (o una voz con dos mayores tensiones). Las dos se proyectarán individualmente y conjuntamente; el énfasis y la dinámica se determinarán por los integrantes. Lo imperioso es que la voz se desenvuelva entre todos: sintetizada (coral) en ciertos momentos, fracturada (individual) en otros. La Carta tiene mil voces y una a la vez.

Todo ocurre en una celda invisible. Sucede en una cierta ciudad / mente / persona / multitud / mineral / espacio. No existe el tiempo. La Carta es algo eterno. Su voz es azuloscura; ser testigo de la constante aceleración de su encarcelamiento.

El fin del antiteatro será proponerles a los integrantes del grupo así como a la communidad / público la mayor parte en la obra no como actores y oyentes sino como autores y creadores. De esta manera nace el antiteatro y su meta: crear / sostener / lanzar una electricidad vascular / acústica / visual; del interior de la frente / espalda; descifrar lo imposible; un sudor ronco en las sienes del mundo; el hielo ardiente del hierro humano que encarcela / descarna; La Carta.

Juan Felipe Herrera
Febrero 1979
San Francisco, California

Zumbará tu garganta /
voltearás hacia diferentes horizontes /
hincada / sentada / acostada / jorobada /
escribirás sobre un hierro invisible /
sobre la pared que encara al universo /
zumbará la pared: un océano vertical /
         Te escribo sobre esta mesa de mares
        un párrafo entre las tablas de arena

buscarás los ojos con los dedos /
caminarás / correrás a frenéticas
velocidades / quizás ciega / tartamuda /
      un peregrinaje de ojos hacia la voz

tendrás un nudo en la garganta /
el nudo palpitará / crecerá / te estarás
sofocando / explotarás con gritos /
       acá afuera cuando alguien grita
te transformarás en ramas elásticas
de llanto / sonidos grótescos se escaparán
     las ramas se mojan de labios gris
     y velos

te embarazarás / te convertirás en una
ave / volando despacio /
     las palabras abandonan las vigas de
     hombres y vientres como gaviotas con
     susto/ vientres de trueno preso /
     la sal esclava

tu cuerpo se entretejerá con otros /
gemirás / seguirás escribiendo sobre algo
impalpable / duro / sudarás locamente / resollarás locamente /
te atraparás en una caja invisible /
te empujará / te prensará / con tus manos
con tu furia / golpearás contra ese cubo
de espacio espeso /
     es viernes / quentino
     tus 18 años en la celda palpitan
     como puños niños

velozmente te enlazarás a los otros
en un nudo / luego estallarás contra

la pared / tus hombros /
tu espalda / azotarán / tus uñas
rasguñarán la caja transparente /
despacio / tu sangre disminuirá /
te enfermarás / toserás / gemirás / olerás
a hospitales / te estarás muriendo /
        aquí también hay una tuberculosis
        de hierro

empezarás a desmoronarte / de repente
te caerás / los otros se quedarán
indiferentes / congelados / te convertirás
en una violenta piel de cuerpos /
te devorarás a los otros / a los inmóviles /
los tragarás / los ahogarás con risa /
        la risa de la araña
           la risa de la araña
              la risa de la araña

aumentará la risa / tu piel / animal de
cuerpos / empezará a girar / rápido /
se estrellará contra el paredón /
la pared de una oficina / con máquinas
de escribir / máquinas-hombres /
máquinas-mujeres / administradores y
secretarias sisearán /
        puñales que nacen de los pezones de
        los administradores / las secretarias
        desnudas en una taquigrafía
                de eslabones

sobre la pared descubrirás algo como un
calendario / apuntarás hacia un día
particular / te agacharás / serás máquina
con ojos delirantes /
pronunciarás su nombre en roncas / largas /
altas / efímeras voces /
        es viernes

torcerás los ojos / despacio / abrirás
una puerta / tentarás sillas (de cuerpos) /
al sentarte te volverás anciana / tomarás
una taza de café / fracasarás controlando
los dedos /

cuando los viejos se mecen
en sillones oscuros y de vez en cuando,
miran sus manos que tiemblan

caerá la taza / se despedazará /
te hincarás buscándola / no podrás
apretar las manos / gemirás / contemplarás
tus brazos inútiles / despacio / esforzarás las manos
hacia los ojos: explotará el aullido del pasto /
las quijadas del pasto que gruñen

sudará el pasto un cierto frío / te
acuclillarás / buscarás un cigarro
en la bolsa / escudriñarás la cartera
por un cerillo / te inclinarás hacia
la luz / agarrarás una foto / la
acercarás a los ojos / temblarán
tus manos / se te escapará la foto /
la cogerás en el aire / algo en tus
manos / resucitará / se dilatará /
se convertirá en algo radiante /
será una gaviota: la divisarás
desaparecer en el cielo /
y luego se acordarán de tus cejas
y tus puños guitarras que tocaban
sol y luna
cuando nosotros sólo pedíamos tierra

bajarás la cabeza / ojos al suelo /
caminarás / perdida en triángulos /
la pared te sorprenderá / la empujarás /
sudarás / te determinarás a derrumbarla /
con tus brazos ancianos / con tus venas /
estallarás / volarás / al fin estarás libre /
saltarás / tartamuda / de alegría golpearás
a los otros / ganarás hacia al universo /
nacerá una pared / una pared circular /
te comprimirá hacia el centro del mundo /
la arrastrarás una pequeña distancia / te
comprimirá: estarás enfrascada en una
flor de hierro / se cerrará / se abrirá /
no te soltará /
un pétalo infinito
entre dos candados imaginarios

la flor pulsará / estrujará / oprimirá
zumbará lentamente / aumentará el zumbido /
te convertirás en una fila marchando zigzag / serás un ejército solemne de estandartes
                                    abejas quentino
                         abejas somos
               como zumban en la cera manca
                    fabricando la bandera de yodo
avanzarán las filas / se unirán ferozmente /
se dividirán / una cargará rifles M-16 /
apuntarás a los otros / a los hambrientos /
a los tartamudos / a los valientes / dispararás /
         entre la recámara de directores
                    y perfume
          penetrando sus manos la armazón
               de un M-l6

con los rifles / el ejército golpeará
a los muertos / el ejército gruñirá /
se torcerá / se hinchará / celebrará
con rabia
          la garganta de somoza

entre carcajadas unos comenzarán a
escuchar / otros olerán algo en el universo /
apuntarán a lo oscuro / quizás hacia alguien /
avanzarán despacio / con rifles / lo seguirán /
gruñirán /
          "dedicamos de ahora en adelante
          nuestros esfuerzos en mantener,
          divulgar y defender todos los
          postulados de la doctrina . . .
          dedicamos de ahora en adelante
          nuestros esfuerzos en mantener,
          divulgar, y defender todos los
          postulados de la doctrina".

los muertos despertarán / se arrastrarán
con sus armas / descaragarán contra el ejército /
matarán algunos / con tiro rápido el ejército
acabará con todos / menos uno / se escapará /
lo fusilarán /

del ejército muerto despertarás: lo velarás
en llanto /
       y explotando en la calle
       30 años de humo y sangre
       nada cambia / quentino
       quentino
       nada cambia / sólo tú / ayer murió tu padre
en un hospital de guardias / hoy

los otros se dirigirán hacia diferentes
horizontes / hincados / jorobados / quedarás
sola / velando al cadáver / sentirás un
zumbido en el espacio / los caminantes
gemirán / frenéticos repetirán fragmentos
de palabras / abandonarás al cuerpo /
el zumbido acelerará / tomarás unos pasos:
correrás detrás de los otros /
       camino las calles
       busco los ojos / y
       los busco
      cuando hay más luz los busco

gemirás / gritarás / nadie te escuchará / nadie /
el zumbido explotará / te caerás en rodillas /
seguirás / te caerás otra vez / gritarás / los otros
pegarán contra la pared de columnas invisibles /
lucharán / quebrarán sus armas contra el espacio /
sangrarán sus huesos / alzarán sus ojos / hombros /
brazos poco a poco / abrazarán a la pared /
encorvarán sus muslos de saliva / sus senos de
sueño y gamuza / sobre la muralla / la besarán /
le murmurarán / se sonreirán / se consolarán /
tratarás de desprenderlos / les gritarás /
tartamuda / te lanzarás hacia el universo /
con tus brazos abiertos / con tus ojos blancos
de esperanza /
el muro invisible te atrapará zumbando ///
       pero la gente se acostumbra
       a las rejas
          eternas
       entre los ojos
     y el verano /

B STREET SECOND FLOOR MURAL / 14x14

> 9F
> flat surfaces
> two chairs
> the table with one thin hand thinking
> in front
> her hair black endless
> falling into the crevices of light
> the floor
> full of rumor hexagons & quadrilateral pieces
> of wind
> scrapes the windows & cuts her eyes
> her wrists
> yellow doors warm with short men
> bleeding dreams
> in ashtrays
>
> the throat in the radio & gray saxophones
> sing

LA FURIA DE LAS ABEJAS

> cuando ardían los hombros de los edificios
> cuando los pechos de las mujeres hicieron tigres
> cuando el niño escuchaba con las navajas de los ojos
> cuando el brazo anciano derramó rifles en los
>   hospitales
> cuando la voz del juez se hizo negra salamandra
> cuando los guardias vomitaron la ropa de las aves
> cuando el viento clavaba el convento con gangrena
> cuando emilio ciego marcó el sol entre las tumbas
> cuando la mina de sal se concentró en la punta de
>   tus venas
> cuando la soga del llanto se hizo mujer en tu
>   garganta

Helena María Viramontes — First Prize: Short Story

Birthday (excerpt)

(Momentarily, there are only two things I am sure of; my name is Alice, and all I want to do is sleep. I want to sleep so badly that I am angry at their conspiracy to keep me awake. Why so early? I want to knot myself into a little ball and sleep. I will. I will knot myself into a little ball and sleep. I will become you, knotted stomach.)

finally bonded
drifting afloat i become
and how much i love it
craft cradles me drifting far
far away
the waves rock me
into an anxious sleepless sleep and i love it
God, how much i love it
brimming baptism roll   swell   thunder reaching
up to the vastness   calm
    i relax beneath the fluids that thicken
    like jelly   thickening
    am light and transparent   ounceless
    spinning with each breath you exhale
    i move closer to the beaches
    and i love it

I rub my stomach because it aches. (Would I like to stay Alice, or become a mama?) I rub my stomach again as I sit on the couch, perhaps unconsciously hoping the rubbing will unknot my . . . my baby? no, doesn't sound right. Baby-to-be? isn't the same. Isn't. I sit—my arms folded—on a vinyl plastic couch which squeaks every time I cross or recross my legs. One of my legs swings back and forth. My breath is misty and I exhale hard to watch it form into smoke. Unfolding my arms, I lift my hands to my face and my fingers massage my eyelids. Blurred. Slowly focusing the room. A living room converted into a waiting room. Across from me a small fireplace. An off-white wall supports a single picture of snow and church. Dusty. Everything is dusty. In an isolated corner, a wire chair stands. Big room; practically empty. One dirty window pasted with announcements. I am the intruder.

"I don't know why, that's all." And that was all it had come to. "Now will you please stop bugging me?" Her voice became thorny with the last six words and she was now more annoyed than hurt. How many times had she asked herself the same question? That same question that became implanted in her mind and soon germinated into a monstrous sponge, leaving no room for an answer.

He finally lifted his eyes off the lawn and shifted his glance to her face. Slowly, he continued: "It's the twentieth century. . ." Again he shook his head in disbelief and his eyes glanced over her shoulders and into nothing. "Why weren't you taking anything? You know better." He paused, wet his lips and sighed, "You're a girl. You're supposed to know these things."

"I don't. I don't know why." She felt sorry for him and her voice became increasingly soft. "What do you think we ought to do?" He looked down at the blotches of dirt and grass, staring hard, as if the answer lay beneath.

"You'll have to get an abort—"

"Wait. Just wait." A ton of bricks fell tight against her breast and she could not breathe. "Let's . . . we gotta think this over." There was a long pause between them. The wind blew weak leaves of the tree they sat under and she thought I would like to be that leaf in mid-air swaying so softly. But only weak leaves enjoy the moment of freedom faster; only they die sooner. She realized now, suffering from this heaviness in her heart—this freedom—that the decision was ultimately hers. Hers alone. Her eyes that had first pleaded desperately under the tree now looked upon him as a frightened child.

"Alice." She turned to him and a reassuring smile appeared on her face. She hugged him tenderly and whispered, "You're just making it worse for the both of us." Hers. The wind blew a colder breeze and both trembled, enveloping themselves within an embrace.

A girl with long, stringy hair enters the room followed by a chilly draft that slaps me on the back. I hope I don't look that bad. Sits on the lonely wire chair. I smile at her with lazy lips but the encouraging gesture is not returned. Oily hair. (Looks like she used mayonnaise for shampoo.) I belch out a giggle. Alice—now's not the time to joke. I keep swinging my legs until my heart swells and I choke. Oh my God—

God. What am I doing here? Alone and cold. And afraid. Damn, damnit. I should have stayed a virgin. STUPID, stupid—virgins have babies too. Enough, Alice. Keep warm, Alice. No sex, Alice. Punishing me. For loving, God? Fucking, Alice. Fucking Alice. Stop it, Alice. Alice. Grow up, not out. Alice.

Alice

God isn't pregnant.

Alice

"Alice. Alice Johnson."

"Me," I nod my head and smile. I think I'm going to win.

1979-80

David Nava Monreal   First Prize: Novel

A Pastoral Tale (excerpt)

CHAPTER 17

Miguel was four months old when Raúl graduated from school. Raúl wore his best suit, a wide tie and cufflinks embedded with imitation diamonds. A dais and a microphone were set up in the schoolyard and folding chairs were used to accommodate the audience. Several eucalyptus trees surrounding the graduation area shed their svelte leaves like tumbling showers of excelsior. It was late summer dusk, sprinklers watered the lawn and fat pigeons sat watching from the roofs.

The director of the program and Miss Buford sat on the left side of the dais while the eight students sat on the right. Three months prior, the loquacious divorcée ran off with a policeman and the Negro with the bad eye moved back to New Orleans. The director stood up to make his speech. The spectators squirmed. They were anxious to begin the celebrating.

"I am happy to say that all eight students on stage passed their courses with flying colors. Most of these people had never made it to the fifth grade. But with hard work and encouragement they accomplished more than we had expected." He paused and gave a quick glance to his watch. "Let it not be said that hard work in America has died. These students are living proof of that. But the truly inspiring thing about today is that these people will now get a second chance at life. Before, they were nothing but sociological statistics. Now they are competitors in the labor market. All of us know that the American government is not perfect, but this small insignificant ceremony proves that it is trying."

There was a salvo of insipid applause.

"But without further ado I would like to introduce the person who is to hand out the diplomas, the person who is most responsible for the success of this year's class, Miss Buford."

Miss Buford stepped up to the microphone wearing a white muslin dress that was cut low at the top and raised at the bottom. Her sun-soaked breasts were pressed tightly against her bodice and her shapely legs were in full view. She looked more like a seductive actress than a teacher. Rosa, sitting in the front row, turned her face as a playful breeze pushed Miss Buford's hem high over her knees.

Tossing her head back, Miss Buford began. "It was a joy teaching this class. Everyone tried hard and I think everyone had fun. As for me, I learned more in this one year than I could have in ten. Education should begin at the grassroots level, not in places where money is plentiful. I hope I did something to help in these lines. These students, sitting here, would not have had a chance if it wasn't for this great program. I would like to thank my director who gave me this wonderful opportunity to prove myself and especially the students who enriched my life."

The women clapped and several men whistled.

"Now as I call out their names, will the students come up and receive their diplomas?"

"Ron Thatcher."

"Bill Thatcher."

"Joe Méndez."

"George Álvarez."

"Chris White."

"Sam Luna."

"Carl Lory."

"And Raúl Nava."

When the ceremony was over everyone went into the cafeteria to drink punch and eat cookies. The director was in one corner discussing politics with a man with long hair and sandals. Miss Buford was being looked at and pawed by most of the men of the graduating class. Rosa held the baby in her arms as Raúl poured her a glass of punch.

"Oh, I'm so happy for you," Miss Buford said to Raúl as she kissed him on the mouth.

Raúl stood gawking at the perfumed Venus.

"And congratulations to you, too, Mrs. Nava," Miss Buford said, taking Rosa's hand.

"We named the baby Miguel," Rosa said with a frown.

CHAPTER 18

Raúl's business career began as the assistant manager of the jewelry department of a well-known chain store. The director of the educational program had told Raúl that he could find him a job as a salesman, but Raúl was not expecting such an esoteric product. The first day on the job Raúl was like a fish out of water. He was under the supervision of a thin, intense man of thirty who was proud of his glib ability to make sales. The man was high-strung and he would constantly fly into tantrums. He could not understand why Raúl found it so difficult to learn the jewelry business.

"All you have to do is convince the people that they need to buy a diamond or a watch or any piece of jewelry," he would say.

"But I have never worked in the public before," Raúl would try to explain.

"It's Goddamn easy. Just don't be so damn shy!"

"I can't help it."

"Okay, okay, I understand. You've spent most of your life working in the fields. I should have known that when I hired you through that damn government program!"

"I'm sorry," Raúl would say.

"Just go back to work."

The process was slow, but eventually Raúl began to learn more about his job. He studied a manual on diamonds and discovered that they consisted of points, facets, and carat weight. He even began incorporating the salesman's jargon of "fire," "scintillation," and "clarity" into his daily conversations. Within two months Raúl was repairing watches and making small sales at the counter.

After six months Raúl was allowed to run the department by himself. He opened up the counter, put up the displays, rang up the sales on the cash register and kept the books. Soon enough he built up the reputation of being a conscientious worker. One day, much to the delight of the manager, Raúl made five sales that amounted to over five thousand dollars.

As time passed, the jewelry department was known for its Mexican clientele. Mexicans would come from all over the city and surrounding communities just to buy a watch or a wedding ring from Raúl. He had become indispensable and there was even talk of him being promoted to a managerial position. Raúl himself was slowly being taken in by his own self-importance.

Raúl took to wearing rings on every finger on his hands and he liked displaying gold watches that made his wrist look tawdry and obvious. He paid special attention to his clothing and he would have his hair styled once every three weeks. He flirted with the women in the store and sometimes he got the impression that some of them were taking him seriously. His selling technique was to fawn and flatter the customer. He attained special gratification whenever he sold an expensive diamond to someone who made the purchase not out of necessity but out of the need to impress.

Raúl's observations of his new environment were gathered over the years. Customers walked in and walked out but the one most valued was the one with the most money. That was the reality of things. He began to understand that this was not a country run by the beauty of trees or the serenity of nature or the profundity of loving and being loved. It was not a country that celebrated the birth of a child or the heat of the sun or the passionate wail of joy.

It was not the same world where he had courted Rosa and silently nourished the depth of his heart. This was not a nation of posadas, friendships and meaningful conversations. It was a world of grappling, struggling and survival. It was a life of poses and intricate games. It was a ruthless cycle that spun around the axis of money. Raúl often scorned this society that bent you, drained you of your simple humanity. In the mornings, Raúl would awaken with a bad taste in his mouth. It was as though poetry had turned to prose.

One day as Raúl busied himself polishing the silver he saw Miss Buford walk into the store. She was strolling hand-in-hand with a man that looked twice her age. She saw Raúl and quickly approached.

"Raúl, how nice to see you," she said with a glowing smile.

"Good to see you," he replied.

Turning to the tall man she said, "Raúl was one of my first students."

"Nice to know you," the man said dryly.

"This is my fiancé, Raúl. We plan to be married next year," Miss Buford explained.

"Congratulations," Raúl said shaking the man's hand

"How are Rosa and the baby?" Miss Buford asked.

"Fine. Miguel will be five years old next week."

"Fantastic. I see you're doing okay."

"I'm the manager," Raúl lied.

"Wonderful! I knew you would amount to something."

Raúl blushed.

The man tugged lightly at Miss Buford's arm.

"I have to be going, but it was nice seeing you again," she said.

"Take care," Raúl said.

As they walked away Raúl was very sure that if circumstances had been different, she would have been his.

Rubén Medina
First Prize: Poetry

Báilame este viento, Marián

DANZÓN

Era como esos domingos
en que Padre nos llevaba al béisbol
y mis hermanas y yo
descubríamos el esplendor bajo la yerba
pedazos de agua que nos llevaban
a odiar nuestro origen de caracoles
Padre era hermoso y grande como un autobús

Madre cariñosa como una mujer de paredes
Las calles eran tranquilas
como un sueño de organilleros
Los muchachos abrazaban a sus novias
tratando de imitar la lluvia
de un impresionista anónimo
Y para la tarde Padre se ponía un traje limpio
y agua de colonia y los zapatos brillantes
como reflectores de cine
y se iba a gozar con otras mujeres
Y Madre se quedaba llorando
maldiciendo una y otra vez su mala suerte
y recordando los buenos tiempos
cuando ella era soltera joven y hermosa

LLUVIA

La abuela teje sentada en el sillón
como una vieja diosa tarasca
aunque más parezca un pavo real urbano
y entonces llueve
y yo respiro profundo como una piedra
ando por los muebles como un río
y las manos de la abuela
siguen tejiendo y tejiendo nubes
que para marzo serán un mantel
para el hijo soltero
mientras la ciudad recuerda a sus muertos
entre la melodía monótona de la lluvia

De repente la abuela deja de tejer
mira para la ventana
y entonces suena un relámpago
y yo corro por debajo de la mesa
la abuela viene hacia mí
y desaparece el miedo por las paredes
igual que el sol evapora el agua del asfalto

La abuela sentada en el sillón
como una vieja diosa tarasca
aunque más parezca un pavo real urbano
sigue tejiendo y tejiendo
y yo me meto a la boca un pedazo de madera
que alguna vez fue el botón de un radio

De repente sus manos paran
y se me queda mirando

DAY OFF

a mis hermanas

Este miércoles 6 de febrero,
quiero decir la mañana que levanta
los artesanos y pescadores
en este invierno de pájaros que anuncian el trópico,
en que un anciano desenvuelve el silencio sobre
    la mesa,
pan del día
y las palabras de los amigos
que nos ayudan a vivir:
"Y el poeta derribado
es sólo el árbol rojo que señala el comienzo del
    bosque"
mientras bebe café
y la realidad irrumpe como el canto dulce
de Charlie el pájaro
tatuando la luz del día. He escuchado a los pájaros,
como conmueven los pájaros—murmuran los
    ancianos.

Vale la pena estar vivos.

Quiero decir, vendrán muchos más días
de descanso en que no habremos de ir
a limpiarle el culo al patrón,
servirle café, perdón, decaf a la esposa
y ser amable con la hija cuando su humor lo permite.

Seremos ancianos borrachos con el cabello
increíblemente negro.

Juan Manuel Bernal
First Prize: Poetry

Confesiones de un seudopoeta: Digresiones de un demente

(excerpt)

ÉL Y YO

Pues, hoy, les advierto que me propongo a pasar por alto a él, y escribir mi propia versión de los hechos. Deben de saber que para seleccionar palabras soy malísimo. Mis amigos me llaman: El lacónico.

Él no sufre de soledad, es estudiante universitario. Se sabe de memoria (tiene cierta obsesión de historiador) y en orden cronólogico las obras de Borges, García Lorca, Pablo Neruda, Octavio Paz y otros escritores de la misma envergadura. Nótese que a veces hablo como él; mas me choca su jactancia.

Él es conversador, versátil e intrépido. Yo, prefiero el cielo y el silencio. Al otro, le fascina recitarles a las mujeres, viajar por mundos fantásticos, beber vinos, hacer el amor en toda su geometría posible, escuchar jazz. Además, es epicúreo: comidas suculentas a diario. Me deja las sobras. Les parecerá inverosímil, pero nunca nos hemos sentado juntos; yo me arrincono en la cocina, y él como rey se sienta en el comedor.

En contraste, soy abstemio. A las mujeres les tengo miedo (recitarles nunca podría). El jazz lo escucho solo, cuando me siento nostálgico. Soy ermitaño. Salgo, únicamente, cuando él se queda en casa. Al otro, le fascina emplear-como-papagayo típico lenguaje técnico, telarañeado con alusiones clásicas. Es un dicciobsesionado.

Él desea ser catedrático. Yo me conformo con ser un líder revolucionario. La otra tarde, a quemarropa le tiré una directa.

"¡Qué dices! ¡Un duelo a muerte!"

"No peleo con tortugas", replicó.

Estoy hastiado de tanto antagonismo. A patadas y trompadas le he corrido de la casa un sinnúmero de veces. Mas, como un can vuelve a meterse subrepticiamente. Hoy por la noche le reclamaré: "¡Saca tu facón maldito!"

"SMUGGLE POET'S FATHER . . . "

Vómito inodoro,

       hasta al can le supo insípido:

can sin cola y boca y toca.
"Smuggle poet's father
        into dreamland, Odiseo!"
¡Si fenece mi padre os asesino!
¡Loa a tu madre, hermano!
¡Loa a tu padre, hermano!
        ¿Qué ha sido de ellos?
¿Enfermos están?

    CÁNCER
    CIRROSIS
    NEUROSIS
    TUBERCULOSIS

¡Nadie lo sabe, supo, hubo sabido
        (ni el ángel de la guardia)!
¿Cuál es el exégesis que dan los burgueses?
        Princesa tuvo aborto
        Príncipe revienta de gordo.
            ¿Galenos por doquier,
curando enfermedades sempiternas?
¡Si fenece mi padre os asesino!
Óseo semilunio anólogo
        de tus infortunios:
                Zenón en cama momificada.
                Aquiles en lama contaminada.
El mío, el tuyo, el suyo
se nos van
            sin que podamos
        articular ¡RÍA! ¡RÍA!
Se sabe que el infierno no existe.
Se sabe que el infierno no existe.
Se sabe que no sabemos de lo que
estamos hablando.

REVELACIÓN SOLICITUDIONAL
                ¡Pobrecito del diablo que lástima le tengo!
                                —Pito Pérez
    Nombre: Cholo Asecas
    Posición: Desempleado   Former Job: Ingeniero Constructor (en el barrio)
    Educación: 7th to 9th (skipped 8th purposely), Socially promoted from
        unfunctional moron to functional illiterate.

Estado Civil: Singlemarriedseparatedsinlibrealbedríobarriobsesionado.
Edad: Cronólogica: 25
      Mental: 16
      Física: 37
Afiliciación política: undecided—inclined to apolitics.
Religion: Kung Fu—Bruce Leeoniano
Hobbie: Gang Fu
Deporte Favorito: Ibid.
Planes para el futuro: Hasn't had time to sit down to reflect about the
      future.
Awards: 5
      Who's Who in Gangfu 1975-1976
      Who's Who in Ununited Barrios 1976-1977
      Who's Who in High School Dropouts 1977-1978
      Who's Who in Alcoholics Synonymous 1978-1979
      Who's Who in Best-Covered Story 1979-1980
      Favorite Slogan: The 1980s: The Decade of the Hispano

A THANH LE

Carnal, carnalito, vietnamés:
Sufres el mismo mal que todos
        los POBRES.
            Andas por los mares,
como peregrino,
            queriendo beber,
saciar tu hambre,
        con un palmo de agua en las manos.

LETANÍA, LOCURA COMPRENSIBLE

Mecanografía en mis senos, la historia de historias / estoy en el threshold
—encrucijada de mi vida / cipres[es] soslayan through oblicuos eyebrows.

Es insabible, no mecanografíes en los senos de los senos / vayamos por
cosas: la destructuralizacíon nos encauza al caos / se están
autocondenanándose al olvido perpetuo / irritable eres trovador (si el Cid
viese el poema épico que le escribiste, os pidiese un duelo / si yo pudiera
trotro-va-ría en lenguaje fluído / los duendes mitológicos, digo nuestros
antepasados, los griegos se equivocaron al decir que Julio Verne no
existió. Espérense me equivoqué, les conté el cuento incontable / verde
verdolaga a la deriva / unoceroveintiochoesminombre / ¿no existen
seudónimos en esta sociedad?

Ignoro la postura que debería de tomar el escritor / la literatura como arma / nazco on strike / protesta social / aquél por requisito social se adhiere / 2 personas muertas / a ideologías momificadas / causada por unsafe conditions / o ideologías regenerativas / revisen mi curriculum vitae / como les había dicho; la versión oficial cambió: los tipos fumaban marihuana en el trabajo / Ten stabbed each other / "fui preso infiltrador, who's who in CIAnuro S.A.; asistente general del asistente general" / ¡qué finalice el genocidio! lector, lectora subraya la letanía, locura comprensible.

Me imagino que no se podrá escribir letanías por siempre. Ya que se da el caso, específico y veraz, de que todo en la vida / perdóneme tengo hipo / ni te leerían, escríbeles en endecasílabos, en rima / tiene reglas. Empecé como poeta / una chiquilla mujer me lo dijo / no es que te defraude Federico le creí / tú sabes cómo García Lorca / en una ocasión es la vida / tus circunstancias eran muy diferentes García Lorca / pero mentía por hábito; te confieso que le besé mucho más nunca le conocí / le prendí una vela a Venus para ver si regresaba / su hijo le pregunta ¿qué es un poeta? / regresó ella, pero no su amor / la madre le contesta: tú eres poeta, niño.

Antónimo y Sinónimo —seudointelectuales, producto de la sistematización de la mediocridad— están sentados en la cafetería de City College, discutiendo cómo beneficiarse del capitalismo / ironía no intencionada.

"Me dicen el rompereglas (y deben de saber hasta por eso me pagan / cuando me mude de casa les dejaré mugre, cabrones / que si odio a alguien . . . poquito menos que el atípico individuo / oye, tú has de ser deudo de FRANCISCO DE QUEVEDO Y VILLEGAS por el estilo barroco, por escatológico / no me creerán pero me pagan por trovar frustraciones / aprendan a Cervantes, él nunca aceptó ningún centavo, ni aún del Santo Oficio / Don Quixote trató de sobornarlo / por estar en contra de todo vas a parar en la cárcel, ya verás revoltoso".

Caballero solicita, cortesmente, dama prostituta para tres encantadoras noches en elegante burdel-hotel. Insigne dama solicita urgentemente, gígolo para cuatro divinas vacaciones, pagadas por el esposo, en inolvidable resort / Jazz. Jazzista, Jazzero. Jazzera. Jazzefue. Javino.

A toothless girl saca de su bolso un paquetito; al principio le da vergüenza. "$10.15, y si no me paga le subiré de impuestos".

Vagabundo innovador; carga todas sus pertenencias en una cobija. Ríanse. Vale la pena. ¿Estás embarazada de un niño que nunca parirás?

La conocí de vista. Subía los escalones a las cinco en punto todos los días. Solía reírse después de leer su correspondencia (aunque, ¡nunca supe quién le escribía!). Se fue con muchos adioses, ninguno dirigido a mí. Un niño desea mostrar sus zapatos de mariposa al mundo. Todo mundo lo ignora.

Dos homosexuales nunca se besarían en la calle / mentira, déjenlos en paz / moléstenlos. An individual claims that we never went to the moon / el Pentágono le mandó una orden oficial / los Beogeanos colectan piérides para ahogarlas en los piélagos ecuménicos / "sea tan amable de presentarse ante las autoridades por refutar que la luna no fue visitada por cosmonautas primermundistas" / no sólo eso, sino que después de ahogarlas las hacen mermelada / un hombre conviértese en cucaracha / otro en caballo / los cholos en centauros / a poco te gustaría que como hombre / exitosa invención: mujeres en japón / te cambiarán tu nombre: de Paz a Pacífico / hay un ancho vacío, ¿verdad? / las injertaron / y una mujer acepta el cambio de nombre como hecho natural / con tigres, fue una invención fracasada. "ÚNICO MATRIMONIO QUE SOBREVIVE LAS INMUNDICIAS Y LOS MARTIRIOS" / las jitanjáforas son huecos en los sueños / Octavio ocupó el puesto intelectual, como en galería de tiro al blanco: soldadito —de crí crí— Alfonso Reyes / los Beogeanos en tumulto; la razón: porque no llegó el cheque a tiempo (sinónimo de orgasmo político) / LOS SUBE Y BAJA DE LA VIDA; LAS TENTACIONES DE LA HUMANIDAD / "soy el príncipe de la imitación" / escepticísimo innato / se le negó la entrada al teatro Colón al ingeniero del Descubrimiento porque traía consigo, identificación del siglo XV / la reina de reinas (y no de belleza) le dió en pápiro italiano. Cortés respaldó al ingeniero, a ambos metiéronlos al calabozo de la Santa Inquisición por comunistas de la Derecha, / y en latín técnico para la obra *Fausto*. Borges fue el maestro de ceremonias / ¿qué si me ciño al realismo mágico? ¿a la vanguardia? ¿al modernismo? ¿las recetas literarias con garabatos de doctor reprobado? / dictó su conferencia en gaucho. Malinche, después de todo lo que le hizo: golpizas (primer hombre en la historia encarcelado por abusar a la mujer), pagó la fianza: concubina para toda su vida y traidora del ilustre y oprimido pueblo mexicano / digo innato porque con analizar el vocabulario basta: ¿a poco? ¡no me digas! ¡sí como no! ¡cuéntame otro! / EL MATRIMONIO ES: EL DE ECCE HOMO CON MAGDALENA.

A Pito Pérez lo ascendieron de puesto: Director de Alcohólicos Eternos, he runs the program with a three million dollar budget for ten million alcoholics / los dos bestsellers (a ver multiplechoicistas, oigan bien) son: a) *Los Miserables* b) *Cien años de soledad* c) *Yo Boccaccio* d) *La cucaracha, el caballo y el centauro*.

Una mujer acaricia a unos gatos, y golpea a su hijo / competencia para ver quién tiene más credenciales / a cincuenta automovilistas se les pregunta que a dónde se dirigen / local pusher en busca de legal bidders / ninguno supo / Bartolomé de las Casas fue el que apuntó el primer gol / absurdo hoy, absurdo ayer, absurdo mañana: absurdo siempre / el gol fue descalificado por fuera de lugar / ya no niego a Dios, lo acepto a él / ella, si es que tiene los brazos cálidos / a cien ciegos los engañan poniéndoles una estatua de Buda en vez del hijo de María / para que se refugien los refugiados (salvo dictadores) / "No me digas tu nombre ni tu natalicio. Tampoco, cuándo estudiarás ni qué clase de música te gusta más. Dime que julio es mejor que agosto. Que nuestras charlas son incomparables. Dime que te vas, cuando no te mire." / Los fanáticos del béisbol están electrocutados al televisor / "¡Paletero convicto por vender paletas de marihuana!" / ¿Sabrán los no-poetas las ansias que existen en un poeta? Ignórolo, igual que ignoro si las gaviotas planean su migración anual. / Desengáñense, el paletero es inocente. / "Hubo tiempo en que pensé todos los días y las noches en ti. Hubo día (maldito día, por eso lo recuerdo) que te fui infiel (por no pensar en tí). Asesiné cuatro inocentes flores y tres gusanos".

> Tejen a todo México con
> madera vieja / ten orgullo /
> da identidad / como México
> no hay tres / a tu nación /
> UNHAPPY OVER / la historia
> puede ser aplicada a cualquier
> tiempo o era / el equipo
> mexicano nunca ha perdido /
> el presidente usa pasta dentrífica /
> se están quemando los
> ¿Hare Krishnas? / ¿Qué es un chansonnier?
> ¿Qué es, o cuál es la maquinación
> o raciocinio de tejer a México?

YO SUGIERO [. . .]

> "Yosoyradicalperoencasa. Corrección:
> en mansión. Ya se aclararon las mansiones de Pablo Neruda".
> "Con recibir el cheque mensual estoy contento; ¿qué a cual ideología
> me ciño?
> a ninguna, porque no las entiendo; mas
> conjeturo que con un poco de estudio
> seré-su-servidor-múltiple ideólogo.
> ¡Entiéndame, es una pregunta retórica!"

¿Cómo exlicar qué aciaga, experimentación fúnebre ha sido la historia de los pueblos pisados por minúsculos gigantes? Absorto, entre tregua y fugado está el profesor: "Ya déjenme de criticar a mí y a mi clase. Ya les hice patente mi solaridad: yosoyradicalperoencasa. Polemicen sobre lo absurdo del ensimismado romanticismo contemporáneo. ¡Ataquen eso, y no a mí! Ataquen a los Ísipos y no a mis vacaciones en Cancún! ¡Ataquen al ataque y no al atacado! Ataquen a las piérides; a las xenofilias; a los enpopeyados; a los amorines; a las consolidaciones congestivas; a los abusos modestos; a los informes de gobierno —que tienden a letanías—; ataquen a restauraciones apocalípticas; a la vitalidad excesiva; a perezosos dinámicos; ataquen a 'mis manos aplauden solas'; . . . Ataquen al exterminio heterogéneo; a egoísmos reinvicados; a contradicciones substanciales; a subsidios subrayados. "Los profesores, somos muy vulnerables."

[. . .]
Tu cuerpo desvinculado, tembloroso:
besos contradictorios. Yo sugiero que
¡se suicide el poeta! ¿Ustedes qué piensan?

Michael Nava   Third Prize: Poetry

Sixteen Poems

LONG DISTANCE

Deep night at the window
reflects my face, the ember
of my cigarette. In deeper space
the stars burn white and yellow.
Our voices cross like shadows
on the wires, somewhere over Kansas
where I once woke to a blizzard.
And this cold–
ness finds its focus at my spine,
rises like fingers to my throat.
I watch at the window, see
a face that you will never see
mute as roads beneath a blizzard,
all direction gone.

FOR DAVID

I read words I wrote five years ago,
"The clock lays down its arms,"
and it is your arms I remember
your blunt hands on the table

as inanimate as starfish.
It is the middle of December.
Cold stars harbor in the trees.
Across the lawns of California
the wind disperses like a wave
and like an image in dark water
your face forms in the drift of things.

THE LOVER

The lover is the double man
who has four arms, four legs.
Two mouths frame a single breath.
Four eyes stare and stare
as though, should they turn away,
he would disappear.

TWO TRANSLATIONS FROM NERUDA
LULLABY (FROM "TANGO DEL VIUDO" BY NERUDA)

I'd give the sea-wind lifted from
the darkened ocean, coarse with salt
to hear your breathing cross the gulf
between the dark side of the bed
and this side the light keeps lit,
and seek the union with your breath
the horse seeks with the whip.
I'd desert the shadow madrigals
that echo off these walls
to hear you pissing out the back
door, silver to the black
as though you poured slow honey.
The futile swords would then subside
their clatter in my soul, and I'd
evict the blood dove from my brain
that calls things by their vanished names
to people vanishing.

TWO TRANSLATIONS FROM RUBÉN DARÍO
THE ANCIENT WOMAN

The ancient woman told me:
        Observe this desiccated rose
that gathered in itself the season's splendor.
Time, that rents the highest walls of heaven,
cannot deprive this volume of its wonder.

Its leaves decant a purer attar
than the wisdom of your learned books;

the fabric of the dreams I spin I gathered
from a song learned at the rose's lips.
You are a Fate, I said, I am a fate, she said,
and I rejoice with all creation at the spring
by bringing life forth from the dead.

And she transformed herself into a scented queen
and in the subtle air, at the fingers of the Fate,
the dried rose, like a butterfly, took wing.

FOR **W.**

Neither your forehead, intimate, still,
nor your body curled like a question mark,
nor the life you speak of in the dark
are as mysterious a gift as your sleep.
In the vigil of my arms you are again
a child,—and I see you as perhaps
even God must see you, free
of the games of time, of love, of me.

Jesús Rosales | First Prize: Short Story

Parte del proceso (excerpt)

PARTE I: TAL VEZ AL HABLAR MÁS CON ELLOS

SIGUE CANTANDO, ALBERTO

Tú, sigue cantando, Alberto. No le hagas caso a nadie más. Nosotros debemos pedirle a Dios más personas como tú. Cómo da gusto que seas de Tijuana, del T.J. (en inglés), de ser tijuanero, de Tijuana Tech, como algunos lo dicen por burla y también por ignorancia. Dudo que ella haya caminado por la calle Primera y Constitución, por la casa donde tú naciste, por donde don Felipe, el del puesto de la esquina te prestaba "Chanoc". Los domingos, después de limpiar los Fords le entrabas duro a las carnitas. Ella no te vió nunca comer pero tú te acuerdas, ¿verdad? Sí, tú sí te acuerdas, tú no sabes engañar. No, Alberto, ella no sabe lo que es vivir en una vecindad sin hermanos y sin padre, pues él estaba en Bakersfield, no sabías ni por qué. Tu tío era tu padre en esos días. Te llevaba pan caliente a la cama, te sentaba en sus rodillas en esas importantes juntas de la CTM, te paseaba en el carro, "el quince" le decían, trabajando, recogiendo a viejas pintarrajeadas, de ropa grotesca y tacones altos, mareadas de licor maldiciendo el aire limpio del taxi. Tú mismo me contaste estos detalles.

Alberto, tú sí conoces Tijuana. Sabes dónde paran los amarillos, los "coyotes", y a qué hora se debe ir a la telefónica. No, 'mano, no le hagas caso. Ella tampoco conoce el barrio de San Fernando donde ahora viven tus jefitos. A pesar de tantas tentaciones del barrio tú todavía cantas con inocencia y cuando cantas, sonríes. Esa sonrisa es la que ofrece esperanza a muchos de nosotros, porque es sana, limpia, netamente natural. No la quiero comparar con la frescura del mar porque eso sería regresar al pasado, además esas cosas en labios de nosotros suenan mal. Comparo tu sonrisa con el agarrador sentimiento de una tranquilidad afable que se aproxima a falsa angustia. Angustia por vivir un sentimiento tan profundo.

Yo te he visto comer tacos de cebolla y te he visto también en la madrugada pegado a esa vieja máquina de escribir. Cabeceas de día con los libros abiertos. Cuando ni cebollas había entonces si llamabas a tu madre y tu padre la traía al instante con esas ollas de arroz y frijoles. La esperanza, Alberto, la esperanza. Lo que sea de cada quien.

Y ahora te traiciona la Debbie, tu güerita que romantizaba un prototipo, no lo tomes tanto a pecho hermano, eso ya descubrimos que le pasa a cualquiera. Está bien, llora y bebe la cerveza. Mira, Enrique y yo te acompañamos. Es rutina natural de la vieja tradición; Por eso no debes dejar de cantar. No, no nos falles en eso, Alberto. Te ruego que no escuches la canción. ¡Cántala! ¡Cántala! Ya échate el grito profundo que angustia tanto al pecho, pues ya nosotros también sentimos el sofoco. ¡Eso! ¡Eso! ¡Canta, hermano, canta! " . . . vamos a darnos la mano, somos tres viejos amigos que, estando vencidos, creemos en Dios".

POR AHORA DÉJALO

Apoyaba la cintura en el fierro protector de la baja mitad de la puerta de salida. Su pecho, así como todo su pelo, se descubría a todo ese desierto sonorense. La noche era negra, el viento chocaba ciegamente con el tren. Y aunque el tren tercamente taladraba la vía, se sentía sosegado con tremenda serenidad. Respiraba profundamente ese aire fresco que limpiaba todo su pasado. Se sentía parte de la tierra. Se atrevió a pedirle a Dios la pluma de Steinbeck pero comprendía que sólo él podría ser el mexicano.

¿Cómo telegrafiar a sus amigos esos milagrosos relámpagos que alumbraban el desierto? Esa fuerza natural la admiraba en un espacio muy lejano; Sin embargo, sabía comunicarse con él. Era una fuerza y se sintió superior a cualquiera. Fue entonces cuando chupó el limón y le dió otro trago más fuerte a la cerveza. Fue para celebrar pero entonces maldijo a la Debbie.

La maldijo por no tener el interés de saludar al señor que caminaba por el camino con un azadón en el hombro y su nieto en la mano o por no tener la sed suficiente para comprarle un vaso de agua de limón a la viejita o por no tener el hambre para comer el taco de carnitas que el niño huarachudo apasionadamente le ofrecía. Pero era absurdo. Ella no los conocía. Presentía que al llegar comería tacos de a dos pesos y subiría en camiones de a dos pesos y que el elote también le costaría dos pesos. Pero eso no le preocupaba. Sólo lamentaba la clara imagen de Debbie. Sus claros ojos, grandes y brillosos, su pelo castaño, su cuerpo sensual decorado con aquel vestido rojo que tantas veces usó con sus tacones "jeans". Más que todo eran esos tacones "jeans" lo que más destacaba de ella, lo que él más lamentaba.

Pensó en México. Lugar donde compraba helados de los carritos paleteros y a los niños les pagaba por cumplir mandados. Lugar donde le era fácil caminar por las calles y constantemente toparse con la existencia. Y la Debbie surgió de nuevo.

Pedro le llamaba. Chupó el final del agotado limón. Ya la lata vacía de cerveza rodaba en el polvo de Sonora. Desmangó la camisa y caminó por el vestíbulo que conducía a su alcoba. Pedro le ofreció otra cerveza pero no recibió respuesta. La Debbie lo estaba venciendo. Pedro le platicaba sobre el abuelo en el D.F. que aún no conoce, de su tía en Abasolo que ni siquiera sabía su nombre. Le preguntó sobre la taquería en Durango. Quería saber si se podía tomar agua, si era peligroso sentarse en los excusados. Le confesó su preocupación por su mal español, por el peligro que le llamasen pocho o cualquier otro nombre. Más que cualquier otra cosa le preguntó sobre el hombre mexicano, ¿Qué tanto se parece a ti? ¿Les gustan mucho las gringas? No contestaba ninguna de sus preguntas. No tenía control de sí mismo. En ese momento se dejaba manipular por la Debbie americana, por la que hablaba perfecto español.

PARTE II: IMPOSIBLE EN EL EXTRANJERO

RUTINA

La mañana:

Otro día. Se duchó. La señora tocó la puerta de la habitación. La señora anunció, "el desayuno". Almorzó mirando al cielo gris de la ventana. Escuchaba claramente el sonido del antiguo reloj. Ninguna palabra. Acabó y pensó sobre el plan del día: caminar por la ciudad y fotografiar lugares importantes. Se incorporó de la silla. Preparó su mochila, recogió la chamarra y salió de la casa. "Adiós, adiós", dijo la señora.

La tarde:

Ninguna palabra. La señora limpió la casa. Aprovechó la soledad para abrir su pecho al sol.

La noche:

La llave abrió el candado pero la chapa mantuvo la puerta cerrada. "Voy, voy", dijo la señora. Entró a su cuarto. Aflojó la mochila y recogió una carta. "La cena", anunció la señora. Cenó viendo la televisión. La señora fumaba. Ninguna palabra. Terminó su coliflor y patatas. Tomó un largo trago del vino. Permaneció un rato en el comedor. "Buenas noches". "Buenas noches", le respondió la señora.

En la casa en Guinardó se hablan doce palabras por día.

ADÓNDE IR?

Ya déjame, Leticia. Ya quiero llegar. ¿Qué no ves que he caminado todo el día? Yo no sé de dónde sacas tanta energía. Yo dedico mis días a sentarme en las bancas de las plazas de la ciudad y así me siento débil, ¿cómo es que tú puedes ir a bailar? No, Leticia, yo no quiero ir a tomar sangría; el licor no ayuda en estos días. Pero ve tú con Pamela; ella sí es amiga. Besa la copa en que tomes y disfruta su compañía. No preguntes de dónde vengo ni a dónde voy. Me daría pena decirte la verdad. Pero sí te confieso que deseaba caminar por todas las calles de esta ciudad. Trataba de recoger recuerdos, de fotografiar lugares importantes, como los cines y los cafés que tanto frecuentaba. Paré un rato a descansar, a tratar de estudiar apuntes y sólo escribí una carta a la familia. Al recordarte comprendí que por obligación debería de pasear un rato por la calle de Aribau. Esta calle sí causó nostalgia porque ya desde hace tiempo la habíamos leído en ficción. Ahora al verte no sé si el encuentro cambie la situación pues ya he caminado bastante este día. Yo ya quiero llegar. No, Leticia, yo no quiero tomar sangría. Mucho menos ir a bailar. Quizá cuando regresemos a East Los recupere la confianza. Pero no, Leticia, no. Ahora sólo tengo ansias de llegar.

NADA

La última despedida en Barcelona fue en la calle Urgel. Pedro y Merced habían organizado una fiesta.

Ya en la mañana Adrián me había ayudado a llevar las maletas a la estación de tren. Más bien le pedí que fuera a la casa para facilitar la despedida de la casa de la señora Aguado. Eran las diez y Adrián no venía por eso salí a comprarle unas rosas, esas que venden en la esquina. Sería un adecuado regalo de despedida. En dos días de seguro se secarían. Y con ellas, mi presencia en esa casa. Cuando Adrián llegó, le presenté a mi "señora". Nunca le conté que allí comí coliflor y patatas todos los días. Por eso saludó atentamente a la señora. Ella platicó brevemente sobre sus ya acostumbradas despedidas; sonreía y daba un beso, creo que eso era parte de su rutina. Salí de la calle Guinardó como si fuera al cine.

En la casa de la calle Urgel, Pedro, Mercedes, Pamela y yo brindábamos mientras Leticia arreglaba sus maletas. El trago "43" me mareó pues había comido sólo una bolsa de churros en todo el día. Celebramos toda la tarde. Yo prometí escribirles y no olvidarlos. Lo dije al tomar otra copa de anís. Pedro me retrató con Pamela y Leticia. Quizá también era la última vez que las veía. Brindamos muy confiados de nuestro futuro.

Salí antes que otro invitado estropeara mi despedida. Por eso los abracé a todos y me fui a caminar por la calle Pelayo. Cuidadosamente fotografiaba todos los lugares significativos de esa ciudad. Tuve tentación de comprarle un cachito de lotería al cieguito de la esquina pero no creí que se acordaría de mí si lo hiciera. Por eso caminé por las Ramblas hasta llegar a la estación.

Estuve leyendo el *Washington Post* mientras el "Rápido" arrancaba. Mis manos tranquilas jugaban con las páginas del periódico. Compré un bocadillo de tortilla de patatas y dos cervezas "Skol". Miré hacia fuera, estaba todo muy obscuro. Creo que ya habíamos pasado por Tarragona.

PARTE III: SIN DUDA AQUÍ

NO DEJES QUE AFLOJEN, PEDRO

"¿Por qué escuchas tanto a Pedro Infante?"

"¿Por qué lo preguntas? Tú también lo escuchas, y te gusta. No metas el dedo en la retórica que no es el propósito de estas canciones".

"Bueno es que tanta música que podemos escuchar pero nos aferramos a refugiarnos en el pasado. No quiero oponerme pero el hecho es que contradice nuestra vida académica".

"Mira, cuando estaba en la secundaria, escuchaba las canciones 'intelectuales' de David Bowie y aprendí que en 1984 se acabará el mundo. Por eso no quiero discutir. Nos queda poco de vida. Disfruta la música y esconde por allí la retórica".

"'¿Y si le cantaras al profesor Oviedo una canción de éstas, qué crees tú que pensaría?"

"Lo primero que debería de pensar es que una vez, en un lejano espacio, también fue chavo con inquietudes sanas. De seguro le gustaron las morras y les mandaba poemitas. Ya será todo cursi para él pero pasó por todo este proceso, compadre. Ahora. Si le dijera a Oviedo que el filósofo que más ha estimulado mis sentidos es sin duda José Alfredo Jiménez, el ranchero compositor, el hijo del pueblo, me mataría su expresión. Le chorrarían sus 'babas de diablo' para decirlo más a su nivel. 'No hay que llegar primero pero hay que saber llegar'. Estoy seguro que ya alguien lo dijo anteriormente en la historia del hombre. Lo perfecto fue que yo lo escuché primero en español, en voz de Pedro Infante (composición de José) que en la de un Descartes o Kant o cualquiera de su pandilla".

"Pero no sólo él te fregaría. Muchos de nuestros compañeros no saben que las cantamos. Entonces es raro para ellos ese desbordo de emoción. No te has fijado, en las juntas nos han acusado de borloteros sentimentales. En las fiestas cantamos hasta con ronquera y muchos de ellos quieren acompañarnos pero se niegan la ropa que usan y el make-up de las viejas los controla completamente. Creo que debemos aprender que entre más culturas penetramos, más nos enriquecemos. Eso tenemos que aprender si es que uno quiere realizarse en este país. '¿Y qué?' es una actitud bastante estúpida y lamentosa".

"Bueno, pero somos estudiantes universitarios que debemos de saber poder analizar cualquier situación. ¿O no? ¿Qué pasó con el tema interesante de Cortázar defendiendo su posición como autor exiliado pero a la vez considerándose revolucionario, en ese artículo que leímos en clase? Además, ¿qué pasó con el Buscón Pablos, es en verdad un personaje picaresco? ¿A eso venimos a la universidad? A ver si después de largos años podemos orgullosamente mostrar que la 'Benina' de Galdós era en verdad una dulce y desinteresada mujer? ¿O que don Juan Tenorio inconcientemente violaba el sí de las niñas? ¿No es el propósito de venir a la universidad para purgarse de simplicidades? ¡¡Todo es contradicción, amigo!! En mi situación. O dejo de escuchar a José Alfredo o dejo de jueguitos en aulas con deditos en mejillas, disfrazados de interés intelectual. Imagínate. Ayer la clase discutió *Residencia en la tierra*: que si Neruda era poeta a pesar de describir imágenes atroces; que si le prestó pesetas a César Vallejo para desempeñar su bolsillo. Y yo, esa misma tarde regreso al apartamento a escuchar canciones de los Corazones Solitarios. No dejé de sentir una fuerte contradicción. Sentí tristeza, amigo. Lo curioso fue que tú llegaste y te sentaste a escucharlas y desapareció la inquietud. Nunca te lo dije, pero te di las gracias".

"Vamos a callar. Deja que toque la música. Creo que todo es parte del proceso".

Uno nunca sabe

Hablaste con Susana. Te dió ride en su Volkswagen. ¿Será eso un hecho histórico? Bueno es en sí histórico, pero, ¿será ella una futura poeta chicana? Eso es el gran misterio de toda la bola de ustedes. No se atreven a criticar a nadie, ni al más tímido y misterioso porque nadie quiere "meter la gran pata histórica". "Meter la pata" y decir que cierta persona no sirve para escribir literatura. ¡Claro! Nadie quiere quedar en ridículo en su futuro. Toda poesía chicana es fabulosa, dicen. Prometedora, demandan. Todo escrito en chicano es bueno, serio y justificador. ¡Cuidado con reprocharlo! "All is heavy," dice el "Tecolote". ¿Quién será el gran escritor chicano del futuro? Todos pueden o nadie, nadie puede serlo. Por eso es tan posible que la gente pueda escaparse con un diploma de este colegio. No te extrañaría si Susana, o el "Tecolote" o Armando Tan-Tan, o el tal Manuel que todavía no conoces, serán los fregones escritores del futuro. Como diría tu amigo Carlos Cid, "los más chingones".

Pero perdón.

Tú renuncias. Sí. Tú renuncias las actividades de esta noche. Eres tú sin mitote, eso es todo. Y podrías agregar "¿y qué?" pero no vale la pena.

Eres tú sin mitote. No aplaudes a esos futuros hombres ilustres de la lectura de hoy. No fumas la marihuana de Manuel ni de aquellos que la pasan para ser más camaradas, más carnalitos. La renuncias, la renuncias porque los que la ofrecen lo hacen por puro mitote.

Quizá ellos tengan razón en todo lo que hacen. Quizá tú no comprendas la situación histórica. ¿Entonces qué estás haciendo aquí? Te aseguro que no eras el único en preguntarte esta pregunta.

Esta noche, en la lectura de poesía, Roberto Durán te impresionó porque fue sincero en su presentación. ¿Y la autoridad? Empedándose y rifando. O.k. Está bien, eso no tiene nada que ver, pero, ¿para qué poner las caras idiotas? ¡Idiotas de falsa seriedad! Con el licor y la rifa toda palabra es bella, toda palabra es clásica, "tan-tan". Son la crema de los verdaderos chingones del colegio. Son los auténticos chingones por eso los mandas a la chingada, porque resulta que tú crees en una busca más sincera sin ayuda alguna de su pinche falsedad.

¿Y ahora qué? ¿Qué harás ahora? Esa ilusión ya la perdiste. Solitario carnal. Estás solitario. "Tú a lo tuyo y ya tendrás tu recompensa", dijo María, la de España. Solitario carnal, estarás solitario. Tú no naciste para participar con la bola de "escuelanos". Tú sólo quieres ver el futuro en forma muy personal. No quieres tener miedo de vivir tus pensamientos. No quieres pertenecer a ningún club de solicitudes. Eso ya es riesgo tuyo. Por eso al ver hoy a la Debbie no solicitaste una conferencia con ella pues es sin duda el enemigo extremo de tu tranquilidad. Por eso también te gustaría mandarla a la chingada. Pero hablarás con ella. Eso ya lo sabes. Será inevitable, el destino lo demanda. La verás y hablarás con ella. No para hacerla de pendejo, como antes, sino para que le molesten tus pláticas, cada una de tus palabras. Te dicen que la Debbie habla perfecto español. ¡Sí! Entonces que te dé el beso que te debe y que siga desarrollándose en su mierda de ambiente. Eso decíselo hoy mismo, ahora que todavía vive el coraje.

¿Y AHORA QUÉ?

Tal vez al hablar con ellos puedes encontrar respuestas. Ya basta que te pases las horas evaluando situaciones. Deberías de escucharlos mejor. Mira, rezar no lo haces y con Dios no sabes platicar. Visitas iglesias sólo para escaparte de la gente. No hombre, es mejor que hables más con ellos. Ellos sí que te ayudarán a encontrar lo que tú buscas. No dejes que Alberto cante solo. Háblale y dile que no se agüite. Convenciéndolo que olvide su güera, te convences también a ti mismo. 'Ora si tú no quieres, no hay problema, haz lo que quieras. Pero es mejor hablar con él. A la neta, no dejes que tome solo. Por ahora deja que las cosas se desarrollen, ¿o no? Pero después, no te dejes manipular por ningunos tacones "jeans" ni por gringas que hablen perfecto español. A ti te ha tocado mala suerte con ellas. No es bueno intentar otra vez. Hazme caso en lo que te digo. Tus miradas no penetran en ellas. Tal vez al hablar más con ella te puedas convencer mejor. Pero, ¿para qué buscar esos labios de cristal? No 'mano, tú a lo tuyo, ya basta de humillaciones. No me gustaría que le enviaras esa carta a Tetsuo Mizutani. No quiero que vayas a Nagasaki en busca de más alternativas y de nuevos escapes de la rutina. Ya sabes que en el extranjero es casi imposible encontrar respuestas. Te incorporas a otra rutina, a una forma más remota de sentir compañía. Viviendo y caminando no sabías a dónde ir. No busques a otra señora Aguado. No escribas otro resumen. No quiero que no sientas nada. Piénsalo bien y no mandes la carta a Tetsuo Mizutani. Ya no te dejes engañar por nuevas perspectivas. Ya ves que creías que estando fuera de tu ambiente podrías ver mejor el tuyo, pero no resultó. ¿No te acuerdas del problema a tu regreso? Cuestionaste a tus colegas del colegio. Cuestionabas más a tu ambiente, te sentías más centrado en ti mismo. No hermano, esa parte del proceso déjalo para el pasado. No vayas a Nagasaki. Ya no hables de enormes distancias y sus respuestas. Es sin duda aquí donde tendrás que enfrentarte a los problemas. Es parte del proceso decir tonterías y consumir falsas esperanzas. Pero eso se desarrolla. Por eso no tengas miedo de seguir buscando la respuesta a tu soledad. Aquí termina un proceso. Mañana empieza otro. Con la experiencia del anterior y con la madurez del próximo, el nuevo proceso será aún más difícil. Por eso perdona carnal que te diga que aquí nadie encuentra su busca. Pero estoy ya hablando del futuro y tú no me crees.

1981-82

Mary Helen Ponce

Honorable Mention: Short Story

Recuerdo: When Rito Died

I remember when my brother Rito died of tuberculosis in the Olive View Sanitarium. He had been ill when as a child my parents had lived in Ventura, where they settled upon arriving from Mexico. Later it was said that the cold of las limoneras had caused el t.b.

We did not have a telephone, all emergency calls were relayed to us through el Mister Williams, owner of la Tienda Blanca as we referred to Pacoima General Store. He was a good, kind person who extended credit to la gente mexicana of our barrio, who had agreed to give my parents a message from the sanitarium during the final days of my brother's illness.

One night or early morning, Mr. Williams came to give my parents the message: Rito was near death. I remember I woke up when our dog El Duque began to bark and the lights went on in the house. I heard voices coming from my mother's room: soft, murmuring. (There was never panic in our home.) Soon the car was cranked up. I heard it go out the driveway, then fell asleep. When I next woke up, the car was back, as was my father. A deadly silence permeated our home, only broken by the sound of muffled crying.

I don't remember who told me Rito had died. I don't remember if I cried. I was five years old and barely remembered the handsome stranger with blue-green eyes who had been away most of my life. I do remember the soft whispery voices, the shadowy figures that came and went, among them my Tío Luis and Tío Macario, only relatives of my mother in this country, special to her, and to us.

I didn't see my mother for most of the day. I believe she remained in her room where the neighborhood women kept going in and out. The men remained outside with my father and uncles where they huddled together, talking in short muted sentences. Toward evening they built a small bonfire around which they gathered.

Among the men was my older brother Berny who was about seventeen, thus allowed to be among los hombres. I recall I peeked out the door to see one of the men with a bottle which he passed around. My brother Berny declined. Our father was muy recto, strict, so that Berny was not allowed to drink, not even on this somber occasion. The men stayed outside, around the fire. The bright yellow flames gave their sad, long faces a strange eerie look. Inside the black-robed women prayed and kept el velorio.

During the early 1940s, Mexican families such as ours had little money to spend on funerals; most were kept simple, due both to tradition and economics. The wake or viewing of the body was done at home, as it was convenient and less expensive.

I remember the day the carroza came to deliver my brother's body. I was playing hop-scotch toward the back of the house (where I wouldn't be seen or heard) when I looked out to see a black car approach. The driver leaned out to call, "Is this 13011 Hoyt?" "Yes," I answered. Before I could ask what it was they wanted I heard movement inside the house, en la sala. The front door opened to let my cousin Mary (from Oxnard) and sister Elizabeth out. They began to direct the driver. I was told to go "in the back," which I did. When next I looked, the black car was gone. Everything was still. Then I heard crying from inside the house. Soft, forlorn. I stood outside and listened to my mother's anguished cries, "Hijo mío, ay, hijo mío." The cries came and went like waves of sound.

Toward afternoon neighbors and relatives came to pay their respects, among them la Mrs. Harding, principal of Pacoima Elementary where we had attended, a kind lady who had liked Rito quite well. When I saw her inside I too wanted to be among the mourners, so I pushed my way in between the legs of the mourners and into the living room. It was then I saw Rito. He was lying in a dark coffin set atop a wooden bench. Behind the coffin and on both sides hung white sheets with gardenias pinned to the material. Large candles set at the head and foot of the coffin flickered. In tall vases and cans stood fresh flowers placed on the floor, flowers brought by the neighbors who had added crespón to make a more formal arrangement. Atop the coffin lay a silver cross, next to it was a funeral wreath made of white gardenias, and across it a white ribbon with the inscription "Nuestro Hijo Querido." Among the flowers were buttercups, taza en plato as we called the flowers that looked like cups on a saucer, which, together with the white gardenias, gave forth a sickly, sweet smell we younger children referred to as olor a muerto. The reeking, stifling smell of the flowers and sad eyes of the mourners soon forced me to leave the room but not before I sidled up to la Mrs. Harding who hugged me, called me a "sweet child," and admonished me to "help my mother."

That night el Padre Alfonso came to say el rosario. After he had given my parents el pésame, he knelt and began to pray el Padre Nuestro. The women who had been praying throughout the day gave the response. He ended with the Litany of the Saints as we responded, "Ruega por él," and the blessing;

Requiescat in pace. "Amen." He then took his hat with the pompoms (brought from his native France), set it on his head and left.

That night I was allowed to sleep in my mother's bed as there was no room elsewhere; the relatives from Oxnard had remained overnight for the funeral. I recall my excitement at being allowed in my mother's room, so that I began to jump up and down on the bed, until my friend's mother Doña Raquel came into the room and gently told me to go to sleep. She sat with me until I did. In the morning everyone looked haggard and somber in their dark clothes. Chocolate and pan dulce were served, after which the men went into the sala where they carefully picked up the coffin to begin the short walk to our church, el Ángel de la Guardia. The women and children followed the procession to the church door where the bell began to peal, "dong, dong, dong." Even the bell sounded sad. Father Alfonso awaited the body which he then blessed. The Mass of the Dead followed. During communion all went up to receive la comunión that was offered for the soul of the "dearly departed" and which I knew would ensure that the spirit of my dear brother Rito would go straight to heaven.

When mass was over we followed the priest and coffin outside as he sang *In Paradisum*, "May the angels of the Lord greet thee." Then the coffin was placed in the waiting hearse, the same one that had brought Rito home for the last time. My father and relatives followed in another car.

I did not attend the funeral; they said I was too young. Instead I walked home trailing my mother who had decided not to go to the cemetery. She said she could not bear to see her first son interred. She walked with my cousin Mary and Aunt María who appeared to hold her up. When the big black hearse went by she wavered in her step, stopped for a minute. She remained motionless until the hearse had passed, then slowly looked up. I heard her murmur, "Adiós, hijo mío." She then resumed the long, slow walk.

I stayed behind, slowly picking my way between the rocks and grass that grew along the path next to the street, my eyes glued on the big black car that finally turned left—and disappeared.

1982-83

Bone Games

DEDICATIONS

The divinity of light
the falling moonlight
the bleeding womb
the lies flowing
the eyes seeing
the opaque moonlight
hundreds of hands reaching
for the darkness under railroad cars
the panic sounds you make to yourself
as you face sudden death
the sun going down in that woman's
vagina, electricity, the mystery of
existence and sunlight
all these things I dedicate to life
to romance I dedicate my eyes
and cactus I eat with the
stingers not hurting my wings
I circle slowly the water beneath
the desert, maroon blood flowing
in that pounding heart
all these things were listed
malfunctioning machine guns short
glimpses of Jews and Nazis in L.A.,
Protestants and Catholics in Ireland
slugging it out for God
fragile art made from the flames
of burning flesh
all these things were on the list of
dedications and more or less

whichever way you look at it,
the lists full of people
guilty of truth and one lie can
condemn you to restless horses
trotting endlessly at a furious
pace across green grass
you on the back holding onto
political statements and visions or
dreams or maybe just colorful
illusions of red sunsets and ladies
and rainbows strewn freely across
the sky a harp, a chrome harp
atop a heavenly hill as you
zoom in closer you see the
flowers around it and on the
harp you see a list of names
of children almost born and
lists and more lists of poems
and unknown photographers and
paintings and flashing lights and
new names everywhere walking
on the grass

POEM FROM THE BASEMENT

In here the feathers are talking
about pop pop
the return of nothing to say
the illicitness of your conspiracy
piracy concrete vastness
the cape, the fishing line,
can the survival be another
plot, where can we insert
the staples to reach in
to connect the issues the
reality escaping from itself
the corruption of even the simple
bird's song the dreamland in
advanced decay we are in the
dreamland of advanced eagles
rotting in the nest
the mirrors do not lie
the eyes may deceive the desire
to preach about the surrealism

in your big toe darling,
but catch innocence touching navels
in the public transportation system
with hands smoking from an illicit
heat eating the age of this arrival
. . . this fire, this despondent nation
eating itself with someone else's spoon
let's look the other way when the
dead fall off the bar stool and children
assassinate themselves with the prince
frog's testicle, let's turn the pages
of the newspaper as nails are driven
through the coffee, the poison
amputates the mind with the exhibition
of the eye in museums, the narrator
points to the glass case and says
here was their failure and this is
how they lived, here are the skulls of
their hydrogen babies the cold fingers
of their demented elections, here is
the evidence of depleted erection
here are their tears preserved
in gasoline, here was their future
burned with the agony of their own seed rotting
here is the evidence of empires
rising only to fall, here are their,
their lies and their whores
here are their artists,
. . . their leaders and the blood
     of the storm
     here is the story of cargo overturned
here is the decay rampant with lust
here is the song of blasphemous
tyranny here is the innocence
betraying itself and capitulating
to its own suicide, here ladies
and gentlemen is the exit
to the museum

NTERLUDED EXCERPT ON REALITY
     With all the necessity to scribble
     at all dishonest hours of a spent night
     here for seconds

we once held each other
here the night crept in to devour
our own uncertainty about the
European blood
  here I left drops of old
maroon Aztec blood
   there in the solitude
of a lost inspiration we conspire
to flaunt our innocence
there in the blessed sunrise
we awoke chilled by hours of night
desert air to roll over
and wish that our combined psychic
energy could move the logs
into the fire while the warmth
of our passion eluded itself and
we dozed off into a dream sleep
with the sun beating down harder
every second until finally we
kicked aside the blankets and
stood before the growth of air
that flowered and flowed down from
vanishing stars
to stand with us as
we greeted the new sun.

Jack López   **First Prize: Short Story**

The Boy Who Swam With Dolphins (excerpt)

We had been driving for about an hour far away from the smell of the sea as the highway in Baja California headed inland. Hills and cactus and dry oven heat. Heat shimmering in waves far off down the road. Mirages of ocean waves. Then the highway began climbing up, up into the hills. After the road crested we came to an oasis by the side of the road. Perry coasted the car to a stop. This place was painted bright pink with huge green palms all around it. On the other side of the road there was a motel with a big green swimming pool. After we got close enough to the water we could see that the pool was green with algae. At the oasis there was a small veranda with a Coke machine and chairs. We opened the top of the machine and took cold drinks. The owner came out from inside the building and smiled.

"You boys want some food?" he asked in good English.

"No, thanks."

"How about some firecrackers?"

"No, we just want some drinks."

"You want to see a photograph?"

"A photograph? Sure." We thought it was naked girls.

"Twenty-five cents each," he said. He was a small, older man with grey hair, but he didn't seem that old, rather he was stately. His breath smelled of stale beer and he had not shaved for a few days so that grey whiskers reflected light when he turned a certain way. We followed him into the store. There was a fireplace in the center where a fat old lady was making tortillas by hand. The store was a curios shop and he had everything from stuffed iguanas to those cork guns that pop in your ear to playing cards with naked women on them. He even had switchblade knives in a display case. And all this was out in the middle of the desert. I guess he figured a bunch of real dumb tourists were going to come by.

Anyway, we followed him into a back room that had a brightly woven blanket for a door. It must have been his bedroom. There was a single metal framed bed in the center. Newspapers were spread over it and they were wrinkled as if someone had been lying on them. There was a small shrine in the corner with candles and a plaster of paris crucifix presiding over the room. He went to an old dresser that had a smokey cracked mirror over it, opened the top drawer, and took out an envelope. From the envelope came the photo. He showed it to us. It was a picture of a fat old man with a diaper on, lying on what looked like this same bed, in this same room.

"What the hell is going on?" Jay asked.

"Pancho Villa," said the old man. His eyes were glowing with pride.

"Pancho shit," Jay said and walked out. Perry followed, shaking his head.

"Pancho Villa on his death bed," the old man said. "Look closely." I tried to hold the photo but he wouldn't let go of it. Po Boy and I looked very close. There were all these marks all over this guy's belly, and it was a very big belly.

"Bullets," he said, his eyes big and gleaming, thinking of past times.

We bought a bunch of cold drinks and left the oasis. We drove on looking for three rocks on top of a hill and then shortly after that, a dirt road off to the right. About thirty minutes later we spotted the rocks. And sure enough, farther up the road there was a small dirt road leading into the arid hills but toward the ocean.

The road dropped into a valley that had water, a valley that had a series of farms. There were neat little pastures full of cows. We passed acre upon acre of olive trees swaying in the afternoon breeze. We passed dirt-floored houses where rounded ladies swept the dirt in their hand-embroidered dresses using brooms of straw. We drove on and on, crossing a shallow creek once, twice, then three times. It was getting late when finally the road emptied onto a broad floodplain that was bordered on both sides by steep hills covered with chaparral and cactus. We drove on. Then we could smell the salt, hear the sound of breaking waves. We drove over a dirt hill and we could feel the ground shaking from the power of the waves. Then the road took a turn to the right and we could see the waves. It was almost religious, like a miracle. Blue, blue sky with water a deeper blue. A small bay with a peak in the center. The entire bay was alight with diamonds sparkling from the afternoon sun. We thought at the time that the waves were at least fifteen feet, but now, after the passage of time, I know that they were no larger than ten feet. Still, that was the largest wave any of us had seen.

Jesús had been correct in his analysis of the wave that broke in this bay. It was perfect. It was a peak that broke both right and left in deep water but kept lining up all the way into a very fast shorebreak.

Po Boy was in the water paddling out before any of us had our boards off the car. We were hesitant, not knowing what the bottom was like or what else was going to be in the water with us. But soon we were all in the water doing what we did best—surfing. We were taking off on the largest waves we had ever seen and riding them like we did it every day. The bottom was large, smooth river stones that did not hurt your feet. It was funny, but as you rode into the shorebreak, the water rushing back out from the beach would clank the stones together, making it sound as if there were an audience clapping. All of us rode some pretty fantastic waves, but we all got blasted at one time or another. Like the set that came just before sunset which closed out the entire bay. It kept building on the uneven horizon. I was so scared, my heart almost popped out of my mouth. Perry had lost his board trying to roll under one of the first waves to break. Jay was way inside when the set hit. So it was just Po Boy and myself. I was farther out than he was, but he was not scared, rather he had never seemed to be having such a great time. The huge waves made him come alive. I looked down the face of one smoking giant that I just barely made it over and saw Po Boy bail off his board and body surf the drop, shouting at the top of his lungs.

The explosion after the wave broke was tremendous, somewhat like a waterfall. I didn't think I would see Po Boy alive again, but there he was in almost the same position on the next wave yelling his head off. He amazed me. It was a Po Boy that I had never before seen . . . .

It had been pretty late when we arrived, so we only got to surf about two hours before darkness overtook our magical bay with the perfect wave. We were exhausted after the short time of surfing with so much adrenalin flowing. We built a fire of driftwood on the beach and warmed up some tortillas and beans and drank some warm Cokes. We fell asleep under a sky that was not competing with electricity to show us its charms. We were definitely

THE CHICANO/LATINO LITERARY PRIZE 👞 67

smug in the knowledge that we had searched out and found what for us was a perfect wave.

The next morning I awoke to find my sleeping bag completely wet. The fog was in. And it was a thick fog. A slight movement was blowing in from the ocean, pushing small droplets of water past my face. Perry and Jay were still asleep. Po Boy was not in his sleeping bag. I arose, stretched, put on my Levis and sweatshirt, and walked over to the bushes. I came back and cut some kindling to start a fire. The newspaper was damp but finally I got some small flames going. I fed the flames some larger pieces of driftwood and soon had a fire. I boiled water for coffee. Jay and Perry awoke separately, used the facilities shall we say, and then took coffee with me.

"Where's Po Boy?" asked Jay.

"His board's gone, so I guess he's out there surfing," I said.

"He's nuts."

"I don't know if it's balls or lack of brains."

We warmed some tortillas on the fire. Jay spread peanut butter and jelly on his and then rolled them like they were big cigarettes. Perry and I put butter on ours. We drank our coffee in the stillness of early morning fog. All we could hear was the roar of crashing waves. It was strange that the water was so close yet you could not see it, but only hear waves breaking. After a while Perry walked to the water and started yelling for Po Boy.

As it became later we could see that the fog was hugging the coast. Inland it was bright and clear, on its way to becoming hot once again. Yet the fog still clung to the ocean so that we could not see the waves or Po Boy. We all wanted to go. We loaded the car. Perry started the engine thinking that Po could hear it and he would come in. Perry honked the horn over and over. We walked to the water's edge and shouted again and again. Evidently he could not hear us. It wasn't like Po to completely disregard us. We walked up and down the beach looking for his surfboard. No sign. We were all thinking the same thing but no one would bring it up. If only the fog would lift. But it wouldn't.

Luis J. Rodríguez   Second Prize: Short Story

Sometimes You Dance With a Watermelon

"Ayyyyy."

A man's voice, then the tumbling of a body like a sack of potatoes down a flight of stairs.

"Pinche cabrón, hijo de la . . . "

A woman's voice.

"*¡Borracho!* Get out of my house!"

Next door to the disturbance, Rosalba tossed and turned on a squeaky bed, her fragile mirror of dreams smashed into fragments.

"You dog! Get out of here!" the woman's shrieks continued outside the bedroom window, a raspy stammering over the curses.

"But, *muñeca*," the man slurred. "Give me a chance, *querida*. Let me in, *por favor*."

"This house is not for *sin vergüenzas* like you," the woman wailed.

A loud rustling sound pulsated through the window as the man toppled back onto a row of shrubbery. The whimpers of small children behind a torn screen door followed the man's moans. Rosalba carefully opened her eyes. Early morning sunlight slipped into the darkened room through small holes in aluminum foil that covered the window. The foil kept the daylight out so that Rosalba's latest husband, Pete, could sleep. Rosalba turned away from the heavy figure next to her, curled up in a fetal position.

Rosalba was forty years old with flawless brown skin and a body that could be in its twenties. She had fountains of hair down to the small of her back that she had kept long ever since she was a little girl. Only now, gray strands were intertwined with the profusion of dark ones.

Pete worked the graveyard shift at a meatpacking plant near their apartment on Olympic Boulevard. He slept during the day and labored at night until he wended his way home from the stench and heat. When he got there, Pete climbed onto the mattress, propped up by cinder blocks, to the comfort of Rosalba's warm body.

As the noise outside subsided to uneasy quiet, Rosalba felt a yearning to go someplace. Any place.

She carefully emerged from under the heavy covers and grabbed a dirty pink bathrobe with loose threads hanging from the hem. She tiptoed through the room, peered backward toward the bed, then slowly opened the bedroom door to a frustrating medley of creaky hinges. Pete, the lump beneath the covers, rolled into another position then lay still.

Rosalba entered the living room and stepped over bodies stretched out on mattresses strewn across the floor. There lay her twenty-four-year-old daughter Sybil; her daughter's four children, including the oldest, nine-year-old Chila; and Sybil's no-good, always-out-of-work boyfriend, Stony.

Rosalba worked her way to the kitchen and opened a cupboard. Cockroaches scurried to darker confines. The nearly empty shelves were indifferent to calls from her nearly empty stomach. The family survived mostly on nonfat powdered milk for breakfast, tortillas and butter for lunch, and corn flakes for dinner—most of which Sybil bought with food stamps.

"This life is draining the life out of me," Rosalba whispered, as she stared at the vacant cupboards in front of her.

Rosalba interrupted her futile search for something edible and thought about the twenty years that had passed since she first crossed the U.S. border from the inland Mexican state of Nayarit. Her daughter Sybil was five years old then; Rosalba, strong but naïve, was twenty-one.

Rosalba fled her hometown. She fled an abusive husband that her parents had coerced her to marry when she was sixteen. She fled a father who announced he would disown her if she dared to leave. Rosalba finally concluded that the suffocation there would kill her more than being without a father, husband, or even her mother, who sat off by herself, unwilling to challenge the men that eventually overwhelmed Rosalba and her mother to the point of paralysis.

With Sybil, one beaten-up valise held up with tape and rope and her fortitude, Rosalba managed to stake a ride on a creaky old bus with exhaust fumes that leaked into where the passengers sat, making them groggy. Without arrangements or connections, Rosalba exited the bus in Tijuana, near the U.S. border, crowded with women, children, and single men who also risked everything for another life.

Rosalba cried the first night in the street. In her loneliness, she thought about the rancho where she grew up, tending to goats, chickens, and a couple of horses. She thought about their house made of mud and logs, although sturdy, with an open-air dome-covered oven in the patio. She thought about the scorpions and how she had to dust off the bed sheets, how once her mom sliced her skin and sucked the poison from a scorpion bite when Rosalba was a child. She still carried the scar on her back where her mother sewed up the wound with a needle and thread.

Rosalba also remembered how as a little girl she'd take an empty bucket to the village well and fill it with water for cooking or baths. And she recalled walking barefoot along dirt paths with bundles of clothes or baskets of corn that she balanced on her head.

She remembered a time when everything as clear, everything in its place—a time aligned with the rhythms of the universe, it seemed, when she felt her mother's love and her father's protection and a deep internal throbbing to do, learn, and be.

Things changed when she got older. When she became a woman, at the start of her first blood, when she began to hunger for herself. Everything turned toward the men, the chores, and the "duties" of wife and mother. So when she fled her family, she realized, she also fled the fond memories. Rosalba stopped crying and vowed to never let these memories weaken her resolve and force her back to a place where she also felt crushed.

Along with a small child, Rosalba knew she was in danger if she stayed in Tijuana. She followed other migrants through the permeable line that separated the two countries. Eventually, borrowing rides and the kindness of strangers, she ended up in L.A. She realized then that if she ever harbored any notions about returning to Nayarit to her family, she'd have to let them go from that point on.

Unfortunately, Rosalba endured many scary nights staying in dingy hotel rooms with other migrants, mostly women, in downtown Los Angeles. She not only didn't have a man to help but no obvious skills except what she learned on the rancho. She had to survive being cast into a peculiar universe of neon and noise. This was a place where winos and the homeless resided on the sidewalk, where women sold themselves for sex to eat or get stoned, and where people on city buses never say anything to you unless they happen to be drunk or crazy.

In the middle of this, she met Elvia, a slightly overweight but vivacious twenty-four-year-old, who also had a five-year-old child, a boy. Rosalba and Elvia became fast friends. She now had someone to share her concerns, her appetites, her hopes. Elvia was also single and fleeing a world similar to Rosalba's, although more urbanized, being from the port city of Ensenada, Baja California.

Rosalba often took care of Elvia's boy while his mother worked in a sewing establishment in the Pico-Union district west of downtown. She loved watching Sybil playing with someone her own age for a change, to know she could finally have a semblance of a child's life. Everything seemed like it would work out fine, where Rosalba could seriously consider a little bit of happiness and stability.

But this part of her life ended with a terrible tragedy—when Elvia's boy accidentally fell three stories to the ground below from an opened window while Rosalba was taking a bath in the middle of the day. Elvia, devastated, left the place and was never heard from again. Remembering these things was difficult for Rosalba, and shaking her head slowly from left to right, Rosalba focused again on the empty cupboard before her.

"*Chingao*, there was never anything to eat then either," Rosalba grumbled to no one in particular. Even though Pete was now working, his lean check barely took care of the rent, clothing, and bus fares.

She didn't mind the adults not eating, but the children . . . she was prepared to starve so the children could eat.

Rosalba didn't have the same concern for Sybil or Stony. She was certain they were into drugs or other illegal activities.

Why Sybil would end up with an ex-convict like Stony was beyond her. As a child, Sybil was shy and respectful. Someone once commented on the girl's good behavior as she lay in Rosalba's arms while both sat on a sliced-up seat in the smelly bus from Nayarit to Tijuana. Even during their first years in the crumbling downtown hotels, Sybil didn't cause her mother any headaches. She stayed off in a corner, entertaining herself. Sometimes the girl lovingly caressed Rosalba's face to wake her from sleeping on the couch too long. And despite the tragedy of Elvia's boy's deadly fall, Sybil maintained a good disposition.

That didn't last too long.

By ten, Sybil complained about everything. She spent more time on the sidewalks and alleys, with other children from migrants, next to crazies and drug addicts and disheveled men. She learned to talk back to her mother and run away when she didn't feel like falling into line. At about that time, Rosalba tried to teach her about helping others by taking her daughter across the U.S.-Mexico border, carefully escorting other migrants through brush and cactus, and assisting them with their entry into city life. But this only made things worse by opening Sybil up to a world fraught with danger and interesting characters—instead of turning away from this, she relished the excitement and uncertainty.

Soon Sybil began to hang out with older guys. One, an undocumented man who already had children back in Sinaloa, got Sybil pregnant with Chila—she was sixteen, the same age her mother was when she had her. This man was later deported and disappeared from their lives. After that Sybil frequented nightclubs and dance halls. She brought home many a sorry specimen; one of them gave her the other three children she bore—only to leave for Houston with another woman.

Rosalba, who thought her daughter might have learned something from these ordeals, felt further betrayed one day when Sybil brought Stony home. At first glance, Stony seemed nice. But as soon as he smiled, his missing front teeth and beady eyes made him look ominous—like a lizard with fangs. Stony had a look that Rosalba noticed in many Chicanos recently released from the joint. He never worked, but when pushed, somehow coughed up beer money. Rosalba figured Stony sold food stamps to buy booze.

Staring into the vacant cupboard, Rosalba became even hungrier. She closed the cupboard doors then walked toward the kitchen window that overlooked an alley behind their home; the alley was cluttered with burnt mattresses, treadless tires, and weather-beaten furniture.

Rosalba leaned against the streaked glass, fibers of hair dispersed themselves across her face. She looked over the Los Angeles sky, smudged over with smog, blocking out the mountains or greenery in the distance. In a dirt yard, children played and chattered in broken English and half-Spanish, a language all their own like the pidgin spoken wherever cultures merged and clashed.

What a puzzling place, this Los Angeles, Rosalba thought. Factory whistles all day long; the deafening pounding of machinery, with cars and trucks in a sick symphony of horns, tires screeching, and engines backfiring. Added to that were the nauseating odors from the meatpacking plants. Rosalba felt the air thick with tension, like a huge rubber band hanging over the streets, ready to snap at any moment.

Two *winitos* staggered by. They sat down on the curb's edge; one of them removed a bottle of Thunderbird out of a brown paper sack. Across the way a young woman pushed a market cart down the street, her three small children crowded inside. In front of new stands and shops, women in print dresses and aprons, recently arrived from Mexico or El Salvador, sold food and other times from brightly painted stands—*raspadas*, *elotes*, *tamales* or *pupusas*.

On other days, family quarrels erupted, with children rushing out of houses, intermittent screaming from women and men, and police cars turning sharply around street corners.

Rosalba thought about the Barrio Nuevo Estrada gang: tough, tattooed, *caló*-speaking young men and women with their outrageous clothing and attitudes. They were mostly from the Estrada Courts Housing Projects, always fighting with somebody—rival barrio gangs, police officers, one another.

Although life in Rosalba's village in Nayarit had been full of want and ill treatment, the world she ended up in was far more threatening. But she mulled that over a while and accepted this fact: She could never return. This was her life now, in East L.A., with Pete. Sharing whatever she owned with Sybil, Stony, Chila, and her other three grandchildren. No, she would never go back.

But still, although she tried not to, she couldn't help but recall the images, voices, and smells of her village in Nayarit. As a young girl, she'd walk barefoot down a dirt path with bundles of clothes or baskets of corn balanced on her head. So one day she promised: *When I die, take me back to Mexico. Bury me deep in Nayarit soil, in my red hills, and along the cactus fields. Bury me in long braids and in a* huipil. *Bury me among the ancients, among the brave and wise ones, and in the wet dirt of my birth. I will take with me these fingers that have kneaded new ground, these eyes that have gazed on new worlds, this heart that has loved, lost, and loved again—remembering that I once lived and suffered in North America.*

And often Rosalba thought about Pete. A good man, she almost said out loud. Pete was not like the men her daughter seemed to attract. He was also so different from Rosalba's previous two husbands, the one in Nayarit who never saw past his dinner—and an alcoholic in L.A. who lived in the crawl space of her house for a short time until he was shot dead in a barroom brawl.

In Rosalba's eyes, Pete was truly decent. Working nights, gutting steer and hog torsos, pulling out fat-covered organs and yards of intestines, then washing the blood and gore down a large hole with a monstrous water hose—all for Rosalba. And she knew it.

Today, Rosalba needed to get away. The morning beckoned her to come out—to do something, anything.

She sat at the kitchen table—dirty dishes scattered about the tabletop, with bits of hardened tortillas from the night before—and worked on a plan.

Rosalba could take Stony's dented Ford pickup and visit the old furniture stores and used clothing shops along Whittier Boulevard or First Street. Or she could go around the Eastside, gathering newspapers, cardboard boxes, aluminum cans, or whatever she could turn in for extra money. She did this so many times that the men at the county dump site looked forward to Rosalba's visits, to her bright face and brash approach, and the way she mixed up the words in Spanish and English.

Rosalba dressed quickly, gathering a few loose bills and faded coupons into an old nylon purse. She then worked her way around the bodies on the floor to where Chila was sleeping. Rosalba looked at the child's closed eyes and fingered her small hand.

"Buelita," Chila moaned as she awoke. "*¿Qué pasó?*"

"Come, *m'ija*, I need you to help me."

It took a strenuous moment before Chila made out her grandmother's face in the dimness of the room. The last time she saw her grandmother's face like that, she had convinced Chila to help steal old beaten-up lamps and chairs from broken-into Goodwill bins.

"Oh, Buelita, I'm too tired."

"*Mira nomás*—you're tired, eh? You ain't done nothing yet. Now get dressed and come with me."

Rosalba got up and made her way into the kitchen. Chila snarled a weak protest, then tossed a blanket off, unmindful of the younger children next to her, and rolled off the mattress. Chila knew that once Buelita put her mind to something, there was no reasoning with her at all.

Chila dragged herself into the bathroom while her grandmother prepared a couple of tacos to eat later from the leftover meat in the refrigerator. A small girl for nine, she had an impish face with large brown eyes.

"What are we going to do, Buelita?" Chila asked, as she attempted to brush her hair into some kind of shape. She had grown feisty at her age and, unlike Rosalba, refused to wear braids—just long straight hair, wild like the tails of stallions.

"*Adio—adónde quiera Dios*. Wherever God desires," Rosalba said. "What's it to you?"

"Gee, I was just asking!"

Despite such exchanges, Rosalba and Chila were really best buddies; none of the others in the house were close enough to even talk to each other that way.

Rosalba hurried outside to check the pickup truck. The driveway—overflowing with oily engine parts, boxes of yellowed newspapers, and rain-soaked cartons—was in sharp contrast to the empty kitchen cupboard. She managed to reach the pickup and pull herself inside the cab. She turned on the ignition, and the truck began to gripe and growl. Eventually the engine turned over, smoke spewed like a cloud over the driveway's litter.

"Let's go, *m'ija*," Rosalba yelled over the truck's engine roar. "*¡De volada!*"

By then, other members of the household had awakened. Stony was the first to pop his unshaven face through the window.

"Hey, man, quit gunning that thing—you'll break something!" he managed to holler.

Rosalba pressed the accelerator even more as the exhaust thickened. No sleepy-eyed, ex-con, beer-guzzling boyfriend of her insolent daughter was going to ruin her beautiful day, she thought. It was a day that begged her to do something, anything.

Chila flew out of the house, banging the screen door behind her. Rosalba backed the truck out while Chila screamed for her to slow down as she leaped into the passenger side. The pickup chugged out of the driveway and onto the street.

The truck continued down the block, smoke trailing from behind as Stony bellowed out of the bedroom window, "*¡Méndiga loca!*"

The Ford roared through Eastside streets and avenues, across the concrete river to Alameda Street, where old Mexicanos sold fruit on the roadside while factory hands gathered in front of chain-link fences, waiting for employers in trucks to pick them for day work. Rosalba decided to go to *el centro*—downtown.

They passed the long blocks of Skid Row, with the displaced gathered on street corners or beneath a cardboard-and-blanket-covered "condo" on a sidewalk; they drove past the brick-and-stone welfare hotels of painful rememberance. Past warehouse buildings and storefront garment sweat-shops. Rosalba slowly pulled up to the congestion of cars and humanity along what some people called Spanish Broadway.

In the crawl of downtown traffic, Rosalba had time to look out the window at gray-haired Black preacher, who sermonized from the sidewalk with a dog-eared Bible in his hand. She noticed a newspaper vendor on a corner studying the people who walked by as they scanned the latest news in Mexican publications, including the close-up shots of cut-up and bullet-riddled bodies in crime and disaster magazines. Everywhere *norteñas* and *cumbias* poured out of record shops.

"How about a shine . . . shoe shine?" exclaimed a half-blind man. "*Para zapatos brillosos.*"

The streets bristled with families, indigents, and single mothers shopping. Rosalba spotted a man staggering out of a *tejano* bar, followed by another man. The second man knocked the first one to the ground and repeatedly punched him in the face. Nobody paused or did anything to stop him.

Another man pushed his little boy from out of a group of people gathered at a bus stop and had the child pee in the gutter.

Rosalba and Chila cruised further up Broadway, away from its most crowded intersections. *Cholos* stood deathly still inside brick alcoves, elderly women strolled along cautiously with heavy bags, winos lay in fresh vomit nearby. More stubble-faced homeless pushed shopping carts filled with squashed cans, plastic bags, and cardboard. The scenery carried the rapid-fire Spanish of the Mexican and Central American shoppers, the foul words of workers unloading merchandise out of six-wheeled trucks covered with gang graffiti, and the seductive tones of pretty women in tight pants enticing potential shoppers to check out the clothing racks.

Rosalba noticed an empty space at a curb and swiftly pulled into it. A sign on the sidewalk warned: NO PARKING, TOW ZONE. But she pulled up the hand brake and turned off the engine anyway.

"Buelita, the sign says . . . " Chila began, but she saw that it didn't matter. Rosalba walked off as if by ignoring the sign, it would go away.

"Forget her," Chila muttered, and rushed up behind her swift-moving grandmother.

That day burned and bubbled; Rosalba and Chila felt like *chilis* on a hot plate being heated before being skinned. Their stroll became torture, especially since Rosalba would stop here and there to browse and barter over items, the majority of which she had no intention of buying. Rosalba was just glad to get out of the house and interact with the world—just to haggle, if need be. Chila, on the other hand, only thought of the mattress and pillow she left behind.

"It's so hot," Rosalba finally conceded. "How about a watermelon, *m'ija?*"

"Sure."

Rosalba and Chila stopped at a Grand Central Market fruit stand. Laid out in front of them, a splash of colors like works of art, were papayas, mangoes, watermelons, apples, bananas, and oranges. Rosalba picked out a sizable speckled dark green watermelon. She argued over the price with a man, who appeared bored; finally, she assembled her change and paid for it.

"Here, Chila, carry this."

Suddenly, to Chila, the watermelon looked like it was at least a quarter her size. She lifted it with her thin down-covered arms, rested it on her belly, helped by a hefty push from her knee. They kept walking, but after a couple of blocks, the weight of the watermelon, the cluster of people, and torrent of smells—all the heat and hubbub—became an unbearable boiling stew.

They stopped to rest at a bus stop bench.

Chila glared at her grandmother.

"I'm tired, Buelita. The watermelon is too heavy."

Rosalba stood up, glared back at Chila—sweat beaded on her nose—but then pondered a way to ease the girl's burden. At that moment, Rosalba's thoughts returned to Nayarit, to a time when she was a little girl and strode for miles, carrying loads without assistance of animal or man. Then she turned toward the watermelon, pressed like a boulder on Chila's lap.

Rosalba wrested the watermelon from the girl; Chila let out a long sigh.

Rosalba walked a little, and stopped. With great care, she placed the watermelon on her head, then slowly removed one hand. The watermelon wobbled a little, threatening to fall and splatter into green, red, and black fragments on the sidewalk. Rosalba steadied the wiggly thing, then let it go. She took a few more steps. This time the watermelon stayed upright, as if held by an invisible hand.

Chila stared at her grandmother—stunned.

Even more stunning became Rosalba's efforts to rumba—keeping the watermelon on top of her head while her feet and hips gracefully shimmied along the cement walkway.

A crowd gathered around the woman as she weaved past the dollar stores, the immigration law offices, and through racks of clothes and CDs near the street, and rows of pirated DVDs on blankets. Merchants stepped out of their shops looking on in disbelief, preachers stopped their exhortations, and bus stop patrons strained their necks to see.

Car horns greeted, hands waved, and some people simply got out of the way.

Rosalba swayed back and forth to a *salsa* beat thundering out of an appliance store. She laughed and others laughed with her. Chila stepped back into the shadows, stupefied, and shook her head.

"Ayyyyy," Rosalba managed to yell.

Rosalba had not looked so happy in a long time as she danced along the bustling streets of the central city in a loose-fitting skirt and sandals. She danced in the shadow of a multistoried Victorian—dancing for one contemptious husband and for another who was dead. She danced for a daughter who didn't love herself enough to truly have the love of another man. She danced for Pete, a butcher of beasts and gentle companion. She danced for her grandchildren, especially that fireball Chila. She danced for her people, wherever they were scattered, and for this country she would never quite comprehend. She danced, her hair matted with sweat, while remembering a simple life on an even simpler rancho in Nayarit.

Francisco X. Alarcón   First Prize: Poetry

Tattoos

UNTITLED

    poems
    fill up
    pages

    tattoos
    puncture
    flesh

DREAMS OF A CALIFORNIAN POET IN PRISON

*After Derra Caulk in About Time: "An Anthology
of California Prison Writing* (1980)

    each morning
    I wake up
    alone
    pretending

    that my arm
    is the flesh
    of your body
    pressing

    against my lips

SUEÑOS DE UN POETA DE CALIFORNIA EN PRISIÓN

    cada mañana
    me despierto
    solo
    fingiendo

    que mi brazo
    es la carne
    de tu cuerpo
    pesando

    sobre mis labios

RAÍCES

mis raíces
las cargo
siempre
conmigo
enrolladas
me sirven
de almohada

ROOTS

I carry
my roots
with me
all the time
rolled up
I use them
as my pillow

LUZ

teñida de noche
tengo la piel
en este país
de mediodía
pero más oscura
tengo el alma
de tanta luz
que llevo adentro

"DARK"

I used to be
much
 much
  darker
dark
as la tierra
recién llovida

dark
was all
I ever wanted
I would sing
dark
dream dark
talk only dark

happiness
was to spend
whole
afternoons
tirado
como foca
bajo el sol

"you're already
so dark
muy prieto
too indio!"
some would lash
at my happy
darkness

now
I'm not as dark
quizás
sean los años
maybe
I'm too far
up north

anyway here
"dark"
is only
for the ashes:
the stuff
lonely nights
are made of

FLAGS

> stupid
> rags
> soaked
> in blood

BANDERAS

> trapos
> imbéciles
> empapados
> en sangre

PATRIA

> nosotros
> los que nacimos
> marcados
> de extranjeros
> en nuestra propia
> tierra
> los que pagamos
> con moneda dura
> hasta por este aire
> que nos raja y niega
> los que regalamos
> todo lo que todavía
> no nos roban
>
> nosotros
> los que nada poseemos
> los reducidos
> a sombras
> los que llevamos
> en los ojos
> una noche cruel
> y oscura
> sólo nos reconocemos
> en las estrellas:
> sabemos que nuestra
> patria
> está por hacerse

Un Beso Is Not a Kiss

un beso
es una puerta
que se abre
un secreto
compartido
un misterio
con alas

un beso
no admite
testigos
un beso can't
be captured
traded
or sated

un beso
is not just
a kiss
un beso is
more dangerous
sometimes
even fatal

Lucha Corpi
First Prize: Short Story

Shadows on Ebbing Waters (excerpt)

2 November

This morning I stood before their graves. Grandma and Silvia buried beneath my feet. I sat there for a while. It was peaceful and warm. I was ready to get up when I felt a short trembling just below my navel. It was like the soft flapping of wings inside me. Blood rushed to my face and my heart pounded in my chest as if to welcome the sign. And yet, I felt alone. All the people I wanted to share that moment with were unable to reach out and put their hands on my belly and touch you through me, my little one. The years of loneliness I had always managed to shun fell on me suddenly. And for the first time, I felt out of place in my natural surroundings. I did not belong any longer. But where did I belong? Mexico, I thought; I could go to Mexico, visit Grandma's hometown and all the other towns Grandma used to tell me about when I was little. Maybe I belonged there, but I knew I didn't. Mexico was my past, the place that smelled like my grandmother's clothes, a smell of fresh herbs, the smell of wet soil after the storm . . . a refuge.

On my way back from the cemetery, I went past the spot where Silvia and I walked on that afternoon she arrived. Then we had talked all through her unpacking and bathing. And after preparing a light supper we had sat in the back patio overlooking the lake to wait for Laz.

"I had forgotten how beautiful the lake is," Silvia said with a sigh.

"Yes, it is, but you must have seen many beautiful cities and lakes . . . " A silly comment I immediately regretted saying. I didn't want to awaken memories in her and make her long for any other time but then.

"Not as beautiful as this one now," she said and looked at me as if she could read my mind and wanted to put it at ease. "What made Laz want to settle here? He's from Texas, isn't he?"

"Isn't that reason enough?" I answered quickly, and we both laughed. Grandma had always told us how ugly Texas was compared to California and how she hated those rude rednecks who had no love for the land, or for Mexicans for that matter.

"Grandpa Lewis was the exception, of course," Silvia said amusedly, then looked away. "How wrong Grandma was. In the cities of California there is no love for the land or for Mexicans either." She was silent for a while, then asked, "How did you convince Grandma to let you marry Laz?"

"Oh, that was no problem. Laz won her over. He told her he was the exception, too, just like Grandpa. And besides, his family had come from Mexico, too. Anyway, she was getting old and wanted to see me well cared for before she died."

"Does he come from a rich family in Texas? I mean . . . ," Silvia hesitated, "you've never said anything about his family in your letters . . ." I knew she felt uncomfortable.

"Don't be embarrassed. I've asked him the same thing, but he doesn't tell me. He just laughs and says it doesn't matter," I answered in a low voice. I knew Laz was in the house. I could hear the water running, doors opening and closing discretely, and his moving about getting dressed. "I guess I don't know much about his life before I met him."

"Has he ever taken you back to Texas to meet them?" Silvia was intrigued.

"No. He says his parents are dead and he doesn't want to see his brother again. He left home when he was very young and hasn't been back since. He enlisted in the army and was sent overseas. From there on, I don't know much. He says he doesn't want to remember. He only wants what he has today, now, our life together on the ranch." I must have looked troubled because Silvia came over and put her arms around me.

"Maybe he's right. It's not important." She smiled. I tried to find comfort in her words and her warmth, but I couldn't.

"Anyway," I said childishly, trying to cover up my uneasiness, "it's all very romantic, don't you think? I'm married to a man with a dark past!"

Silvia smiled. She walked to the far end of the patio to see the sun setting on the other side of the lake. I stayed close to the door waiting for Laz.

He came out a while later and kissed me. We didn't say a word. I looked at him, gentle, always smiling as if he had no care in the world, and my doubts were dispelled.

. . . Cheated my way out of death   always   darian   loved me like a son   no idealist   went along with me   no children   only me   laz, money is for you   accept it   can't accept it darian   take it   give it to the poor   what you please   don't care   anything happens you are set for life   bloody money darian can't refuse it laz   blood on my soul not yours   go they're near before it's too late   i won't leave you darian   such romantic   go   go   they'll be here soon   nothing left for you here   boat on fire   from the rocks   single gunshot thundering in the inertness of the late afternoon   from rock to rock to the small cavern   darkness   coldness stillness   crouching   a little boy numbness   wanted to cry couldn't   darian   body growing colder   colder crabs forced myself to eat   vomited three times   couldn't hold their raw meat darian nourishing me even after death   eating his body through them tide finally took him back sea and time forever   grave of water should have been mine   crabs snapping off piece by piece while alive   gunshots   early morning   noon   late night   men waging war to build peace   naive like me worst kind of mercenaries we were   pacts with the devil to win the way to heaven something better beyond the sea beyond   and i found you eva and i found peace   i thought silvia wasn't so lucky   lucky no   she was   she died and i live   i live . . .

6 NOVEMBER

Laz stretches his legs, rubs them up and down, as if they were numb. He is ready to get up and walk to the lakeshore as he does every evening. He looks in my direction, but he doesn't move from his chair. He seems to hesitate and then sags back in the chair. I want to run to him, have him hug me, tell me everything will be all right again. But I can't move from this chair, either.

That first night Silvia spent here we stood together by the door to the patio watching her. She seemed so enthralled by the reflections of twilight on the lake waters, and was so still that, for a moment, she looked like one of those beautiful mannequins I saw in a fashion magazine she'd sent me.

I was so eager to have them meet, I was ready to call her, but Laz held me back. Instead, he walked toward her and stopped a few steps from her. He looked intently at her. I stood motionless by the door, and for an instant, I felt like a spectator watching a play. I was the outsider. I saw them standing there, Laz holding her hand, not saying anything. My imagination took off at full speed. Laz had always teased me about my romantic flights. He was right. As stupid as it was, I had already begun to see them as characters in one of those syrupy, romantic novels I used to read as a young woman. And I had forgotten they were my cousin and my husband, and not two estranged lovers meeting after a long and painful absence. I was so caught up in their fictitious love tale I had not noticed they were standing before me, looking bemusedly at me, Laz chuckling and Silvia waving her hands in front of my eyes.

I came back from my reverie only to feel embarrassed; a child caught play-acting, a torrid first kiss with a mirror. But I laughed. I was always laughing then, at myself, at anything that was funny.

Yes, it was a happy and fascinating evening that day my cousin Silvia came home. Through all the trying and painful evenings that followed after she was gone, I have chosen to remember that particular one. I listened to them talk about all the wonderful places they had visited. All of a sudden, Laz was transformed, renewed. He was fifty-one, but his face glowed youthfully. Before me was a man I had been married to for fifteen years, and a stranger at the same time, with whom I was falling in love all over again.

Yet in the back of my mind, questions were beginning to shape painfully and slowly. Why had he denied this part of himself to me? Why had he married me and settled here when he could have had an exciting life elsewhere? I couldn't even give him children. He was nineteen years older than me. Had I become his child-wife instead? God knows, during our married life I had been as foolish and playful as a child. But he seemed to enjoy my foolishness, and I so wanted to please him. It had never occurred to me someone in him starved for something else. But most of all, that night I became aware of my limited experience. A sense of loss was beginning to seize me. It made me tremble.

I have never been able to hold pain, embarrassment, or fear for very long. So by the time I was preparing for bed, I had already dismissed those thoughts as quickly as they had come to mind.

. . . Silvia the semidarkness of the patio the desolate look at one moment intense feverish brilliance in your eyes immediately after your lower lip trembling flushed cheeks dried mouth quiet feeling of desperation just above your stomach it was like looking into my own face i wanted to put my arms around you there is a way out there is instead i stood next to you paralyzed my own pain unbearable it was all coming back the man i was long ago back to haunt me you extended your hand to me distantly a cold hand trembling i held it in both hands we knew silvia not brave like you water am so cold moon shines shines relentless you mustn't lose hope no hope laz dying few months am so cold laz i will hold you silvia i won't go away don't be afraid not afraid laz i don't regret anything in my life pain hurt love disappointment hard work all my life looking for a place like this no need to trade things off explain them away everything simple funny it had been here all along laz i can't see you am here won't go away i want you to go away laz i can't you must don't look back we must spare eva don't tell her promise laz let her think kindly of me she loves you silvia she needs you laz go away go back to the house this i must do alone silvia eva silvia . . .

Gary D. Keller, El Huitlacoche   Honorable Mention: Short Story

The Raza Who Scored Big in Anáhuac

I thought, being raza, that this was my *tierra*. You know, roots, ¡qué sé yo! Now I think maybe I'm just another *extranjero*, one who crossed the wrong-way river.

I came down to learn stuff. Junior term in Anáhuac. At the Universidad Nacional Autónoma [UNAM]—the student movement—¡la revolución estudiantil!—I met and befriended Felipe Espinoso. He helped me with my notes because, speaking frankly, my written castellano isn't the best. "Language loss" is what some professor once muttered to me when I tested out at Cal State University. Felipe was curious about Chicano ways. He called me "güero valín, the Mexican in preppie polo shirts." That made me laugh and I would kid him about the same Yucatecan guayabera that he wore every day that I knew him. We were both attending the same course, Theory and Practice of Mexican Social Class Structure, taught by tal profesor, one Maximiliano Peón, who alerted us at once to the fact that even though his remuneration was not enough to cover the gasoline that the trip cost him, he was proud to be teaching this course at UNAM as a servicio to the youth of his patria.

From the profile Felipe reminded me—it was an uncanny, almost perfect likeness—of a Mayan head in Palenque, a bas-relief with the prominent Mayan nose and receding forehead that I had pondered over in an art book at the CSU library. I had always wanted urgently to visit Palenque. I used to think about its Gothic arches and cornstalk glyphs when I was just a kid, working behind the counter at the Taco Bell, baking cinnamon crispas. Now I found myself in Anáhuac, peering into the eyes of a Maya.

Felipe pressed me hard on Aztlán, and pleased with his avid interest, I was proud to tell him about the meaning of César Chávez's black águila in a white circle, of "vato" and "cholo," the Sleepy Lagoon riots, the finer points of pachuquismo, the fate of Reies Tijerina, the difference between an acto and a mito, Los Angeles street murals, and the old Operation Wetback of the '50s, and the silly tortilla curtain que parió.

In turn, I queried him about the political peripecias of Vicente Lombardo Toledano, the pastimes of Siqueiros when they threw him in the Lecumberri lockup, the subtleties redounding in the national diversion of deciphering every six years who the PRI [Partido Revolucionario Institucional] tapado really was, the new malinchista movement of contemporary Mexican feministas, what Buñuel had really meant in "Los olvidados," and why Cantinflas had plastic surgery done on his notable nose.

One afternoon after class, at the tortería which surely has the best crema in the valley of México, La Tortería Isabela la Católica, only a few minutes from the university library which is a living historic-revolutionary mural, I confided in him a Chicano hope for a binational carnalismo. We were both brought to tears and to a heartfelt abrazo de correligionarios, not to mention compinches.

In class, Felipe Espinoso was quiescent. Weren't we all? In our aula there were over 80 where there should have been 50. The earliest got seats, the next earliest, window sills, then came those who pressed along the walls until the door could no longer be opened and the half dozen hapless laggards who either missed the lecture of the day or tried to catch a semblance of the proceedings from outside, through a window. The university had been built for 120,000 almas; there were over 260,000 in attendance. Classes had been scheduled seven days a week from the earliest morning until midnight.

During the days approaching registration, Indians trod in from the valley, from the mountains surrounding the valley, from the plains beyond the mountains surrounding the valley, from the plains beyond the mountains which circle this Anáhuac. They filed down the mountain roads, dog-tired, without chavos or any other material resources, spurred on by an implacable will for wisdom and upward mobility. Alentados perhaps by rural maestras de escuela they came for the term to UNAM where tuition was basically free. They traveled the roads in huaraches made from the rubber of discarded tires, slept where they could—in attics, hidden in obscure recintos of the university, in the swimming pool when there was no water—waited resignedly for a seat to study in the hopeless library that could no longer accommodate the push of the masses, begged or hustled for the term's nourishment. I have seen this drive that cannot be stemmed by any earthly privation or police state curtain at my heartfelt border, across which God's innocent children slip into the promised coloso of milk and miel, and I genuflect before these campesino multitudes and each day relive their fierce, steadfast resolve, share their dusty anger, revere their pursuit of self-improvement.

Halfway into the course, Felipe made a pronouncement. "Güero, I thought I liked Prof[esor] Maximiliano Peón. I no longer like him. He is deceptive. He is pequeño burgués."

"He comes out here for nothing to teach this unwashed horde and untouched rabble, doesn't he?"

"Sure, he comes out, and punctually. He's all subjectivity and nineteenth-century retórica, spouting about the incontrovertible objective realities of Marxist-Leninist revolutionary materialism. He's a living contradiction, a comfortable gentil hombre, an hidalgo of the professorate, all immersed in bourgeois pieties and comforts, drunk with arriviste parfums and amaretto and frangelico liqueurs. But to assuage his sotted, corrupted soul, to aggrandize his smug persona, to allay his midnight anxieties—because he knows well that his kind and his class would be first to the paredón in a genuine revolution—he sacrifices salary and comes out here to provoke inditos de Lerdo Chiquito so that they may march to revolutionary beats, so that they may be mowed down by imported burp guns. Yes, he'll watch it all on his Magnavox in the parlor. He'll be hoping that he's hedged every bet, that he'll come out triumphant no matter who wins the partido."

I should confess now that Felipe was a fanatic for the jai alai and he had taught me to be a fanatic. His front on imagery troubled me. Of course it was what everybody tried to do at the jai alai, bet on the underdog when the price was low and hope for the score to turn, then bet again on the opposing team at good odds and sit out the game a sure winner no matter which team won. I protested, "But I love his Spanish! My God, his command of the language!"

"¡Coño! Sure you do. You're a poor, hapless Chicano—a güero pocho boy who has never had the opportunity to study your mother tongue with any formality or system until now. Don't be deceived. It's all Porfirian sophistry and pedagogical pettifoggery. He doesn't even speak Spanish anyway. He speaks Castilian. And these poor, ingenuous indios—I include myself here, once a poor simpleton from Quintana Roo—who also are mostly tonguesmen of Zapoteca, Huichol, or whatever, they are mesmerized by the castizo buffoon who wishes to provoke their action for lost causes so he can feel assuaged for having 'done something' about the Mexican social class problem."

"This is wrong," he went on. "Let us have a revolution in Olmeca, or Chichimeca, or Náhuatl even, or Mayaquiché. Anything but the Porfirian castellano of the Mexican empire and the simpering sleight of hand of the crypto-revolutionary."

So, then, Maximiliano fell from his pedestal. But who or what to replace him with?

The Virgin of Guadalupe's day was approaching. We were tertuliando with other left-leaning student intellects at a café in the slanting sun on the Promenade of Institutionalized Revolution, near the cathedral. We could see a pilgrimage approaching like marabunta down the wide promenade. Felipe told me that tonight would be a fine one to be at the jai alai. Probably he should take all my money and his too and bet it on the main partido.

"Why is that, Felipe?"

He turned to the promenade. "They will be betting heavy." The pilgrimage swept down the promenade, eighteen campesinos abreast, marching in for the novena. There were delegations from Tenancingo and Tlaxcala, Acámbaro and Acatlán, Pátzcuaro and Pachuca, and even Pénjamo and Tzintzuntzan. First the crests of cyclists congruous to paramilitants. They had plastic virgins tacked to their handlebars and wheels and pennants that saluted the breeze of their own making. Then came legions of dusty benditos, huffing and chanting the Ave María, each village headed by a priest and an icon. Then down the Promenade of Institutionalized Revolution came herds of goats and turkeys and aggressive geese, bullied by trotting boys and mongrels. The peddlers followed too, hawking tostadas in green or red sauce, sweet potatoes in carts with piercing steam whistles, guava and cajeta, mamey and mango ice, jícama in vinaigrette. Jesting and cursing in the militant sun, the pilgrims marched and peeled corn husks, smearing the tender grain of their elotes with colored sauce. On the special earthen track, the last kilometer to the cathedral doors, the supplicants came by on bloody knees, bearing the indrawn vision. In the courtyard they were doing Amerindian dances against the slanting, sinking cathedral walls. Precisely every ten meters hung white metal signs with red letters neatly stenciled: It is strictly forbidden to urinate against these holy walls.

That night at the jai alai with all our funds in hand I worried and became a little drunk. Felipe doubted too and wondered if we oughtn't be at the cockfights. "On nights of the novena, the Indians come to the cock arena and wager nuggets of gold that they have dug out of the countryside."

"But here too the galleries are filled with countryfolk. Besides, Felipe, we are fanatics of the jai alai. We know nothing of cockfights."

"True enough. All I know of the cocks is that they use one straight and one curved dagger. That's all I know. It's a question of breeders and other intimate variables." Felipe sighed. "Whatever happens tonight, we cast our lot with the people."

"Sure," I said. Right then I felt muy raza, muy Mexican. "Sí, con el pueblo." But immediately I started to wonder, "Do you think the games are fixed?"

"Who would fix them for the poor to win?"

"Maybe the government. On orders of the authority."

"I wouldn't put that beyond the authorities. A devious scheme to enervate the pilgrims. But no. Why should the government subsidize the gambling vice? Besides, it doesn't happen all the time. It's just . . . a pattern. We must realize that by probability we stand to lose. But the odds make it worthwhile. A handsome wager."

"But I don't want to lose, Felipe. If I lose I will have to eat pinto beans all month. I'll have to return to Califas."

Felipe laughed. "Come now, compis. It's not every day that a vato loco can wager with the people with a firm hand. Maybe the match is fixed every night before the pilgrims make the final march to celebrate Tepeyac. Just to brighten the Indian's firm belief in the miraculous. But no, I don't think there's any question of a fixed game. It's simply the milieu, those days when the campo and the aldea come to court, the Indians packed in the galleries, hiding behind masks. I think it's a spirit that descends on the jai alai court. An ether which comes from the galleries and penetrates the players."

"Perhaps a revolutionary spirit?"

"Yes, but lapped up by the gambling vice the way mole is contained and dammed by corn dough. The inditos make their way up to the galleries expecting the supernatural."

I laughed. "What would Gramsci think of this, Pablo Freire, even the barbudo Carlos Marx? Could they construct a paradigm pa'l fenómeno?"

"Hard to say. It's too early in the course."

"You're right, Felipe. On a night like tonight one should be a jai alai fanatic. Have you seen all the grenaderos about?"

"Yes. They've even brought a contingent in from Atzcapotzalco. I'm sure there are two in front of every pulquería, every brothel, every revolutionary square, every Ateneo in Mexico City."

"How many do you think there are at the university library, underneath the mural?"

Saturday night at the Palacio de la Pelota, El Frontón México. The jai alai court was stretched and wide, bounded by three rock walls. The open end was strung with an immense steel net protecting the spectators from the missiles. Occupying the choice seats in the middle of the stands were the vested ones, Arabs and Jews, gachupines and wealthy Mexicans who played the favorite and lapped up the chiquitero money.

There was a roar from the crowd. The intendant and four huge Basques with long straw wickers bound to their wrists entered the court. They marched single file and solemnly along the wood boundary line. Then they turned and faced the crowd, placed their wickers across their hearts in salute, and gave the slightest of nods. There were whistles, jeers, and enthusiastic applause. The players broke rank and began to practice up. It was two mean frisky bucks playing against two stooping esthetes.

Felipe studied the program. "This match is a timeless syndrome: youth versus experience. Only a poet or saint will win this."

"Well then," I asked, "who do we bet on?"

"It doesn't matter, güero. The team that falls behind and permits the chiquiteros to bet their pittances. We will bet on the underdog, the people, and their expectations for a miracle."

"I like that, Felipe. A higher logic. I may be a vato loco, but you are a vate loco. A meta-wager and a melodrama. A dialectic that ends in a materialistic. I like the pastel money of México. It's easier than the hardened green of the dólar."

Redcaps called the odds out, which were an even 100 red versus 100 blue, and the match to 30 points began. The fierce bucks dominated from the very start, and as the score mounted in their favor the odds dwindled, 50, 30, 10 to 100. From the galleries there was a steady projection of sullen mirth. I saw an Olmec-looking type call out, "That old camel should be playing marbles with his grandchild!" and a striking mestizo who looked the prototype of Vasconcelos's raza cósmica imprecated a few times and then said, "Get him a pair of roller skates . . . and a Seeing Eye dog!" Rejoined a weasel who looked more like the critics of Vasconcelos, who coined La raza cósmica. "No, old fool! Bring him Sancho Panza!"

The score was 20 to 12. The redcaps had become bored and sat in the aisles kibitzing with their clients. The guards, instead of standing straight up, were lounging on the very net that bounded the court. And the sharks filed their teeth or counted their fistfuls of wagers on short odds or nonchalantly cracked sunflower seeds. That was when we bet most of the money credited to us for a month of studies and livelihood on the underdog at 80 to 1000. The sharks were glad to take our money. "No lo hagan," a concerned bourgeois gentilhomme advised us. "You're just going to make a tiburón happy. ¡Qué el partido se va de calle!"

A portentous occurrence. The jai alai became like the opera buffa. The old artistes made two points and there was an ominous silence. The redcaps got up from the aisles but called out a few odds. There was almost no betting. They were waiting—the galleries and the short money, seven, eight thousand strong—for another mysterium. The intereses creados squirmed up in their chairs like weasels. This point—it was taking too long, too many volleys! The great and turning point came in like high tide and the redcaps quieted no scuffles no coughs, but the poke of the rubber and rocklike sphere impacted and spread upon the front wall and the long, retrograde arc of the orb obfuscating in spotlights, the skim of wrists along the green middling, and the crack of stone's conjunction with straw. Rolando, the stiff yet still graceful elder, scooped up the ball on the short hop and propelled it swan's neck thick on the middle so it angled sinuously on the low, wide front, bounced within the far outside wood, and spiraled into the netting. The galleries were ripped wide open with Amerindian joie de vivre. The men or beasts within tore asunder their poses and stepped outside themselves. The promised sign! I turned to Felipe. He glowed with cherubic ecstasy. I held his head like a son. The redcaps called out odds: 40 to 100, make it 45, no, 50 to 100. Red and blue tickets passed countless brown hands. The aisles writhed like serpents. We bore the manic coaster to allegorical heaven.

It was like the Westerns, too. The well-off villains in their business suits and gold pocket watches presenced their reserved finale. They put away their pepitas and pistachios, and their eyes popped and their jaws hung awry. "Cover!" they begged the redcaps. They wanted to cover, to hedge. The God-fearing rested easy. None of us doubted the outcome. Social and poetic justice would be done.

Rolando was all about, luxuriating in his renaissance, his regained nerve.

Soon we were winning! The young bucks leaned against the wall and slowly sank to the floor, their innards chafing, their tongues flapping. Holding his wicker high above him like a torch, Rolando traversed the court with the stately mockery of a ceremonious bullfighter. Caught up in the euphoria I began to scream a confused litany of mythic templates; the eagle, the serpent, the nopal, the thunderbird, the "¡Sí se puede!," la MECHA [Movimiento Estudiantil Chicano de Aztlán], el Anáhuac, Aztlán, all jumbled in the same olla. Felipe and I embraced. "¡Vamos a ganar! ¡Venceremos!"

Then, an inexplicable alteration of events. The elders loosened up—¡qué se aflojaran!—got tired, and permitted the youngsters to come back. The game tied up at 29. The ultimate metaphysic! Pee pee was drawn from the caved-in bladders of many. The galleries lost their nerve and hastened to hedge their spleens. The sharks and businessmen, anxious to reduce their losses, covered the Indians, and bet all the Rolando they could. The redcaps shrieked out the odds: 100 even, 100 pesos, pick 'em.

I grabbed Felipe. "Los indios have lost their nerve and are seeking insurance. ¡Tienen los huevos en la garganta!"

"Me too!"

"Let's cover! If we do, we win either way!"

"No way," Felipe said, "let us ride!"

I was in a swoon. "Oh, God! All that pastel!"

"Are you with me?"

I squeezed his hand. My knees were buckling. His face was mauve and bloated. "God, yes!"

I am an innocent, I thought. The ingenuous fanatic. For the moment I loved him so, I could have given him my life.

The ultimate point began.

Rolando served the ball, a giveaway straight to the opposing front man. We should have lost, instead the ball dribbled obscenely out of the unnerved wicker.

"We won!"

The young buck climbed and clawed the net in a twist of fury. Futile as Bergman's squire.

I turned to Felipe. "You won! You knew the old boy'd do it!"

He didn't seem terribly happy, though. He pointed at Rolando leaving for the dressing room, wiping his brow amid hosannas. "It took a lot out of him."

I felt funny. Felipe and I split the money, 50-50. The devalued pastel wad of Mexican money barely entered my pocket. I had more in the wallet; there were bills in my shirt pocket. Child supplicants stood willfully at the exit next to the Palacio. I emptied coins into each calloused hand.

"Don't do that," he said.

"Why not?"

"It's bad form. It makes you look like a gringo."

"I know that. It's only because tonight I've scored big."

"No, never. You'll spoil them."

To win money: that was not enough. Felipe was still angry, knotted up by the match, and slowly I became angry too. It was not enough on the eve of the Virgin's day, despite the magnificent catharsis. Why? No más por no más.

Felipe had been silent while we lined up and collected our bets. Now he almost whined. "Now we must go and fuck some woman. I know a brothel, not too far."

"I don't want to fuck some woman! I'm too buoyant. I want to keep my money. Not tonight, Felipe. I'm too worn."

"Pues sí, compis. That's the way we do things here. The night won't be complete. El rito del jai alai se lo exige."

"I thought you were a poet, a mystic, and a left-leaning intellectual."

Felipe cursed a lot about shitting in the milk of the Virgin and all that folklore. "If you win, you've got to go. Don't leave me to my designs."

"What's this brothel like?"

"Perverse! What güero can claim to have known México without having visited its muchachas?"

"What do you mean, perverse?" I asked him hostilely.

He grinned. "Authentically perverse."

La Madama Lulú's was not perverse. It was repulsive, y me pareció muy típico. Two grenaderos sat on the sidewalk in front of the brothel. Some político or máximo chingón was fucking his brains out. Their carbines lay on the pavement at their sides. They winked at us as we went in. The brothel bureaucrats sat us on an overstuffed Louis XVI and the whores lined up and flaunted us all petite soirée fête in stained miniskirts. "¡Vamos a hacer beibis!"

I didn't have the huevos to choose, so the most entrepreneurial of their lot plopped on my thighs and fondled my member. Soon, having been kneaded like a croissant, it began to acquire that mauve, belligerent feel. "Ven aquí," she coaxed. She took some of my salmon and sandía-colored money and gave it to the bookkeeper. The bookkeeper gave me a red poker chip. Then I had to give the poker chip to the porter, who meticulously opened the door to a broom closet cubicle and handed me a roll of toilet paper. We went inside. I didn't give a shit anymore. ¡Qué carajos! I was resolved. Yet suddenly I realized I was fucking a perfect stranger.

Later we were famished. The high was worn and it had turned cold and raw. There were pilgrims wandering the street, like strays. Felipe and I went into an all-night estancia where they cut newspapers into napkins. We had steaming hot caldo tlalpeño. We had machitos, finely minced tacos of bull testicles sprinkled with aguacate and cilantro in piquante sauce—sympathetic cannibalism. We washed it down with Carta Blanca. Felipe was quiet and grave. He looked frightened. I couldn't fathom what he was thinking.

I kept drinking. After a while I asked him, "Why don't men and women do anything or go anywhere together in this country? Why are the men in the plaza and the women en casa?"

"They do go out together," he protested.

"Sure, to a té danzante at five in the afternoon."

"Those are appropriate hours. I'm sorry that we are not as advanced as your civilization."

"I've told you before, Felipe, it's not my civilization. Shit, I just live there. Don't blame me you sent out a fuck-up like Santa Anna to do an hombre's job."

"Here we still believe in the novia santa."

"You do?"

"Sure."

"I mean you, Felipe Espinoso from Quintana Roo."

"Why not?"

"It seems muy raro I bet. The novia santa. It goes well with la casa chica."

"Don't insult me."

"I'm sorry. You have a novia waiting for you?"

"Sure!"

"Where?"

"In Tulúm. It's small."

"Sure, I know it. There are ruins there. Hay presencia del pasado."

"Tienes razón."

"And how long since you've seen her?"

"The six years I've been here at the university. I take a course and a course and a course. Como tu work-study, right?"

"Not quite. You're going to marry her?"

"As soon as I graduate."

The night was cool and Mexican. Stars appeared like wishes. It was very still, soon it would be early. We walked with our hands in our pockets and our faces down, steadfast in the drunken ambience. We came to a park. The coconuts and the palms were still and etched. Some campesinos with no place to go were trying to sleep on the benches that they had arrogated. There was suddenly a clump of grass in front of me. I plopped on it. The grass tickled my nostrils. I giggled. "Get up!" Felipe sounded alarmed. He pulled me. It seemed like someone else's arm.

"¡Viva la revolución!"

"Be quiet, won't you!"

"What do you mean, quiet? Is this a police state? ¡Viva la revolución! ¡Viva la Virgen de Tepeyac! ¡Viva Tontantzín! Let every good fellow now join in this song: vive la companie. Good health to each other and pass it along, vive la companie."

"Get up!"

"No, you come down. Down to my level."

"All right. If you quiet down."

I laughed. "Where I live they say Mexicans—that means Chicanos of course, not you real Mexicans—were made to pizcar tomates because they're built low to the ground. What do you think about that?"

He flashed his winning grin. "I'm curious about your Chicano ways."

"Well. When are you going to graduate?"

"Soon, if you keep quiet so no one steals my money tonight."

"Did you walk to Mexico City from Tulúm?"

"Well, no. Actually, I got an aventón."

"And were you like the indios that come streaming in from the picos and the valles around registration time?"

"Most assuredly."

"And did you live like them, begging, and hustling, and working?"

He smiled. "Well, nobody gets to find much work in this city."

"So then?"

"So I'm still hustling. Only I'm an advanced student now, senior class."

"¿Qué me dices?"

"I'm sorry, güero. We were playing only with your pastel money."

"Only my money? But I saw you pitch in your share."

"That was merely sleight of hand."

"I see. So then, at 29 up, you weren't really that nervous."

"Oh, I was very nervous."

"Yeah, but not as nervous as me."

"No, I wouldn't think so."

"No, you wouldn't think so. After all, for you it was win or tie."

"Something like that."

"And you don't feel bad?"

"I feel very bad. I need for you to know how bad I feel, even now, after winning, despite winning. Not only the money, but my life's dream, enough to live on so that I can take a full course of study and graduate. Porque, compis, tú eres mi cuate, ¿sabes? O, como dicen los tuyos, soy tu carnal."

"How can you say this shit to me now? Do you know I'm debating whether or not to kick your fucking head in?"

"Pues, ponte chango, carnal. Pa' la próxima más aguzao, vato. Porque ya aprendiste. That's what Buñuel meant in *Los olvidados*. Like they say in these parts, más cornadas da el hambre que el toro."

"Don't hand me that pestilent shit. You simply hustled me. I'm just as poor as you. You knew if I lost that match I would probably have had to drop out and return home. Either that or starve."

"And you're not used to starving. Sure you're poor—I realize that. But you work. As a stock boy, at Taco Bell, as a piss-pot polisher. Lo que sea, entran los chavitos, haga cola para el financial aid. You're poor like Cheech and Chong. We use the same word, poor, but we don't mean the same referent. I mean devastated, a nullity without the remotest identity."

"Why are you telling me all this stuff now? You won your ticket. Why couldn't you have just let me keep on thinking you were a fucking prince?"

"Pues, por pura vergüenza. You may not believe it: allí en la casa de putas, where much profound Mexican thought takes form, I thought about it long and hard. But you deserve more. You are a fine fellow, very young, ingenuo, and my sense of shame and your need to know, they joined forces. It may not be as pretty as pastel illusions or the half-breed Virgin who showed herself to the cosmic race, but I felt I owed you the truth. Por eso bajaste al Anáhuac, ¿no?"

"And besides, you have enough money now, ¿verdad? You've got your graduation ticket and you can give up your contingency pigeon, right?"

He looked crestfallen. "I'm sorry. Los malos hábitos are difficult to overcome. I want to go to school intensively now and graduate and no longer do what I used to have to do."

"Well, I guess the course is over. It's been . . . well, it's definitely been a learning experience."

"Get up, güero, please."

"Why should I? I want to sleep. Here, entre las palmas."

"They won't let you sleep here. Some grenaderos will come by. They'll take you to the station and keep the pastel money which you think is so much softer than the dollar."

The grass began to smell of manure. I got up.

On the ninth day I discovered I had contracted the gonk. That was quite a letdown. The same day the pilgrims returned to the countryside and the grenaderos abandoned the university library with its revolutionary mural. I watched the campesinos as they trod out of the capital. The drunken revel was over and so was the holy fervor. They were tired, broke, bearing loathsome lesions on their knees that peered out of their trousers, which had worn away in their penitent sojourn in the Virgin's sanctuary. They looked like a crestfallen army in retreat. They resembled those Vietnamese multitudes on the run that we used to look at, guilt-ridden and repulsed, on the evening news.

When the last of the campesinos and their geese had moved on I could then cross the Promenade of Institutionalized Revolution to the barrio pharmacy where they were caring for me. All my money seemed to be dissipating in penicillin and in little luxuries to assuage the discomfort. Every day I walked sore and open-legged to the pharmacy and pulled down my trousers in the back room. The attendant, una celestina fea y arrugada who looked like the incarnation of gleeful disapproval, would put the needle in.

"How many cc's are you going to give me?"

"You need a million cc's this time up."

"No chingues. You'll have the needle in my bun for over five minutes. It'll be an hour before I'll be able to move my leg."

"¡Cómo que no chingues! That's what you should say to yourself, güerito. ¡Porque chingue y chingue y mira el resultado! O como decimos por aquí: Quien se acuesta con pulgas . . . "

"Spare me the dénouement. Let's get it over with. Look, why don't you just give me 500,000?"

"You want 500,000? I'll give it! You know how many machos come back here three weeks later, open-legged, and bawling because the pus is back again and dripping out of their putrid chiles?"

"God no, give me the million. Anything."

"Here it goes, y no chilles, ¿eh? güerito valín. Porque como sabes, tú tienes la enfermedad de los meros machos." She began to laugh with great moral gusto. As my leg turned numb I realized that in Mexico the man wasn't always in the plaza and the women only en casa.

It was just a few days before my term was up and I was to return to Califas. I bumped into Espinoso in the library.

"Hola, vate loco."

He looked embarrassed, almost searching for a space to slink into. "Hola, vato loco. It's been some days since I've seen you."

"Well, yes, I've been spending time at the old farmacia. I got the gonk, thanks to you and your macho ideas and your disgusting putas that you believe are sensuously perverse."

"Well, I figured. I got it too. La mierda de gonorrea is epidemic here."

"Well, that's the best fucking news I've heard all week!"

"You think so? You want to reenact the Alamo here in the library? Fuck it, man, be happy it's just gonk que se quita con penicilina and not what they say you get on the other side of the river, herpes. Let me tell you something, güero, and this is God's truth. Since I've been here, six years in this hostile valley, that was the first time I got laid."

"Not enough billetiza, right?"

"Right. It wasn't a financial priority."

"Sure, you didn't have a sufficiently dumb gringo to hustle big enough at the jai alai. Well, you must be busted by now what with shots and poultices and all. Here, let me stake you again—what the fuck, the Chicano baboso never learns." I flipped out a pink and canary bill with the likeness of Venustiano Carranza and stuffed it in his guayabera pocket.

"I'll accept it as a wedding present on behalf of my novia and me."

"Yeah. I was sure that you'd accept it okay, Mr. Savoir Faire."

"I don't mean to hurt you, güero valín. But, ¿sabes lo que tú eres . . . en el fondo?"

"No, Mr. Maya. No idea what I am en 'el fondo.' But I'm sure you're gonna tell me, Mr. Sabelotodo."

"En el fondo tú eres . . . ¡turista!"

Time softens the sense of injury and lets the little nostalgias form the veins and lodes that make the past palatable. If I had an address to write to, I would have sent him a card or something. But there was no address, maybe the empty swimming pool, o como dijo esa noche, una nulidad sin identidad remota, and barring that I would find myself in the library, which seemed like an unsullied cavern, to sit and ponder, open the page in the art book to the Palenque man, frame ideas, sometimes talk silently to the stone head.

When you give meaningful events the profound reflection that they require, the many details that you missed in the ongoing come into relief and give a new bent to the hurt. In the labyrinthine library of my soledad I uncovered and relived the discreet portents and signs. How he envied and admired attributes that I didn't remotely realize. "Güero" he called me, though in this country I could not remotely pass for fair. And my blue jeans and knitted polo shirt were such a center of attraction, the ballpoint pen that contained three cartridges: red, black, and green. Finally, I gave it to him. The way he liked to introduce me to girls on the campus—girls, I conclude now, who were not his friendly acquaintances as I had thought at the time, but barely accorded him the minimal courtesies of fellow studenthood. He would introduce me, I realize now, with a touch of the panderer, and how they would take to the exotic Chicano, the güero valín with a rather hairy chest who maybe reminded them in his knit shirt of some phantasm image they had conjured in their head, a Robert Redford, well-heeled, privileged, and native in Spanish. You were waiting there, Felipe, furious and sotted with envy, bridling your lust—how you must have kept so much venom under wraps—hoping that I would puncture the maiden ethics of niñas de bien, maybe score, maybe there would be a scrap of carrion in it for you. For you hadn't been laid in six years!

How you queried me, Maya, about so many things like routes and rivers, fences and sensors, coyotes and pollos. Were you trying on Chicano, my friend? Were you speculating on the North? How proud you were, como un tío paternal, when you arranged a little public trial for me at the tortería, bade me eat the chile más piquín de la tortería. And when I passed your little test and won a round of student applause, did you not say, "See, he's no gringo now, he's earned his bones." But it was nothing! I've been eating those pequines my whole life!

Now I feel so mortified that I could have confided in you—¿qué?—after two or three days of acquaintanceship at most, such intimate yearnings as my whole carnal hope for Mexican-Chicano compañerismo. ¡Qué ingenuo! Now I know, máximo peón, that even in oppression, even if there are only two oppressed peas in a constricted pod, they will disaggregate into an oppressor and an oppressed, a siervo and a señor, a leader and a led. That is the nature of oppression and of the oppressed, the theory and the practice. That they know only what they know and act on what they know, a great chain of oppressed people, a great daisy chain of being that leads not straight to St. Thomas's sandía-hued heaven, but low, up and down picos, down and up valleys, across llanos, and even across rivers where the current runs in opposing directions. Yet, truly escarmentado that I am for having so readily and unselfconsciously confided in El Otro, that moment in the tortería, that heartfelt abrazo over tortas de lomo . . . How is it that two oprimidos of such divergent estirpes, of such varied formation, could have, if just for a transitory term, communed? I cherish that shared governance of perceptions even though to obtain it requires a racking sojourn into memories filled with penitence and humiliation. And I think of a passage in Hemingway where it is observed that where we are weak, there where nature surely breaks us, and if we fare with good fortune, and go on the mend, there, where we were weak, we are now the strongest. And although in the end it's all the same for nature will break us, definitively, it will not be at the junction where once we were weak and now we are strong.

Amigo, I don't quarrel with your many truths or the intensity of your motives. Of one thing, no cabe duda, I am poor like Cheech and Chong—thank God for it, bless that level of poverty that still subsidizes the notion of humorous solutions.

Well, yes, there is one perception that I quarrel with. ¡Yo no soy turista! In truth you were the tourist, amigo, as well as the tour guide and the conning lout. A most engaging and eager one, the way you genuinely investigated my nature, but like any tourist, even an enlightened and avid one, you compared the landscape by a self-same standard. Your sense of the picturesque, the empathetic, and the offensive were all measured out in the same pastel currency. But the estranged is different from the tourist. It is his lot to wander forth, to cross rivers that flow up course, seek out his own image in the dubious landscape of the other, search for a currency that isn't there. Por supuesto, the Chicano needs to gaze into smoky mirrors that reflect no peer. Know this, venerable Maya head that has perdured for 1200 years on a coated ivory page in a slick art book in a library: I am strong where I've been broken and I'm not prepared to cave in.

1984-85

Poems

PINCHED TOES

At the start of the day
I yelled at little Benjie for spilling his cereal,
then I pulled Gloria's hair too hard when it wouldn't
twist into an even braid

Baby Lala got on my nerves for wetting her diaper
twice before breakfast and for spitting up her rice
and milk all over my last clean dress

and let's not even think about last night

I didn't want to kiss Rudy at all this morning
because of the way he asked if there was any
fresh tortillas and could I make a better lunch today
'cuz he was getting tired of how I made his sandwiches

not to mention that the man still can't find
his own clean clothes and it's because
they are nesting under last week's calzones

And if Josie wants me to watch her little pack of
animals again I'm gonna sell 'em to the Circus Vargas

I'm gonna bite the dog too

I hate K-MART shoes

SOLTERA

The rain is a quiet whisper in my ears tonight
si quería
I could shatter soltera and dance in the rainlight
desnuda

and tonight

when soft July slips through the tiny holes of my
window screen I will call for violin and angels
and dance with God because He is the only he

remaining

and tonight

I lower my bird self onto the thinly carpeted
floor under my bed and pedal an
invisible bicycle until I scream and curse
the He and the he because my legs no longer
fill with blood

because my heart has failed me

TERROR EYE

Tina
used to dance to the Four Tops with that shaky
little hip-step she made up one morning while we
stayed home from school and glittered our fingernails

we used to go out with the same boys
sharing them on a rotating basis
we wore gold earrings dark lipstick black heels

great for dancing
and Tina would laugh forever on account of her
joyous disposition and the night air

sometimes we had to hold our breaths for about
a month and a half before we could breathe again
but it was always worth it

I don't visit or call or in any way communicate
with Tina anymore, not since her husband
showed me the damp narrow tunnels in his eyes

he wanted me to understand something about how
a man has needs and desires that have nothing to do
with nothing at all

except no job no money no self-respect or
some such foolish thing, I saw his plan of action
and what is there to do but reject the

heroic rapist and draw yourself away from the
crocodile who cries himself a river
because you have seen the poisoned shadows in his eyes

Last time I saw Tina she wore dark glasses
that didn't cover her purple eyes or blue cheek
and there really isn't any way to hide a broken arm

she ran away from me
so after I washed my dishes all I could do was
light three candles and remember

Tina used to dance to the Four Tops with that
shaky little hip-step and laugh until forever
with the coming of the dawn.

Juan Felipe Herrera   Second Prize: Short Story

Memoir: Checker-Piece

It took place in a tan two-story East L.A. Victorian. Somehow, the four of us were participants in an odd game in which all the players had to intersect at this particular cube-like dwelling.

It was a checker-piece in the center of a checkered infinity. All the houses seemed to be exactly alike, as if they had been pressed through a sharp grill in the stratosphere and softly and silently flattened into a two-tone grid in the hottest ground of Chicanoland.

Everything was patterned: veridian green lawns snipped with the grace of a ballerina, probing T.V. antennas plucking messages through the smog, and a score of plump off-white 1952 Plymouths; everything aglow beneath the perforated and hazy Plexiglas box in heaven.

Tomás Mendoza-Harrell had invited me to come over. I had met Tomás a year earlier, in 1970, at Royce Hall Quad at UCLA during the early planning stages of a raucous trip to Chiapas. He said he had a film project in mind for me.

He had gone through the usual Chicano male initiation rites held at Santa Colby, an Ozzie-and-Harriett, two-bedroom house in Santa Monica, which a brown horde converted into a hallucinating den of first-generation E.O.P. [Equal Opportunity Program] undergrads drinking papaya tea and sangría, eating Quaaludes and tortillas, listening to Santana and Satie, talking about

Quetzalcóatl and revolution as we planned the next raunchy Molotov attack on the Greek fraternities and as we ditched Juan Gómez-Quiñónez's Mexican-American History-B class.

He picked me up in his rebuilt Volkswagen bug, La Cucaracha.

At the time I was living in Venice trying to eke out an enlightened existence on E.O.P. loans, macrobiotics, Crayolas, poetry, and a holistic relationship with Lynne Erlich, a Jewish-Russian-Mexican-Chicana poet who had just broken up with the lead singer of the 103rd Street Watts Band.

As usual, once in the belly of La Cucaracha, we became two phosphorescent rap machines unraveling new ideas for the sweltering lowlands of Aztlán.

Tomás's green eyes punctuated the plan: "Look, ése, I want you to meet Geraldine Kudaka when we get to the house. She's gonna do camera while I direct. Anyway, it's a Neo-Mayan Chicano urban thing. We'll talk about details later."

I told him to roll down the window.

He had already been trying to teach me Ken-Po Karate and the heat was bloating my sore 130-pound-brown rice-fed bod. It was an interesting film concept, I said, but at the moment La Cucaracha and its envelope of air overpowered me.

Everything was too real. It was as if we were traveling inside of a Magritte painting, careening through a freeway made of cotton spiraling into a labyrinth of neatly scissored origami residences.

La Cucaracha whips through the maze. Tomás's green lights go on again: "Watcha, you are wearing khaki pants, okay? No shoes, no shirt, ¿me entiendes? You are walking through a tunnel with a hood over your face, but there is a way out. You are alone, groping through a dark cosmos, you hear voices, moans, things are clawing at you, you are trapped in a damp chamber of voids, secretions, and suffering figures. What do you think?"

I realize that the rap we had a couple of weeks ago at Santa Colby on the Mayan concept of the Underworld, Xibalba, is about to go on screen.

"And then," he blurts readily, clutching the plastic donut he uses to steer the Cucaracha rocket, "we are going to tie you up on a boulder in a hiding place I know of in the Santa Monica Mountains. It's perfect for this scene."

"What about Geraldine?" I ask. The wiry Chicano space pilot quickly responds: "Never mind, once we get you tied up, I want you to start screaming, snarling, shaking your head violently, left and then right." "Uh huh," I mumble, gazing at the architectural precision of the eerie landscape we are approaching.

Tomás continues, crouching forward. He looks like he's about to ski into the windshield. "Remember Anthony Quinn in *The Hunchback of Notre*

Dame and how he distorted his body?" he adds, on the verge of standing up and jamming his head through the roof.

"Simón, yeah, I know," I ponder through the glass.

"Well, that's how I want you to move your torso and upper body while La Geraldine whips you." He lifts his thin left eyebrow professorially as he elaborates, "You know, this is the most important part of the film."

"You ain't kidding, carnal. It sure don't sound like 'Viva Humpty Dumpty'," I quip and stare at him.

Tomás settles into his seat again. He appears to anticipate a negative vote on the film. I turn and look out the little window again. Everything looks so identical.

I think about contrast.

Last summer Tomás and I were walking through La Plaza Central in San Cristóbal de Las Casas after bribing a pilot to fly us to the Lacandon Jungle. I bought the day-old *Excelsior* paper from Mexico City. As I paged through it thinking of a shortcut to Comitán, the take-off point to the jungle, an odd rectangle of letters slipped into my mouth. I whispered,

"MUEREN VARIOS EN MANIFESTACIÓN CHICANA."

Rubén Salazar is blown into careful confetti squares in the smokey web of the Silver Dollar Bar by the L.A.P.D. swat-pig.

I see a thousand stitches being sewn over the bleeding streets, tying up the swollen sidewalks like skin.

I think of Little John Angulo somewhere in Westwood writing his last metallic note on the jagged blue line of his left arm. And no one would hear his last poem of desire and no one would applaud his hard pride as he fixed his eyes on the dead wall forever.

La selva Lacandona appears.

José Pepe Chan Bol paces the makeshift airstrip at Naja in the heart of the Lacandon Mayas. He has come to accept malaria in his village like a predictable storm. He has become accustomed to playing Christian Baptist preacher and reciting the Bible from Maryland in the thatched-roof temple that his sons built. The only thing that bothers José Pepe Chan Bol is the air.

It smells like a fuse burning.

He can hear the green time bomb ticking among the vines of the forest. Near Chancala, he can hear Joaquín Trujillo, one of the government's Latino henchmen, drink post and stake out Lacandon land for timber, dolomite, and rubber. And not far from the airstrip, José Pepe Chan Bol can see where the fuse has scarred the earth, stripped the land, and left a road of stiffened patches for the next bulldozer from San Cristóbal.

But on the freeway of East Los [East Los Angeles, California], looking out of a luminous Aztlán space shuttle called La Cucaracha, no matter how hard I try, no matter how hard I attempt to focus, I see no contrast.

I think of Venice again.

I could be eating some fluffy brown rice with a touch of tahini sauce with a half-glass of water. I could be in my closet converted into an art studio sprinkling glitter on my latest Chicano Matisse crayon nudes. I could be brushing Lynne's thick black eyebrows as I prepare to do one of the special Chicano-Bogart lines like, "What's a chavala like you doing in a cantón place like this?"

But I am here next to a kamikaze compadre zooming on a one-way mission to the gut of Aztlán as he unravels one of the aesthetic battle plans in the Chicano Movement's war against the Kapitalist dragon.

I crack open a bottle of warm spring water that I always carry in my hand-woven bag, and take a swig.

"Check it out, carnal. Who's going to hear me scream and snarl à la Anthony Quinn under a dirty black burlap sack, humping on a rock in the middle of nowhere in a five-minute 8mm film done by some oddball from San Francisco regarding some kind of urbo-Mayan-Chicanoid chingadera that you came up with?"

I lean back. I look through the stained amber sunroof. La Cucaracha is on cruise control. Tomás peers at me with one eye as he scopes the freeway for the next off-ramp, humming one of those whimsical tunes you hum to paste desperate moments together. I lean over and whisper to the Aztlán pilot, "I love it, I love it."

We break out into our Cinco de Mayo special mariachi yell and rattle out some of the finer aspects of the scenario. In no time we glide into the front emerald lawn facing the antique tan and square Victorian.

Alejandro Murguía is sitting on the bed with his back to the windows. He is a lean young man. He reminds me of a campesino that I met in Chiapas who said he loved to be alone in the fields of maíz and that he wasn't himself in the big towns like San Cristóbal. Alejandro is dark. He has the aura of a human lizard dressed in a silk suit. He appears elegant, motionless, and foreboding.

He lures out a few syllables, "How's it going, man?" I decide to do one of my one-word Bogart moves, "Suave."

No one is speaking, although I can see through the corner of my eye that Tomás is gesturing wildly to La Geraldine about the film project.

The heat is unbearable. Everything has taken on a slick brush stroke of thin oil. Even the walls suddenly appear with a new glazy coat. We seem to be rotating around each other like carousel dolls.

La Geraldine comes over and slowly hovers over Alejandro. I want to think that they are lovers, but a distinct feeling takes hold of me—all of us look so out of place here. Alejandro stops the daze. "Look, why don't you come up to the city? We just took over a building, a place for artists and writers to live and work and get it together. ¿Qué te parece?"

Everyone joins in and talks about another battle plan in the Mission District of San Francisco. Alejandro mentions his essay on political theater, soon to be published by Pocho-Che Editions. There's only time for a cigarette, a few gestures. Suddenly, it is over.

I take another hit of mineral water.

I think about heading back to Venice. This old Victorian is a mystery. Who lives here, anyway? Maybe the basement leads to an underground chamber and the secret opening to one of the seven magical caves of Aztlán. Or maybe it's a classy depot for winos and Movement gente rented out by a Chicano Studies professor with tenure. Tomás and I walk out to the front porch. I look back. Alejandro seems to have moved only a few inches. You can see his steely profile against the brilliant white curtains. He studies Geraldine as she speaks. It is about 2:30 in the afternoon. No one is out.

La Cucaracha looks funny parked next to the plump line of 1952 Plymouths.

I can feel the giant tan checker-piece looming behind us as Tomás puts the car into third gear.

Margarita Luna Robles   Second Prize: Short story

Urbano: Letters of the Horseshoe Murder

April 15

M'ijo—

I don't believe this is happening. I've been so upset I can't eat or sleep. I don't know if I'll be able to go to work tomorrow. I don't even want to go outside of this house or even get out of bed. I can't face anyone. I can almost hear what everyone's going to say. Everyone always tells me you're up to no good, always in trouble, a real troublemaker. Some of the younger kids' mothers say you're a bad example for their kids. Then they look at me. I'm the bad mother, it's my fault.

God knows I've tried. I've worked so hard! Why do you keep doing this to me? I work to support you, on top of always having your meals and clothes ready and the house clean. I do it all for you! Maybe that is the problem—I do too much, I don't give you any responsibility. I do it so that you can study and be someone. I guess that's the end of your studies. You know how hard Tavo and I worked to get you into that school. They didn't want you 'cause of your record—now look!

This is bad all the way around. Mike's pissed off. I don't blame him. He's been more than a father to you, he's treated you right. Look how you pay him back.

Wait till your father hears about this. I haven't called him. Why should I be the one who always "gets it together"? Then no one appreciates it and I get blamed. Forget it. I quit. I can't take this anymore. I'm not going to talk to him. He doesn't care. He never took any responsibility for you after he left. I don't expect him to now. He's got three sons and a wife. He doesn't need the problems you make.

Randy, please tell me it wasn't you. I believe you. You're all I have. I have Mike too, but you're my baby. You and I have been through some times together. I can remember holding you so tightly while you slept, you were just a baby. I'd be so afraid of the dark I'd lay there crying, sometimes all night. Then I'd be afraid that I would die and there would be no one for you. I love you. I'm still here for you. I'm praying hard for you. *Be Good*—for me!

God be with you.

Love,
Mom

April 17

My dearest Randy,

I love you. I'm so scared. The police came by asking me all sorts of questions. I didn't know what to say. All I said was I don't know anything and that we were at a party in San Francisco. I said that I don't know my way around in the city so I don't know where the party was at 'cause I didn't know anyone there. I was so scared I started to cry. Then my dad got really pissed off and told them to leave and get in touch with our lawyer.

My parents are really upset about this. But it's not just this. They don't want me to see you anymore. They never have wanted me to see you. I wish they would leave us alone. I get tired of all this shit.

To top it off, your friends don't like you being with me. They always just ignore me, as if I'm not there. The girls don't even talk to me. They just stare at me, as if I don't belong there. I can understand that maybe they want to be with you, but it's not my fault that you want to be with me.

Randy, please tell me it's going to be all right and that you and I are going to be together. I love you too much to let you go. I don't want to be without you. I'll always be here for you.

Please write.

Yvette y Randy
PVM

April 18

Dear Randy,

How's it going, mi locote? What can I say except all this shit broke loose. The whole clica is acting like they got a stick up their ass. Everyone tries to be cool but they're scared. No one knows what happened. Three of our homies got picked up for the shooting at the Studio 47. No one from the barrio was there and Yvette told me you guys were in San Fra at a borlo.

See, if you had been with me your face would've been seen and you'd never have got picked up. The only trouble you'd be in would be with Yvette. But you could really work that out easy, the way you always do. I know it's none of my business but why her? She's so out of reality. She could be fucking white for all I know. Whenever you bring her around it's like she's smelling CACA.

Maybe you lay that trip on her, not to mix or hang out 'cause the "loca" may rub off on her. And she's so clean, so untouched by the barrio, and that's what you want. If that's what you're doing, that sucks 'cause I know and I have a good time when we're together. I know I make you feel good, cabrón. I also know it bugs you that I hang out with the vatos and I call it as I see it. The way I see it is I'm here. I'm waiting for you. Whenever you're ready.

I hope you get out soon. I miss your face.

Love,
Mousie—VHS

April 19

Randazzo,

I was glad to hear from you, homie. I guess by now it's getting to you, being locked up. Counting those fucking bricks gets real old too quick. The rap you've got keeps you away from the rest of the vatos in there. By the way, I knew Puppet got picked up for questioning but he's not out yet. This is a desmadre for the barrio 'cause la placa is playing "surveillance" in the Horseshoe. The vatos aren't even able to hang out at the park without the pigs busting in. We can't even walk the streets without being stopped. Last night one of the chavalos got stopped and frisked at gunpoint—the vatito is only 13!

Then they wonder why we don't got any respect. You know me, ése, I've been around a long time, I've seen a lot. ¡Qué chinguen su madre, fucking putos! I could tell you a lot of stories but they'll only censor them in the mail room there. I'll tell you when you're out. These are things you gotta know to survive 'cause now you got a chaqueta with la ley. So, you're gonna be getting it from la placa once you're back on the streets, so prepare yourself. You're also gonna get mierda from some of the homies. You gotta understand that the heat's on in the barrio, paranoia has hit everyone, and then there's the vatos who want rank over you. They're gonna use this in their favor. You know who they are but not everyone in the barrio knows.

The challenge is yours, homes.

Después,
OSO—VHS—SJ—14

April 19

Dearest Mom,

I got your letter. I guess you're pretty worried. I'm sorry. I know I keep blowing it. But, I didn't do it. You'll see. I'll be out of here in no time. They don't have anything on me, I'm just a suspect. There are no charges.

Never mind about what people say. I keep telling you that's a real problem you have, always worrying about what everyone will think and say. I hope you're feeling better and that you're going to work. This is nothing. I swear.

Tell Mike I'm sorry and I'm glad he's there for you. He's firme, even if he's not a vato loco and never was. He's been good to me, always let me be me.

Don't worry about el jefito. He's never around when I need him so he shouldn't say anything about anything. If he wants to help, fine, if he doesn't he should butt out. His sons aren't so bad—they are my half-brothers, even if we never see each other or spend time together. Have you seen Stretch? He looks just like me, but bigger and I'm a vato loco and he's a jock. I like him. I always wanted a kid brother, I mean he is a kid brother but he's never around. You know what I mean.

Dad probably knows. The word gets out quick in the streets, Stretch knows. Don't bother calling him. Let him call you. Don't worry, okay? I'll be out soon. I miss your cooking.

I love you, Mom.

Your son,
Randy

April 20

Q-Vo Oso—

I got your letra, homes. Good to hear from you. I swear I needed to hear from you. People write, you know what I mean? It's different with you and what you got to say. You know what I'm going through. I'm going fucking crazy in here.

I've been in here one whole week, I mean I've been in here longer than that before but not like this. I think they're playing games on me. I still don't got a court date, and there are no charges. They can't keep me here too much longer. You don't think someone is throwing a rata on me, do you? Or, maybe they think they can get someone to say I did it and it'll be pretty soon so that's why they won't let me out. The last time I broke probation, I skipped the county line and fucked up by driving off the cliff in Santa Cruz. I guess that could have been worse, I could have killed myself. But it's illegal to keep me here like this, but they're still doing it. They said just the fact I broke probation again will keep me here. This fool told me I broke probation by going outside the county without a legal guardian. You know how I told you I was at a party in San Fra? My probation officer hasn't even come around.

I guess what's really bothering me is that it's Saturday night and I ain't getting any. Mousie wrote me. Boy, she's something else . . . I told you. She don't make it hard for me—ha ha, actually, she makes it very hard. She takes care of it, too. She's got huevos, she could have been a vato. She'll tell you off in no time. She's good to me, but I know she ain't fucking loose. She says she'll wait for me. What do you think?

Yvette wrote to me too. I love her. She is so nice and different than any of the other rucas. Except Mousie. I want Mousie in reserve, you know, when Yvette can't make it. But, oh boy, Yvette. She's soft, like a dream. She smells like warm milk, and she tastes so good. Every time I kiss her, it's like I don't want to stop, like being lost in a cloud that floats, forever. Boy, I better stop. This only makes me think that I ain't got either one. Tonight I'll thank this fucking system for not tying my hands up.

Do me a favor, homes. Get in touch with Father Mateo at the church and tell him I need to see him. I need to talk to someone soon. He's the only one they'll let in.

Drop me a line.

Your Homie,
Randazz-O
VHS—San Jo—14

April 20

Randazz-o,

What's going down, ése? Seems you're on a streak—puras chingaderas. Could it be you're getting a little too sloppy, not covering your tracks?

This is the third time you get picked up in one month—for different cargos. ¿Qué pasa, ése? The word out on the streets about this rap ain't too good. You're getting in over your head, vato. The first time was grand theft, the second was suspect in a case of arson, and now this.

You know what they say, locote, the third time is a cinch. You're in: Big Time Felon. You're not even eighteen! I guess that gives you rank in the streets, in the barrio. Rank don't rank where you're at. I could have told the homies about you—you're a bit too pushy too soon. Your timing is off and timing is what you need to be on top. You bring desmadres on yourself and you bring it on the rest of us. Barrio Horseshoe is hot with the pigs 'cause of you and nobody's liking it. Between you and me, homes, I think you're better off in there.

Of course, this could be a game la ley is playing, trying to put a torcida on you for good. Lock you away. Being the leader that you are in Horseshoe, they want you off the streets.

But, I don't think so. Like I said, this is between you and me. When you get out, IF you get out, we'll take care of business. Just you and me. Suave.

Al rato,
PaYaSo
San Jo Norte—14—VHS—Y—Qué

A DIALOGUE WITH NO ONE AT THE PARTY IN THE HORSESHOE

Date:	April 20
FLACO:	H-e-e-e-y, party time. Let's get down.
TINY:	Alri-i-i-ght, look who's here, el Rocky.
CINDY:	It's about time someone had a good party.
MELINDA:	I know, it's been a rough week.
MOUSIE:	You ain't shittin', I miss Randazzo.
ROCKY:	Randazzo? Fuck. Three of our homies are locked up.
TINO:	Hey, man, we ain't locked up. Cut loose.
LITTLE MARY:	Don't be so cold, how would you like it?
ROCKY:	Hey, man, you're getting too much foam in the beer. Pump it right.
J.R.:	Beer? Who's got the goods?
LA SHORTY:	What goods you talkin' about?
OSO:	No la rieguen. You know the fuckin' pigs are out.
RICO:	That's what I like: order.
LITTLE MAN:	Hey, Mousie, you wanna dance?
PINO:	With all these lovely ladies here, who wants to dance?
MANUEL:	Change the fuckin' record.
BEAR:	Yeah, put some oldies on.
EL RAY:	Dim the lights, let's get close.
PAYASO:	Hey, Mousie, I heard who you been fuckin' with.
MOUSIE:	It ain't you, puto.
LA SHORTY:	Alright, Mousie.
LITTLE MARY:	That'll show you.

CINDY:	God, Mousie, you got a lot of nerve.
VERDUGO:	Some rucas around here think they got huevos. They don't.
DREAMER:	Leave the rucas alone. Let them have huevos for breakfast.
PAYASO:	They can have mine right now.
OSO:	Córtense el pedo con las rucas. Show some respeto. It's good for las rucas to be strong.
EL RAY:	My, my, look who's here, la Rosie looking mighty fine.
ROSIE:	Hey, Ray. Cyclone and Beto are out there waiting on some of the other guys.
PINO:	Hey, Cyclone better not be packin' tonight.
CYCLONE:	Someone say something about me packin'?
BETO:	If some of you ain't packin', that's your problem. Chisme has it that . . .
TINO:	Yeah, we heard, Vickie's Town is coming down tonight.
OSO:	Who's worried about Vickie's Town? I heard Lomas is after them so they ain't moving outside their turf.
LA SHORTY:	Yeah, but I heard that Lomas got a pleito with us too.
VENADO:	Things are hot in San Jo, okay? No barrio has it good with any other barrio. Pinchi Lomas always has a pedo with us so every fuckin' time we get down, they run crying.
MANDO:	Hey, man, this is a party.
OSO:	Shut your fuckin' mouth.
CINDY:	Who's pumping the keg? We're still getting too much foam.
EL RAY:	I'm pumping . . . the keg, Cindy, the keg.
BETO:	I'm feeling really fucked up.
CYCLONE:	It was that shit you were smoking.
ALBERT:	Who's got fuckin' shit to smoke?
OSO:	You guys better cool it.
MOUSIE:	You nervous, Oso? Have you heard from Randy?
MANUEL:	Hey, the never-ready sisters are here. Get it, Navarette, ne-va ready?
LINDA:	You can hear this party on the other block.
STELLA:	Who's got the whites?
MIMI:	Whatever you do, don't get redded out.
PINO:	I got some dust.
ROCKY:	Heddy and some of the other varas from Little Town are here.
MIMI:	I saw Chino and his brothers out there, too.
LINDA:	That's alright, Little Town locos are fine.
MOUSIE:	It's good that smaller clicas get it together with us.
MANUEL:	Except for Barrio Libre.

OSO:	Shut the fuck up.
ALBERT:	This is a good party, people are dancing and singing and getting high shaking up the dust.
BETO:	That dust was good, made me think of my mother.
TINO:	That dust got around tonight.
EL RAY:	You guys blow it with dust.
CINDY:	You wanna dance, Ray, or are you waiting on Becky?
MOUSIE:	Angel baby, my angel baby.
LITTLE MARY:	OOO-HOO I love you, OOO-HOO I do.
MELINDA:	No one could love you like I do.
LINDA:	Alright, turn the music up.
OSO:	We can't have the music louder or the pigs are gonna down.
TINO:	Or Vickie's Town.
ROCKY:	I got my shank.
CYCLONE:	I got my cuete.
PINO:	I got my dust.
BETO:	I got my ruca.
DREAMER:	But did you bring your huevos?
OSO:	Look, it's after twelve, maybe we should call it a night.
TINO:	But there's still beer in the keg.
ALBERT:	And there's still plenty of dust.
HEDDY:	And there's still plenty of rucas here.
OSO:	Is that all you guys think about? Drugs, cuetes, and rucas?
LITTLE MARY:	Wow, there's about 50 people here tonight.
MOUSIE:	There's cars parked for two blocks clown.
LITTLE MAN:	EVERYBODY STOP! TURN THE MUSIC DOWN! CUT THE LIGHTS!
CINDY:	What's happening? I gotta go, I gotta go.
LA SHORTY:	Shut up, Cindy, get down!

Sound heard: BLAST! BLAST! BLAST! BLAST! BLAST! BLAST!

MOUSIE:	Little Mary's down!
MANUEL:	Flaco's hit!
BETO:	I told you guys, you better be packing.
OSO:	Nobody panic! Just stay down on the floor. Girls, you're not doing anything for Little Mary by screaming. Get to the phone.
ALBERT:	What's going on, man? Is it the dust or is this?! Oh, man, get me off of this shit, I don't want to die.
CINDY:	My mom told me not to come.
EL RAY:	My mom told me to stay home, come on, Cindy.

DREAMER:	FUCKIN' VICKIE'S TOWN—THE WHOLE GANGA IS HERE! WHERE'S THE FUCKIN' PIGS WHEN YOU NEED 'EM?
OSO:	THIS IS A SET-UP. FUCKIN' NARCS. THEY'LL LET EACH OTHER OFF FIRST! MOUSIE, DID YOU CALL THE PIGS? STAY DOWN AND SHUT THE FUCK UP OR WE'RE GOING DOWN!
MOUSIE:	Little Mary's still breathing . . . Operator, this is an emergency. There's been a shooting, we need an ambulance. Two people are down, there's a war outside, there's shooting.
LINDA:	My God, Flaco's not breathing. FLACO-O-O-O-O, FLACO-O-O-O-O!
CINDY:	Oh, Flaco, please don't die.
CYCLONE:	DON'T GO OUT THERE, BETO! BETO, BETO!
STELLA:	BETO'S DOWN. BETO, BETO, BETO, BETO!
ROCKY:	STELLA, GET DOWN!
OSO:	FUCKIN' ROCKY, LET BETO BE. DON'T GO OUT THERE, BETO, DON'T GO!
MOUSIE:	GET THE FUCKING POLICE HERE RIGHT NOW. WE'RE ALL GONNA DIE. 3-3-0 SPENCER, NOW!
CYCLONE:	EVERYONE QUIET! SHUT UP! WE GOTTA THINK! OSO, PINO, CHINO, RAY, LET'S GIVE IT TO THEM! BARRIO HORSESHOE RIFA Y QUÉ!
EL RAY:	You ladies stay low, watch Little Mary. Let's see, Mousie, get a towel, and press here, like this, you got it? Cindy, leave Flaco alone. Linda, watch Cindy, get her calmed down.

Sound heard: CRASH! CRASH! CRASH! CRASH! CRASH! CRASH!

CHINO:	Oh, man . . . Look at my ranfla . . .
MOUSIE:	Get away from the window, Chino, you're gonna get your brains blown out.
OSO:	This is it, homies. Get your cuetes, fileros. Out in the garage, get the tire irons and the axe. ¡Vamos a darles en la madre!
STELLA:	The ambulance is here.
EL RAY:	Here comes the police force. . . . Oh, wow! I hope they don't blow our vatos away. Vickie's Town culeros just split.
OSO:	TRUCHA! We ain't gettin' them here tonight!
DANNY:	FUCK. Look at all the pinchis ranflas.
OSO:	Look at my fuckin' house, man.
PINO:	What the fuck brought this down?
HEDDY:	Rocky and Beto are hit. . . . Rocky's doing real bad . . .
VENADO:	Pinchi Tinto de Vickie's Town had a pleito with . . .
OSO:	No, officer, we don't know what happened; we were just having a party . . .

Sunland

Tuve la sensación de haber vivido este momento en otra ocasión, de haber pisado cuidadosamente, primero con el pie izquierdo, luego con el derecho hasta encontrarme parada en el pavimento familiar. Sería déjà vu, como decían los gringos, quizás, o tal vez otra vaga ilusión de la vida. Sí, eso debía ser. Me fijé a mi alrededor. Era el motel dilapidado que hace años había sido convertido en una fila militar de apartamentos de una recámara. Les sonreí a los niños descalzos que jugaban enfrente de las puertas de tela. Éste era el lugar donde se reunían los pobres blancos, las madres que dependían de la ayuda del gobierno, los borrachos del pueblo y los hombres que golpeaban a sus esposas —éste era el centro de constantes asaltos de inmigración y aquí me encontraba yo, en el mero centro de todo, sintiéndome como si una vez antes había estado aquí. Toqué rápidamente en el marco de la puerta de tela, tratando de ignorar la música ruidosa que venía del parque, al otro lado de la calle donde los adolescentes de pelo largo se juntaban con sus *six-packs* de cerveza y sus estéreos a todo volumen.

El sonido de los pasos de mi abuelito me recordaron la razón por la cual había venido.

—Pásale, hijita —me dijo y corrió la puerta de tela.

—Quiúbo, Dalín, —le dije, usando el apodo para el hombre que todos conocían como don Luis. Le di un beso en su mejilla de indígena tan bien conocida por mí.

—¿Cómo te has sentido, jita? Siéntate —me dijo el Dalín, apuntando a una silla—. Me da gusto que viniste. *How you like it?*

—Está suave, Grandpa —le contesté, sentándome a su lado en el viejo sillón. Empecé a recorrer la pequeña sala, tenía una televisión blanco y negro, un sofá verde y descolorido, las paredes pintadas color crema empezaban a pelarse. Desde donde estaba, pude ver una ventana pequeña, pero estaba bien tapada con unas cortinas para que no entrara la luz. Cerca de mí estaba un calentón de gas en el piso junto a una puerta media abierta que daba a un pequeño cuarto de baño.

Se oían unos ruidos del apartamento de al lado.

—Gente loca. Siempre haciendo ruido —me dijo el Dalín, leyéndome los pensamientos—. ¿Ves la estufita que tengo, jita? —continuó, apuntando al pasillo que daba a una pequeña cocina—. Hace muy buena comida. Pero me traen Meals on Wheels al mediodía, así que nada más hago la cena. ¿Cómo has estado, jita? ¿Por qué no te acompañó Raúl?

—Raúl —suspiré sin contestarle. Recordé aquella noche cuando sentí por última vez el dolor de sus manos que bruscamente me acariciaban los senos hasta llegar al bulto que cargaba dentro de mí. Para qué decirle que ya hacía meses desde que lo había visto, mejor mentir, ¿acaso no era la vida una bola de mentiras, una bola enorme que rodaba y rodaba, apachurrando todo lo que encontraba en su camino?

Me vi levantarme. Escuché el sonido de mis pasos sobre el piso de linóleo de la cocina. Heché un vistazo a la pequeña estufa, a los muebles, a las paredes sucias, manchadas de tanto sufrir. Pensé entonces en el cuerpo desnudo de Raúl, su sexo duro y ansioso por penetrarme.

—Ven, hija, siéntate —insistía el Dalín, jalándome del lado de Raúl—. Anda, te voy a traer unas galletas que hice, son como las que te hacía la Nana.

Regresé a la sala y me senté otra vez. Callada, miré al Dalín entrar a la cocina y empezar a abrir los trasteros. Fue entonces cuando se me vino a la memoria la última vez que había visto a la Nana viva y sana. Estábamos viviendo en la casa verde detrás de la botica. Una noche, el Dalín había traído a la Nana y la había dejado con nosotros mientras se iba de borreguero, informándonos que ya no la podía dejar sola. Desde ese día, la Nana había vivido con nosotros, pasando hora tras hora sentada en el sofá como bulto, la mirada fijada en la televisión, perdida en su propio mundo. Yo había tratado de hablarle, pero ella no me había hecho caso. Antonio le acariciaba el cabello, la besaba en la mejilla arrugada cada vez que salía con sus amigos. Luego, una noche, mi mamá nos había rogado que la cuidáramos por un rato mientras ellos iban a la casa de sus compadres, pero no quisimos, yo me quería ir con Mercedes a un *sock-hop* y Antonio estaba apurado por irse con sus amigos. Por eso, cuando se la tuvieron que llevar en la madrugada casi muerta al hospital para que los médicos la examinaran como cadáver y pudieran confirmar su hipótesis, lloré, maldije, me rasguñé las entrañas hasta sentir la sangre escurrir y caer en gotas gruesas sobre mis pies. Pero Antonio no había dicho nada, ni un suspiro se le había escapado, aún cuando la visitamos por última vez y vimos el maldito cáncer que empezaba a escaparse por todo su cuerpo. Desde ese día sentí a Antonio diferente, como si él mismo hubiera probado la muerte.

Casi no vimos al Dalín después de la muerte de la Nana. La mayoría del tiempo se iba de borreguero a diferentes pueblos, huyendo de sí mismo, de las memorias de aquella muchacha joven de la cual se había enamorado aquel día al lado del río en la Tierra del Encanto. Años después, circuló el chisme que el Dalín tenía una novia, una mujer cuya familia era de Nuevo México. Cuando mis tíos se enteraron, se lo reclamaron, pero él no lo negó, informándoles que pensaba casarse con doña Soledad. Mis tíos se habían enfurecido, peor aún más mis padres. ¿Cómo podría el Dalín pensar en casarse con otra tan pronto después de la muerte de la Nana? Le habían gritado, llamándolo un viejito loco. Pero a mí eso no me había importado. Yo los había ignorado. Me estaba convirtiendo en una mujercita llena de sueños de irse a California, de casarse e irse lo más lejos de ese pueblito muerto. ¿Qué me importaba a mí la vida del Dalín, menos la de mis padres? Sólo las constantes peleas con Antonio interrumpían mis sueños torpes. Antonio no era como yo. Él no podía sobrevivir de sueños como yo. Él era impaciente, siempre me molestaba cuando se aburría y por su frustración de no encontrar un trabajo. Yo sabía que estaba harto del betabel y, como el resto de sus amigos, resentía que nadie en los pueblitos de Colorado le diera trabajo a los mexicanos que no fuera trabajo de campo. Era al principio de los años sesenta y no había en esos pueblitos racistas un Martin Luther King, Jr. Pero yo no era como Antonio, yo sí podría ignorar todo esto sin dejarlo destruirme. Yo todavía asistía a la escuela secundaria y no dejaría que nada destruyera mis sueños.

La voz del Dalín me rescató del pasado. —Ándale, jita, come —insistió, dándome un taco—. Quiero que conozcas a mi amigo, don Pedro, también es de Nuevo México. —Antes de que pudiera probar la comida, se acercó a la puerta y lo llamó—: Compadre, venga. Compadre . . .

Unos momentos después, apareció un señor moreno y a pesar de su cuerpo delgado y jorobado, sentí la presencia de lo que antes había sido un hombre fuerte, noble, como aquellos caciques aztecas del pasado antes de que la historia los atrapara como lo había hecho con él y con muchos otros tatas indígenas. Me vi parada a su lado, sobre la inmensa pirámide del sol murmurando la antigua poesía que los indígenas habían creado para adorar a sus dioses, me sentí libre y llena de esperanzas. Le extendí la mano y me apretaron unos dedos largos que no parecían querer soltarme, como si lo ahogara un río y solamente yo lo pudiera socorrer. Le retiré la mano. De repente, quise huir, esconderme como había hecho esa mañana cuando Mamá me había rogado que saliera para decirle adiós a Antonio antes de que se fuera a la guerra.

—Siéntese a platicar, compadre —le ordenó el Dalín.

—No puedo, compadre. Estoy esperando a mi hija.

—¿Está seguro que no es a la gringa Dorothy que espera, compadre? —le contestó el Dalín, guiñándome el ojo y tocando a don Pedro ligeramente en el hombro.

Don Pedro dejó escapar una risa seca que le sacudió todo su cuerpo haciéndolo temblar hasta que por fin se escapó al aire libre. Vi la risa resonar contra las paredes sucias, la pequeña ventana, hasta que por fin cayó muerta a mi lado. Estiré la mano para tocarla, pero algo me detuvo.

—Ay, don Luis, cómo es usté —le contestó don Pedro. Había volteado a verme otra vez—. Bueno, señorita, mucho gusto. Me tengo que ir, don Luis.

Le estiré la mano a don Pedro y me quedé viendo su cuerpo frágil que, sigilosamente desapareció detrás de la puerta de tela.

—Pobre compadre, esa vale mierda hija que tiene, viene nomás para quitarle su cheque. ¿Viste lo flaco que está? No quiere comer bien. Yo le doy de la comida que cocino porque esa porquería que le traen las viejitas del Salvation Army no sirve. De todos modos come poco. Temo que se vaya a enfermar y se lo lleven al *rest home*, ni inglés sabe. Yo que tan mal hablo el inglés, hasta le gano.

En ese momento parecí escuchar la voz de Antonio y lo vi sentado en el piso de tierra jugando con sus soldaditos verdes. Quise resistir, quedarme con esas imágenes frágiles del pasado, pero la voz del Dalín me jalaba a su lado. Le vi la cara y desesperadamente traté de encontrar a aquel orgulloso tata indígena que me había criado, el que se paraba a bailar con los indios de Nuevo México que venían a bailar cada cuatro de julio en la feria. ¿Sería posible que él sólo existiera en mi memoria? Sí, eso debería ser.

—¿Cómo está doña Soledad? —balbuceé, deseando cambiar de tema—. ¿Todavía le habla diario?

Respiró profundamente antes de contestarme. —Pobre Soledad, desde que le dio el último ataque se quedó paralizada. Según dice el chisme, han regresado todos porque la vecina que la cuidaba ya no puede con ella. . . .

Los cuatro hijos de doña Soledad habían llegado durante la noche, resbalándose silenciosamente como culebras por todo el camino de tierra hasta llegar a la casita de su madre. En un rincón de la pequeña cocina habían aventado sus maletas sin preocuparse por colgar su ropa o siquiera sacar el cepillo de dientes. Mecánica y cuidadosamente se habían abrazado, una palmadita en la espalda, "¡pos, cómo estás gordo! ¿Qué no haces al jog?" mientras pensaban, viejo pelón, nomás viene a sacarle dinero para mantener a esa puta. La gorda dominaba la conversación con pláticas de su hijo, el ingeniero de computación, de su hija la pianista, de su *pet poodle* Fifi, y mientras tanto, todos se fijaban en sus zapatos baratos, su pelo pintado y su *playtex girdle* que a cada rato se le subía, pellizcándola y haciéndola rascarse las nalgas. A la flaca se le atoraban las palabras, "po-po-bre-a-má" y cada vez que hablaba se escapaban unas carcajadas del grupo. Al verla palidecer y empezar a retorcerse con temblones fuertes, todos se callaban. El más joven, hombre con bastante educación, echaba chiste tras chiste con intención de romper el silencio de envidia y enojos que habían creado entre sí mismos, pero al ver que nadie le hacía caso, cambiaba de tema, "¿Vieron *That's Incredible* anoche? Salió un hombre que podía soplar *100 bubbles* por segundo".

Para continuar su *happy reunion*, los cuatro hijos procedieron en fila hacia la recámara de su madre. Doña Soledad permanecía en la camita tapada con una colcha gruesa y lo único que se revelaba debajo de su camiseta blanca eran los indicios de unos senos, secos y apachurrados por los años. A su lado quemaba una vela de la Virgen de Guadalupe cuyo olor se mezclaba con el de los orines anaranjados del vacinero que quedaba al pie de la cama. Doña Soledad tenía los ojos abiertos, con la mirada fija en la pared, como si estuviera revisando los retratos que la rodeaban, el de su esposo, que, con los bigotes negros y su sombrero de paja, se parecía a uno de esos antiguos oficiales de la Revolución Mexicana. Al otro lado, colgaba la vieja foto de su matrimonio. ¿Recordaría a aquella muchacha joven vestida de blanco y repleta de esperanzas? ¿O pensaría en el día que murió su esposo lejos de ella en aquel asilo que olía a medicinas y enfermos?

Hablando en voz bajita, se acomodaban a su alrededor, "pobre amá, qué flaca está", decía el pelón mientras encendía su Muriel cigar. La gorda, soplando a un lado el humo que empezaba a llenar el cuarto, le acomodaba la colcha, "¿Necesita algo, Amá? ¿Le puedo traer un cafecito?" La flaca, apretándose el paño contra sus narices agudas, le acariciaba las trenzas largas mientras que el joven murmuraba, "pos a todos nos toca, *c'est la vie*, ¿qué no?"

Después de quedarse parados quince minutos a su lado (Y habían sido exactamente quince minutos porque había sonado "*Beep, beep, beep*" el reloj del joven), regresaron los cuatro hermanos a la sala para finalizar sus planes.

—Quesque los vecinos ya no pueden con ella, así que tenemos que decidir algo —exclamó la gorda.

El pelón, que era el hijo mayor, se rascaba desesperadamente la barriga y después de una larga pausa, —Es mejor que se venga conmigo, que muera en su país.

—¿Y qué va hacer allá tan lejos? —preguntó la gorda—. Yo me la podría llevar a California por un tiempo. Tengo una casa grande, *bi-level, three bathrooms, the girls would love it!*

—Estás loca —contestó el pelón—. Tú ni para limpiarte el culo tienes tiempo, siempre pa'llí, pa'cá, con ese bonche.

—En mi opinión, Happy Haven es el lugar para ella —gritó el más joven—. ¡Tienen *air conditioning*, saunas privadas para los viejitos y *bingo games every Wednesday night!*

Este güero, sí que está retardao, más burro que el burro, pensó el pelón al encenderse otro puro. La flaca quiso expresar su opinión, me-me-pa-re-re-ce, pero otra vez se dejó dominar por los temblones y la tos. Avergonzada, huyó a la cocina.

De vez en cuando, mientras discutían el destino de su mamá, uno se deshacía del grupo para asomarse al cuarto de la anciana. Pero por más que trataran de quedarse a su lado, recordando esa imagen espiritual de su mamá moliendo maíz con toda su destreza indígena, el olor del vacinero los hacía huir de su lado.

—Tenemos que tomar una decisión —repitió bostezando la gorda sin quitar la vista de sus dedos hinchados que adornaba con el más reciente color de *Avon, Purple Magic—* y tiene que ser pronto porque mi hija tiene un *recital* el lunes.

De repente, saltó le joven sobre la mesa —*I've got it!* Una lotería, ¿por qué no tenemos una lotería y así dejamos que el pueblo haga la decisión? Venderemos billetes y el que gane decidirá su destino —se rascó la cabeza. Había momentos en que le sorprendía su propia inteligencia.

Los cuatro hermanos dejaron escapar unos sollozos de alivio, —Sí, buena idea, de algo le sirvió estudiar al güero. Que decida la gente de Sunland.

Se decía que desde 1848 se había tapado un lado del sol y por más que trataran los científicos pasando horas, días, meses examinando el sol por sus inmensos telescopios, no podían encontrar una hipótesis que explicara la falta de luz en algunos de los barrios de Sunland. Hubo un año en que habían calculado la posición exacta del sol al instante que soltara su canto el gallo. Pero la oscuridad permanecía y a lo largo del tiempo se dieron cuenta de que este fenómeno existía por todo el suroeste. Había llegado aquella tarde en pleno día y lentamente se había acomodado en los rincones, en los muros, aún en los rostros humildes de la gente de Sunland que poco a poco se acostumbraban a vivir sin luz. ¿Para qué tener cortinas, lámparas si la oscuridad entraba por dondequiera? Dormían con ella, hasta se sentaban juntos a la mesa. Sólo en las vecindades al otro lado del pueblo brillaba tan fuerte el sol que, según contaban, tenían que usar palas para recoger las rosas enormes que florecían las 24 horas al día.

Ya hacía meses que los habitantes de Sunland habían notado una enredadera mágica que lentamente se subía por todas las paredes de la casita de doña Soledad. Convencidos de que eran las esperanzas, (pos, ¿cómo fregaos podría crecer una planta donde no había luz?) habían ido algunos a escondidas y escarbado cuidadosamente hasta sacarse un pedazo de la planta milagrosa. Desgraciadamente, al tratar de crecerla en sus yardas, echándole agua cien veces al día, se les había muerto.

Las noticias de la lotería corrieron de boca en boca. Muy picados, los habitantes de Sunland se pusieron en cola durante toda una semana para poder conseguir un billete. Estaba dividida la gente; algunos seguían la opinión del joven, ya está acabada, mejor que se la lleven al *rest home*. Otros con su corazón mexicano gritaban, "¡Viva México! ¡Qué muera en su país, que se la lleve el pelón!" Los más progresistas favorecían el aire californiano donde se decía que habían tantos avances tecnológicos, que quizás podrían ponerle partes biónicas a la viuda; tenía razón la gorda. Pasaban muchas horas discutiendo el caso en los campos, en el correo, en los escusados oscuros tratando de decidir el destino de doña Soledad.

Había llegado la fecha para escoger el billete ganador. Las cámaras de *Channel 7* rodeaban el escenario, frenéticamente tratando de entrevistar a la gente de Sunland que ansiosamente esperaba saber los resultados de la lotería. De repente, apareció un trueno en el cielo oscuro que fue seguido por otros aún más fuertes. Los habitantes de Sunland, sorprendidos por la luz que producían los truenos, soltaron sus billetes y con gritos de Ave María Purísima, salieron corriendo a sus hogares mientras que empezaba a llover gotas gruesas que se convertían en pequeños ríos. Los hijos de doña Soledad, también asustados por la tormenta inesperada, huyeron al lado de la gorda. Acomodándose con insultos y pellizcos debajo de su inmenso paraguas californiano dejaron que el viento los soplara hacia la casa de su mamá donde los dejó caer en bola sobre el apestoso lodo. Al levantarse, soltaron un grito: la casita estaba completamente tapada por una enredadera gigantesca que subía hasta perderse en las nubes.

Los cuatro hermanos tuvieron que esperar hasta que cesara la inundación diluviana antes de reunir a toda la gente de Sunland. Con machetes y *bulldozers,* batallaron en el lodo por muchos días hasta que por fin abrieron un paso al interior de la planta mágica, pero al pisar adentro, lo único que hallaron fue el vacinero de doña Soledad.

Me vi abrazar al Dalín y en ese momento exacto sentí un olor fuerte y otra vez tuve esa loca sensación de haber sentido la misma náusea en otra ocasión, de haber sentido el mismo asco al ver los orines sucios de la Nana.

—Estás loca —me dije en voz baja.

Al subirme al carro, vi al Dalín acercarse al banco afuera del apartamento donde don Pedro se había quedado dormido esperando a su hija. El Dalín le tocó suavemente el hombro. Todos esperando algo, ese algo que nunca parecía llegar. *"Someday my ship will come in"*, me decía mi papá.

Gustavo Segade

First Prize: Poetry

Poems

STATE OF THE ART (FRAGMENT)

> *. . . ego fecit totum, et magno cum amore.*

I dream of borders,
the zones on both sides of,
astride the lines,
for the ancient limits do not
tell us who we are,
we, the unknown humans,
cloud people, wandering in the labyrinth
not knowing our configurations;
not knowing our things:

O goddess, we sing our things. . .

for we are people
who have created most of our world;
we believe ourselves
to be our things
necessarily
re-creating us in their
images:
A teacher says my son does not "process"
the school material properly.
The doctor japanesedly outlines my possible
mechanical and psychic malfunctions,
reluctantly prescribing
better living through chemistry
for what he knows

are psycho-social dysfunctions that
I would rather fix
with a fix,
a joint:

fifteen years of hiding
in the enlightened fog
of mota
marihuas, yesca,
high grass, good shit
freedom in smoke,
since my freedom
and
the freedom
of all the edged-out,
the marginal
minorities and majorities
of everywhere
never happened,
and
never
will.

I have always been angry,
or was it always?
When did the anger begin?
Did it start as pain?
            feet hurting-cold in the grey slush
            under the elevated tracks on Third Avenue
            the shoebacks split and mother couldn't
            help that.
            Other kids having bikes.
            Other fathers, cars and steady jobs,
            while Oscar didn't have the pennies
            to get his bike chain fixed
            to get to work,
            dodging the neighborhood dogs in the night
            going to grease cars for Mr. Ford
            in Tampa, Florida.

The Cubans thinking the Puerto Ricans
were "dirty niggers,"
and the Boricuas imagining

the Cubans as barbarian invaders;
both hating the Yankees,
the "Americans" who,
just like everyone else,
believe their own bullshit,
their own idea that they are Number 1.
One-Up in everything
from color to language,
work habits to toilet habits
momism and bombism.
The Rich and the Powerful
seeing all of it
as beneath them,
which "it" was,
still is.
et in saecula saeculorum . . .
Pain walks a long, winding,
bitter path to anger.
All who walk it share the experience;
yet
anger isn't everybody's reaction;
some suffer silently
others grow to love the trek
carefully carrying the Man's rifle
until He needs it to kill
an elephant, or a deer,
or one's
uppity,
rebellious
brother or sister.
But my "number" is to be
macho-heroic;
my models make me
desire to be
Prince Valiant, Cyrano, and Gary Cooper,
Achilles, El Cid, and Che Guevara
starring in a Disney flick.

The first poets of the Viri,
the Homers, sing the anger
of a demigod
whose prideful taking of offense
at the foolishness of his leader,
leads to

blood at home and on the streets.
Formed in his image,
I turn
the anger
into rage.
For us,
today's children of Peleus,
the burning desire
to be free
is
as it was
in the beginning,
ever will be,
unsatisified
rage

II

The Movement anger and the mota were so good;
they went together,
but you don't remember dreaming
you get so directly in the flow
you are the river always becoming . . .
many drown
many just keep on surfin'
some must swim to the side
to dream and observe,
to work at making life
head-on.

"It"
is not,
after all,
a river.
It
is
the
river,
the shores,
the trees
the snake and the bird,
quetzalcoatl,
the two-legged imagining
creature with the power

to dream
it is
dreaming
it . . .

I met a poet.
We flowed together,
but were different.
He was full of mania
touched, anointed,
the sacred oil sweetened
his hair and cheeks,
giving him the power
to create
identity
flowersong
art

The other night
. . . now that the dragons
visit me again at night . . .
I visited him in the madhouse
realizing that it was part two
of a dream I had a few nights before;
the same irridescent rainbow dragon
winding down the streets of Chinatown, L.A.

He tried to escape and I turned him in,
called out to a black cop riding by;
reported the little bastard right back
to the nut ward where he belonged,
where he belongs
for being one or twenty
or a thousand steps
ahead of or behind his times
and
my rules of sanity.
It was so horrible
in there
the people lewd,
screeching and whining,
prescribed dopers,
street dopers
thieves;

the keepers,
as ever,
crazier than the inmates.
He knew his own,
but he wanted out
. . . don't we all?
He wore a little black fedora,
a week's growth of beard.
Still running things,
pushing the system around,
using my visit to escape.
They wore long,
greyish white gowns;
I was staying over night
lying on a cot
with my face to the greenish wall.
A woman's cunt appeared through
a hole in the wall;
I fingered her wet clit,
turned on
feeling guilty
then he had to try to escape,
so he followed me out,
by the sleepy keeper,
down the long marble steps,
like out of a courthouse,
down to the street,
where I called the cop,
and turned him in
for the things he had done to me
out
here.
Then the dragon wound down the street,
the people in it having a good time
being Chinese

He and We made
Chicano
a
word
spoken
in tongues of fire.
One of the few words left
which activates minds

in Spanish, English,
Polish, French, German,
and
many other ways of speaking.
We did the job:
we made some minds have order;
some people took a name
but not mine
because I know
the labels
are for power,
for making a buck, a house,
a family
but not for self,
which has no name
tao tao not tao
the great nonsense syllable
jehovah

It has no name,
no form nor color to show us,
but we sense, we know,
we think and form things,
so we made Him,
we
men
who have the power:
Buddha, Jesus, The Lord Krishna,
Marx, the Beatles,
all-the-same-one-fellah
Mickey Mouse, Aphrodite,
Zoroaster, Baalzebub.
Still
some
cannot do without
them,
the Father
Zeu'piter
Male Sky God
and
His Pantheon
mentioned
Above

CROSSING

Tijuana, Baja California, October 1983

Sitting in Galvan's state
car corner of Emiliano Zapata
and Cinco de Mayo
in front of
the Papelería Acuano
right in the byzantine heart
of Baja and the Border
twenty miles
and
twenty cultural
light years
from
home
      same weather
      same sky
      different smells
      different sounds
guy ambles across the street
newspaper clutched under his arm
white loafers, pants pressed
middle-class man
thinking hard about his thoughts
taking it easy on a Saturday afternoon
a
minute later
old poor man
trudging in rumpled khakis
and
faded blue suit coat
nondescript hat
and couple of days' beard
not sad
just anxious
just there

Galvan catches me trying to read
the street names
get in the car, loco
drive on to buy a sesame seed candy
and two kilos of corn tortillas
down the block
mouth-watering warmness

wrapped in butcher paper
we each eat two
moving through town
dodging
always dodging cars
and potholes
and the long line
to get
to
the
line
around the east gate
reserved for special cases
for special people
funcionarios públicos
and such
Galvan still has official papers
he pulls it off somehow
and we get to go around
only five cars
from the great divide
Enrique buys a newspaper
from a street kid on the line
and soon we get
to the grey US man
in the US grey uniform
who wants to know
our relationship
I sense that
friends
is not
enough
official business
university and government
counts
we cross to highway 805 North
into the first world
at 55 miles per hour
faster than the speed
of history
    same air
    same sky
    different sounds
    different smells

1986-87

David Nava Monreal   **First Prize: Drama**

Cellmates
A Play in One Act (excerpt)

Encarcerated, RAY *is forced to confront his past with the appearance of a mysterious cellmate known as* LUKE. *This excerpt from the play takes place as* RAY *begins to explain his real crime, a crime of emotion, committed against his wife,* DOREEN, *and their child,* LOLLY.

RAY: *(Sobbing. Has a need to explain.)* We was livin' in Bakersfield, California. I had just pulled a big job in Texas. There was money comin' out of our ears. Doreen was happy. She kept singin' Tammy Wynette songs all the damn time. *(Music grows louder.)* She was so fuckin' happy 'bout the baby. She'd go 'bout decoratin' the bedroom, puttin' flowers in the kitchen. I didn't like it. There was somethin' 'bout it I didn't like. *(Pause.)* When the baby was born it got worse. She just kept it at her breast all the damn time. She combed her hair. Cooed lovin' words to her. It was as if they were stuck together like siamese twins. *(Pause.)* I took to drinkin'. I liked the night life. The honky tonks brung me some good times. *(His story slowly dies out.)*

LUKE: What were ya thinkin' 'bout when ya were drinkin'?

RAY: Nothin'. I just thought 'bout gettin' drunk.

LUKE: Wasn't ya thinkin' that ya was jealous of a litter baby?

RAY: I ain't never thought that! Doreen was crazy for that child. Tit wasn't a normal thin'. She took it everywhere. Wrote litter songs fer that baby.

LUKE: Wasn't she givin' ya no more love, Ray?

RAY: Doreen loved me all right. She said she did. But she just couldn't convince me that Lolly was mine.

LUKE: Whose was she?

RAY: Some motherfucker's. Some woman thief. Some past lover that Doreen loved mo' than me. *(Pause.)* I was goin' make her suffer fer her whoredom. *(Pause.)* But I ain't never kilt her.

LUKE: How'd ya geet even?

RAY: I done thin's to her.

LUKE: What thin's?

RAY: Thin's that ken really hurt a woman.

LUKE: Thin's like what?

RAY: I ain't gived her no love when her body craved me. I never gived her no money fer the baby. I spent all the money on liquor and I layed with every bitch I could find. *(Pause.)* I done got even, that's what I did.

LUKE: What did she do?

RAY: She cried, that's what.

LUKE: She never tried to leave ya?

RAY: Never. She just fall on her knees and begged me to understand. She told me there was no lover and that Lolly was mine and no one else's. She told me she was a good woman who loved no one but me. She even told me I was the first one.

LUKE: And what did ya say?

RAY: I called her a liar!

LUKE: And as time passed?

RAY: *(Pause. Slows down the verbal tempo.)* She started actin' real queer.

LUKE: Queer? How?

RAY: *(Louder.)* Just queer!

LUKE: Explain or I'll blister yore back!

RAY: She took to sobbin' all the time.

LUKE: Sobbin'?

RAY: Like a baby. When we lay in bed she sobbed. Her chest shook and her whole body trembled.

LUKE: And what'd ya do?

RAY: Nothin'.

LUKE: Nothin'? Ya didn't even give her comfort?

RAY: She was like a crazy woman. I didn't want nothin' to do with her. She'd fall on her knees and beg to me. She'd tell me to please believe that Lolly was my child. "Honey," she'd say, "I ain't done nothin' with nobody but ya."

LUKE: And?

RAY: And I'd laugh. I'd tell her that Lolly was a bastard and she was nothin' but a five-dollar whore.

LUKE: And that would make ya feel good?

RAY: Fer a while. Then there was a time that I felt better not even lookin' at her face.

LUKE: And the baby? What happened to Lolly dunn' this time?

RAY: She'd cry all the time like her Mama. She didn't have much to eat. Started lookin' real skinny and feeble lookin'.

LUKE: Did ya ever hit her?

RAY: *(Loudly. In protest.)* No! I ain't never hit that child!

LUKE: Ya ain't tellin' me the truth.

RAY: I ain't the kind of man to pick on children!

LUKE: *(Raising the whip above his head and striking* RAY *on the back.)* Tell me the truth ya son-of-a-bitch!

RAY: *(Recoils in pain.)* Leave me alone!

LUKE: *(Strikes* RAY *again.)* I said tell me the truth!

RAY: *(Screams.)* Leave me be, for God's sake!

LUKE: *(Holding the whip in the air.)* Did ya strike that child?

RAY: *(Sobbing. Trying to control himself)* I struck that child 'cause she irked me. 'Cause she sickened me to the pit of my stomach.

LUKE: *(Raising the whip a little higher.)* What did ya do to that child?

RAY: I slapped her.

LUKE: What else?

RAY: I done burnt her with cigarettes and made her sleep in the closet.

LUKE: *(Striking* RAY.*)* Ya scum son-of-a-bitch! Ya deserve to die! *(Strikes* RAY *again.)* That's not all ya done! Is it? Ya struck the child and tortured her mother!

RAY: I didn't mean to. My mind weren't rat.

LUKE: Yore mind ain't been rat all yore life!

RAY: *(Sobs. Is in great pain. He begins reciting the following speeches like a rosary. Like a sorrowful litany.)* It was in the last months that I knew what I had done. Doreen wouldn't talk no more. She just lay in bed or look out the window most of the time. Sometimes I even tried touchin' her, but she felt cold. Colder than ice. Colder than a dead body. *(Pause.)* Lolly was now two years old and the poor child could barely walk. Doreen would have her sittin' in the corner of the livin' room wearin' a bathrobe stained with food and shit. The child would just drool. When she'd seen me walk into the house she'd cry or hide herself away under the bed. *(Pause. Sobs.)* I knew I had done wrong.

LUKE: Go on!

RAY: Then a woman gived me a call one day. *(Pause.)* Doreen answered the phone. She gived it to me with tears runnin' down her face. The woman said she wanted to meet me at the restaurant where she done worked. I met her there at seven o'clock. She was a young girl, not more than nineteen. She sat me down and tells me that she just come from the doctor's. *(Pause.)* She told me she was pregnant and had gotten an abortion. *(Pause.)* She said I was the father. *(Pause.)* I had myself checked the next day. There weren't one thin' wrong with me. *(Sobs.)*

LUKE: *(Raising the whip.)* Go on!

RAY: When I got home that night all the lights were on in the house. Everythin' was quiet. I took off my hat and put it in the closet. I called out to Doreen. I felt in my heart that I wanted to give her a kiss. I called out for Lolly. She was my child . . . my baby. *(Pause.)* There was nobody home. I went into the kitchen and seen this note. It was Doreen's hand-writin'. "Honey," she wrote, "I love you dearly, dearly my love. Ya are my man. But I jest can't take it no more. I made ya mean to me, I'm sorry. I thought 'bout lovin' another man but somethin' inside me is dead. I feel twisted, honey. I had to leave. Please forgive me. Bye." *(Pause.)* Then I went into the bedroom and there I seen them. Both Doreen and Lolly layin' in the tub filled with blood. My gun was on the floor. Doreen had put a bullet through the baby's head then turned 'round and kilt herself. *(Pause.)* They were both dead. *(Pause.)* A killin' of the spirit. *(Pause.)* Lolly's eyes were still open. *(Pause.)* She looked like a plastic doll sittin' on a shelf.

LUKE: *(After a long pause.)* I'm goin' beat ya till my arms fall off! *(Begins whipping RAY.)*

RAY: *(Sotto voice. In a chant-like rhythm.)* Oh, Lord let this be forgiven. Cleanse me of this grievous sin that I have committed. This sin that stays buried in every innocent soul. That sin that is the root, the essence of man's inhumanity to man.

LUKE: *(Striking RAY.)* Yer the killer!

RAY: It was a killin' of the spirit.

LUKE: *(Continuously striking RAY.)* Son-of-a-bitch!

RAY: *(Chanting.)* It was a killin' of the spirit like the soljers who dies fer an idea. It was the killin' of the spirit like the old man that dies without a witness. It was like the killin' of a thousand spirits that die 'cause no one has food with which to feed their dreams. It was the killin' of heaven. Of human hope. It was the killin' of a mother and child.

LUKE: Yer the killer!

RAY: *(Closing his eyes.)* And may each man be blessed with a cellmate. God have mercy on my soul.

LUKE: *(Striking RAY again and again.)* Yer the killer!

RAY: Protect me from my sins.

LUKE: Yer the killer!

RAY: From my wanton miserable soul.

LUKE: *(Stops the whipping. Begins to lower his pants.)* There is only one way to punish ya.

RAY: *(Horrified.)* Oh, God, no!

LUKE: Only one way to teach ya a lesson.

RAY: No, pleasssssse, not that!

LUKE: *(Lowers his pants to his ankles and positions himself behind RAY.)* Those who do the screwin' should be screwed.

RAY: *(Hysterically.)* No, no, no! Help me! Someone, pleasssssse! Help me!

The lights fade. A country-western song plays softly. The lights brighten on the far right side of the stage. Two prison guards are playing cards on a wooden table. RAY's screams can be heard over the music.

1ST GUARD: It sounds like Ray Wilson again.
2ND GUARD: Cell number 42.
1ST GUARD: Every night the same damn thing.
2ND GUARD: For the past two months.
1ST GUARD: *(Dealing out the cards.)* Shall we go investigate?
2ND GUARD: What for?
1ST GUARD: Maybe he's hurting himself.
2ND GUARD: Forget it.
1ST GUARD: You never know.
2ND GUARD: Forget it. Leave him alone. *(Screams. Soft music.)* Plays cards. *(More screams. The music.)* He's having bad dreams.
1ST GUARD: *(Looking casually at his cards.)* Yeah, you're right. It's probably his conscience killing him.

(The lights slowly fade. More screams. The music. Curtain.)

Carlos Morton
Third Prize: Drama

Johnny Tenorio
A Play in One Act (excerpt)

A contemporary rewrite of the Spanish classic, Don Juan Tenorio, *the following scene begins* JOHNNY*'s examination of conscience. The scene takes place in Big Berta's Bar, where* BERTA *helps* JOHNNY *confront his life and death.*

JOHNNY: The curse!
BERTA: ¿La maldición?
JOHNNY: I'm damned for all time!
BERTA: Do I detect repentance in your voice?
JOHNNY: *(Screaming.)* Hell no!
BERTA: ¿No? (BERTA *starts lighting the candles on the altar. Incense burns.)* Quizás entonces tu deseo se hará realidad.
JOHNNY: What wish?
BERTA: Your death wish.
JOHNNY: What are you talking about?
BERTA: Life after death, la inmortalidad. I lit these velas to show you a vision. See how brightly they burn? Smell the copal incense, the kind

the ancients used in their sacred rites. Pray, Johnny, ruega a la Virgen de Guadalupe, nuestra señora, Tonantzín.

JOHNNY: ¡Mis ojos!

BERTA: Pronto vas a ver. Now we wait for the souls to return. They'll come to say a few final words.

JOHNNY: I don't want to hear it, Berta. No one ever really cared about me, not my father, not Ana, none of them.

BERTA: *(Serving him food and drink.)* Cálmate. Sit. Mira, I fixed your favorite comida—tamales y atole. Eat. Los otros están por llegar.

JOHNNY: All right. That's more like it. Be sure to invite Louie. Except that he has so many holes in his stomach, I doubt that the food will stay in.

BERTA: No debes burlarte de los muertos, Johnny.

JOHNNY: Hey, Louie! I'm calling you out, man! Berta made some ricos tamales and hot atole. Better hurry before I eat it all up! *(LOUIE, wearing a calavera mask, enters.)*

BERTA: *(Noticing LOUIE.)* Ah, Louie, there you are. Te traigo un plato. You boys have such big appetites, hay que calentar más tamales. *(BERTA exits.)*

JOHNNY: *(Still absorbed in his food.)* Yeah, Louie, sit down and . . . *(Suddenly noticing him.)* Oh! Another appearance, eh? What's with the costume, still playing trick or treat?

LOUIE: ¡Te dije que no te acercaras a Ana!

JOHNNY: *(Pulling out a gun.)* Chíngate, cabrón, nobody tells me what to do! *(LOUIE lunges for JOHNNY, who shoots LOUIE in the head.)* I told you not to mess with me! *(LOUIE does not fall—he keeps advancing.)* Jesus Christ!

LOUIE: Remember, I'm already dead! ¿Qué te pasa, Johnny? ¿Tienes miedo? ¡Tú, el mero chingón! *(Grabbing JOHNNY by the throat.)*

JOHNNY: ¡Ayyyyyyy! ¡Déjame! Let me go!

LOUIE: *(Dragging JOHNNY over to the table.)* ¡No me digas que sientes la presencia de la Muerte!

JOHNNY: Get away from me!

LOUIE: *(Grabbing JOHNNY by his hair.)* Come! Come! Que ésta va a ser tu última cena. *(Pushing his face into the plate, forcing him to eat.)*

JOHNNY: What is this horrible stuff?

LOUIE: Tamales de ceniza. *(Forcing him to drink.)*

JOHNNY: Ashes!

LOUIE: ¡Atole de fuego!

JOHNNY: Fire! Why do you make me eat this?

LOUIE: Te doy lo que tú serás.

JOHNNY: Fire and ashes!

LOUIE: ¡Morderás el polvo!

JOHNNY: No!

BERTA: Ya se va terminando tu existencia y es tiempo de pronunciar tu sentencia.

JOHNNY: My time is not up!

LOUIE: Faltan cinco para las doce. A la media noche no se te conoce. Y aquí que vienen conmigo, los que tu eterno castigo de Dios reclamando están. *(Enter* ANA *and* DON JUAN, *also calaveras. They block* JOHNNY's *escape.)*

JOHNNY: Ana!

ANA: Yes, it's me.

JOHNNY: ¡Papá!

DON JUAN: Sí, mi hijo.

JOHNNY: *(Tries to jump behind the bar. Enter* BERTA *dressed as La Catrina with skull mask.)* Berta!

BERTA: No hay escape, Johnny. You must face them.

JOHNNY: You too!

BERTA: No estoy aquí para juzgarte, Johnny—they are.

DON JUAN: Un punto de contrición da a un alma la salvación y ese punto aún te lo dan.

LOUIE: ¡Imposible! ¿En un momento borrar veinte años malditos de crímenes y delitos?

JOHNNY: Berta! Will I really be saved if I repent?

BERTA: Yes, but only if one of your victims forgives you on this the Day of the Dead.

JOHNNY: *(In a heavily accented Spanish.)* Entonces, perdónenme ustedes, yo no quiero morir. Deseo pedirles disculpas a todos los que hice sufrir.

LOUIE: Empezaremos conmigo, que soy el más ofendido. ¿Por qué me acuchillaste? ¿Por qué te me echaste encima?

JOHNNY: There's no excuse. But it was a fair fight among men. You wanted to be like me, Louie, but you lost, and that's the price you had to pay.

LOUIE: ¿Vean? No tiene excusa. Que le aparezca la lechuza. Si de mi piel hizo carnicera, ¡él también será calavera! *(The feeling of this last scene is that of a bullfight.* JOHNNY *is the bull and the others are wielding the cape, pike and banderillas.)*

BERTA: ¿Quién sigue?

ANA: *(She is dressed like a whore.)* I am next.

JOHNNY: Ana. You don't want to see me dead, think of our children.

ANA: I am thinking of them. I would rather they not know you, for fear they will become like you.

JOHNNY: No, no, no! I swear to God—I'll change!

BERTA: You repent?

JOHNNY: Sí, I promise to go home and be a good padre y esposo.

ANA: Mentiras! I've heard all this before. He'll go back to chasing women and drinking first chance he gets.

JOHNNY: Ana, don't you see I have to change, my life depends on it.

ANA: No, Johnny, you're addicted to your vicios. You contaminate everyone. Look, I gave you all my love and you turned me out to turn tricks!

JOHNNY: But the Mafiosos were going to kill me. You agreed to do it. I didn't force you!

ANA: You manipulated me, Johnny, like you did all the others.

JOHNNY: But, Ana, don't you see, it's a curse that's been passed down from generation to generation. I'm a victim, you're a victim, ¡todos somos víctimas!

ANA: That's right, blame everybody but yourself!

JOHNNY: Ana, honey, think about it. You tried to control me, you wanted to channel my energy.

ANA: I wanted a family!

JOHNNY: But I'm not an esposo. I am a hunter!

ANA: *(Laying into him with a vengeance.)* Si mi corazón murió en esa carrera, ¡el mujeriego también será calavera! *(A mournful cry escapes JOHNNY's lips.)*

BERTA: ¿Alguien más? Time is almost up.

JOHNNY: ¡Papá! How can you stand there and say nothing after what you did!

DON JUAN: Ya lo sé, y me arrepentiré hasta mis últimos días. Después que murió tu madre, traté de encaminarte hacia una vida mejor. Fracasé. Seguiste la vía chueca.

JOHNNY: Hypocrite!

DON JUAN: Johnny, dile a Dios que te perdone, como Él me perdonó.

JOHNNY: You want me to ask God for a pardon?

DON JUAN: Es lo único que tienes que hacer.

BERTA: Go on, Johnny, ask for forgiveness.

JOHNNY: But I don't believe in God!

DON JUAN: Entonces estás perdido. *(JOHNNY sinks to his knees. Bells toll softly in the distance.)*

BERTA: Johnny, Johnny, you don't really understand what's happening, do you?

JOHNNY: Berta, will you forgive me? *(Throwing himself at her feet, groveling, as though wanting to get back into her womb.)*

BERTA: Johnny, tú nunca me has ofendido.

JOHNNY: I trusted you, Berta. I told you everything.

BERTA: That's right, mi'jo. I cleansed you by listening and understanding. You see, I am the eater of sins, la que se traga los pecados.

JOHNNY: Oh, Berta, you're the only woman I've ever loved! *(Turning to the other skeletons, who have remained deathly still in a silent tableau.)* You see, somebody loves me! *(To* BERTA.*)* Does this mean I'm saved? Does this mean I've cheated death?

BERTA: No, Johnny. No te burlaste de la muerte. You are already dead.

Carmen Tafolla   First Prize: Poetry

Poems

HOT LINE

(to my first-born, first-dead, para m'ija)

The mark of you is soft and bright on my body
    The ridge is smoothe up my belly
        disruptedly even
    deep and rich in color
           and unforgettable
              like you.

The feel of it against my curious fingers
    is not like skin—
        but different—
    like promises and memories
        and passionate peace in one.

The scar is somehow like concentrated satin—
    a yard of it per half centimeter—
        rare, distinct, and full of voice and story
        "Cada cosa en este mundo"
           (decía esa viejita que conocí)
           "tiene voz, virtud, e idioma."

This mark of you on me
        is full
          of story
    and
    of
    love.

It is your gift to me. Each night I
can reach down and feel it, listen,
and hear your message

on this our own
        private

red
hot line.

NINE MOONS DARK

—This is what it takes to make a child

Nine new moons of dark hot wind
and careful mouthfuls, hoarded, pointed,
sent direct to fill the small one.
Empty *jarros, ollas,* make the magic prayer,
and corn tortillas carry forth alone
the gifts of all.

Grace from spiritdancers gives the balance
over holes and rocks
that make the street,
to keep the swollen womb
from falls and blows.

One treasure-bought
small handmade *vela,*
lit in prayers to
Indian Pregnant Virgin,
still in name the goddess free
pre-fires and pre-cross,
Guadalupe
Tonantzín.

And last, a blessing
from the eldest face of corn.
Hand, even warmer, gives the
touch, the shape
of welcome.

> Past the rabid dogs
> the knifecold brows
> the hungry pouts
> searching for purse—
> there is none.
> Past the street lights' angry metal blare,
> Past the profit eyes
> that buy the babes
> before their birth,
> grabbing,
> appetize a bill for 50, 20, any
> strange-faced tender
> under trembling fingers

of the ones whose other
children starve at home
and some, caught hard between
foodsilence and
fullarmscrying,
follow, into
a car.

Past the doors of public *Hospital Civil*,
pulling her *rebozo* tighter
round her dropping belly, rising life,
her tiny claim intact.
Nineteen years seems
long enough to wait
for this small cry,
the very first,
feels the head emerging
strong

the tiny heart pounds out
its shout of proud survival

      small investment, kicking
      whisked away
      passed hand to hand
      change arms to arms to beds
      and on the road, new papers, forms
      a neat 10,000 chopped
      in many stops and stages
      to Northern Nursery's Lie:
      money buys it
      all.

      And somewhere at the *Hospital Civil*
      a scream undying burns:
      This one's not mine!
      This dead one pulled from your *hielera*
      for the cool fleshmarket's use…
      The scream goes on, unchanging, strong,
      as if to heat their hells
      and rip their walls
      and reach the wind, to touch
      that one of hers,
      so far.

Nine new noons of Indian-color-earth enfolding
warm as blood and turquoise-feathered prayers
and all they give her
is that purpled baby, cold
from the refrigerator,
thrice-abandoned one, reused
to move their market

that baby
cold
touched soft at last
by her painpartner fingers
whom even her
long burning scream
of rage and love
cannot
warm.

SWEET REMEMBER

Sweet remember
when you ask our little girls to be
so sweet,
sit neat,
cry easy,
and be oh so pretty on a shelf

When our young women who are decent
are to always be
in company
of strong young men
who can
protect them

When parents breathe
a sigh of relief
to see their daughters married
and now safe
and someone else's
responsibility

When girls and women
are expected
to play at home, which others should protect,
to always breathe in innocence

and be shielded from heavy news, and death,
to sing and paint
and, when appropriate,
to scream and faint

Sweet Remember
that Marta Díaz de C.
had her legs spread
on an electric bed
as someone probed with great delight
to see her scream
till dead.

Sweet Remember
that Cristina R.L.O.
was taken in the night
from her parents' home
and husband's bed
and forced to talk with massive rape,
incontinence, indecency,
and forced to faint while hanging by her knees,
wrists tied to feet, till circulation ceased

Sweet Remember
Elsa B.
whose naked 3-year daughter
was immersed
in ice-cold water,
as the Sergeant pulled her tits and whispered in her ear,
"Whore, come sleep with me
and do it sweetly
or we will not let
the child's head up
until she kicks no more."
And when she did,
they threatened a
Portrait in Two:
Whore and Child Whore—
side by side in bed—
with plenty of volunteers
to tear them both
right through the core
mass party rape in
stereo
and screams

galore
"and then we'll know
where we can find
and kill
your husband."
And sad and sick,
to save her child,
she spoke.

And Sweet Remember
young Anita S.
who was raised to think her womanhood
was in her breasts
and inside panties and to be covered
in a dress
and then,
because the village teacher was
a critic
of the government,
and a family friend,
she was "detained,"
and called a Marxist,
had her breasts
slashed at with knives
and bit by soldiers eager
for their flesh
and had then "Communist"
burnt with electric pen
and shocks
into her upper thigh
and her vagina
run by mice,
and live to know
her womanhood
was in her soul.

And Tina V., María J., Encarnación,
Viola N., Jesusa I., and Asunción
who screamed first and did not think to strike
who'd never fired a gun or learned to fight
who lost their husbands, parents, children, and own lives
and oft times dignity or body parts or eyes
and some whose pregnant nipples tied with string
were yanked toward opposing walls
and back

till babes were lost
and blood was running black.

Sweet Remember
this is why
I do not ask
my child to cry
to sit sweet helpless and be cute
to always need a male escort
to think that only he protects,
not she, herself, and not she, him
to think herself so delicate
so weak,
to hold as inborn right a man's protection
or his pity for a tear on pretty cheek

But I will teach her
quite instead
that she is her own brave life
till dead
and that there are no guarantees in life
nor rights
but those that we invent
and that the bravest thing of all
to think, to feel, to care, and to recall
is to be human
and to be complete
and face life straight
and stand on solid feet
and feel respect for her own being
temple, soul, and head
and
that she owns her strong brave life
till dead

GUATEMALA

there are no political prisoners
only men's heads that show up sewed
into the now-pregnant bellies
of their fiancé's corpses

only hands that open
from the jungle floor,
fingers crying "*¡Justicia!*"
as they reach like vines trying
to break free

only butchered organs
pressed into the earth
beneath the feet
of "government" officers

only Ixil Indians in rebellion,
their red woven messages of humanness
in whole Indian villages corralled, beheaded,
for existing too full
of straight-backed dignity

There are no political prisoners
There are no *problemas de derechos humanos*
There are no repressions in free democracies
There are only Presidents
who scratch each other's backs,
blindfold each other's eyes,
laugh uncomfortably,
puffing the finest
popular-name cigars
and cutting too-human heads
from the non-human bodies
of non-justice.

Alfred Arteaga   Honorable Mention: Poetry

Cantos

CANTO PRIMERO

Primero. Arrival.

Arrival.

First, the island.
The cross of truth.
Another island.
A continent.
A line, half water, half metal.

An island of birds, "Ccollanan."
An island of birds,
"Ccollanan Pachacutec!"
Sounds above an island, in
the air, trees, "Ccollanan Pachacutec!"

Female sounds. "Ricuy
anceacunac yahuarniy richacaucuta!"
An island of female birds, imagine
the sounds, the air, the trees, at times
the silence, the slither in thorns.

So perfect a shape, right
angles, the globe yields to so
straight a line, look. One
line, zenith to nadir, heaven,
precipitation. The only other,
straighter still than that horizon
we see at sea, perfect: paradise.
That horizontal line, from
old to new, he knew would yield,
yes, so perfect a move, he
knew, yes, so perfect a shape
yes.

Trees caught his thoughts.
Birds and onshores brought them
from the boats. She knew those
thoughts, heard those songs.
Could there be one more island?
Birds, sounds, perhaps pearls,
gold? Eden-Guanahaní, perhaps
another? "O my Marina, my new
found island. License my roaving
hands, and let them go, before,
behind, between, above, below."
West.

América, América. Feminine
first name, continent named
for him. América.
Here, Santa Fe. Here, the true
faith. I claim, in the name of
the father. Land of thorns,
in the name of the son.

The edge of this world
and the other, is marked

in water: ocean, river, wave to
her, she waits on the other
side. Aquí, se llama la Juana,
de apellido Juárez, india,
prieta y chaparra, la que le encanta
al gringo, al gachupín.

Island of cactus, genus
Chauhtémoc. Island of rose,
land of thorns. Pedro de
Alvarado, an eagle, la
región transparente, a
night of smoke. Marina
Nightear, an ocean contained
in one woman, as it was in
the beginning, world
without end, fallen
eagle.

So feminine a shape. So female
a bay. Another shape: gliding
birds. Another: touching trees.
True name of woman, Vera Cruz,
body of a woman. "He named me
Xochitepec, yes so we are all flowers
of the mountain, all a woman's body,
that was one true thing he said in
his life." Above, birds,
leaves, above so woman a form.
Las quince letras: not the seven words:
Contestó Malintzín, "yes
I said yes I will Yes."

En el nombre
de la Virgen de las Espinas,
ella que en buena ora nasco,
this archeology is born: here
tibia, here ball courts, codices,
teeth. Inside, the caves are
painted. Here is an architecture,
see, toco, toco,
tocotín:

Tla ya timohuica,
totlazo Zuapilli,
maca ammo, Tonantzín,
titechemoilcahuíliz.
Mati itlatol ihiyo
Huel ni machicáhuac
no teco qui mati.

En la sangre, en las espinas
de la Virgen de Santa Fe,
these names are written:
América Estados-Unidos, née
México. I name her
Flower of the Mountain,
Coatepec-Cihuatepec-Cuicatepec
Amor Silvestre,
Terra Nova,
Cuerpo de Mujer.

The edge of this world
and the other, is marked
in metal: on this side America,
on this side América.
Nights they spill from
San Diego and Los Angeles
threading the steel mesh
como nada, los verdaderos
alambristas, buscando el cuerpo
de mujer, buscando,
Xochitepec.

Raymundo Gamboa — First Prize: Short Story

50/50 Chance

It's true that he returned immediately from Las Vegas yearning for the quieter, familiar place with an ocean to go with the sand. In the meantime, he had to be somewhere so he leans against a traffic lightpost on the Eagleston's Body Works [on the] corner of Golden State Freeway and 18th Street in Bakersfield, where lizards go to die.

Strawman's simple appearance, despite all it lacks, is adequate. His thin hair balds along the top, at the crown. The head looks more like a spherical mass of bone strategically located on his shoulders. From his hips, just above the beltless pant waist of his corduroys is a lip of fat. Though chilly, he sports only a "Last Act of Defiance" T-shirt and torn, multi-colored Converse court shoes, without socks and with frilled laces.

He removes the Marlboro butt, though long enough for several more puffs, from his gap-toothed mouth as he decides to lift his thumb, to flash his juice card, making his move to the Pacific Ocean. One more good night of hitch-hiking, of signaling his optimism. He sneezes the ash off the 'boro, dropping the cigarette from his left hand and the S.B. [Santa Barbara, CA] cardboard sign from his right as he runs from the sport pick-up that has pulled over just ahead. Of course, they play leap-frog with him. After a couple of hops, he jumps into the back, they throw him a poncho, and hand him a *sin semilla* joint through the cab's sliding window. His life becomes harmonious with the wintry evening while traveling on the cheap.

At first, the wind whines a memory of innocence. Once a youngster walking in an alley, he came across a tomcat, white and fluffy, with its fur frilled from being on the outs. He'd say to his friends, "It came with the name Carnation." It disappeared as casually as it had appeared. Months after, he had decided it had been killed. It wouldn't have just left him. Straw ran across another one in the same alley. Even to Strawman, it looked exactly like the first one though he knew it wasn't. He thought it cute to name it Reincarnation, just for the wittiness of it, but his parents wouldn't allow it. They thought they broke his infatuation but he'd call it by that name in their absence. That was the first time he went with the motion of the ocean, readily conceding, in return for personal peace.

Once in Santa Barbara, an American's Riviera, Strawman starts to strongly feel the urgency in his mind. He thinks, "It has always been there, kind of, really." He doesn't understand, but he knows.

Lately, during his relapse of skulling the neighborhood, not the thoughts themselves, verified one of his fears. The sky, alley, and roofs are quietly empty. Yes, Straw's eyes absorb disturbing possibilities. Strawman endured the lightning, the pounding rain, and pronounced winds as they heightened an awareness of the light and shadows. But his eyes threatened his mind with the browns, greys, and blues of the neighborhood. Even after the storm, he cannot ignore the recurring black tracery of the branches on the skeletal winter trees.

Dawdling is thinking too. With decisiveness, Straw says to himself, "I will not be fed to the lions." Unleashing emotional freight, he storms about the alley, kicking wood, cans, and cardboard boxes, shaking wall pipes, then paces aimlessly before becoming momentarily stoic. Then he begins to direct indictments at the walls in the voice of a street vendor, and at the rate of an L.A. lawyer. That desperate action underlines the absence and need of that boyhood bond with guys that shared a precarious lifestyle—those arrested, on the run, that have jumped bail, killed, or were killed, those here one day and gone the next. They could never plan too far ahead in their tragic romance with life. "What happened?" he asked himself, desperately kicking a trash can. Then the sound of a siren galvanized him into action.

Again, his time of submission waivers. He will get professional help later. As much as possible must be accomplished on his own. Since the death of Kennedy he noted the cruel truth: even the death of a president leaves the desired impact. It's the active life. Temporarily, he will go on. Soon, he will pull back.

Strawman positions himself on the sunny side of a corner building on lower State and Bath Streets. The reason is obvious—places like that are popular think spots. It is where divine insight ingeniously borders the insane observation.

While his stomach craves a Spam sandwich with chips, the Perrier bottle, filled with water, appeases his want. It is temporary. Strawman will soon be back on his pride diet, pure park water, fruits and juice from markets' discarded lemons, soup from the Mission, and milk from creamers he'll pick up at coffee shops before he is told to leave. Occasionally, he will deal for a small bottle of Gatorade to help his body retain salts, but will never beg for good or panhandle money. His is a proud life, not a glamorous one.

A reflection off a window makes Strawman look across the street at a cigar store. He'd lived through the advent and popularization of the space program, color T.V., The Beatles, Woodstock, $.74 per gallon of gasoline, the Pill, T.V. zappers; now, it is his personal computer which astonishes him with a thought. His concern is beyond the recurring soda pop observations which go flat, not fizzing to maximum pressure. Then he forgot what he thought he remembered.

Customarily, he rubs the pressure ridges on his forehead. This time he diligently recalls a conversation with Brian, a Berkeley buddy, a conscientious Native American, beyond the kind with a vaccination mark under his armband. Brian was proud of that. He believed in the Spirit and the spirit of man, the epitome of all existence. "We believe in freedom and exhibit grace," he quipped as the poetic light from the Mohawk Gas sign lamentably dramatized his landscaped face. A hurt breaks into his thought. Strawman's memory is lit with the bold, circular sign which looked like a luminous buffalo-head nickle. The sign is a tragic neon totem to idealistic Americana. It stands for Americans who like to live with the past, not in it. Strawman laughs, lightly, but cathartically. It is rare. And it's okay because they had laughed then. Shortly after the past conversation, Brian registered as a conscientious objector, which the draft board appropriately processed. Soon afterwards, Straw accepted his one-year tour in the Viet Nam hell. He returned, like many others, with nerves as twisted as Kudzu, and lowered expectations of his country and himself.

Straw returned home to drugged crazies that he only came close to understanding. During a summit session, one of them suggested he read the Faustian legend "Blue Blazes." Initially, Straw didn't because he was in a stage of his life when he despised trains, not to mention train stations, because of all the jumping on and off trains he was doing. He had to be continuously on the move. Anyway, reading about someone else's last moments of a tortured existence focused on the pain and sacrifice of unrealized expectations wasn't what he needed.

An additional insight flashed upon Straw about the spirit of Native Americans as he noticed the cigar store Indian. The carving itself was more than the silent advertisement that nicotine in its various forms was available inside; it was a symbol of peace, after nearing their extinction.

"Oh yeah, peace," Strawman said hollowly to himself. Maybe that thought was exactly why he like the cartoonized Presidential Seal: a toothy mouse in its "Last Act of Defiance" was flipping off the eagle which clutched it, with one talon. Importantly, the cartoon was true to Truman: the eagle looked toward the olive branch, toward peace; it held the arrows in the other talon. Yet, on the T-shirt, power had replaced diplomacy, though the two stayed together.

The cold took his thoughts.

Again, that day, Straw begins to suspect that the frigid evenings have seeped through his scalp, into his brain, making him squirrelly. Timely, he remembers that crazy people don't know they're crazy. They think everyone's like them. But they remain anxious because of the ongoing, threatening feeling from the question, "What's going to become of me?"

A piece at a time, Straw is dealing with the dilemma that Nicaragua had posed for him. His decision not to go there to fight was justified in that, this time, he would surely die in combat. So he stayed. And for a while he'd collected money, signed manifestos, and had even written revolutionary poems.

When the sadness of knowing what he is capable of doing yet not able to do overcomes him, he must get on the move. The temporary calm achieved by movement makes the difference though he is not purified, just removed. And the cleansing that was to take place didn't. Very often, from then on, his life pendulates from resignation to surrendering to the madness of being all the way back in the future.

Strawman feels his bones loosen from his muscles and sag against his skin. That's what happens every time he allows his mind to trail off into the safe, thoughtless dark of his netherworld. He remembers, as if to further encourage himself, the sadism and the lack of common sense associated with the invention and introduction of the guillotine. It's said that the sadist French inventor, not too packed with common sense, cut off his hand to demonstrate how cleanly it worked.

Thought in silence no longer intrigues Straw. In the past, it used to allow him conscious control of himself. It used to, but not so much anymore. Every day, while sitting on a bench on the boardwalk, he'd sit and read any newspaper. One day, while aware he was turning the pages at set intervals, not even pretending to be reading, someone walked by and commented, "You have the paper upside down," as if suspecting the inner section was right side up. It no longer mattered. For a time, by then, he was beginning to look pensively between the lines and columns. But one thought would not consistently emerge from the convention.

Later, he went back to the same bench, at the same time of day. Acting troubled and looking confused he'd stare, from an athlete's crouching position, at the composition of the sidewalk. Straw was good at skull cinema. "Are you alright?" someone would eventually ask. And he would invariably answer, "Yes, just watching a turtle drowse," to keep it academic.

For variety, he would customarily sit and stare at the waves. To catch people's attention he would sit as if hypnotized. "Are you okay?" someone would intermittently ask. "Yes, I'm looking at the earth from outer space," he'd answer then add, "we're a water planet," as they stepped up their stride to get away.

Progressively, he begins to lose that impulsive ability to twist and to turn everything. The more he contrives, the less he sees the difference—the more thought tortures him. At times, he has to make a canny effort just to keep a hold on himself.

While standing like a tragedy in rags at the front of Casa María Furniture, Straw is no longer merely a rootless memory on the make, for the day's sake. He does not recognize Mr. Milktoast, his psychologist of old, walk up with two men.

"What are you doing?" Mr. M. asked curiously, with the uniformed men standing at a comfortable distance.

"I came back to S.B. to experience the ocean with the sand," Straw said, though startled by the interruption.

"Where have you been all this time?"

"There for years and around for months."

"Around where?" Mr. M. asked suspiciously.

"Floating around like a butterfly . . ." he said having forgotten the ending. There was one.

"At a collector's convention?"

"That too," Straw answered.

"Straw, you don't look well," Mr. M. stated, standing akimbo, but caring.

"C'mon Judd, it's always been like this," Straw answers, looking vacantly, while trying to decide why he accepts being called Straw and not by his name: Miguel Distraw, Michael, but never Mikey.

"But tell me where you've been," Mr. M. coaches.

He remembers a trick maybe Judd taught him years ago on how to avoid acting on anger.

He counts to ten. The anger is genuine because it doesn't go away. Judd's persistent questions are taking away the privacy of his mind, the time for clearing thought for which he'd returned to Santa Barbara.

Unknown to Strawman, the time he'd taken to think through his anger and to come up with an answer angers Mr. M.

"I've been developing a big camera that can take a picture of the person as it takes the picture," he fires back, carelessly, meaning to say, "a picture that is as big as the person." But that doesn't make any more sense. Or does it? They exchange words with abandon.

"What have you been doing?" Mr. M. asks again, this time less patiently.

"I won't answer any more!"

"Why not?"

"You've playing with me."

"With you, how?"

"Okay. I've been developing a lie detector test for probation officers."

"Why?"

"Ass. I remember your game."

"What?"

"You turned my self-committal into your promotion."

Boom! There is was there, he'd finally remembered. Judd had penetrated Straw's memory through the residual conflict of a broken promise. But, then, Straw is not clear about what happened, exactly.

"It's as clear as black and white," Strawman says, with the expectant hope of their initial contact now gone from his eyes.

"What?" Mr. M. asks.

"You're going to try to take me in," Straw predicts a challenge.

"Try?" Mr. M. questions, annoyed, not without justification. Last time, Straw had been handcuffed to a chain around his waist and shackled at the feet, all standard procedure at Review Hearings, and he'd almost ripped Mr. M. a new asshole.

"Yeah, try," Straw says belligerently.

"Straw, we'd better get off the street, we can talk some somewhere else."

"Talk. You mean ask more questions."

"You don't understand that I've always tried to help you. Calm down." That command put a gun to Straw's head.

"Why? You gonna flush my blood on the street again?" But Strawman is not sure again! He's not sure if he remembers it was Judd. Was he thinking he remembers? Anger, as uncontrolled emotion, is as threatening to him as waves of a storm are to a sailor. He is still second-guessing himself the moment before they take all choice from him.

As if a prerequisite to what was to come, Straw pisses on himself. It tickles down his left leg, tickling the hair folicles.

Before he's totally aware of what is happening, an eager officer has him from behind, securely, but not abusively, in a controlled chokehold. Before the struggle is over, the other officer has a swatch of Straw's hair in his hand. The next thing he feels is the loss of his survival arrogance from a knee to the genitals. Sometime after, Mr. M.'s third pair of hands are on him, his punch goes beyond registered pain, numbing the side of Straw's face. For seconds, Straw expectantly waits the arrival of pain to assure him he's still capable of feeling.

In the jail's C-cell, commonly known as the rubber-room, he hisses through his nose to let out the desperation that blurs his vision. He itches from the dried urine on his leg, so he pisses anew. Disgust builds up to create a tension inside which makes him feel like he's sitting in an idling bullet train. His strands of muscles seem to be coming apart. There are no windows to look beyond himself. Before that can happen, he starts to run nowhere, he pounds the wall, he yells. Nothing except incomprehensible sounds and activity penetrates his awareness. He's now sure exists, the isolation make it so. That's the repeated message no matter what he yells, says, or does.

Most of the time that self-assurance is impossible.

A lapse of sanity overtakes him. Straw rants something about man splitting the atom in order to break down the secret of matter. For hours, intensity of feelings and behavior do not cease. Intoxicated with himself, he passes out, not realizing that the initial confrontation that he sought with himself has been made.

Awakened by a cool draft, he's refreshed. His C-cell is too well ventilated, but for then, it's fine. For a moment, the wafts of his body's dried sweat pierce his nose like the worst moments in a small restroom. Then, his attention focuses on emotions reverberating within. To relax his body, he turns from his side onto his back. The camera's unblinking, intruding eye overhead. Their minds hover over his. Being observed requires vigilance. It's ironic, but true. For those who are watching with concern, he sits on his naked bottom, positions himself like Buddha and hunches into a patient's pose. All that is to suggest to observers he's ready, that he wants to be trusted to control himself.

Hours, probably days later, the slitted window through which he has rejected medication, but has sometimes accepted food, opens. This time it stays open. He cups his family jewels.

"Do I take my cue from how you look or what you've done?"

Straw takes his time to answer. His knotted nerves are loose at the ends.

"Are you my shrink?" Straw asks, as if for assurance.

"Yes, I'm the psychologist."

"You're the one who can negociate my freedom," Straw states.

"I am?" she asks, rejecting total responsibility.

"You are. And you're the one that can wrap me in plastic, like a vegetable in a supermarket, and send me on down the highway to Camarillo." That state mental hospital will always be there.

"I can't do all that. You'll have to do your share. What I write in your profile is up to you."

"This Club Med is my satellite home, not a transport station."

"Mediterranean Club," she repeats for self clarification, "I hadn't thought of it that way."

"Sure," he answers smiling, while the intruding sound of an inmate's plastic shoes is clopping on the cement floor. He doesn't say they're as loud to him as horse hoofs on a stone road. "It's like being a king here. We're fed, kept warm, clothed, kept relatively healthy, and even entertained . . . or are entertaining," he continues.

"Thomas, roll it up!" he hears down the hall, then adds to her, "I don't need to be here anymore. When can I go?"

"When you talk to me. . . more freely than you did the other 'shrink'," she teased.

"You mean answer more questions?"

"If you'd rather not talk to me, then you can go back to Mr. M.'s caseload, back to not talking to him," she offered blandly.

"First, answer my question," Straw proposes.

"Ask," she invites.

"What's your name?"

"Mary Boles," she answers.

"Doctor?"

"Of course," she responds and smiles. "You're going to call me Mary, please."

With that, she quickly moves out of the group of nameless people that observe and address him sparingly, those that he ignores as their eyes roam in and out of his isolation. That's one way to build trust to start with.

"Solitude," wrote Nietzche, "makes us tough towards ourselves and tenderer towards others." That's where Straw's trust had come from and made him more optimistic, more human.

The next day, thanks to Mary, he rebounded from the rubber room. He was dressed in a carrot-orange jumpsuit, but he was on his way to get new clothes and to a cell with others like himself. His wiry body would be able to breathe through the cotton, navy-blue smock, rugby-reject T-shirt, wet-dreamt boxers, wind-worn pants, construction worker socks, and brown or black plastic sandles made in The Republic of China.

Straw continued his recovery. Sometimes he felt guilty because role playing was not what he wanted to do with Mary, not even once in a while. Maybe it was enough that he knew. He always knew though he couldn't always do anything about it. With the tension relieved, physically and mentally, he is ready for the final scene of this recurrent uncontrolled role as an alien. At all times now, Mary and others give him plenty of opportunities to be totally sane, and Straw is for the most part. It's not advisable to get sane too quick. In mental recovery, there's an inherent suspicion of an affinity for doom. For that reason, Straw uses restraint when there's an opportunity for gain. He withdraws when trying to maintain, and he pushes, gently, when there's something to be lost. His thoughts seesaw for control, but are effectively processed behind the scenes. Regaining that control is costly and guarantees nothing, but it is worth it.

Things get as clear as black and white, he thinks, noting that they're both colors. And another thought about color wedges in. Yellow walls throughout the jail are not enough for sporty inmates. They're too safe. The color unbalances fast-tracking desire. For them, that's costly on the street. Oh well, maybe that's not his problem, or maybe not yet. That, and many other little nervous thoughts are turned to rough and cracked skin between the fingers and at the elbows.

Weeks later, Straw finds himself sitting in front of Mary. Now, he too, is behind an unlocked door, a true status symbol of a candidate for freedom. On his ankles, he feels the draft scampering by like a mouse. Though uncomfortable about that, he doesn't say so. By merely filling in a name on a form, a psychiatrist cannot only place, but also maintain a hold on his life. Along his upper lip, within his mustache, beads of sweat spring from that thought.

Carefully and calmly, Straw answers Mary's endless questions, careful not to question them and to restrain the hope from his eyes. Mary's "Let's see," and Straw's distraction, from her alternately removing and replacing her eyeglasses, are okay. It's trying, but okay. She pauses the fiddling briefly, then resumes with a question, a brief pause, then doodling, then a question; often, there's direct eye contact, then a question—a question—then a question. Straw can't think of all the right answers, so he looks out for the question, the wrong question. The emotions explode and subside. It's Straw who must maintain in the struggle for acceptance into her magic circle of the saved.

They are in solo flight, within one another's informed inner circle. Straw's is one of consciousness; Mary's is of euphemisms and professional ideas, without the language she uses in her reports. She pauses, he continues to think.

"Never, for the sake of peace and quiet, deny your own experience and convictions," wrote Dar Hammarskjold in *Markings*. For Straw, that recent reading is a melancolic remark that massages his mind. He accepts it. For that reason, the scent of his young life which smelled of roses was almost deleted several times in his life, almost, but not quite. There is still more to live before his actions disembody that spirit, or exercise it sparingly. Just as he is seasonally brittle, he can be seasonly tough.

Strawman relaxes his patient-to-doctor posture to appreciate the years of effort. He clearly feels the future and it speaks to him: peace is working harder on oneself, not being smarter. The sincerity of that feeling and insight wells in his chest. He gently eases himself forward to the edge of the chair, relaxes his legs by bending them at the knees, and shifting his weight to the balls of his feet, Straw doesn't forget to leave his arms limp at the elbows and his hands on his legs, with the fingers open and relaxed. He asks, "If I stood outside, at the front of this building, could I see the Pacific?"

1987-88

Poems

CHIMAYÓ, NEW MEXICO

Decked in October light adobe grows gold.
On a wall a fresco of Jesus in thorns,
red chiles strung in decades,
apples in buckets,
green chile roasting to peel and freeze,
the air sweet as come.

Santuario de Chimayó,
steeples, like pencils,
sign the sky.
This is a pilgrimage, not a tour,
make the sign of the cross.
Behind the church a mountain
kneels in a field.
Sap on my fingers, plucking mushrooms
from timbers,
someday when I sleep with you
it will taste like this.

ONE DIMENSIONAL MAN

His smile, a minus sign, cancels
whole populations.
I was useful once, a tape recorder
he talked at and played back,
a rear-view mirror announcing
his face at stop lights.
On a self-improvement spree
he took me up like tennis
or a Third World cause.

159

I, the colored help,
Guadalupe, quota, folk art,
more chic than a Santa Fe healer
he saw on the sly,
my Guatemalan cottons
matched his ties.

Bastard. Strip-mining wasted
your heart. How you love
to subtract. Ordering soldiers
to save a village you strike
the match. You always liked me
on my back, with an instamatic
you snap, snap. Sentimental,
you pocket my eyeteeth,
you finger my onyx. Liberal,
you do not steal it, you donate
my bracelet to a Mayan exhibit.

Silviana Wood   First Prize: Short Story

And Where Was Pancho Villa When You Really Needed Him?
(excerpt)

To me the first day back to school is like a holiday, even better. Everyone gets to wear something new and tries to act more grown-up than the year before, but they forget and start hitting you and running around, so everything's the same. The new teachers are so mixed up they're always missing papers or books and don't even know your name. Everything is a lot of fun, and that's why the first day is the best day of the year. Next to the last day.

In all the world I had three best friends: Maromas, Penguin, and Peanut Butter, and we were together again in the sixth grade. This was going to be a good class even with fat Hortensia Martínez who wet the bed still and stunk like a skunk so nobody wanted to sit next to her. And even with suckass Fidelia Medina who was always the teacher's pet because she was so smart. She told on everybody and nobody could beat her up 'cause she had a father who could speak good English, and would come running to the school to make the principal paddle the winner of the fight. By this I mean that the winner was *never* Fidelia.

Our new teacher was late and it was just like a party. Fidelia was showing off her new green crocodile notebook that had a special pocket inside for her pencils and erasers that nobody could borrow. It even had a pencil sharpener and the green crocodile notebook was stuffed so full of clean paper that it could hardly get zippered close. Fidelia *had* to be rich—she never wore socks with holes in them.

We were happy too because this year we got to be on the second floor of the school with nobody else but the library. And we knew that on fire drills, the most exciting thing in the year, we would get to leave the building by climbing down the fire escape stairs along the wall outside. Everyone else would just get to walk out normal. I was lucky too because I didn't have to go to Carrillo School where my cousins went. Everyone knows Carrillo School has a dead nurse ghost who haunts the toilets. Next year we would all be in the junior high across the railroad tracks. That's if we passed.

It was very noisy when the new teacher walked into the room. Maromas had almost convinced Peanut Butter to meet him later under the bridge instead of going to her dumb Catechism class, and Penguin was teaching me magic tricks, like the one where you tell him what row your card is in and he can tell on the third deal which one is your card. We all shut up when we saw our teacher; we didn't breathe. She was so beautiful, like a movie star. We kept looking at her; she smiled.

She carried a small box with her things: a bottle of lotion, a sewing kit, a box of Kleenex, a desk calendar, a white vase with red plastic roses, and a clay kangaroo with pencils and pens in its stomach. She spread these things on top of her desk and put other things inside the drawers while we waited. Then she wrote her name in big letters on the blackboard: Miss Folsom. Her fingernails were long and polished the same color like her lipstick. She got a Kleenex and wiped the chalk from her hands. Again she smiled to us.

"My name is Miss Folsom. Can everyone say 'Miss Folsom'?"

"Miss Folsom," we repeated. Fidelia was the loudest.

"Fine. And now I have to learn *your* names." She read her list. "Oh, oh. I can see problems already. Well, I'll just have to seat you in alphabetical order until I've learned your names. When I call your name step up to the desk I'm pointing to. Please be patient and we can change around later after I've learned your names."

She began to read our names: "Goo-ee-ler-mo? Gooeelermo Al-ma-zan?"

We all started to laugh when we figured out what she meant.

Except for Guillermo who didn't know it was *his* name she was saying so funny. Fidelia pointed to Guillermo. And lucky for him that we already called him "Yemo" or else he would've been called "Gooey" for the rest of his life for sure.

"Just what does Gooeelermo mean?" Miss Folsom asked us.

"Guillermo means William," said Fidelia who knew everything.

"Ah, William. A noble name. Take the first seat, Willie."

After Guillermo, she changed Francisco to Frankie; Juan became Johnny; Joaquín became Jack; and then it was like a game with all of us waiting to see what our new name would sound like. Maromas, who could spell all the words in the world and knew the alphabet already knew where our names would make us sit. So he pretended to be like a traffic cop at a parade, blowing a whistle, waving his arms, and moving us to the new desk even before Miss Folsom who was still trying to read our names. Maromas was funny that way.

"And what is *your* name?" Miss Folsom asked him, probably thinking she could make him sit down.

"Maromas. Maromas means somersaults," he said as he made an ugly face at Fidelia before she could answer for him.

"Somersaults?" Miss Folsom laughed out loud, real pretty. "No one could possibly be named 'somersaults' now, could he?" She checked her list anyway, to be sure just in case. Maromas wiggled his ears at us and stretched his mouth like a rubber band. Miss Folsom couldn't find his name so she let him keep directing traffic.

"Juan Cardenas?"

Penguin shuffled his feet and walked over to the desk.

"Thank you, Johnny," said Ms. Folsom.

If anybody wants to know, no one, not even his mother, knew where Maromas got his name, but Penguin got his name from the time he ran away from Fort Grant, the reform school. They say that they used to lock up the boys' shoes so they couldn't escape through the cactus, but Penguin ran away barefoot through the desert anyway. When he got to Tucson his feet were all cut up and swollen and he walked like a penguin in a zoo.

At first he used to beat up anybody that called him a penguin, but later he changed his mind and liked his nickname. He even got a penguin tattooed on his arm with India ink after he was captured and sent back to Fort Grant.

"Virginia Jaramillo?"

Never mind how Miss Folsom said *that* but it was Peanut Butter's real name. And if you want to know why she was called Peanut Butter, it was because the guys in the junior high school said she was just like the commercial on television about some peanut butter: "smooth, creamy, and easy to spread." And the name stuck even though some of us didn't get the joke.

Miss Folsom finally figured out that Maromas was really Antonio Salazar so everybody in the last row had to move one seat down to make room for him. Fidelia was in the last row where she didn't belong, and we were laughing at her 'cause Miss Folsom had skipped her. Fidelia walked up to Miss Folsom's desk when she saw Miss Folsom put her list in the drawer, and to get even with us, Fidelia did her usual showing off.

"My name is Fidelia Medina. Fidelia means 'faithful' but everyone calls me 'Della,'" said the liar 'cause that was the first time any of us had heard her being called *that*. And God punished her for lying and sat her right next to stinky Hortensia Martínez. Fat Hortensia's name stayed almost the same except that now it sounded like 'whore'.

Miss Folsom had finished off the names quick. Chop, chop and she was done. By the end of the week we were all using our new names. Some of us even forgot our old ones. Except for Maromas. He just pretended to be deaf when Miss Folsom called him Tony.

So that was how our last year in elementary school started.

1988-89

Una vez, en un barrio de sueños . . . (excerpt)

*(*Una vez, en un barrio de sueños *. . . consists of an introduction and three short plays, with a cast of ten to twelve actors. [. . .] And please also note that the playwright has attempted to recreate the voices of the Chicano working class with authenticity and respect; therefore, the syntax, spelling, and pronunciation should remain without change. The play takes place in a small southwestern town in 1971. Set is dimly lit, soft guitar music; actors enter with stylized movements to music.)*

NARRATOR: Una vez, havía un muchachito muy flaco y muy cochino que se llamaba Federico Narices de Perico, y que vivía en el barrio más pobre y miserable en un desierto donde el sol quemaba las viñas y hojas de la madreselva, y nada se atrevía a crecer aquí sólo algún o dos árboles de piocha. *(Lights up.)*

NARRATOR: Aquí no havía padres; todos los hombres jóvenes se havían ido a la prisión en Florence, desaparecido a California, o convertido a cheques de mantenimiento del govierno.

NARRATOR: Las mujeres jóvenes se quedaban adentro de la casa todo el día, alejadas del resecante sol, mirando las telenovelas que casi las hacían llorar . . .

FEMALE ACTOR: Will you love me forever?

MALE ACTOR: Yes, Ericka, yes, yes, forever.

FEMALE ACTOR: No, you won't. *(Lights up.)*

MALE ACTOR: Yes, my love, I will.

FEMALE ACTOR: Will you love me even after you learn my terrible secret?

MALE ACTOR: Yes, my sweetheart, I will love you. Please marry me.

FEMALE ACTOR: But the shame.

MOTHER: But you can't marry her. She is your . . .

ANNOUNCER: And now a word from our sponsor. *(Same male and female will do a dandruff shampoo commercial.)*

FEMALE VOICE: *(As though reading female actor's mind. Notices male sitting next to her.)* Hmmm, I think he's cute.

MALE VOICE: (Also as though reading male actor's mind. Notices girl.) Hmmm, I think she likes me. *(Female actor fluffs her hair and smiles at male actor. He is horrified to see: dandruff! He exits. She exits in tears.)*

ANNOUNCER: Tune in tomorrow, etc.

NARRATOR: *(Returning to story.)* Hasta en la tarde, cuando entonces se pintaban sus caras con el maquillaje Avon y se vestían en vestidos muy pretty del Lerners, y se paraban afuera como ficheras en un cabaret. Pero sin música.

NARRATOR: Y los viejos se sentaban afuera todo el día, sin miedo al sol porque su piel ya se havía cambiado a cuero de zapato, y se sentaban allí, las sillas ladeadas a la pared, esperando que nada pasara, asoleándose como cachorras perezosas en las tumbas de un panteón.

NARRATOR: Esperando. Todos esperando. Porque en este barrio no havía sueños. No miento. Sí, havía sueños. Pero eran sueños que sólo se hallaban en un botecito de pintura. Aquí nadien crecía joven y nadien soñaba despierto.

NARRATOR: Desde un principio, Federico era un pendejo.

CHORUS: Allí va el pendejo, allí va el pendejo . . .

NARRATOR: En las mañanas veraniegas antes que el swimming pool abriera a las doce, o más tarde si el lifeguard de la universidad tenía una buena cruda por los estudios, en lugar de dormir tarde o vagar por la vecindad en busca de cosas buenas pa' robar, Federico se sentaba en cuclillas en frente de su casa y jugaba en la tierra entre la banqueta y la pared de su casa, y hacía pretend que era un ranchero muy rico.

Con un palito puntiagudo, trinchaba zurcos en la tierra seca, y sembraba hojas arrugadas de las piochas, y las regaba con interminables recorridas a la llave en la yarda detrás de la casa con una lata vacía de la sopa chicken noodle soup de Campbell's.

NARRATOR: Inútil es decirlo, pero las hojas de piocha jamás hecharon raíz.

NARRATOR: De todos modos Eddie Spaghetti y Tony Baloney pronto pasaban, bamboleándose, con sus sesos fritos por inhaling paint, con narices rainbow colors. Y pataleaban con gusto la plantación de Federico, y luego marchaban como madriles borrachos, riendo locamente.

NARRATOR: ¿Como qué?

EDDIE AND TONY: Like drunk baboons.

NARRATOR: Ahhhhh.

NARRATOR: Luego Federico se iba a nadar hasta que el swimming pool cerraba a las seis y regresaba a su casa un poco más limpio pero muriéndose de hambre. Se comía los frijoles helados directamente del refrigerador porque su madre no se los freía antes de la hora de cenar.

MOTHER: *(Reclining on sofa, smoking, watching T.V..)* Es tu culpa; tú nomás tienes hambre por andar nadando todo el día. Todo mundo sabe que te da hambre, es como tomar vitaminas, la misma cosa. Tú tienes la culpa.

CHORUS: *(In conga line.)* Tú tienes la culpa. Tú tienes la culpa. Tú tienes la culpa.

NARRATOR: Ella decía mientras veía la televisión, resoplando sin fin sus "cagarillos", tomando sus Pepsi-Colas.

NARRATOR: Los días de summer vacation terminaron, y la escuela empezó el día después de Labor Day y ahora Federico se tenía que sentar en su desk, bored to death, sus pies dolientes por tener que volver a usar zapatos otra vez. Con la excepción de Geography, Federico odiaba la escuela.

NARRATOR: ¿Y por qué le gustaba la geografía?

NARRATOR: Porque en la clase de geografía Federico podía ver otros mundos, otras tierras, y en su mente, él creía escaparse del barrio.

NARRATOR: *(Laughing.)* ¿Escaparse del barrio? Qué absurdo. Nadien se escapa del barrio. ¡Ni las cucarachas!

NARRATOR: Anyway, cuando el día terminaba, corría pronto a su casa antes de que el Eddie Spaghetti y Tony Baloney pudieran golpearlo por no tener dinero que darles para comprar más pintura to inhale, o porque el Federico nunca quería juntarse con ellos cuando ellos tenían una lata nueva de pintura.

MOTHER: Es tu culpa, por no defenderte. *(Gives him money.)* Corre, ve pa' que'l Chino y traime una paca de cagarros. Malboros.

NARRATOR: Federico iba a la tienda, y como si tuvieran antenas, el Eddie Spaghetti y el Tony Baloney sabían que estaba allí, y lo golpeaban cuando salía de la tienda. Además, le robaban los cigarillos de su madre, y luego ella lo jalaba de las greñas por haber 'perdido' los cigarillos y porque tenía que dejar la televisión antes de que la película terminara. Todos los días, le parecía a Federico, lo golpeaban, y algún día, Federico bien sabía, tendría que defenderse. Y él tenía miedo. Mucho miedo.

NARRATOR: Y en este barrio vivía un viejo muy antipático que no tenía nada que hacer mas que sentarse afuera en su porche y leer hasta que sus ojos débiles se cansaran. Luego allí se sentaba con sus ojos medios cerrados, sin moverse, y esperaba como un reptil mesozoico para que las moscas pararan cerca de él y . . .

ALL: ¡Juácate!

NARRATOR: Matarlas con su matamoscas. Don Anselmo era su nombre, sencillamente, y él era odiado por todos los buquis del barrio. Don Anselmo estaba bien enterado de esto y esto le hacía sentirse muy, muy contento.

DON ANSELMO: *(Brushing fly with fly swatter.)* E Pluribus Unum.

NARRATOR: Decía mientras echaba a un lado las moscas muertas del barandal. Impacientemente esperaba que la campana de la escuela sonara porque al merito enseguida de la banqueta, en la tierra más cerca a la calle, don Anselmo havía ordenado a su yerno, el hallelujah, que pusiera inmensas piedras, más bien penas, por ninguna razón mas que para hacer tempt a los buquis que venían de la escuela, a subirse en ellas y brincar de una a la otra, para que don Anselmo pudiera despertar, y pararse, y gritar fuertes malas palabras. *(Kids jump from one block to another.)*

DON ANSELMO: Cabrones, bastardos sin padres, hijos de la chingada, pachucos, voy a llamar a la polecía.

DOÑA REBECCA: Anselmo, por favor.

NARRATOR: Así le rogaba su esposa flaca, doña Rebecca Nalgas Secas desde adentro por la ventana. Éstas eran las únicas palabras que se oían de ella, jaladas en un tono martirizado. Ella sabía que si don Anselmo se agitaba demasiado, comensaría a toser, volviéndose rojo, y tuviera que meterse para adentro. ¿Adentro?

DOÑA REBECCA: ¡Dios no lo quiera!

NARRATOR: Bueno, un día Federico se tubo que quedar after school a escribir las palabras que no sabía spell veinticinco veces cada una, y para cuando hizo finish, todos, incluyendo Eddie Spaghetti y Tony Baloney, se habían ido a sus casas y Federico se fue andando slowly a su casa.

NARRATOR: Al llegar a la casa de don Anselmo, vio que don Anselmo estaba bien dormido, y entonces Federico se subió a la primera piedra. Luego se sentó en la segunda para estudiar la tercera. Las rocas estaban llenas de agujeros, y él estaba sintiendo la textura áspera y arenosa muy atentamente que actualmente perdió algunas de las palabras cochinas de don Anselmo. As a matter of fact, don Anselmo ya había terminado con su repertorio general y estaba desesperadamente tratando de pararse de su silla y el matamoscas se le cayó y él estaba muy gordo para poder agacharse y levantarlo.

DON ANSELMO: Cabrón, sí, tú, cabrón. ¿Qué estás haciendo con mis piedras?

DOÑA REBECCA: Anselmo, por favor.

FEDERICO: Estudiándolas.

DON ANSELMO: ¿Quién eres tú que crees que sabes algo de mis piedras?

NARRATOR: Don Anselmo le preguntó pero sabía perfectamente bien que el muchacho no iba a saber, pero le caiva bien porque no se havía arrancado como los otros miedosos.

FEDERICO: Yo sé que son piedras volcánicas.

DON ANSELMO: ¿Volcánicas? A ver, pruébamelo.

FEDERICO: ¿Ve estos hoyos? Cuando el volcán esplotó, hace mucho tiempo, la lava se derritió y cuando le dio el viento helado, los gases calientes adentro se hicieron bombitas y se reventaron en estos hoyitos, o algo así.

DON ANSELMO: *Ben travato, linguini.* ¿No me entiendes? Es italiano. Quiere decir que lo que me acabas de decir es bien pensado. *(Pause.)* ¿*Capici*, Alfredo Fettucini?

FEDERICO: Me llamo Federico. ¿Es usted italiano?

DON ANSELMO: No, soy mexicano, como tú, pero yo sé muchos idiomas, de aquí, *El Diccionario de Frases Foráneas. (Shows* FEDERICO *book.)*

FEDERICO: *(Impressed.) Dictionary of Foreign Phrases.* ¿Puede decir otra cosa? ¿Puede decir algo de volcanes? ¿De Vesuvius? Está en Italia, ¿verdad?

DON ANSELMO: ¿Vesuvius? Seguramente está en Napoli: *vedí Napoli e poi muori!* Eso es lo que yo quisiera hacer: ver a Napoli y después morir. *(Turns to house.)* Rebecca, dale al muchacho unas galletas para que se vaya a su casa. (REBECCA *passes cookies, only her hands are seen.* DON ANSELMO *closes his eyes.* FEDERICO *eats cookie, picks up fly swatter and places on porch rail.* DON ANSEL-MO *opens his eyes.)* Tú me gustas. Puedes venir a visitarme después de la escuela y me puedes decir todas las cosas que estudias, y yo te enseñaré todos las idiomas que yo sé. Is it a deal? *(Puts out right hand.)*

FEDERICO: *(Shakes his hand.)* Yes, it's a deal.

DON ANSELMO: *(Stands fiercely, like a samurai warrior.)* Sayonara!

FEDERICO: Sayonara! *(Mimics* DON ANSELMO, *walks away.)*

DON ANSELMO: Y no te vuelvas a subir en mis cabronas piedras. *(Chuckles to himself.)*

(FEDERICO *exits happily eating other cookie.)*

NARRATOR: Y Federico se fue pero volvió muchas veces a pasar el año de escuela. Ahora que Federico tenía a alguien con quién hablar, alguien que lo escuchaba, que le contestaba sus preguntas, le gustaba la escuela y geografía también se hizo la clase favorita de don Anselmo. Cambiaban información seria al empezar la visita, pero después, mientras comían danish rolls con peanut butter y miel de abeja, la plática se volvía poco absurda, chistosa.

DON ANSELMO: *(Telling story.)* . . . Y luego, desde arriba en las nubes, se calló hasta el suelo, y no le concedió los tres deseos porque no era buena persona. *(Both laugh.)* Y tú, Federico, si tú tuvieras tres deseos, ¿qué fueran?

FEDERICO: ¿Tres deseos? Nomás tengo uno y ése es darle por toda la madre al Eddie Spaghetti y Tony Baloney, especialmente al Eddie Spaghetti porque él es el que le da las órdenes al Tony Baloney que me pegue.

DON ANSELMO: Ah sí, Eddie Spaghetti. Él es tu *bête noir*, ¿verdad? (FEDERICO *puzzled.*) ¿Te acuerdas la lección francesa que tuvimos? *Parlez vous francais, si vous plait?*

FEDERICO: Sí, me acuerdo. El Eddie Spaghetti es mi bestia negra, mi *bête noir.* El que me asusta.

DON ANSELMO: Sí, pero eso es sólo una parte. No te olvides que la bestia negra no sólo es algo que le tenemos miedo, pero es algo que tenemos que conquistar.

FEDERICO: Lo sé. Pero él es mucho más grande y más fuerte que yo. *(Changing subject.)* Pero dígame, don Anselmo, ¿cuáles son sus tres deseos?

DON ANSELMO: *(Dreamily.)* Yo quisiera volar como un pájaro, nadar abajo del agua como un pescado, sin un tanque de oxígeno, y quisiera tocar el piano como un pianista de conciertos. Y quisiera sembrar una semilla, aquí en el barrio y verla crecer.

FEDERICO: Pues aquí nada crece. Además esos son cuatro deseos y usted dijo tres.

DON ANSELMO: Lo sé, lo sé. Pero si uno puede desear tres cosas, ¿por qué chingados no cuatro? *(Pause.)* Y tú, ¿nomás uno?

FEDERICO: Bueno pues, mi segundo deseo fuera poder caminar por todo el mundo, a todos los lugares que hemos estudiado.

DON ANSELMO: ¿Y regresarías? ¿Aquí, al barrio, a. . .?

FEDERICO: Sí, don Anselmo. Yo regresaría a este barrio, y a usted, mi amigo. Y no me pregunte por el tercer deseo: nomás tengo dos. *(DON ANSELMO glares, waits. Pause.)*

NARRATOR: Como darle por toda la madre al Eddie Spaghetti y Tony Baloney era casi imposible, Federico concentró en su segundo deseo, de viajar por el mundo, y como nadien sabía más que don Anselmo de tierras extranjeras, los dos pasaban horas planeando el itinerario. *(Both ad lib, with world globe.)*

DON ANSELMO: Y en Argentina, ¿qué vas hacer?

FEDERICO: Sentarme enseguida de una bonfire con los gauchos de las pampas y comer muchos, muchos sirloin steaks.

DON ANSELMO: ¿Y en Japón?

FEDERICO: Voy a ir a restaurantes y voy a escojer un pescado fresquesito o un lobster de allí del agua y me lo voy a comer crudo con soy sauce, igualito que los japoneses.

DON ANSELMO: Y en Europa. Los museos, las iglesias . . .

FEDERICO: Voy a comer pastries con custard adentro y chocolate por fuera, sentado en un café en banqueta 'al fresco' mirando la gente pasar.

DON ANSELMO: Comiendo, siempre comiendo. Cómo estás hambreado, muchacho.

FEDERICO: En cada país que yo visite voy a comer y comer, y cuando regrese eso es lo que voy a recordar. La comida.

DON ANSELMO: Bueno, mañana me dices más, muchacho, aunque sea de puro comer. *Auf wiedersehen.*

FEDERICO: *Auf wiedersehen. (Exits.)*

NARRATOR: Un día Federico se paró en frente de don Anselmo con un cartón de leche con tres matitas tristes.

DON ANSELMO: A ver, déjame ver qué trais allí, Federico. *(Pinches leaf and smells fingers.)* Tomate. La palabra viene del náhuatl, tú sabes: *tomatl.* ¿Te acuerdas que te dije de ellos?

FEDERICO: Sí, señor, escribí un reporte para social studies.

DON ANSELMO: Y recibistes una "A", ¿verdá? Los indios sembraban tomates desde antes que ni naciera Cristo. Y los europeos creían que los tomates eran venenosos. Idiotas. ¿La vas a sembrar?

FEDERICO: ¿Crecerán?

DON ANSELMO: Eso depende de ti, enteramente en ti. *(Waves fly swatter to end visit; annoyed.)*

FEDERICO: ¿Me ayudará?

DON ANSELMO: Es mucho trabajo. Tú sabes lo que pasa en este barrio —nada crece, tú mismo lo dijiste. ¿Cómo puede crecer algo aquí? El caliche en la tierra seca, el sol, la gente que no le importa nada, el polvo —chingado— es inútil, te digo.

FEDERICO: No lo es. Sí, crecerán; nomás dígame qué tengo que hacer y lo hago. ¿Por qué no me quiere ayudar?

DON ANSELMO: *(Hesitates.)* Sí, te ayudaré pero va a ser muchísimo trabajo. ¿Crees que lo puedes hacer?

FEDERICO: Sí, sí. Nomás dígame, y lo haré. Yo sé que dije que nada crecería aquí pero podemos hacer try, ¿qué no?

DON ANSELMO: Sí, muchacho, podemos hacer try. *(Shake hands on deal.)*

FEDERICO: Yo antes sembraba las hojas de la piocha pero nunca he sembrado algo real.

DON ANSELMO: Ni yo tampoco; tú eres el primero. *(Pauses.)*

FEDERICO: *(Solemnly.)* Don Anselmo, yo le juro que usted y yo vamos a comer los tomates de estas plantas.

DON ANSELMO: Cuidado, un juramento es sagrado. Ay veremos si vamos a comer tus tomates. Ay veremos.
(DON ANSELMO *hits porch rail with fly swatter.*)

Josefina López   Second Prize: Drama

Simply María or America's Dream (excerpt)

In the middle of downtown Los Angeles, CARMEN, and her daughter, MARÍA, search the busy streets to reunite with her husband, RICARDO. This scene portrays their initial experience of Los Angeles, California.

(The following is the making of a city. Actors will take on many roles. It will be organized chaos. Noises of police and firetruck sirens, along with other common city noises are heard. The stage lights up with vendors selling on the streets, and all sorts of unusual and not so unusual people found in downtown L.A. on Broadway Street. CARMEN and MARÍA become engulfed in the scene, appalled to see where they have come to. Placard reads: LOS ANGELITOS DEL NORTE.)

PERSON 1. : Broadway! Downtown L.A.!

VENDOR 1: Cassettes, *¡cartuchos, dos dólares!*

VENIDOR 2: *Anillos de oro sólido.* Solid gold. Not plated.

CARMEN: *Perdone, señora,* could you tell me. . .

BAG LADY: Get out of my way!

PROTESTOR: Homosexuality is wrong! No sex! No sex! *¡Se va a acabar el mundo!* The world is coming to an end! (*Separates CARMEN from MARÍA.*)

CARMEN: María! María, where are you? *(Searches frantically.)*

MARÍA: Mami! Mami! (*Cries for CARMEN.*)

WOMAN 1: Buy this! *¿Sombras para verte como estrella de cine?*

WOMAN 2: Hair brushes, all kinds, a dollar!

WOMAN 3: You want to buy handbags?

WOMAN 4: *¡Vámonos!* Here comes the police. *(All the vendors on the street run away.)*

MAN 1: Jesus loves you! (*Hands CARMEN a pamphlet.*) He died for our sins!

CARMEN: *¿Qué?*

WOMAN 1: That RTD bus is late again!

DIRTY OLD MAN: Hey! Little girl! You want to get married? The world is coming to an end and you don't want to die without having experienced it.

CARMEN: María! María, *¿dónde estás hija mía?*
CHOLO 2: East L.A.!
TWO VALLEY GIRLS: We love it!
CHOLO 1: Hey, *bato!*
TWO VALLEY GIRLS: Party and let party!
CHOLO 2: *¡Oye, mi carnal!*
PERSON 2: *¡Viva la huelga!* Boycott grapes!
PERSON 3: Chicano Power!
TWO VALLEY GIRLS: We love it.
PERSON 3: Chicano Power!
TWO VALLEY GIRLS: We love it.
PERSON 4: A little culture for the *gringuitos.* Tostadas, *frijoles!*
ANGLO BUYER: How much? *¿Cuánto? ¿Salsa? ¿Cerveza?*
CARMEN: ¡María!

(MARÍA *runs scared and bumps into* CARMEN. *They hug each other.*
RICARDO, *dressed in* charro *outfit enters and gives some yells as if ready
to sing a* corrido. *All the chaos of the city stops, and all the city people recoil
in fear.* RICARDO *becomes the hero rescuing* CARMEN *and* MARÍA *from
their nightmare.*)

TWO VALLEY GIRLS: We love it!
CARMEN: Ayyy!! What a crazy city! It's so awful! People here are crazy!
      (*Almost about to cry, she embraces* RICARDO.) But Ricardo, I'm so
      happy to be here.
MARÍA: (*Trying to get attention.*) An ugly man chased me!
RICARDO: But you are all right?
MARÍA: Now that you are here.
RICARDO: Carmen, we are finally together like I promised.
CARMEN: Ricardo, where's our home?
RICARDO: Follow me. (*They leave the stage, props are set up quickly.*)
NARRATOR: They're going to the housing projects: Pico Aliso, Ramona Gar-
      dens, Estrada Courts. No one likes it there, but it's cheap. *'Ta barato.*
      (*On the screen the following title is displayed:* LITTLE HOUSE IN
      THE GHETTO.)
RICARDO: Here we are.
CARMEN: *¿Aquí?*
RICARDO: Yes, I hope it's all right. It's only for now.
MARÍA: (*Smiling.*) I like it! Look, Mami! There are swings and grass.
RICARDO: There are a lot of kids in the neighborhood who you can play
      with.
MARÍA: Really, Papi? Would they want to play with me?

RICARDO: Sure. *(Noticing* CARMEN's *displeasure.)* What's wrong? You
    don't like it?
CARMEN: Oh, no. I'm just tired from the trip.
RICARDO: How was the trip?
MARÍA: *(Cutting in.)* It was great!
CARMEN: Great? You threw up on me the whole way here.
MARÍA: Except, I don't understand why the bus never got off the ground.
    Where are the Angels? And where are the clouds? And the gate? And
    the music . . . like in the stories Mami used to tell me. I thought we
    were going to heaven. I thought you had been called to heaven
    because you are an angel. Are you an angel?
RICARDO: Yes, I'm your angel always.
MARÍA: So if this isn't heaven and you're an angel, what are we doing here?

Alberto Ledesma   First Prize: Poetry

Poetry for Homeboys on the Foul Line

JOSÉ

Every night at eight José
slouches under an altar,
a crucifix, on stacks
of *National Geographic,*
Sports Illustrated
and *Life*,
murmurs Ave Marías
to Padre Nuestros,
rosary tangled
in his fists.

He stares at
Wrigley wads,
ghost stains,
maybe shoe-prints
on the wall,
possessed.

At ten locks himself out
of his cluttered home, his
San Judas Tadeo and
La Virgen de Zapopán,
rides his '56 Bel Air
to High Street

joining the chorus boom
of the Wanderer, the Pretender
and Duke of Earl,

stops at every
well-known corner and
sells crack.

82ᴺᴰ Avenue
no one walks their dog on
pink-brick paths;
no one sits
on white wood porch steps
to eat watermelon in July;
no showers sing,
no tamarind grows
on fertile soil.

Mine's the street of charcoal hope
where rusted
Buicks and Impalas
hide chocolate-stained faces.
It's a trail of asphalt crumbs
on Sunday mornings,
a boulevard
of neon leopards
at the midnight peak.

Mine's the street of
whispered deals,
a wrinkled place where
children learn to
spot police before
they go to school.
It's a dandelion heaven
where no tulips bloom.

Here
the winter sun
hides the clouds
of childhood friends
who fade into
the hug of
ecstasy.

AY-AY-AY!

Caught by Saturday night's tele-película
Mamá said Huisquilco,
the town she left behind,
seemed a little closer,
but Mazola and Bubba's Hair Replacement
verified the distance,
noted that when happiness was black and white,
pueblo folk huddled inside adobe theaters
and witnessed visions of love
for a peso:
Jorge Negrete and María Felix
burst the walls of passion while
Pedro Infante sang:
You passed by my side
with great indifference,
your eyes didn't bother
to look at me.
I saw you;
you ignored me.
I spoke to you;
you ignored me.
And all my bitterness
drowned inside of me. . .

One summer's winter
a velvet-voiced boy
became a charro.
He wore his sombrero
like the rooster his crest
and spoke to mamá
of a green cactus Eden
beyond the hills,
of silver he had found
in the shells of turtles
and of desert pulque
sweeter than calf's milk.
Like morning dew he came,
an oasis rippling coolness
on mamá's parched earth.

In the silent wisdom of her spirit
another fable was wrought.
Her charro,
mahogany on the couch,
snored harmonies
and surrendered no ay-ay-ays of love.

Liliana Valenzuela | First Prize: Novel

Zurcidos invisibles (excerpt)

La pared crujió. ¿Era un sueño? Todavía era tan temprano, ni siquiera las siete. Dolores miró de reojo al reloj. Miró la cama vacía de Marta. ¿Dónde está Marta? Ah, está haciéndoles el desayuno a los dos inquilinos y a Rafael. Ya han de haber salido al trabajo y ella estará lavando los platos. La lámpara se balanceaba del techo, despacito, de la puerta a la ventana. Dolores trató de enfocar sus ojos en la lámpara pero no podía distinguirla bien. ¿Dónde estarán mis lentes? Dolores los buscó a tientas sobre su buró mientras oía otro tronido. Más fuerte. Inconfundible. Se quitó las lagañas, se puso los lentes y vió la pared de enfrente partirse en un zigzag de cemento, de pronto pudo ver la casa de sus vecinos a través del agujero. La casa rugía, y los gritos de los vecinos se colaban por hoyos y grietas. Las camas de Dolores y Marta bailaban por el piso, las píldoras amarillas, azules y rojas de Marta salieron del botiquín y se estrellaron contra la ventana, las medicinas de Dolores cayeron junto a la jarra de agua que dejaba sobre el buró.

"¡Marta! ¡¡Marta!! ¡Ven a bajarme!" gritó Dolores desesperada mientras sonaba la campanita que usaba para que le trajeran la comida. La campanita se ahogaba como la voz de un monaguillo en pleno mercado de la Merced, enterrada en escombros y pedazos de cemento que caían por todos lados. Nuestra casa es fuerte, pensó Dolores, es de las casas buenas, de antes, no se va a caer, no se puede caer.

Abajo, Marta se agarraba de la puerta del refrigerador mientras los platos caían como abanicos al piso. Pedazos de tazas, de cristal cortado esparcidos por el suelo. Agarraba con la otra mano una botella de leche que se desparramaba por la cocina. Marta escuchaba los gritos de su tía a lo lejos perdidos entre la orquesta de vidrio, el cemento encabronado y la tierra que rugía para tragarlo todo. La tierra tiene hambre, pensó Marta, y regó el resto de la leche en el piso. Le echó los restos del huevo, los frijoles, el café, quiso que se lo tragara todo y la dejara en paz. Marta pensó en subir al cuarto y ayudar a bajar a su tía. Pero no lo hizo. No quiso que su tía viviera ya más. Quería que se la tragara la tierra. Que se la comiera junto con los frijoles y la leche y que no regresara nunca más.

Marta trató de salir de la casa pero se caía una y otra vez en el piso. Los pesados muebles se deslizaban crujiendo sus viejas maderas, las polillas saltaban para salvar sus vidas, el gato lloraba en el jardín, el candelabro cayó en el piano de cola y ella sonrió. No volvería a escuchar esa música que la atormentaba, el piano estaría mudo. Sus rodillas llenas de moretones, gateó hasta llegar a la puerta delantera. Me largo, pensó Marta, y se atravesó corriendo al camellón de las palmeras.

"¡Martaaaa! ¡Marta!" gritó su tía por última vez mientras el techo de tejas le caía encima como castañuelas. Las medias, las pañoletas, las corbatas salieron por la ventana. De los closets de Marta, de Dolores y de Rafael salieron discos de Elvis, cartas de enamorados clandestinos, dildos, tequila, minifaldas, tacones de aguja, postales de Las Vegas, aceites olorosos y manuales del Kama Sutra. Una enorme viga de madera cayó sobre el estómago de Dolores y la pared se derrumbó enfrente de ella.

Gritos de espanto salían de todas las casas. Marta estaba acostada en el camellón, la ropa rasgada, el rimel corrido sobre su cara, riendo incontrolablemente.

Hoy en la tarde viene Leti con los chiquillos a merendar. Marta tiene que ir por leche, los tamales y preparar el atole. Tía Dolores ha estado muy exigente todo el día. "Marta, tráeme mis lentes". "Marta, hazme un chocolate". "Marta, ¿ya le diste de comer al gato?" A Marta ya le anda por salir de la casa.

"Voy por la leche, Tía", dice Marta mientras agarra su monedero, las llaves y la bolsa verde del mandado y sale a la Avenida Sinaloa.

"No te tardes", dice Dolores, sorbiendo los últimos tragos de su chocolate.

El sol se cuela por las palmeras que desfilan por el camellón. Marta pasa por el puesto de las flores, la panadería, la refaccionaría, la farmacia del Perpetuo Socorro. Al caminar va sonando su monedero, contenta de respirar aire fresco. Cruza la Avenida Nuevo León y llega a la Tamalería Flor de Lis. Pide 6 de chile rojo, 6 de verde, 2 oaxaqueños y 5 de azúcar para los niños. Compra la leche en el súper de al lado y decide pasar a Woolworth's por una malteada de fresa. Entra a la tienda en Avenida Revolución, pasa por la sección de los dulces rojos, las paletas mimí, los pirulís, y se sienta a la barra. Al lado derecho una pareja come unos tacos de pollo y al izquierdo una viejita come una dona. Marta sorbe lentamente la malteada, apretando el popote con los labios y dejando los pedazos de fresas para el final. La señorita de Woolworth, con su uniforme a rayas verdes y blancas y su gorrito de la misma tela la mira de reojo. Su cabello rubio pintado sale de su gorrito en caireles. "Te gustan las malteadas, ¿verdad?" le pregunta mientras enjuaga la licuadora. "Sí, me encantan, trato de venir cada que puedo, pero mi tía está enferma y casi no me deja salir", dice Marta. "Ah qué caray, así es con los parientes, yo también tengo una tía que se queja todo el tiempo, que si la reuma, que si los juanetes, gracias a Dios no vive con nosotros", dice la señorita sobándose la espalda y riéndose. Marta sonríe.

"¿Por qué te tardaste tanto?" le grita la tía Dolores desde su recámara. "No te puede uno encargar nada. Distraída que eres. Ándale, ayúdame a bajar que ya van a venir Leti y sus niños a merendar. ¿Trajiste los tamales?"

"Sí, tía", dice Marta mientras se muerde el labio inferior y pone los tamales en una olla tapada para que no se enfríen. Saca la leche de la bolsa y por poco se le resbala al suelo. La mete temblorosa al refrigerador y sale desesperada escaleras arriba.

"Anda, Marta, ayúdame", dice Dolores, empuñando su bastón.

"Sí, tía", dice Marta, mientras la levanta del brazo de su sillón y respira su olor a clavo oxidado. Marta está agitada y con trabajo baja a su tía Dolores a la sala, la instala en su sillón preferido, perpendicular al círculo de los otros sillones y sillas. Le trae una galleta con un vaso de leche y sube rápidamente al cuarto que comparte con su tía.

Saca las pastillas de puntitos azules con amarillos y se traga dos. Tal vez hoy necesite tres, piensa, que con la emoción del día, de la malteada, Woolworth, la calle, el regaño, y por si fuera poco al rato llega mi hermana Leti con sus chiquillos. Los niños se portan bastante bien. Pero luego tocan música en el piano y eso le pone tan triste, sobre todo el "Claro de Luna" de Beethoven, no lo aguanta, las tripas se le aflojan por dentro y no quiere sino llorar.

Marta se retoca el maquillaje, dibuja una larga línea negra sobre sus ojos, los labios un rojo castaña. Se echa perfume bajo de las orejas y baja a preparar las botanas.

Mi tía Martita nos trae cacahuates, pedacitos de queso, aceitunas y vasos de orange crush o coca, aunque hoy también nos dieron rompope. Mi tía Martita bebe rompope también. Mi mamá platica con mi tía Dolores que está en su sillón de reina, de ladito. Trae sus lentes oscuros y anda toda de negro, aunque ya hace mucho que se murió su esposo, yo ni lo conocí, dicen que era bien borracho. Mi tía Martita casi no habla, sólo cuando le preguntan algo, nos trae las botanas y se ríe cuando nos ponemos las carpetas que hay en los sillones en la cabeza, como si fuéramos a ir a misa. Mi mamá nos arrebata las carpetas despúes de un rato y nos dice que nos estemos quietos.

Mi tía Dolores habla de lo caro que está todo, de cómo le duelen las manos y ya no puede coser igual que antes, de que ahora sí la van a operar de las cataratas, y de España, de cómo su papá era rico y tenía tierras y se vino a México a hacer más fortuna y de cómo todo es mejor allá. Mi mamá le da la razón en todo porque no le gusta pelear ni contradecir y además es su tía.

Mi tío Rafa baja por las escaleras y nos saluda. Mi tío Rafa y mi tía Martita viven con mi tía Dolores desde que se murió mi abuelo y se vinieron a México desde Celaya. Mi tía Dolores renta además dos cuartos de la casa. A veces hay unos japonesitos, otras veces estudiantes o maestros, pero ella dice que los japonesitos son los mejores, tan educados y ceremoniosos que ni se les siente que están ahí.

Al rato tocamos el piano. Yo toco "El Cisne", "Canción de Primavera", "Para Elisa". Este piano suena mejor que el de la casa porque el techo es bien alto, casi como una iglesia, con un balcón interior, y además es de cola. Está cubierto con una mantilla de España bordada con flores rojas, amarillas y blancas. Mi tío Rafael, de traje café y corbata aunque esté en su propia casa y haga calor, se sienta al piano. No sé qué espíritu le entra cuando toca que aprieta la boca y resopla por la nariz como un caballo desbocado. Levanta la cabeza hacia el techo y cierra los ojos, mientras que da unos acordes endemoniados y no se equivoca ni una vez. Suda y suda y sus dedos se mueven de un lado a otro tocando el "Movimiento Perpetuo", "El Sueño de Amor" y el "Rincón de los Niños". Le aplaudimos con muchas ganas y le pedimos "La Danza del Fuego", "El Estudio Revolucionario", y él sigue tocando, disculpándose que disque no ha tenido tiempo de ensayar pero yo creo que sí ha ensayado pues no se equivoca nunca.

Mi tía Marta tiene una cara como que quiere llorar. Dice buenas noches y sube las escaleras a su cuarto. Dicen que la música la altera mucho, sobre todo cuando Rafael toca "El Claro de Luna", que está mal de los nervios y con la música se pone peor. Me cuelo arriba y la llamo, "Tía Martita, ábreme, no seas malita, y subimos a la azotea a ver a los colipavos todos blancos y esponjados, ábreme, no estés triste". Oigo que repega un mueble contra la puerta, pesado y ronca, ya no puede entrar. "Tía, ¿por qué? ¡Ábreme!"

Ya se encerró, no quiere ver a nadie. Me siento afuera de su puerta y desde el balcón interior veo y oigo a mi tío Rafa dar los últimos acordes del "Claro de Luna": *Luna que te quiebras sobre las tinieblas de mi soledad, ¿adónde vas?* ¿Cómo va esa otra canción? Luna que quiebras el corazón de mi tía, lo haces cachitos, alumbras unos charcos llenos de recuerdos. . .

"¿Qué te hicieron, tía Martita? Dice mi mamá que extrañas a tu papá que murió cuando eras tan joven, ¿es cierto, tía? ¿Te descuacharrangaste todita por dentro? ¿Por qué tienes esos ojos de panda?"

¿Cuándo fue que pensé por primera vez, "mi tía Martita está muerta"? Nunca le dije a nadie.

Benjamín Alire Sáenz

Alligator Park (excerpt)

In 1984 or maybe 1985, I don't remember the year, the years seem far away to me like they never happened, but they happened—I know they happened. Anyway, whatever year it was, I think 1985, we were living in Tecapán and I heard my mother and father talking about all the rumors—I was always listening to other people's conversations—the rumors about the guerrillas. My mother said there was talk, lots of talk about the guerrillas and they were assassinating people. My father shook his head like he already knew it. My mother kept talking about how the guerrillas had begun to bother people and sometimes took them out of their houses and encouraged them to join. I heard those things many times afterwards and I knew it was all true. It was true. They tried, the guerrillas, to convince lots of my friends to fight the government and after a while I didn't see some of them anymore so I guess some of them did join. I don't know, it's confusing, but I do remember those things. I remember those things. I dream about them sometimes but I don't know what the dreams mean, but they scare me and so now I don't pray.

I had a friend of mine, well, not a very good friend, but a friend and he was a teacher at our school. I liked him real well because he liked my ideas and he was very good to us, but he always seemed a little sad even when he laughed. Me and another friend of mine were talking to him before school one day and that day six men came into the school courtyard. The men were all covered up and they had handkerchiefs on their faces and all I could see was their eyes, and the eyes weren't old and the eyes were soft, but they had weapons, maybe rifles, maybe guns—I can't remember—and the men shot and killed our teacher right there in front of us. And the teacher was right in the middle, saying something, but I don't remember anymore what he was saying and I guess it doesn't matter because he just fell. It was the first time I ever saw blood and I saw a lot of it afterwards so now I hate the color red, and the men, the men took some of the students, maybe six of them, all about my age, between ten and fourteen years old because those were the ages of the people who went to our school, and me and my friend, Arturo, ran and hid. What we did was run and hide and I remember thinking that I was going to be dead like my teacher so I ran. Arturo was right behind me and all I could think of was bullets and the eyes of the men. We hid in some fields of a farm outside of our town and we sat there all day until night came and we never said a word.

Jaime put down the notes he'd taken down that morning. He didn't feel like reading any of it anymore. It bothered him. He thought of Franklin and the distant look on his face when he was telling him his story. He had explained to Franklin that political asylum cases weren't easy and that it would take a long time, and the first thing they had to do was write down his story.

"Can't I just tell the judge everything?" Franklin asked.

Jaime tried to explain that everything had to be on paper, and Franklin answered that he couldn't even speak English much less write it.

"I know," Jaime told him, "that's why you have me. You tell me and I'll write everything down, and then I'll put it into English and then we'll fix it all up and organize it so it will all make sense."

"None of it makes sense," Franklin said.

Jaime nodded. "We have to pretend it makes perfect sense. We think that way in the United States." Jaime laughed at his own answer. Franklin laughed, too. They laughed for different reasons.

"Why is your name Franklin?" Jaime asked.

"That's what my mother named me."

Jaime smiled at his answer. He was only a kid, fifteen years old, and already he'd seen everything. But he still didn't know what was behind all the questions. "Yes, I know, but why did she name you that? It doesn't sound like a name from someone who comes from El Salvador. I mean, like my name: Jaime. My parents are Mexican so I have a Mexican name, but 'Franklin'?"

Franklin nodded his head. "Well, my mother joined this new church in our town, a church the gringos started, and one of the elders said Franklin would be a good name when I was born, so my mother named me Franklin like the elder said, but I never went to my mother's church, but I liked my mother, and all I have left of her is the name she gave me." He paused, "If your mother was Mexican, and you were born in the United States, aren't you American?"

"Yes," Jaime nodded, "I'm an American."

"Do you like being an American?"

Jaime popped his knuckles. "Yes," he said, "it's very nice." He lied, but what else was there to say.

Franklin smiled and nodded.

Jaime pictured Franklin as he had looked when he let him in the door that morning. His dark Mayan features impressed him. He carried himself with ease—grace—but when he spoke he almost apologized for it. He showed up at the door saying, "But you don't have to help me if you can't, I understand, it's just that someone said you might help me and they gave me your name and told me where you lived." Franklin had apologized several times before he had even walked in the house. Jaime offered him a cup of coffee and watched in amazement as he poured four spoons of sugar into the cup. He looked around the living room and asked, "Are you rich?"

Jaime thought a minute and said, "Yes, I'm rich. Not rich like the people who own banks but rich enough." If anybody else had asked that question he would have laughed.

Franklin was immediately drawn to all the paintings on the walls. Jaime noticed him staring at them and asked him if he liked them.

Franklin nodded. "Yes, I like them. Did you pay a lot of money for them?"

"No, my brother gave them to me. He's an artist."

"Will he teach me how to paint?"

"I'll ask him if you want."

"And how much do you charge for helping me?"

Jaime thought that Franklin already knew there was no charge since whoever told him to come had also told him his services were free. Perhaps he felt better if he asked the question. "Nothing, I don't charge you anything. You just have to come and sign all the papers, and then when we're ready, my wife, the lawyer, will represent you in court and you can both go before the judge and the judge will decide whether you can stay or not. But once we put in your application you won't have to be hiding from the Migra anymore."

Jaime thought of their morning interview. He looked at the words he'd dictated on the yellow legal pad. He asked himself why he did this, and why he let people like Franklin interrupt his life. He shook his head. He was tired of analyzing himself, and he was sick of other people's insights into his motivations. His mother said it was because he was a good person; his friends said he did these "things" because he was guilt ridden; and his sister said he had a need to do "radical things." "What's the use of asking myself why I do things when I know I'm going to keep on doing them?" he said aloud. He shook his head in disgust. "But they never let any of them stay, anyway. They always get shipped back like unwanted mail." He arched his back and stretched his arms out towards the ceiling. "Maybe this time, we'll win. Sometimes asylums *were* granted, after all. Why shouldn't it be Franklin this time?"

Franklin should be out playing football, he thought, or discovering girls or something like that. He should be doing all those things that fifteen-year-old boys do. Instead, he's hiding from the green vans of the border patrol and coming to perfect strangers asking them for help. He looked at the yellow legal pad and re-read the first paragraph. He made notes on a separate sheet of paper. "I'll need some dates," he whispered to himself. "I'll have to make him remember the exact year, maybes won't do for these kinds of cases. He's going to have to remember the exact day his teacher was killed." He took a few more notes and then put the pad down. He fixed himself a cup of coffee and stared at his brother's paintings. The colors were soothing: Indian blues. He wished Franklin could live inside one of those paintings and live in peace. "Goddamnit! Why did they have to go and name him Franklin?" He took a drink from his coffee cup and fought the urge to have another cigarette.

"What in the hell is a Mayan with a gringo name doing in El Paso?"

1989-90

David Meléndez   **First Prize: Drama**

No Flag (excerpt)

SCENE I

(It is late night on the Gerathy Hill. A small campfire is lit which dances on TONY *and* MIGUEL *who squat down and smoke cigarettes. Various books are scattered about them along with bottles of wine and beer. Both boys are nineteen.* TONY *is short with a stocky body and a thin mustache. His smile is wide, happy and he looks upon* MIGUEL *with hope.* MIGUEL *is tall, thin, with a trusting face but hard eyes. He is brooding and slightly nervous.)*

TONY: *(Putting down a book.)* There are more, Miguelito. Isidro and Georgie-Boy are set. Everyone knows the safe houses if something goes wrong, and if you're caught, not a word without the attorney around.

MIGUEL: I know, I know. I don't want to hear about the plan anymore.

TONY: If they catch us, they are going to kick our ass. But no names, no addresses and nothing about the Gerathy Hill.

MIGUEL: I know, Tony. *(Pause.)* It's quiet tonight. It's hard to understand how things get this quiet. I know something's happening. They're just whispering now.

TONY: You're tired, Miguelito. Tomorrow it will happen.

MIGUEL: Really, they're just whispering. They're whispering it in the ears of their lovers right now. They're whispering about tomorrow. The word's getting around.

TONY: Come on, Miguelito. It will all happen tomorrow. *(Pause.)* I have to tell you something.

MIGUEL: I don't want to talk about the plan, Tony.

TONY: This is not about the plan. *(Pause.)* Miguelito, after this summer, regardless of what happens, I'm leaving City Terrace.

MIGUEL: But, Tony, we have no place to run. Not with all this . . .

TONY: *(Interrupting.)* I have to go. *(Pause.)* I'm leaving for Cuba.

MIGUEL: You can't, Tony.

185

TONY: I have to go. In a way you're right, Miguelito. Even if everything succeeds tomorrow, there will not be a place for me. I can tell. I see it in the others.

MIGUEL: Tony, everyone listens to you and they follow our . . .

TONY: *(Interrupting.)* All I do is help with the message of City Terrace and you're right, Isidro and Georgie-Boy and the others listen to me and they follow what I say, but I am a dark shadow to them. They are afraid of me.

MIGUEL: No they're not, Tony. You're hard on them, but they understand.

TONY: Listen to me, Miguel. I am a dark part of their hearts that they are scared to face. They know I am necessary, but they are still afraid. But you, Miguelito, you have my rage, but it grows in you in a different way. It blooms tender and gentle in you. *(Pause.)* Most of the time, they look at me frightened. I am a demon weed to them.

MIGUEL: Tony, we did this together. We made the plans and. . .

TONY: *(Interrupting.)* It's inside of you now, Miguelito. It's inside of you. This thing has a heart now, Miguelito, one I could never give it. I leave no heart. I pass and leave no trace except for the cinders of my camp-fires.

Tomorrow, Miguelito, if there are cinders on the street, walk through them and leave them alone to soak up the blood of the others. Your mother left, Miguel, and your father's a bastard. *(Pause.)* You have this hill, and tonight you have this fire, and tomorrow you will have the cinders.

MIGUEL: Tony, you can't leave. Not with so much happening. Without you . . .

TONY: *(Interrupting.)* There is you now, Miguelito. That I is why I can leave. This is not my place.

MIGUEL: I don't want to lose sight of you when we're out there tomorrow.

TONY: You won't.

MIGUEL: *(Pause.)* I took my things from the house tonight when my father was gone. *(Laughs to himself.)* Fuck, I'm calling him "my father."

TONY: You're right. He's not your father anymore.

MIGUEL: I'm worried about my little brother.

TONY: Fabian is a good boy.

MIGUEL: He came up to see me today. He brought some sandwiches from the house. I could've cried.

TONY: He'll be alright.

MIGUEL: He took a big chance. You know how the old man is about food and money. *(Pause.)* When he came up, I looked straight at him and, I swear, I couldn't remember what it was like to be ten years old anymore. I'm glad I got out of that house. I'm going to stay here now, in the tent.

TONY: You can't stay here after tonight.

MIGUEL: But the hill . . .

TONY: *(Interrupting.)* They'll come here looking for you. Somebody will get caught and they'll talk about the hill. They'll wait for you. They're going to know about you, Miguelito. You'll have to hide in the projects.

MIGUEL: At Maravilla?

TONY: That's too close. They'll look there first. Go to Ramona Gardens. They'll protect you. I told Isidro and Georgie-Boy. They'll look for you. They'll go anywhere you go.

MIGUEL: This is going to be big, Tony.

TONY: I know.

MIGUEL: *(Pause.)* What we're doing doesn't come from a song or a prayer, Tony. It's instinct. Isidro and Georgie-Boy have that. You have that too.

TONY: Yes.

MIGUEL: Things can become so sentimental around here. There can be nothing sentimental about what we do tomorrow. Nothing optimistic. *(Pause.)* We'll never rest again.

TONY: You have to tell them that.

MIGUEL: Who?

TONY: Everyone at the bottom of the hill.

MIGUEL: *(Pause.)* They don't need us to talk. They need to see us strike up a furnace, and they have to see the light. *(Pause, then plays with the fire.)* I don't want to talk anymore, Tony.

TONY: We are going to be born tomorrow, Miguelito.

MIGUEL: I don't know, Tony. But they're whispering down there. *(Laughs to himself.)* You know those plans we have will last for a few minutes. When we're down there and the smoke comes up and fills our eyes, we'll forget everything.

TONY: That's what I mean, Miguelito. They'll follow you. Even if everything fails, they will look for you.

MIGUEL: *(Pause.)* What can I say to console them? *(Pause.)* They need to hear these whispers.

(BLACKOUT)

SCENE II

(It is the following morning at Los Compadres, a tired little bar in City Terrace. The bar is filled with young men off from work. They are drinking beer and playing pool for money. The bartender, LOUIE, is bored reading a folded newspaper and is unaffected by the chatter of the boys and rancheros playing on the jukebox. LILLY, the waitress, is beginning to age but still has a sturdy, attractive body. She sits at the far end of the bar, smoking a cigarette slowly. From time to time she sways to the songs on the jukebox. It is late afternoon and soon the sun will be going down.)

LILY: *(After a long drag.)* Is there anything good in there, Louie?

LOUIE: Nothing.

LILLY: All those words and there's nothing?

LOUIE.There's something about the guy who killed King.

LILLY: Nothing about César Chávez?

LOUIE: Nothing today.

LILLY: Goddamn it. Anything about those walkouts?

LOUIE: Nothing.

LILLY: Nothing about those kids from Garfield High?

LOUIE: Not today, Lilly.

LILLY: Goddamn it! Then what are these newspapers writing about?

LOUIE: I told you. The guy who killed King.

LILLY: Those newspapers are missing something, Louie. Don't ask me what but something is happening out on those streets. Two days ago I was walking by the Boulevard Theater, and I heard some students whispering out in front. I don't know what they were saying, but they were planning something. You could tell.

LOUIE: How's that, Lilly?

LILLY: You can just tell, Louie. The way they looked around the streets, like they were looking at an old mountain they used to climb. Like someone took away their mountain.

LOUIE: There's no mountain near the Boulevard, Lilly. That's an old street, and in case you can't tell, it's as flat as any other street in town.

LILLY: You know what I mean. You know the way young people look when they dream, and you know what they look like when they get angry. They scared me.

LOUIE: *(Smiling.)* You're beautiful, Lilly. You still bring in customers who want to come in and look at your legs. You can sell anything to anybody when you wear that outfit. You can even sell the pope a double bed. But you're starting to show your age when you talk like that.

LILLY: I get the feeling something's going to happen.

LOUIE: *(Looking up from the paper and becoming slightly irritated.)* What's going to happen, Lilly? What? If something were going to happen, it would say so right here in the paper.

LILLY: I told you those newspaper guys don't know what they're talking about. Did they write about the kids who got beaten up by the cops on Arizona and Third? Did they write about the kids that they took away from East L.A. College last week when they had one of those . . . those. . . . What do you call them? Those sit things.

LOUIE: Sit-Ins.

LILLY: Ya, Louie. That Sit-In stuff.

LOUIE: Of course not. There are bigger colleges doing that with more kids. That's what's gonna get written up.

LILLY: And what about those kids in front of the Boulevard Theater?
LOUIE: Whispers, Lilly. There's nothing in a whisper.

Rubén Benjamin Martínez   Third Prize: Poetry

Plaza Mayor

THE BORDERS

I walk down streets
newly paved and placid,
imagining destruction . . .
walls crack,
ants pour from the fissures,
neons explode in purple flame,
smiles tremble, are torn
by a millenia of teeth,
cars sink into cement
melted by boiling rain,
the hands of clocks fall,
eyes are blinded by firewind,
diaries scream
families hide
words no longer
say hello,
but all around me,
the work continues. . .
sweet tar is brushed
over the mirrors,
mall metal is polished,
the economy purrs content,
sympathetic promises are hissed
while the footsteps of the nation,
heedless of the splintered floorboards,
dance to a frenetic beat.
I imagine these things
when the two worlds
in and outside of me meet:
the complacency of one
destroyed by the urgency of the other,
the death of one
brought to life
by the death of the other. . .
the borders move.

LAGO DE ILOPANGO, EL SALVADOR, 1971
Child with quick
excited steps
nears the lakeshore.
Grandfather, far behind,
net slung over shoulder,
takes two steps
to the boy's eight.
Wavelets lap, birds cry.
Cool morning air
evaporates fast.
Grandfather smiles
the boy's feet slap
the dusty path
clouds of dust
hang in the breezeless air.
Soon, the heat
will suffocate.
A fish breaks
water's surface,
catching the first flash
of dawn.
The sun, orange
with the slightest
tinge of red, slowly
rises over the mountain.

Carlos Nicolás Flores   First Prize: Novel

Cantina del Gusanito (excerpt)

II

" . . . So you plan to stay in Escandón?"

"I don't think I could live elsewhere."

"Américo is a pragmatist," said Porfirio. "A tragedy because he is a highly intelligent man. He could have been a distinguished intellectual."

"Nonsense," Américo sat up in his chair. "If I were a pragmatist, I wouldn't be in Escandón. I would have earned my Ph.D. from Harvard at twenty-five and been working elsewhere. I would have done everything everyone expected me to do, except act on my deepest feelings." He turned to Señor Gallardo. "Getting a Ph.D. meant having to live in the north, possibly stuck up there forever in all that snow. I came to Escandón to get away from the gringos."

Señor Gallardo looked at Américo. "What's wrong with the gringos?"

Américo wished he had kept his mouth shut. Neither Porfirio nor Señor Gallardo had ever understood his feelings about living among the gringos. His companions were Mexicans; he was a Mexican-American. More than a river separated them. "Nothing, except that I didn't fit among them. Porfirio is right. I will never leave Escandón because I hate it too much. Here, every time I wake up in the morning, the thought that I live in Escandón hits me in the face like a chingazo. In the north it's easy to get lost in the delusion that everything is all right. Not here. Here every day the enormous contradiction of what I am and what the border is overwhelms me. Somehow, unless I face it every day, I don't feel alive . . ."

Señor Gallardo shook his head. "It's too bad you feel that way. You shouldn't let anything interfere with your professional advancement. Maybe you'll get an opportunity, a fellowship like the Licenciado's, to complete your doctorate. You're still young. It's never too late."

There were so many things Américo would like to have said but couldn't. He would like to have told them how, during his two years at a university in Dallas, he lay awake late at night listening to radio stations beaming in from the border and swore that once he got back, he would never leave it. He wanted to tell them about the evening he was walking along a street in Dallas on his way to the opera with some Anglo friends and was halted in his tracks by the sound of Mexican music. His friends went on, and he stayed at the small restaurant, listening to the music and eating homemade tortillas. The next year he dropped out of the university and returned to the border.

Américo tried again. "It's taken me a long time to become part of something. I'm just beginning to feel this is where I belong." He grinned. "Where in the north could I find a friend as entertaining as Porfirio Montemayor, a native son of Mexico? Or a cantina as appealing as this one?"

The two men stared at him. Porfirio, then Señor Gallardo, smiled with satisfaction.

II

Porfirio requested a bottle of mezcal. Señor Gallardo looked warily at Américo. A bottle meant that they might be obliged to spend the rest of the afternoon listening to Porfirio's rants. Having noted the hesitation, Porfirio pulled out a wad of pesos and cast them on the table. "I'll pay for the bottle."

Señor Gallardo picked up the pesos, counted them with a serious face, then went behind the bar. He brought a bottle and put it, along with the change, before Porfirio. Resuming his chair he said, with a look of pride, "The best in the house."

Porfirio examined the bottle. "Gracias. I always drink the best. Poetry demands it."

As he poured mezcal in his jigger he added, "Caballeros, if I told you that the worm inside this bottle were alive, that at any moment it might begin wiggling and want to swim out of the bottle, coming out of the bottle's mouth like Frank Sinatra, like that preposterous worm you have painted outside, Señor Gallardo—"

Señor Gallardo chuckled.

"—neither of you would believe me, would you?"

Señor Gallardo, with a subdued smile and his eyes hidden behind his glasses, listened to the rigamarole of metaphors. Américo took out a cigarette.

"Caballeros," said Porfirio again. They waited. He raised his jigger in a solitary toast-like gesture, consumed the fiery liquid, flushed, and then filled the glass again. "Half of my friends are dead."

Porfirio struck a somber note. The smile flickering about Señor Gallardo's mouth subsided. Américo, caught off guard by the unexpected revelation, wondered if Porfirio were up to his old tricks again.

"Some of them, in the early years," Porfirio continued, "died at Tlatelolco. Later, most of them died alone in their apartments in Monterrey, in Mexico City—their skulls split in half by the Mexican government. I fled. I might have been shot at Tlatelolco. I spent the night before the massacre with a woman, a Cuban refugee, and in the morning I was too drunk to be with my dying friends."

Américo had never heard that before. If it were true, Porfirio had been more closely linked to Tlatelolco than Américo had imagined.

"When I found out the government sought me in Monterrey, I returned to Nuevo Escandón. My parents hid me. I survived. I shouldn't have. I became a phantom, worse yet, a worm, like that worm in the bottle, pickled in our famous Mexican bitterness."

"Mine was the generation of '68. Nightly I have asked myself, 'Where did my generation go wrong?' Were we merely sacrificial victims of indigenous avatars, as someone has so pompously written? Today, the most mediocre university students of my generation are rich. Among the best who survived, many are underpaid teachers, irrelevant idealists in these state tecnológicos. I am one of them, having been unofficially pardoned by the government. I am a citizen in good standing as long as I keep my mouth shut."

Américo remembered the late afternoon that Porfirio returned from Monterrey where he had just helped organize a demonstration against the government. When had it been? 1971 or 1972? Porfirio had been standing at the cash register in his parents' discotheque, pleading with his mother for drinking money when Américo walked through the front door. The faces of the latest Mexican and American rack and foil stars filled the posters on the high walls. As they paused on the sidewall outside, Porfirio suddenly raised a clenched fist and growled, "We must always be chingue, chingue, chingue! We must never stop chingando!" Américo had looked upon Porfirio's defiance with morbid curiosity but had seen it for what it was, a lot of posturing.

"For a while," Porfirio went on, "I thought I had become one of the walking dead of the massacre at Tlatelolco. I thought the struggle was over. But today, almost a decade later, something continues to happen upon which the future of everyone on these two continents depends. The current revolutions are the most obvious front of the struggle, and the most violently and simplemindedly opposed. That in itself is remarkable—that there are still people willing to fight and die in what has been described as Latin America's second war of independence."

Though it was difficult to tell what Porfirio's role had actually been, Américo had always been fascinated by this aspect of Porfirio's life. He himself had witnessed the students' protests in Mexico from a great distance—from inside walls of a mental ward of an American military base. The slaughter of hundreds of students by the Mexican government at Tlatelolco had so repulsed him that the event took on the quality of fiction, like the Spanish conquest of the Indians.

"American priests," continued Porfirio, "don Mexican rebozos and their white feet appear in huaraches as they pass out the host with one hand and point to the blood in Central America with the other. Tons of cocaine and marijuana cross the international bridge every week, headed straight for the American soul, an unstoppable subversion if there ever was one. The signs are everywhere. Even the Indians have read it in the stars; they have recorded it in their myths and codices. Volcanic eruptions, earthquakes, unheard of and incurable diseases. In this hemisphere, we are not talking about a stupid little bedraggled revolution, with sombreros, huaraches, and cartucheras. We are talking of nothing less than the Revolution of the Americas, a crisis and a change of such a magnitude that history will make a left turn where we expected it to go right. But," he paused, his eyes shimmered, "to speak about the Revolution of the Americas is like speaking about that worm seeking its liberation from that bottle of mezcal. No one believes it. No one expects it."

Porfirio fell silent and drank his liquor slowly. Américo thought of something he wanted to say, but he picked up his Tecate instead. Across the bar throbbed the electronic hysteria of the Dallas Cowboys game, the air conditioner, and the inexhaustible jukebox.

Graciela Limón
Third Prize: Short Story

Concha's Husband

The night was a dark, sultry August evening filled with the dampness of the Jalisco highlands after a heavy storm. The year was 1923. Outside of Concha's tiny house the cobblestones reeked with the acrid odor of litter and droppings of mules and horses. Now and then a dilapidated old Ford could be heard lumbering down the street, and its driver—a stranger in town, no doubt—wondered why so many people were crowding into the doorway dimly lit by a yellowish, fly-speckled light bulb.

It was the wake of Concha's husband. The dark figures stepped in from the gloomy night, each silhouette filing past Concha's hunched-over form whose face was hardly visible, hidden as it was by her black shawl. Beside her sat four boys. The last was so young that he still sucked his thumb. He was looking around him without understanding that his father had been dispatched to reckon with his maker just that morning.

"*Señora, lo siento mucho.* My deepest sympathy for you and your little sons. They've lost their father and you have lost your husband. *¡Qué pena!* Life has so much suffering but God is good and only He knows why these things happen."

"*¡Qué vergüenza,* don Doroteo! That husband of hers was terrible, and just look at her. She weeps as if the most virtuous of all men had just died. If I were in her place I would shout with joy. *¡Qué vergüenza!* He was a good for nothing! He . . . *Sí, sí,* I know that the dead are to be left to God. Well, he's dead and gone and I'm sure he's burning in hell."

The townspeople squeezed into the uncomfortably small room where the body was laid; and since there were but a few of that town's inhabitants who had not known the dead man, the room was packed beyond its capacity. Both men and women vividly remembered Concha's husband, so that now that he was dead each one of them had his or her own reason to take one last look at their town's greatest womanizer.

Memories filled the small room to the brim. The women's recollections were charged with the shame of having succumbed to lust, a strong sense of guilt which then mingled with the desire to do it all over again, if only for one more time. On the other hand, the men's thoughts were filled with the wrath felt by those cheated. It was an anger also filled with gloating; a pleasure in knowing that at last someone had laid Concha's husband in his grave, just as he deserved. Some of those men, however, had to admit that they were secretly jealous of Concha's husband because he had possessed that mysterious something that made women come panting after him just as if they had been dogs in heat. As those dark-skinned men with drooping mustaches looked down upon the body, they remembered the dead man's unsightly buck-toothed smile that had seduced so many of the town's beauties, and they were torn between hate and envy.

"*Bueno para nada,*" came a murmur from a bearded clenched jaw.

"*Pero se te cae la baba, ¿verdad? Ya quisieras tú tener lo que él tuvo,*" was the response from another tight mouth.

On the other hand the women . . . ah, the women, theirs was another story, because what memories were harbored deep within those hearts! That night the town's females encircled the body like a ring of black crows, each woman believing that she had been the one and only of the dead man's loves. Concha's husband had been that way; he had the gift, the knack, the magic, because no matter if the woman were young or middle-aged, he had only to look into her eyes, and inexplicably she began to sigh and purr like a cat ready to mate. The truth was that in that bleak town there were hardly any virgins left because Concha's husband had lain with just about every eligible woman and girl. Fat and fragile, young and unmarried, old and married, with many children even, Concha's husband had been a *chingón*; he had enjoyed them all.

Most prominent of the weeping circle that surrounded the dead body was the matron with heavy breasts, the one who now wept inconsolably and who was nearly twenty years older than Concha's husband. He had one day surprised her behind the chicken coop, but he had only to place his warm hands on her drooping breasts before she hung out her tongue and said, "*Sí, sí.*" What happened next was so sinful and lecherous that if her old baker of a husband ever suspected even the half of it, he most surely would roast her in one of his ovens. But ah, even now the heavy-breasted older woman still felt herself go wet just looking down at the dead body of Concha's husband.

Next to the matron stood the beautiful young daughter of the mayor, and anyone could see that she was barely this side of being a child. What a plum she would have been for the young man standing beside her who even now was looking forward to a life of respectability and reasonable success in that town of small men shackled to miserable patches of stony earth. What a prize that young, convent-bred girl would have been to any man. But no, unknown to that ambitious young man, Concha's husband had robbed him of such a liberation from the doldrums of wretchedness, because that young man was destined soon to discover on the night of his marriage that his beautiful young wife was incomplete, that he had received a damaged package, that the goods were tainted, and he would be laughed at, scoffed and mocked. Pitiful, ambitious young man. The worst was that as he stared down at the body of Concha's husband, that young man did not yet realize that he, just like the rest of the men in the room, had been plundered and that the thief was Concha's husband.

It should be told that it happened to the mayor's daughter as it always happens to the innocent—unknowingly. It came on a Sunday morning when she had left the church after mass and had stopped to gaze at the beautiful flowers that were being offered to her by an old Indian woman, flowers that were a perfect buy for the day. All of a sudden, out of nowhere one hand extended the coins to the *vieja*, while the other offered the flowers to the mayor's young daughter. When she looked up she saw bright buckteeth and a smile so different, so enticing that she had no other alternative but to accept the flowers.

The next thing she knew they were behind the church's sacristy, back there where no one ever goes, and she was allowing Concha's husband to lift her skirt. The nuns in her school had forever admonished against such a thing, but there was nothing the mayor's daughter could do to stop what was happening. When it first began, pain shattered her virgin's body, but it was nothing compared to the delight that followed, and the mayor's daughter loved what was happening. She loved this man with long teeth, and while she was feeling all that pleasure, she thought that the poor convent sisters had been wrong, misinformed and cheated.

Standing very close to the mayor's daughter within the weeping circle was the Indian girl from no one-knew-where. However, it was known in the town that the girl had several brothers, rough, taciturn, knife-carrying Indios who kept a close account of their sister's goings and comings. She was Concha's maid, because even though the house was small there were four boys for whom Concha had to care, the meals to prepare, the clothes to wash in the river, and so many other chores to which attention had to be given. Yes, a maid was necessary just for those demands. But there was yet another important reason for a maid in Concha's house; her husband was an inspector for the tequila distillery in the capital city, and in that town of plain men of hardened, calloused hands, a man of stature such as Concha's husband, of course, had to have a maid in his house.

It had happened with the Indian girl just as it had with the others: unexpectedly, quickly. One day she was making the tortillas for the noon meal when she suddenly felt a warm breath on the back of her neck, and when she turned her head to see what it was, there was Concha's husband with his alluring front teeth shining in the kitchen's gloom. He whispered something into her ear, and slowly, as if welded together, they edged towards one of the darker corners of the dingy kitchen. Then it happened, right there on the chilly tile floor, and the Indian girl had never felt so much pleasure in her life, even though she was remembering all the while that the tortillas were burning.

So it was that those women, old and young alike, stood around the dead body of Concha's husband, each one remembering, each one wishing that it could happen again. It had been worth it all, they thought, even for those who had been unmarried and unable to explain from where the child—for there were many children—had come. In truth, it was impossible to tell just how many of the children that crowded the church's schoolroom were unknowingly brothers and sisters. All anyone knew was that the children were orphans if their mother was unmarried, or if the mother was married, that its father was a man to whom the child bore no resemblance at all. What those countless children could not know because they were as yet innocent and ignorant, was that they all looked uncannily alike, and that they in turn all looked like Concha's husband. It had to be admitted even by the town's

Doubting Thomases; most of the children—girls and boys—had the same face, which gleamed with the well-known overhanging front teeth.

And if the women were as yet yearning for Concha's husband even now at his *velorio*, the men, as it is already known, were a different tale because most of them, if not all of them, hated the now dead man. Indeed, they had reason to feel nothing less than loathing for Concha's husband because had he not truly cheated them of their honor? Had not Concha's husband deprived each man of his claim to be the one and only macho of the town? Every one of those men had taken pride in the women he had conquered, the many girls he had seduced. Each one at one time or another had boasted to the other men of the town, "*Quítate, que aquí viene mi gallo.*" But for those bitter men the unforgivable truth was that it had been Concha's husband who had made them all look like pale little girls at a First Communion ceremony. It had been he who had run off with the coveted prize of being number one with the women of the town. Most degrading to those coarse men was that for them the man now laid out dead on the cold kitchen table had been nothing less than a disgusting office worker. Those men who were creatures of the land, tough and weathered, proud of their ability to take pain, of their capacity to get drunk and sing all night long with the mariachi, and to rule in their home as proud as fighting cocks—they had been made to look tame by that buck-toothed *catrín* whose nails and hands looked more like those of a woman than of a real man.

Concha's husband had enemies, many enemies, who wanted him dead and who now looked about curiously wondering who had been the real *valiente* who had pulled the trigger on the good-for-nothing. Those cuckolded husbands, those duped young men who had dreamed that they would be the first to gain entrance into that beautiful young thing, those dishonored fathers and brothers, all hated Concha's husband—and envied him. But they begrudged the hidden hand that had killed the lecherous dog even more; that unknown someone who had blown out his brains with a Remington revolver and set all the women to weeping, and the men to thanking God for taking the prowler off the streets of their town forevermore.

In that humid, impoverished Jalisco town, no night had ever been as the night of the *velorio* of Concha's husband. In the dim light of the smoking kerosene lamp the features of the old baker, of the owner of the *tiendita*, of the town's only mail clerk, and of all the other men who daily broke their back in a futile attempt to clear a wretched crag of earth so as to plant *maíz* or *frijol*, all those faces looked like yellow, hardened Indian masks rather than faces of flesh. Their eyes were slits, sharp slanted gashes as in the faces of ancient oriental nomadic peoples whose taut bronze skin clung to faces marked by high cheekbones and wide, tight lips that betrayed an ancestral demand to be avenged.

Every one of those men had desired the death of Concha's husband with all the energy and strength of his heart. Each could have been the one to rid that town of its scourge, but only one of them had been macho enough to pull the trigger. Each man knew it, and inwardly hated himself for not being the one destined to bring tranquility to this town of black-shawled weeping women.

As for Concha, time seemed to reverse itself, transporting her back to her early youth. She was at that moment remembering when she had first met her husband. No, he had not been handsome in the sense that most people think of the word but there had been something about him that had captivated her; it could have been the way he walked and carried himself, or perhaps the manner in which he looked into her eyes. Now that Concha was reminiscing, she was almost certain that it was her husband's smile, a mouth filled with teeth, that had most fascinated her.

Concha's husband had entered her life when she was barely fifteen years of age. He hadn't been much older; perhaps five or six years beyond Concha's age. But even then he already had a reputation for his womanizing, and it had been Concha's father that had admonished her against any relationship with such a type. But Concha's father's words were useless because by the time they were uttered it was too late. Not that anyone should think that Concha had done anything wrong or had been intimate or any such thing, but rather that she was by then in love beyond words with that young man. She was, as she at the time told her confessor in church, dying of love.

So Concha's husband was married. It must be said that when he married Concha he did so for the first time, because by the time his brains were blown out years later, the record incontestably proved that he had married several women after Concha—without the benefit of divorce—because Concha's husband, among other things, had also been a bigamist.

During those first years after her marriage, Concha had been happy with her husband. She liked the way he showered her with affection and attention, and the way in which he sweetly addressed her as "*mi reina.*" In the beginning Concha felt confident that her father most certainly had been wrong in rebuking her husband, who brought her fresh-cut flowers daily and constantly smiled his charming smile. Yes, Concha had been very happy for that first brief period.

But then it happened. Concha got pregnant, and very soon she began to puff up and to wobble about in a most ungainly manner. It was at that time that her husband one day failed to come home; he neither left a note nor took a stitch of clothing with him. Besides being shocked beyond words Concha was devastated, as it can be imagined, especially when she was told by the town's gossip mongers that her husband had run away with don Lencho's wife. Don Lencho was the proprietor of the only *cantina*, and to make things worse those same wagging tongues informed Concha that don Lencho's wife had not been loose, but rather a model of virtue up until the time she saw the well-known grin of overhanging front teeth aimed at her. After that the tavern keeper's wife seemed to be paralyzed, as if she had been stung by a poisonous scorpion. When those same tell-tales saw the woman leave on the morning milk wagon, they saw that she was enraptured with love as she was held tightly in the arms of Concha's husband.

So Concha had no other alternative but to return to her father's home, where she was given a sermon sternly warning her against the weaknesses of her sex and the many temptations that come to a married woman who is alone. She stayed with her father as she awaited the birth of her child, which came shortly thereafter. Concha gave birth to a fat little boy who in time looked just like his father.

Thus did the years pass for Concha. One day when her boy was three years of age, and while she was buying tamales at the town bakery, Concha was suddenly shocked by the force of two male arms which enveloped her from behind, wrapping themselves around her waist like two mighty ropes. When she was able to wiggle around to face her attacker, her heart knew no end to its joy when she realized that it was her husband. Concha's husband had returned and she would no longer be alone in her valley of tears. She opened her arms and her whole being to her husband and, since don Lencho had quietly slipped out of town several years before, there was no one to even ask as to the whereabouts of the love-smitten *cantina* keeper's wife.

Concha once again set up house with her smiling, affectionate husband and boy, resuming the serene life they had led before she had been struck by pregnancy for the first time. But how true is the saying that we're born to weep and moan in this wicked world, because Concha's happiness was short-lived and her cross once more became an intolerable burden to bear when she again found herself to be with child. When her body once more became puffy and bloated, yes, Concha's husband again disappeared, this time with one of the nuns that taught the town's girls how to sew and stitch baby clothing. Concha wept many bitter tears because she desperately missed her husband's hypnotic smile and his tender caresses.

When she returned to her father's house to give light to her second child—who with the passage of time also inherited his father's face—Concha was obliged by her father to pack her and her boys' few belongings, and along with her father to emigrate north to the land of the *gringos*. When they arrived in Los Angeles, Concha was able to find work making ladies' girdles, thus paying for the considerable amount of food required by her two fat children. But when the old hags say *"Dios los hace y ellos se juntan"* how wise are their words, because when the second of Concha's boys was no more than two years of age, the poking front teeth and soft fondlings again made their way back into Concha's life. It mattered little that she and her family were in a strange land far from Jalisco, and it mattered even less that they were surrounded by strangers, because her husband nonetheless found her. And since her heart had no limit to its love for her husband and because she was the essence of patience, she happily took him once again to her breast, even though this time her actions occasioned her father to suffer a seizure that caused him to die in his sleep one night.

Soon after that sad event it became apparent to all that Concha's husband had found himself to be a plant without roots in the lifeless land of the *gringos*. Once again Concha was compelled to pack her and her boys' things into a small cardboard suitcase, and along with her husband they responded to an ad in the newspaper that offered free car transportation back down to Jalisco, in exchange for sharing the task of driving an old Packard touring car.

The little family, along with the old *gringo* gentleman who owned the shabby and worn car, trudged first in an easterly direction on the American side toward Nogales, a small town straddling both Arizona and Sonora. The tiny party crossed the border there and continued on to Cananea, a rocky, barren town which is still in the state of Sonora, then on to Jalisco. In all it was a slow, harsh and hazardous journey, but Concha's husband flashed his smile during the arid daytime, and at night he murmured soft words into her ear as they made love in a small tattered canvas tent that flapped in the howling desert winds.

Now at her husband's *velorio*, as Concha sat looking upon his body, his head sheathed in bandages so that the three gunshot wounds would remain unseen, she recalled those incidents of so many years ago. She found, however, that inexplicably the years that followed their trek south blurred, and that the details were not as clear as the first part of her memories. She remembered, of course, that after their wanderings up there in *el norte*, she, her husband and her two boys had returned to their former town where they once again set up house, and where her husband returned to the job at the distillery. Her memory recollected that those years also brought two more pregnancies, each separated of course by the easily foretold absences of her husband. Concha could no longer tell who the women or the girls had been, but she, like everyone else in the town, knew that her husband had again managed to seduce and fill that woman or girl with wild promises of love.

Through it all, Concha had remained steadfast, forbearing, and above all virtuous because, not surprisingly, she sometimes suffered from the pangs of temptation during the long absences of her husband. She, even now as her husband was about to be buried, was not an old woman. On the contrary, she was yet a young woman filled with the drives of her sex, and it must be said that Concha was beautiful. She, however, fought off those demons and forced herself never to take notice, much less respond to the few but ardent advances aimed in her direction by some of the town machos. The truth was that she was more than irreproachable in goodness; Concha was a woman in love. She was in love with the soft voice, the purred words, the seducing front teeth. Concha was in love with the nights she spent with her husband and she gladly would have given anything to spend the rest of her life having buck-toothed, fat little boys if only she could have prevented her husband from vanishing each time she was afflicted by pregnancy.

And of course it happened again—her husband's disappearances, that is— because even after her fourth little boy was born, and even though at the time she hadn't been pregnant, despite that, it had happened once more. It should be told, however, that Concha's husband really did not entirely clear out on that occasion, not the way in which he had done previously. Oh, he left Concha's bed and house, most certainly, but upon that last time Concha's husband did not bother to leave town. Instead he remained in full view living sinfully with a married mother of five children he had lured from the neighboring town of Arandas.

Even now at the wake, when the Remington revolver had done its work, now when Concha knew that the room was swirling with the murmurings and the hate-filled thoughts of transgressed men and women; even now, Concha still reeled under the weight of her confusion at the thought of his brazenness and gall, because the truth was that her husband had never before committed such an overt deed. And even though she refused to admit the painful truth, yet the wagging tongues had informed her of the couple's open violation of moral decency. Concha had been told in detail of how both her husband and the other woman promenaded in the town plaza, and of how they fondled and kissed one another publicly. Concha also had been fully apprised of the anger of the town's men and women—especially those women who, like Concha, were still in love with her husband.

"*Señora, lo siento mucho.* My deepest sympathy for you and for your small sons." Concha was torn from her trance by the repeated words of condolences. "Believe me, *señora*, it must have been a case of mistaken identity, or perhaps it was a matter of envy because your husband was such a diligent inspector. It could be that perhaps he even refused a bribe. At any rate, *señora, lo siento mucho.*"

The hollow, condoling voices droned on and on with words that were meaning the opposite of what they uttered; words that were really saying that, yes, her husband deserved to die; that, yes, it surely must have been the hidden hand of a justifiably outraged father or husband or brother that had surprised the seducing jackal that morning as he stood waiting to cross a street. The muffled murmurs added to Concha's fatigue, filling her with an enormous desire to be left alone, to return to her solitude, to think and to remember. The yellow-brown faces whirled about her. The air in the room was rancid and stifling. It seemed to Concha that the women glared at her accusingly. Their looks seemed to place the full burden of blame upon her shoulders. She, who had been a loving, patient and forgiving wife. She, who had faced all rebuke and criticism and chastisement for the sake of her husband, now it was as if she were being held responsible by those jealous females for the demise of their prowling debaucher.

The kerosene in the lamp began to empty, the wick sputtered and the light diminished. Men with large calloused hands took hold of their women and slowly the cortège of black shadows receded and the room began to empty. *"Buenas noches, señora Concha." "Hasta mañana en el entierro." "Qué Dios la bendiga y la guarde una santa."* The funeral silhouettes made their way past the makeshift bier, past what used to be Concha's husband, past the four fat boys, past Concha. Slowly and with much hesitancy did the town's men and women leave the side of the prostrate and bullet-riddled body of Concha's husband.

"Fue un cabrón," was the last muttered, muted insult cast upon the dead body.

Concha was finally left alone with her four boys. Her head was swimming with the day's events. Her body ached and yearned for rest. As she silently walked about the gloomy house locking doors and securing window shutters, she longed to forget that her husband's body would remain under the same roof with her. That thought made Concha anticipate the next day's sunlight with all her soul. Perhaps in the morning matters would look better, possibly life would hold out a different path for her.

She put her four fat, toothy boys to bed and entered her room. Concha's forehead was cold and clammy, as if the hand of death had laid a caress upon it, and her eyes were inflamed from weeping. She removed all her clothing and stood naked as on the day of her birth, remaining that way for awhile; perhaps for a minute, perhaps for an hour. Then she stooped over and picked up the bundle of ugly black clothing and took it to the wardrobe, which she opened silently and carefully. There on the bottom shelf was another packet, one carefully wrapped in an old canvas bag. As the young widow placed her mourning clothing down with one hand, she picked up the other wrappings, and with both hands unfolded it. It was the Remington revolver that her father had given her shortly before his death. His soft words still echoed in her memory, "Take this gun, *m'ija.* One never knows the future. I've taught you how to use it. Maybe the day will come when you'll see yourself forced to use it."

Concha skillfully and deliberately clicked open the gun's chamber, and she saw that it was almost in the same condition as when her father had given it to her all those years before. It was the same, except for one detail: after this morning, there were three bullets missing.

Concha clutched the weapon with both hands, leaned her aching, feverish head against the closet door and whispered, *"Mañana será otro día."*

1990-91

Manuel Ramos

The Ballad of Rocky Ruíz (excerpt)

CHAPTER ONE

> *Ojitos bonitos*
> *que me están acabando*
> *ojitos bonitos*
> *que me están matando*
>
> *"Ay, ojitos"*

I don't recall all the subtleties and particulars and some of the events are screwed up in my head—out of sequence, out of synch. Hell, there were too many late nights and fuzzy mornings, and even back then I had a hard time keeping it straight. Life had this rough texture, like Velcro on a screen door. But there is one detail that stands out in my mind as clearly as if I was staring at her this minute, across the room, waiting for her to finish taking off her clothes. Those eyes—the round, moist, glowing brown eyes that will haunt me as sure as *la llorona* prowls dark alleys looking for bad children; eyes that will stay with me until Chicanos reclaim their lost land of Aztlán—forever. There are days when I look over my shoulder and I catch them watching me, driving me up the wall, chilling my skin, making me forget every other woman I knew or met or loved. I know those eyes.

And the blood. I remember the blood. . . .

Toby Arriega's jury came back in about forty-five minutes—guilty on enough counts to send him away for at least another eight years, maybe a little more if the judge hammered him with aggravations.

The trial had exhausted me. I was too old for this—taking on work simply because it walked in the door, busting my butt trying to find a witness to back up Arriega's alibi, pouring over police reports, talking to the names listed by the D.A., calling Toby's brothers and sisters for help, piecing together a defense out of nothing, and getting paid just enough to keep me on the hook until the trial was over. Then the damn jury took less than an hour to decide my effort was worthless.

It was a tough case from the beginning. I didn't particularly care for my client or his relatives. They were a hoodlum bunch from the Westside and they knew more about the criminal justice system than most judges. They had no qualms about cussing out their lawyer in the courthouse hallway.

I suggested to Toby that he cop out to one of the assault charges, but the old con would not go for it. He was already a two-time loser—what the hell did he care? He knocked over the convenience store, of course. What I couldn't understand was why he beat up the clerks and trashed the place. Toby denied the rough stuff and said wrecking the joint was the work of a kid, maybe one of the clerks, or another stickup man, angry that Toby beat him to the punch—in any case, it wasn't Arriega. But I couldn't prove that. The clerks fingered Toby, said he locked them up in the back room and pistol-whipped them before he rampaged through the aisles of dog food, loaves of bread, and comic books. And Detective Philip Coangelo finished the job with a very crisp and formal recitation of the incriminating remarks Toby had made when they busted down his door and dragged him away to the city jail.

I ended up in the Dark Knight Lounge, hunched over bourbon and beer, fed up with my scraggly assed existence as a borderline lawyer who represented guys who should have gone to the public defender, or housewives who finally had had it with their fat and usually unemployed husbands. Yes, I was feeling sorry for myself, almost as sorry as Toby would feel when they shackled him in the van for the long, quiet ride to Cañon City and the State Pen. At least he knew what he would be doing, and where he would be doing it, for the next several years. I didn't have a clue.

I finished my shot and ordered another, nursing the beer. My gut burned with the liquor's acid. My bones, from eye sockets to ankles, were sore. You'd think Toby had worked me over after the verdict came in. It was only my forty-one-year-old body letting me know, in the cute way it had, that I drank too much, ate all the wrong foods, represented too many of society's dregs, and let the little tensions of life overwhelm me. I stared into the bottom of the empty shot glass, looking for a sign, a hint, anything that might lead me into tomorrow with more than a hangover and an empty wallet.

"You look lousy, Luis. Ain't no big thing, man. It couldn't be that bad." Tino Pacheco wasn't exactly what I had in mind. He was an old friend —damn, who wasn't?—but I had a hard time handling more than a few minutes with him. Unfortunately, Tino would hook into a person for days —months—and his edgy, tough-guy act eventually rubbed off on whoever was with him. Tino had this influence on people. He had a way to make a person talk and act crazy.

Our hands met in a half-hearted attempt at the Chicano handshake, but we didn't quite remember all the intricacies. "Tino. Long time. What's up?"

I put up with Tino because of the old days. When we were young, Tino and I had ended up crawling on the floor more than a few times, usually after a dirty, ugly fight in a bar where the white kids were too sensitive for Tino's insults or the Chicano brothers decided they had had their fill of him.

He had a gleam in his eyes, like mica dust, and he was either higher than a kite or in love. I was drunk enough to be amused. He pushed the girl in my direction, and I knew that Tino's problem was not drugs, not right then. He hung on to a Chicana many years younger than either of us. I checked her out, not expecting much, and I was pleasantly surprised. In the shadowy smoke- and alcohol-induced glaze of the bar, I saw that Tino finally had done something right.

Long, black hair framed a thin, seductive neck. Her slender body snuggled against Tino with the right bit of casualness to whet my curiosity.

"Luis, old buddy, I want you to meet Teresa Fuentes. She just graduated from law school, man. A lawyer like you. This is the guy I was telling you about, baby, Luis Montez. Attorney-at-law and old-time revolutionary pal of mine."

I looked at her face and, you know how it is, there are times when the people, atmosphere, and emotions all come together at the right instant, and you swear that life really is fine after all. The four black musicians on the small, barely lit stage kicked off their last set with a moody, bluesy jazz harmony that set exactly the right tone. The bourbon cruised my system, mellowing out the rough parts and tricking me into thinking that the city was the only way to go. And I stared into the most beautiful pair of eyes I had seen in years of chasing every manner and style of woman, tearing apart two marriages and who knows how many affairs, living through broken hearts and breaking a few, too. But those eyes turned me into a twenty-one-year-old loco, a dude on the prowl, and the world again was inhabited by beautiful, sensual women. The most beautiful, the most sensual was right there in front of me, rubbing her thigh against macho Tino, to be sure, but now she had met me, and, if Tino was pendejo enough to steer her my way, well, ése, así es la vida, man.

She offered her dark, manicured hand and I took it, compared its color to mine—almost a perfect match—rubbed it, and held it for a few seconds more than was appropriate. She smiled at me and about ten years of crust fell off my skin. "Very nice to meet you, Mr. Montez. I've heard a lot about you." I assumed from Tino, which meant I already could be trash in her eyes.

"Luis will do, Teresa. And don't believe anything Pacheco tells you unless he can produce two witnesses, unrelated." Tino socked me in the arm—"Hey, bud, don't give Teresa the wrong idea"—and a puzzled, worried look creased her forehead. I wanted to touch her face, to assure her that the thing between Tino and me wasn't serious, that it had started somewhere back in the history of our lives too ancient to remember. I massaged the charley horse in my shoulder left by Tino's punch. The guy always had been a pushy son of a bitch.

The night turned into a hazy, gritty smear of strong drinks, loud music, and smoky bars. We bounced around from one joint to another, Teresa drinking one for the three Tino and I guzzled. She was quiet, aloof, and I appreciated the way she surrounded herself with mystery. I tried to stay cool, but I was lost in the booze and every ten minutes or so I caught myself wanting to grab her and kiss her and rush her away to my place.

I couldn't ditch Tino, and the longer the night lasted the more belligerent and hostile he became. A half dozen times I had to pull him away from some guy he was going to bust in the mouth, or from the victim of one of his unprovoked verbal assaults who was ready to clobber him with a beer bottle. It was obvious he was trying to impress Teresa, but all she gave him was an occasional hug or a little kiss on the cheek and plenty of exasperated sighs. I guess it was enough for him.

Lolly's Taco Shack on West Thirty-Second Avenue has the best jukebox in town—James Brown and Los Gamblers, Al Green and Freddy Fender. At three in the morning, it's usually crowded with Mexicans whooping it up from the dance at the G.I. Forum hall, suburbanites tasting the edge, and professionals celebrating the fact that everything has gone their way. Teresa and I ended up at Lolly's to put a cap on the night with something other than alcohol. We munched away at menudo, enchiladas, and green chile, listening to a background of kitchen noises and the excited babble of culturally deprived white folks soaking up the color and smells of Denver's Little Mexico.

I tried small talk, but my concentration was shot. Those eyes. I would start to say something and then realize I had been staring at her in silence, taken in by the flashes of color and midnight deep in her eyes, and finally, awkwardly, I would look away or say something stupid.

I figured it was safe to ask about Tino, since he had passed out in the backseat of my car. "How long have you known Pacheco? He doesn't seem to be the type that would be in your circle." The cloud that passed over her face told me I had again turned to stupidity when I had nothing else to say.

"Exactly what is my circle?" Something about my half-hearted attempt to insinuate she lived in a separate, more refined world upset her.

"Okay, okay. How about a simple how did you meet Tino?"

She shrugged, took her time about answering. "He's my landlord, if you can believe that. After the job offer from Graves, Snider and Trellis, I asked around about an apartment, a quiet place to study for the Bar exam. When I finished school, I moved up here quick, without much. Someone at the office told me about the Corsican Plaza. Tino's asked me out every week since I've been there, but I was so into the Bar, I didn't do anything else for two months. That's over now and I needed to unwind . . . so I took him up on his offer. And here we are." She smiled like a kid who had found a shiny new quarter in the sofa.

Before I lost myself again, I tried talking. "Tino's a little intense, sometimes. I've known him for a long time. He's basically all right. Loyal. Does the best job he can." I wanted to tell her old Movement stories, brag about our days as Chicano radicals fighting cops and university deans. I let it go. The old days are harder and harder for me to drag up, especially with a young sweetheart scarcely old enough to remember the big names like César Chávez and Corky Gonzáles, let alone care about the grunts of the revolution.

"Sure. I don't have a problem with Tino. He reminds me of my brothers in Brownsville. Talks and struts just like them. A Chicano." That explained that.

She must have been at the top of her class. Had to be close to coax a rise out of the old guys at Graves, Snider and Trellis. The offer was most likely contingent on her passing the Bar. She didn't seem fazed by that. She really was relaxed almost mellow and I was knocked out by her attitude. After I took the Bar exam, it was a month before I could relax, before I quit rehashing the questions and rewriting the answers in my head, convinced I had blown it. And I did not have the pressure of the best job I had ever been offered riding on the results. I was headed for the legal-aid office and the poor and under-privileged—if I could pass the damn Bar. Teresa had already forgotten about the exam.

She would be the first minority woman in the firm, so a certain amount of stress would come with the package. Little things like advising the most racist client one of the unhappy partners could steer her way, or fighting off the heavy-handed sexual maneuvers of her colleagues. But if she showed any ability at all, she'd have it made for the rest of her professional career, provided she didn't mind representing insurance companies and corporate employers, and counseling rich codgers about taxes and estates. Several years before, I would have railed at her about selling out, but I didn't have that in me anymore and, as far as I was concerned, she was far too beautiful to argue about political questions that had been debated again and again before she was born or when she was a kid.

"Is your family still in Texas?"

"My mother and one of my brothers are down there. Everybody else has spread out around the country."

"You'll like Denver, Teresa. It's a beautiful city, plenty going on these days. Not much like Texas, though, particularly Brownsville."

I bet myself that she was a good daughter of a traditional Chicano family. Fluent in Spanish—knew about vatos and cruising and the Chicano male-role playing that her brothers must have shown off whenever they had a chance. A woman I could fall for, forget the eyes.

With some women, you think you know exactly what is going on in their heads; you see it in their faces, the way they wrinkle their foreheads, or frown at the corners of their mouths, though often you cannot do anything about what you think you know. Surprise, or joy, or the hurt is right there and it helps clumsy slobs like me deal with them. We struggle to overcome the disadvantage we have whenever we are in the company of women who turn our blood to frozen honey.

Teresa offered no such help. I had not learned the kinds of things I wanted to know about her and she gave up nothing about herself unless I asked. She would be good in court or across the conference table. Opposing counsel would pay trying to figure her out before she lowered the boom. I promised myself to avoid that situation.

The eyes—shining in the restaurant's bright white lights, creating lewd and wonderful visions in my imagination about what the two of us could do with each other. They flared up again at the mention of her hometown. I dipped a piece of tortilla in my menudo and pretended to eat.

"Have you been down there, Luis?"

"Years ago. When I was in college. I had a friend from San Benito. He took me through Texas when we were out on the road. A little Chicano roots trip to Mexico and other points south. Long time ago. Maybe you know his family. His name was Ruben Ruíz. We called him Rocky. You know anybody named Ruíz?"

For the first time that night, she missed a beat. She tried to shovel food in her mouth and answer at the same time, and it didn't work. Her spoon rattled on her plate. The beers were finally catching up.

"No. Not from down home. I don't know any Ruíz. But you're absolutely right. Denver is nothing like Brownsville." She reached across the table and grabbed my hand. "I should go home, Luis. I think I've had it, probably overdid it my first night out since I've been locked up with my Bar outlines and law books. And we have to take Tino home."

I held on to her hand. "Right. Good old Tino. We can drop him at his favorite corner. He's used to sleeping it off in the gutter."

Twenty-five minutes later, as I half-carried, half-dragged him into her apartment and then plopped him on her couch, I seriously wondered why we hadn't thrown him in the street. Then I reminded myself that we were buddies, carnales, revolutionary comrades, and it would not do to toss him away, no matter how much of an asshole he was, no matter how much I wanted to tell Teresa that we needed to learn more about each other and why didn't I spend the night and show her how sweet an older Chicano with about ten drinks over his limit can be, given the opportunity.

"You sure he'll be okay here? I can take him to my place, let him sleep it off on my back porch. You hardly know this guy."

She laughed as she threw a blanket over the snoring lump. "Quit worrying. He's my landlord. I see him every day. His apartment is one floor under mine. If we knew what he did with his key, we could take him to his place. It doesn't make sense for you to cart him around town so you can bring him back here in the morning. It'll be all right. I can take care of Tino." I left knowing damn well that she could and thinking that Tino better not try anything with her once he came out of his stupor. Something about the strength of Texas women had always brought out my admiration. Or was it the eyes?

Graciela Limón   Third Prize: Novel

A Voice in Ramah (excerpt)

PART ONE

Thousands thronged to the Basilica of the Sacred Heart . . . and joined a silent procession behind the cortège as it was taken to the Metropolitan Cathedral. The sealed gray casket of assassinated Archbishop Oscar Arnulfo Romero rested on the steps of San Salvador's huge Cathedral, a wreath of red roses at its head. Suddenly the outdoor funeral service was transformed into a tableau of horror: exploding hand bombs, wild gunfire, terrified crowds stampeding in panic. Before it was over, 35 people had been killed; 185 others had been hospitalized . . . others disappeared.

Time, April 14, 1980

San Salvador, El Salvador
March 1980

Even though the size of the crowd was immense, a strange silence prevailed. Only the hushed shuffling of the mourners' feet and that of their intermittent prayers broke the stillness. The streets surrounding the Cathedral were clogged with people who had come from every sector of the city, and from beyond San Salvador. There were those who had left kitchens, factories and schoolrooms. *Campesinos* had walked distances from valleys and volcanos, from coffee plantations and cotton fields. They all came to accompany their Archbishop on his last pilgrimage through the city. Most of them wept, crouching close to one another; some in grief and others in fear. They pressed and pushed against one another hoping to see something, anything that might give them a sense of direction. They were nervous, knowing that every doorway could be a sniper's hiding place.

From the Basilica of the Sacred Heart, where the Archbishop had lain in state, the grievers filed toward the steps of the Cathedral's crypt. The murmur of whispered prayers and stifled sobs rose, crashing against the shell-pocked walls, swirling and tumbling in mid-air.

"Padre nuestro, que estás en el cielo, santificado sea tu nombre . . ."

Bernabé Delcano struggled with the crucifix he had been assigned to carry in the funeral procession. He was holding the cross high above his head, even though its weight made his forearms ache. His hands, which clutched the cross tightly, were stiff and white around the knuckles and fingertips. The young man, like his fellow seminarians, was dressed in a cassock which slowed down his movements. The intense heat made his head throb, and the public speakers that blared the prayers of the Mass only increased his discomfort.

He continually looked back into the crowd, making sure that his mother was not far from him. Bernabé felt assured each time he saw Luz's round face returning his glances, knowing that she too was keeping her eyes on him. Once, he held on to the crucifix with one hand and quickly waved at her with the other, but he didn't attempt that again, since the gesture almost made him drop the cross. Sweat formed on his neck and trickled down the inside of his shirt to his waist. He looked around him, seeing his mother's face again, but now the interference of faces and bodies made it impossible for him to get a sense of her feelings.

He looked at the faces of the other seminarians, hoping to catch a glimpse or a look that would indicate that their confusion was like his. Instead he saw blank, expressionless eyes. Only their lips moved in automatic response to the Our Fathers and Hail Marys mumbled by the priests at the head of the funeral procession. Bernabé looked beyond the faces of his classmates to those of the people. Some were lining the streets, but the majority walked behind the priests and the nuns, the seminarians, and altar boys. Looking at those faces, he was suddenly reminded of a painting. Once he had taken an art class in which his professor had dismissed the unit on cubism with one word: excrement. Yet, Bernabé had been fascinated by the pictures and examples shown in the textbook, and had spent hours in the library of the seminary reflecting on them. One of the selections had been entitled "Guernica," and the caption beneath the picture had identified it as the work of Pablo Picasso. Bernabé knew little regarding the artist, except that people argued as to whether he was a Spaniard or a Frenchman. What mattered to Bernabé, though, was the painting.

In it were fragments of human beings. The portrait showed incongruously shaped heads, rigid, outstretched arms, dilated eyes, twisted lips, jagged profiles, all scattered without apparent meaning. It also showed parts of an animal, the face of a horse. Bernabé had noticed that the animal bore the look of terrified human beings. Or was it, he had wondered, that the reverse was true, and that human faces looked like animals when they sensed their slaughter was near. The odd thing, he had thought at the time, was that those broken pieces of human beings could not be brought together again, even though he had attempted to imagine a head attached to some arms as he tried to piece together a human figure.

Now, as Bernabé marched in the cortège, he realized that these people around him were really fragmented: faces, eyes, cheeks, and arms. They were broken pieces just like in Picasso's disjointed painting.

"*Ave María, llena eres de gracia . . .*"

The cortège wound through the streets, past the indifferent eyes of the wealthy, and past those who pretended to be wealthy. Their tight lips betrayed a feeling of disgust. It was a pity those faces said to Bernabé, that the Archbishop had not heeded his finer instincts, his better judgement. Their eyes betrayed their beliefs that priests had best stay out of politics and confine themselves to Mass and to forgiving.

"*Gloria al Padre, y al Hijo y al Espíritu Santo . . .*"

Bernabé began to feel fatigued; faces blurred in front of him. The endless prayers droned monotonously in his ears. The cross seemed heavier with each minute. As he moved along with the rest of the mourners he began to stumble on the wet pavement. His fingers went numb and his perspiration made the cross slip in his clutching fists. Suddenly, he dropped the cross and fell on his knees. His cassock got entangled around his ankles and the press of people from behind kept him down, forcing him to crawl on his hands and knees.

Bernabé jerked his head right and left. Unexpectedly, a loud blast shook the ground under his hands. A grenade exploded in the midst of the surging crowd at the edge of Plaza Barrios facing the Cathedral. The blast was followed by machine gunfire and rifle shots that came from several directions making the mass of people panic. Hastily, the Archbishop's body was picked up and taken into the church by four bishops. Most of the mourners, however, were unable to reach the sanctuary of the Cathedral, and could not find shelter anywhere. They swerved and lunged in every direction, screaming hysterically.

Mothers crouched wherever they could in an attempt to protect their babies. Men and women pressed against the Cathedral walls hoping to find cover behind a corner or a sharp angle. Young men, mostly guerrillas, pulled out hand guns, then fired indiscriminately into the crowd in an attempt to hit members of the death squads with their random bullets. Uniformed soldiers suddenly appeared, also firing automatic weapons into the crowd.

The plaza was soon littered with bodies of the dead and the dying. People pushed and trampled each other in a frenzy to survive. No one thought. No one reasoned. Everyone acted out of instinct, pieces and fragments of tormented beasts driven by a compelling desire to live. All the time, the blasting and the firing of weapons and grenades continued.

Bernabé, crawling on the asphalt, was caught unaware by the first blast. The shifting weight of bodies pressing above and around him made it impossible for him to rise. Then bodies began crashing upon him, pinning him down. Suddenly, he felt intolerable pain as someone stepped on his hand, grinding the bones of his fingers against the pavement. He screamed as he attempted to defend himself with his other hand, but it was to no avail. The boot swiveled in the other direction, stepping on Bernabé's hand with an even greater force. The crowd dragged him back and forth, finally smashing him against a wall. Managing to pick himself up with his left hand, he leaned against the stone wall and looked at the bobbing heads and twisted limbs. The panic was at its peak.

"¡Mama-á-á-á-á!"

Bernabé's scream was hoarse and choked; it emanated from his guts, not from his throat. He didn't know what to do, where to go. His wailing rose above the howling of those around him, and he continued screaming for his mother

The pain in Bernabé's arm was intense, forcing him to remain against the wall despite his urge to run. He remained motionless, feet planted on the bloodied concrete. His body was bathed in sweat and his face, neck and hair were caked with dirt, grime and blood. Bernabé began to sob, crying inconsolably even though he was a man of twenty years. He screamed because he feared he was going to die, and he didn't feel shame, nor did he care what anyone might think.

Suddenly the thought that his mother was also in danger cut short his panic. Bernabé lunged into the crowd, kicking and thrashing against the bodies that pushed him in different directions. He screamed out his mother's name, using his able arm to raise himself on whatever shoulder or object he could find, trying to get a glimpse of her. But his mother was nowhere in sight.

Bernabé was able to get away from the plaza, slipping through a break in the encircling cordon of soldiers. He ran around the fringes of the square several times. He rushed up and down streets, and into doorways, shouting her name, but his voice was drowned out by the din of sirens, the horrified screams of people, and the blasts of machine guns. Bernabé shouted out his mother's name until his voice grew hoarse and his throat began to make wheezing, gasping sounds.

He suddenly thought that she might have gotten out of the plaza and run home. So he scrambled toward his house, hoping that he would find her waiting for him, but when he arrived there the door was locked. With his good hand, he beat on the door. When his fingers became numb with pain, he banged with his forehead until he felt blood dripping down his cheeks.

Suddenly a brutal shove sent Bernabé sprawling on the pavement. When he looked up he saw a uniformed soldier standing over him. "What are you doing here, Faggot? Better pick up your skirt and find a church to hide along with the other women. If you don't get your ass out of here, your brains are going to be shit splattered all over these walls. You have until the count of five. *Uno, dos, tres . . .*"

Bernabé sprang to his feet and ran. He kept running even though his breath began to give out, even though the pain in his arm was intolerable, even though he knew his mother needed him. Panic gripped at his guts and his brain. He knew he had to keep on running.

After the horror had spent itself in the plaza, stunned men and women searched in the lingering blue haze for a son, or a wife, or even an entire family. Among them was Luz Delcano. She called out her son's name, her soft weeping joining that of others, like the rotting moss that clung to the stone walls of the buildings surrounding the square. Luz Delcano went from one body to the next, taking the face of this one in her hands, turning over the body of another one. Desperation began to overcome her. In her fear she remembered the loss of her first son, Lucio. Now Bernabé, her second born, was also gone.

1991-92

Terri De La Peña   **First Prize: Short Story**

Territories

*V*ENTANAS

My partner Luanne Jackson and I got the radio call on a cool Tuesday night. She flipped on our overhead lights and swung the black-and-white east on Broadway in Santa Monica, right past the new business complex.

"Lots of dark corners on that street, Ron. All kinds of hiding places."

"Yeah." I stared out the dusty window. "Wish the city would get wise and get more street lights. Bad guys really like to play when it's pitch black out."

"Don't get personal now." She glanced at me across the squad car's interior. "You know I hate 'black' used in a negative way."

"So don't *you* go around accusing my homeboys in the department of 'brown-nosing'. *I* don't like 'brown' used as a put-down either, Ms. Jackson."

We laughed together. Lu and I had been partners a long time. Neither of us thought it an accident that a black woman and a Chicano had been paired off. We liked to think we were an effective combo, especially in our own neighborhoods. No one in S.M.P.D. [Santa Monica Police Department] seemed willing to argue otherwise.

"There it is, on the right."

Lu parked the squad car in front of a two-story, wood-trimmed apartment building. Hibiscus bushes and Italian cypresses bordered its entry, and a bare bulb shone from the building's eaves, offering dim illumination.

We approached the building and I took a quick look at the mailboxes. "Number five is at the top, Lu."

She followed me up the stairs to the first apartment facing the street. At the top of the stairs we wound up on a narrow deck. It had a couple of plastic patio chairs, a rusting hibachi, and lots of potted plants. A sliding glass door faced the deck; its miniblinds were at a slanted angle. Through them I saw a Latina in a turquoise turtleneck and black jeans peer out. She had an edgy look on her face.

"I'm Officer Ron Velez," I said when the woman unlocked the door. "My partner's Officer Luanne Jackson." The more I looked at the Latina, the more familiar she seemed.

"Come in, please, Officers." She extended her hand toward me. "I'm Pat Ramos, the one who made the call."

"Patty Ramos?" I grinned suddenly, recalling a black-haired little girl who threw a mean curveball.

For a moment, she stared at me before covering her mouth with one hand. "Are you related to Margie Velez? She was in my class at St.Anne' s."

"Right." I liked looking at her pretty eyes. "I'm Margie's big brother."

"Well, unfortunately, we didn't come here to reminisce." Lu tossed me a reprimanding glance. "Ms. Ramos, you reported you were being harassed?"

"Yes." Pat Ramos took Lu's cue and got down to business. "By a man who lives across the street." She stood by the wide front window as she spoke. On reflex, it seemed, she tugged at the miniblinds and pulled them shut. "I've caught him looking through las ventanas before. No sense in making it easy for him."

The Ramos girl had grown into an attractive woman. No wonder men noticed her. Some loser she had dumped over was probably giving her a hard time. I sensed her anxiety and let my voice grow gentle. "Why don't you tell us about it?"

When she hesitated, Lu acted like she'd read my mind and cut in, "Is he your boyfriend?"

Pat Ramos sputtered a fast denial. "It isn't *that* at all. I . . . " she turned candid eyes to mine. "You see, I'm a lesbian. This guy knows it. He's been harassing me—and my friends."

I was glad Lu kept up the questioning. Pat Ramos's admission threw me for a loop. She had been my kid sister Margie's playmate. Except for her short hair, she sure didn't look like a dyke to me.

Lu kept her pen poised over the notepad and avoided eye contact with me. "Why don't you tell us the whole story, Ms. Ramos."

Meanwhile, I let my eyes roam around the apartment. I took in the floor-to-ceiling bookcases and figured they were crammed with stuff about women's lib, abortion rights, all that plus lezzie propaganda. On other walls Pat Ramos had hung framed certificates and several photos of women. I wondered who they were.

She offered us seats. Lu acted like she hadn't heard that. We remained standing while Pat Ramos paced the small living room and her story.

"This guy has stared at me ever since he moved across the street."

"Do you know his name?"

"Gus Becerra—according to one of the neighbors." She crossed her arms in front of her and kept pacing. "When I come home from work, he stands in front of his building and watches me pick up my mail. When I go out, I see him looking at me while I'm getting into the car—and sometimes when I come back, too. He gives me the creeps. Now it's worse."

I leaned against one of the bookcases. "What happened?"

"The mail carrier accidentally delivered some of my mail across the street last week. I'm not sure if it wound up in Becerra's mailbox or what." She stopped her pacing and faced us. "I subscribe to lots of feminist and lesbian newspapers and magazines. This guy Becerra somehow got his hands on a couple of them. When I got home from work that day, he was standing by my mailbox. He had ripped up my magazines. He threw the pieces at me. From what he started saying, I knew he had read them first. He wasn't going to let me forget that." She paused, and without looking at either of us, continued in a quieter voice.

"He called me names—all kinds of names. He stood next to me while I unlocked my mailbox and kept up a constant verbal attack. I was scared, Officers—very scared. I took my mail, rushed past him, and hurried upstairs."

"Did you say anything to him?" Lu asked while she scribbled on her pad.

"Only when I thought he was going to follow me. I turned around on the stairs and said, 'Don't even think about it.'"

"And then?" I spoke before Lu could.

"He said what I need is 'a good, hard fuck.' He said he wasn't about to try that himself 'cause he didn't 'want to get AIDS.'" Ramos sighed. "I know I shouldn't have said anything else. By that time, I was really furious. I called him an ignorant asshole. I told him his brains were between his legs."

Lu raised one brow. "Did he do anything in response to that?"

Pat Ramos nodded. "He started up after me. Good thing I already had my keys out. I unlocked the door as fast as I could and slammed it behind me. I didn't hear him go away for a long time."

"When did that occur, Ms. Ramos?"

"Last Friday. I reported it," she added with what I thought was a trace of sarcasm. "When no officers showed up, I went to stay with a friend. I didn't see Becerra when I left, and I didn't see him when I came home the next day either. Meanwhile, I told several friends about the whole thing. They all wanted me to stay with them. I just don't want to get into the habit of doing that. Know what I mean? I need to feel *safe* in my own home. I've lived here five years. There's never been any trouble before."

She hardly took a breath. "Then today, Becerra was waiting in front. He started yelling at me again by the mailboxes. I went upstairs fast and phoned my friends. Two of them came over. He started in on them too."

Lu's dark eyes studied hers. "Exactly what did he do?"

Pat Ramos sighed and rubbed her hands against her jeans. "He called them the same names he'd used on me. 'Mother-fuckin' dykes.' 'Pussylickers.' I think you can get the picture."

"Yes, ma'am." Lu kept her eyes on the woman's. "Did your friends provoke him in any way?"

"No. I warned them not to before they came over. I don't want any more trouble. My friends didn't want to leave till you showed up, but I sent them home. I was worried about them." For the first time, Pat Ramos sounded tired. "How can I avoid trouble when Becerra keeps hanging around my mailbox? All I'm doing is trying to get my mail."

Lu studied her. "Has he touched you in any way?"

Pat Ramos shook her head. "No. That doesn't mean he won't. I hate all this, Officers. It's like living in a fortress all of a sudden." Her eyes did not waver when she gazed at us. "I want him stopped—before he does anything else."

I sensed her fear and tension, but still was puzzled about her current lifestyle. What had changed her from the scrawny kid I remembered? She had been raised in the same neighborhood as me, played softball with my sister, shared identical family values, and a Catholic education. What had made her cross the line into an unknown territory?

Lu must have been aware of my wandering thoughts. She stuck her notepad in her belt and opened the door. "Ms. Ramos, we'll go talk to Mr. Becerra right now. Whether he knows it or not, he's in violation of your civil rights."

"I doubt if he cares, but thanks."

Before I closed the door behind me, I glanced at her. "We'll be back."

"How'd you like that little trip down memory lane?" Lu muttered as we crossed the quiet street.

"Sure as hell took me by surprise." I shook my head in bewilderment. "That Patty Ramos used to pitch a mean ball, Lu. Didn't see any of her softball trophies on those shelves."

Lu cut her eyes at me. "Mmmhmm. Plenty of lesbo-type books instead."

"Yeah. She sure doesn't look like a dyke to me."

"No more than you look like a cop, cholo-boy." Lu grinned and led the way to the apartment building where Becerra lived.

"Good evening, Officers," we heard someone call when we got there. A stout sixtyish woman in a yellow sweatsuit came around a corner of the building and paused by the low brick border. She held a leather leash with a tiny mongrel on the other end. "I'm Faye Preston. Can I help you with something?"

I nodded to her. "We'd appreciate it, ma'am. We're looking for a man named Gus Becerra."

She looked rattled when I said that. "Hate to admit it—he's one of my tenants." She glanced around to be sure no one overheard. "If it wasn't for the asinine rent control laws in this town, you'd better believe I'd have thrown him out by now. He acted all sweet and polite when I rented to him a few months ago. He's changed his tune since."

"Ma'am?" Lu took out her notebook again.

"He's a mean son-of-a-bitch—pardon my French. Lives in Number Three with his wife and little girl. I go out of town a lot—Las Vegas, Laughlin—you know, once us seniors escape the rat race, we like to gamble. The other tenants say he beats up on his wife whenever I happen to leave. Makes me worried sick about that poor woman and the little daughter." Faye Preston sighed with genuine concern.

"Whether it's true or not, Officers, I don't really know," she went on. "He keeps his windows shut, drapes snapped tight. I might be the landlady—lot of good that does—can't even see inside that place. Never been able to overhear anything either—my hearing isn't what it used to be."

"Anything else, ma'am?"

"Is there ever," she said. "Other folks on the street tell me he yells at their kids all the time. Some of them won't let their little girls play anywhere near here because of Becerra and his foul mouth. What's he done now?"

Lu gave her a cordial nod. "We'll take it from here, Mrs. Preston. Thanks."

Faye Preston kept talking while she watched us head into the building's courtyard. "From what the neighbors tell me, I wouldn't let my own little darlin' puppy near that big lug."

When I turned to wave at her, she gave the small mongrel's leash a tug, as if to emphasize her point. "Don't worry, honey. I'll clean up after Petunia." She saluted me and pulled a plastic pooper-scooper out of the paper bag she held.

I grinned. "Good for you, ma'am."

Becerra's apartment was tucked away in the far corner of the first floor.

Lu pushed the doorbell to apartment three. "Landlady's damn opinionated about this guy."

"Becerra sounds like a real beloved figure," I remarked, still half-smiling.

In seconds, what was left of my grin faded. We came face to face with Gus Becerra. His bulk with its thick neck and flabby middle squeezed itself into a khaki security guard's uniform. He had a close-cropped head and heavy-lidded stare. Right off, I tagged him for a cop wannabe, fixated on keeping his neighborhood clean single-handed. I wasn't a bit surprised to hear his radio blaring the local police frequency.

"What can I do you for?" Slack-jawed, Becerra stood in his open doorway, giving us the once-over.

Even in the shadows, I could tell by Lu's face she had no use for this guy. Not that she was crazy about protecting dykes. She cared even less for macho-types who intimidated every female on the block. I made some quick introductions. Then Lu took over.

"We're here to investigate a possible violation of California Code Section 51.7, Mr. Becerra. A young lady across the street says you've harassed her and her friends."

"You call that mother-fuckin' bull dyke a 'lady'? My ass." Becerra spit out his words. "That bitch is out to snatch every little Susie-Q on this street. I've seen how she looks at all the teenaged girls around here. And you should see the sick trash she reads. Did she tell you I tore it up? Fuckin' A, I'd do it *again*. Sick and tired of all these dykes and faggots going public, trying to lure innocent kids. You ought to lock *her* and her kind up. Jesus Christ, I have a baby daughter and—"

"Excuse me, Mr. Becerra," Lu cut in. "You have no right to read or destroy another person's mail. That's a Federal crime—outside our jurisdiction—but that young lady could file a complaint against you for that alone. You have no right to intimidate her either. Do you know what a hate crime is?"

"Blah, blah, blah." A high-pitched laugh burst out of Becerra's ugly mouth. That crazy sound made me step a little closer to Lu.

My partner did not let him shake her. "A hate crime is violence or intimidation by the threat of violence committed against another because of race, color, religion, ancestry, national origin, political affiliation, sex, *sexual orientation*, age, disability—"

Becerra's eyes almost bugged out at Lu's emphasis. "You tryin' to tell me that fuckin' dyke has civil rights? What about the safety of this neighborhood, huh? What about my daughter and all the other girls on the block? I want them to be safe, not lured into that sleazy dyke's apartment."

"Regardless of your personal opinion, Mr. Becerra, that young woman," Lu said through gritted teeth, "is entitled to the same civil rights as you are."

"She's a pussy-lickin', cunt-chewin' dyke. I don't give a shit about her so-called god-damned rights. How'd you like that snatch-sniffing *señorita* to take a grab at *your* tits?" He jabbed his middle finger at Lu.

"Keep your hands to yourself, Mr. Becerra."

"Shut up, you black bitch."

I moved nearer to grab his attention and give Lu a chance to cool off. "You keep this up, Mr. Becerra, and we'll have to take you in."

"Fuck you, stinkin' beaner—"

"Mr. Becerra, whether *I* like it or not, we're both Latinos—so you just cancelled out that ethnic slur. My partner and I are going to leave now. We'll give you some time to calm down and think this over. ¿Entiendes? Listen good, hombre."

He smirked while I faced him down.

"You are not to threaten nor in any way intimidate the young lady across the street. You are not to stand by her mailbox and harass her or her friends.

Otherwise, Mr. Becerra, you're in violation of her civil rights, you're liable for arrest, and she can file a civil suit against you. ¿Comprendes?"

"Ain't goin' to listen to a greaseball coconut and a fat-lipped oreo—that's what you both are. Doing the white man's shit work. Get the hell out of my face!" He slammed the door hard.

Lu and I looked at each other. My adrenalin was pumping and I could see the veins in her neck throbbing.

"You okay, Partner?"

She nodded. "He's too damn stupid to realize he's the wrong color to be a bigot. I could've handled him *myself*, Ron."

"I know you hate the word 'black' used in a negative way—especially when the word 'bitch' is added to it."

"What did I *do* to deserve such a considerate partner?" She grumbled as we crossed the street to Pat Ramos' apartment.

"If Becerra doesn't quit the harassment, Ms. Ramos," Lu advised, "you may have to obtain a temporary restraining order to make him keep his distance. He's hopping mad right now. He didn't like hearing you could sue him for violating your civil rights."

"Homophobes like to think they're above the law." Pat Ramos looked weary. "All I want is for him to leave me alone."

"Well, if he doesn't, give us another call. I sure wouldn't mind taking that guy in," I drawled. "In the meantime, concentrate on what you can do to protect yourself."

She sighed while I went on.

"Have the owner of your building put some bright lights outside. Some landlords don't realize they're legally responsible if tenants are injured on their property. Becerra might think twice about hassling you if the building's exterior is as well-lit as Dodger Stadium. Why don't you tell the landlord we mentioned that?"

She nodded.

Lu kept her hand on the doorknob as we were about to leave. "In the meantime, be careful. Let Becerra spout off all he wants—don't answer him. His intent is to rattle you, Ms. Ramos. Don't give him *that* satisfaction."

"It won't be easy, but I know you're right. Thanks again, Officers." Pat Ramos leaned against the door jamb and at last smiled a bit. "Say 'hi' to Margie when you see her."

"Sure." I handed her my card. "If Becerra keeps up his weirdness, don't hesitate to call. That's what we're here for." I took the stairs two at a time after Lu.

Off duty, Lu and I had coffee at the IHOP on the corner of 20th Street and Santa Monica Boulevard. The waitress left the pot on our table and we split a piece of hot apple pie between us.

"Pretty down in the mouth tonight, Partner. Still trying to figure Ms. Ramos out? Hope you weren't sweet on her once upon a time."

"You *do* have a fat lip, Lu."

She chuckled and poured herself another cup of coffee. "Also hope you're not getting into a macho mood and going back there to 'straighten' her out."

I lit a cigarette and took a long drag. "So what if I did?"

"Give it up, Ron." She reached over and touched my hand. "Man, you need to find yourself a woman again—not her. Ever since you and Lydia split up, you've been in a funk."

"Don't talk about Lydia."

Lu took her hand away and leaned back in the booth. "We've been through a lot together, man. When Wardell was killed, I would've gone crazy if it hadn't been for you. You were the one I counted on then, remember?" Her large eyes grew soft. "I care about you, Ron. Shit, if you were just a little darker—and if I didn't know so damn much about you—I could go for you myself."

I laughed at that.

"I do know some fine lookin' Latina sisters—from my old neighborhood in South Central. Told you before—say the word and I'll introduce you to them."

"Lu—butt out and finish your coffee."

She grabbed my cigarette and snuffed it. "Only if you promise to put Pat Ramos out of your mind. She's a fox—no doubt about it. *You* just ain't her type."

"I wonder why Margie never told me about her."

"Maybe Margie doesn't know. Looks like a lot happened since their high school grad night."

"How do you figure it, Lu?" I lit another cigarette and she bummed one off me. She quit smoking at least twice a month.

She exhaled slowly. "Some folks are born different. Some never figure out *why* they feel different from everyone else. Sometimes it's 'cause they're the only black family in the 'hood. Other times it could be 'cause they're skinny and everyone else is fat. Or maybe it's like the Ramos chick—she goes for women. Must be kind of a shock to realize you're *that* different. Must be double hard when you're brown, too. All I know is, I have a hard time with black bulldaggers. They freak me."

"Why's that?"

"Probably 'cause black folks have called *me* that. They see a black woman in uniform and they right away label me. Shit." There were sparks of anger in Lu's eyes. "Black women *have* to be tough, man. *I* sure don't have to be a bulldagger to be tough." She downed some coffee. "That Pat Ramos—she's damn tough herself. Can you see her telling that scum Becerra his brains are between his legs?"

We laughed together.

"She was a feisty little kid, too. She'd just better not let her temper get the best of her where Becerra's concerned." I finished my smoke. "Ready?"

Lu nodded and stood up. "My kids must be wondering why I'm not home yet. 'Course, I'll blame you."

"Who else?" I winked.

The living room windows of my sister Margie's house were dotted with red paper valentines, her older daughter's handiwork. When I noticed "Uncle Ron" had been neatly lettered on one of the larger hearts, I smiled.

"It's a good thing you phoned, or I'd never be opening the door this late." Margie gave me a quick hug and gestured me inside. "¿Qué pasa, hermano? Can't you sleep?"

"Thought I'd pop in on my way home. Am I keeping you up, Margie?"

"Pues, no. I've been busy with the baby—he's teething." Margie was wrapped in a quilted pink robe and looked sleepier than she would admit. "It's a good thing Pete's on duty at the fire station. Otherwise, he'd never get any rest around here. ¿Quiéres una cerveza, Ron?"

"I'd love one." I slumped on her overstuffed sectional couch and rested my head on its back. Though I missed seeing her kids, I was grateful to have a chance to visit alone with my sister. It wasn't often the two of us had that chance.

"How's Lu?" Margie came back with a glass of Miller's. She handed it over and sat beside me.

"Still worries bringing up her kids alone, but—hey, Lu's doing it fine—like she does everything else." After I took a swig of the beer, I set the glass on the low coffee table. I gave my sister a quick look and came right to the point. "How come you never told me about Patty Ramos?"

Margie's drowsy expression vanished. "What about her? Something happen to her?"

"She's a dyke, Margie."

She glared. "Correction: she's a lesbian activist."

"You know then."

"Sure. Where've *you* been?" She took on the same combative attitude she used whenever we argued about politics. "Pat pops up all over. She's been interviewed on KCRW and on cable talk shows. She even spoke in the human sexuality class I took at Santa Monica College."

"Jesus." I took another gulp of beer.

"Ay, Ron. You act so surprised." Margie's face eased into amusement "Don't you remember what a tomboy she was?"

"You were a tomboy, too."

"And Pat was my friend when we were kids." She glared again. "What're you saying, anyway?"

"I'm saying Lu and I took a call from Pat tonight. A fat pendejo across the street's been harassing her. He knows she's a dyke and he's trying to intimidate her."

"Ay, Dios. Is she all right?"

"So far." I leaned toward her. "Margie, why didn't you ever tell me about her?"

She sighed and curled her bare feet beneath her. "When I saw how you reacted to Lydia's brother coming out of the closet, I decided there was no point in telling you about Pat."

I stared across the room. "Lydia—and Beto—have nothing to do with this."

"Yeah, sure, Ron." She tossed me a skeptical look. "Why do you think Lydia divorced you? You couldn't handle Beto's dying of AIDS. He was her only brother. She loved him—and you couldn't even handle *that*."

"Look—I don't want to talk about *them*. I mean it, Margie."

"When do you want to talk about them, huh?" My sister was not about to let go. "Don't you think it's time to start? You lost a fabulous woman, Ron—a woman like Lydia isn't easy to find."

I got up so suddenly Margie flinched. My back to her, I stalked across the room and gazed at the silly cut-out valentines taped to the picture window. "Lydia never told me about Beto, not till he got sick."

"She was being protective of her brother."

I turned around. "Protective?"

"You're a cop, estúpido. Lydia's quite aware of *that*." Margie took a sip of the beer I'd left on the coffee table. "You have a certain at-ti-tude. Lu has it, too. You both swagger around Santa Monica like you own the whole town."

"You're such a damn bleeding heart, Margie. Jesus! Ever since you've been taking those college classes—"

"What's wrong with getting an education?" she challenged. "There's life beyond the Police Academy, you know. Or maybe you *don't* know. Obviously, you don't if you're so shook up about the existence of Chicano gays and Chicana lesbians right here in our home town."

I looked away from her and didn't say anything for a long time. I kept eyeing those little paper hearts and wondering where Lydia was, what she was doing. And I didn't want her on my mind anymore. I didn't want to think about anything.

"Look, Margie, it's late." I moved to the door. "We both need our sleep. I'm going home."

"Fine." She reached my side faster than I expected. "Ron, next time you come by—let's *really* talk. You need to."

I wasn't about to commit myself, and leaned over to kiss her instead. "Do you still see Pat Ramos?"

She met my gaze. "Once in a while I run into her at the mall, or somewhere like that."

"Still friends?"

Margie shrugged. "We don't have much in common anymore. I *do* like her, Ron. Always have. I think she still likes me, too." She touched my cheek. "You look tired, hermano. Get some rest."

"You too, Margie."

After being at Margie's for that little while, I felt even more pissed off. She took every chance to tell me how wrong she thought I was about everything. I gunned my Cherokee up the coast to Sunset [Boulevard], then swung around and headed back to town. It was past midnight when I aimed the Cherokee down the unlit street. I found a spot next to a fig tree, right below Pat Ramos's window.

Her kitchen light was on, but I couldn't see her. I wondered what she would do if she saw me, not that it mattered. What mattered was, I didn't want to go home to spend another long night trying to quit thinking about Lydia. Whether I agreed with her or not, Margie's words had struck hard. Lydia hadn't trusted me enough to tell me about her brother Beto. And, damn it, her instincts had been right.

Finding out Beto was a faggot had turned me against the kid. Before that, I had been like a big brother to him, teaching him to drive, lending him money, talking him into staying in school. After I found out what he was, I couldn't even look at him. And when he got sicker, all I could picture was baby-faced Beto getting butt-fucked by some leather dude. Toward the end, Lydia spent every free moment with him, while I signed up for overtime. When he was gone, she told me to get out.

Sighing, I wanted those memories to disappear like the haze from my cigarette. I sat there and smoked it down to the filter. After I snubbed it out, I leaned against the head rest and tried to doze. Next thing I knew there was a light shining in my face. Pat Ramos and another lezzie—a regular Dyke Patrol—stood outside the Cherokee, pointing a flashlight at me.

"Officer Velez?" Pat Ramos called.

"You *know* this guy?" Her long-legged companion seemed wary.

"Yeah, Jackie. He's one of the officers who was here earlier." Pat Ramos watched me unfold myself from the car. "What're you doing here?"

"I'm off duty. Thought I'd stop by on my way home to see if everything was all right. Must've conked off." I stifled a yawn. "Hope I didn't scare you."

"We thought Pat had another creepster hanging around." Her friend Jackie was a lanky white girl with a brush cut. "Came out to investigate." She crossed her arms and scanned me, like she couldn't wait for me to get lost.

Embarrassed to be caught napping, I took the hint. "Everything's fine, I'm shoving off. Good night."

They both nodded and didn't budge till I'd driven down the block. Through the rear-view mirror, I saw them holding hands as they headed upstairs.

Lu and I had a busy shift for several nights. A string of car jackings kept us hopping and we had our usual series of complaints about the homeless panhandling outside of restaurants. We didn't have much chance to shoot the breeze till we picked up some coffee to go a few nights later.

"Her girlfriend's name is Jackie. And Becerra works security at the 7-11 down the street."

"What?" Lu almost spilled her coffee. She gave me a piercing look. "What the hell have you been up to, boy?"

I grinned. "Some informal stake-outing."

"While simultaneously getting the hots for Ramos."

"Nope. Just trying to make the most of my insomnia."

"What *am* I going to do with you, Ron?" Lu was exasperated. "You're going to get yourself in a mess of trouble."

I lit a cigarette. "Maybe you should marry me."

"Sure. And make Wardell roll over in his grave. You are one crazy muchacho." She took one of my cigarettes from the pack I'd left on the dashboard. "Well, has Becerra been up to his old tricks?"

I shrugged. "Think we scared him—for the time being," I added while I offered her a light.

"Maybe you've picked up his fascination with the beautiful Ms. Ramos." Her cigarette's tip glowed in the darkness of the squad car.

"You're weird, Lu."

"*You* need a vacation, man." She was about to say more when the dispatcher cut in. Lu flipped her cigarette out the window and veered the car west on Santa Monica Boulevard.

Sergeant McNeill and Officer Sánchez were already at the shooting scene at the 7-11.

"A regular gunfight at the O.K. Corral." McNeill pointed to the dead man lying spread-eagled in the rectangular parking lot. The paramedic team was busy loading an injured black guy into their ambulance.

"What's the story?" Lu started her questions before she was even out of the squad car.

Sánchez came over and nodded to us. "Possible self-defense. We have several corroborating witnesses, both inside and outside the store. The black dude in the ambulance is a homosexual. He says the security guard watched him through the store window as he drove up and right away started hassling him once he got inside."

"Accusing him of shoplifting?"

"Nope, Lu. Making anti-gay remarks," Sánchez clarified. "The guard followed him out here and kept it up. Pushed him around a little, knocked him down. Looks like the gay dude may have a rib injury. Anyway, he says he carries a piece in his car for protection against this sort of thing—he's got the permit to prove it. When the security guard—who outweighed him by about 100 pounds—tried to grab him again, the gay dude reached inside the car real quick, whipped out the .38, and let the guard have it."

I felt my skin crawl as I squatted next to the big body. "Lu, take a look."

She did not flinch. "Gus Becerra."

McNeill overheard us and stared. "You know him, Jackson?"

"We took a report on him last week. He was harassing a lesbian in his neighborhood."

McNeill whistled. "That dyke sure lucked out. Don't that beat all?"

"You do the honors, Ron." Lu gave me a half smile when she parked the squad car outside Pat Ramos's apartment. "I'll wait out here."

"I won't be long."

"Damn right. I'm counting on that."

"I can't believe he's dead." Pat Ramos seemed dazed as she absorbed the news about Gus Becerra.

"He sure won't bother you anymore."

She rubbed the corner of one eye and looked at me. "This probably sounds cruel and heartless—but you know what? I'm *so* glad a gay man killed Becerra. It's like when a woman kills a man who's battered or raped her. Ya basta. We've had enough."

"Yeah, I know."

She paused and pushed her black hair from her forehead. "Now you can let someone else use the parking place in front."

I acted casual. "How often did you see me out there?"

"Every night, through las ventanas."

"Becerra was bad news for a lot of people around here." Leaning against the door jamb, I spoke quietly. "Got used to checking up on things. It'll be hard to break that habit."

Her gaze was direct. "You have to."

"Pat—"

"You did your job and I appreciate it." She wore the same determined look Lydia had the night she told me to leave. "That's the end of it."

I hadn't begged then, and I wasn't about to this time. When I said good night, I didn't even look at her. She closed the door right behind me and I heard the double-bolt click.

Lu eyed me when I got into the squad car. "How'd she take it, Ron?"

"She's relieved." I reached for a cigarette.

"And you?"

I took a long drag.

"Tough cholo cop."

"All in a night's work, Lu."

"I've caught that toughness from you."

"You *know* it."

When Lu pulled the squad car from the curb, I glanced back at the apartment building. The miniblinds in Pat Ramos's window were drawn tight. I knew I would never see inside.

1993-94

Elaine Romero   First Prize: Drama

Walking Home
A Play in Two Acts (excerpt)

ACT ONE
SCENE ONE

(The play is set in the present in the dunes of the Southwest border and its memory. Historical and contemporary characters inspired by primary sources: journals, letters and interviews by women of the U.S./Mexican border from the distant and recent past. The protagonist, MARIA, *recalls her past through conversation with* WOMAN IN THE SAND.*)*

(MARIA *in blue light.*)

MARIA: I'm seeing him. In the past. I'm just a child. Really tiny. He's enormous. The biggest man in the world. We walk together. By the tide pools. It's easy to lose your balance there because the rocks are rugged and the pools are wet and slick.

    He tries to help. He offers me his hand, but I won't take it. Because I'm an independent little girl. And I don't need his help.

(Blackout.)

(JESUSITA, *an older Latina woman, appears.*)

JESUSITA: The truth.

MARIA: I want to be alone. With her. Keep the truth to yourself for a minute.

WOMAN IN THE SAND: You can't stop the truth.

JESUSITA: Want to hear the truth the way I remember it?

MARIA: No.

WOMAN IN THE SAND: Yes.

MARIA: Not yet. (*To* WOMAN IN THE SAND.) Spare me. Please.

WOMAN IN THE SAND: I can't.

JESUSITA: (*To* WOMAN IN THE SAND.) You look weak. You can take it on?

WOMAN IN THE SAND: I can.

MARIA: What do you mean—can she take it on?

WOMAN IN THE SAND: She means—

MARIA: Yes.

WOMAN IN THE SAND: You'll see.

MARIA: Well, I don't want to hear another happy-ass story about what wonderful fathers you all had.

WOMAN IN THE SAND: You won't.

JESUSITA: That's not my story.

MARIA: Good.

WOMAN IN THE SAND: Go ahead.

JESUSITA: (*To* WOMAN IN THE SAND.) You'll make it to the end?

WOMAN IN THE SAND: I will.

MARIA: What're you two talking about? Take what on? Is there something you're not telling me? (MARIA *looks straight at* WOMAN IN THE SAND *who turns away.*) I want to know everything. Don't hide anything. I'll figure it out. I'm at least that smart.

WOMAN IN THE SAND: You do know everything. It's all laid out for you. It's very easy for you to see. He—

MARIA: He?

WOMAN IN THE SAND: Your "he."

MARIA: He had to prove to the world he didn't care. And then he had to prove it to me. He was just really macho. Tough. That's all.

WOMAN IN THE SAND: Not half as tough as us.

MARIA: You're kidding, right?

WOMAN IN THE SAND: I wish I were.

JESUSITA: My past.

MARIA: She's going back there and we can't stop her?

WOMAN IN THE SAND: Pretty much. (MARIA *resists listening and then finds herself drawn in by the story.*)

JESUSITA: (*Beat.*) We lived in Trujillo when I was little, but when they started to build the lake, the Storrie Lake by Las Vegas, my dad came back and asked for work building the dam. So, we moved back here to Upper Town for awhile. (*Beat.*) My mother got pregnant again, her eighth baby. All girls. Eight girls, trying to have a boy. Only three girls lived. (*Beat.*) I was the first that lived. (JESUSITA'S MOTHER *stands pregnant, holding her back. She lies down. She scribbles something on a pad of paper and hands it to* ABUELA.) In 1918, when I was ten, the bad flu came. A lot of people die on that time. My mother was pregnant when she got sick. And her tears run. (*A doctor works on* JESUSITA'S MOTHER.) (*Pause.*) She was about seven months with the baby. The doctor took care of her and said it was better for her to have the baby than to die with the baby in. So, the doctor gave her something to make her have the baby. She could still talk a little then, so she said:

JESUSITA'S MOTHER: Jesusita, call your tía, tell her that I have my baby.

JESUSITA: That day mi abuela come. Mi abuela deliver it by herself; nobody was with her, just the neighbors, right here in Upper Town.

ABUELA: Push. (*As* JESUSITA'S MOTHER *cries out in pain, her* ABUELA *assists in the birth of the baby. Sound of crying baby.*)

JESUSITA: It was another girl, the last one. I heard that baby cry. The baby girl lasts about an hour, and then she dies. And in a few days, my mother dies. She was thirty-four. (*Two* MEN *enter. They carry off* JESUSITA'S MOTHER'*s body.*)

MARIA: (*To* WOMAN IN THE SAND.) What are you guys trying to depress me or something?

WOMAN IN THE SAND: Do sad stories depress you too?

MARIA: I guess, everything depresses me. (JESUSITA *huddles together with her sisters.*)

JESUSITA: I was ten years old when my mother dies, and the other sister was five, and the little one, the little sister, was three years old. We cried and cried and we were sad.

MARIA: (*Seeing* JESUSITA'*s past.*) You cried all the time when she left. And there was this big gaping hole in your heart, where she used to be. A place only she could fill. That's how you felt when she died.

JESUSITA: Yes.

MARIA: You wanted to die, too. You wanted to leave this world right along with her.

JESUSITA: I did want to die. But I stayed.

MARIA: That was the first time you felt like dying.

JESUSITA: You understand me. (JESUSITA *brushes her sister's hair.*) We were so sad but mi abuela and mis tías were with us.

MARIA: But it's not the same, is it?

JESUSITA: No, it's not the same. (*Beat.*) We couldn't go to the funeral because it was a big storm, a snow in March. We felt such sorrow. I slept with my sisters and helped them. I remember, I give them a bath and comb their hair. Yes, I clean my sisters when our mother dies. (*Beat.*) There is nothing in the world like your mother. That's your best friend. I never forget her, or forget how she looks, or how she holds me. Never. (MARIA *wraps her arms around herself as if she can feel her mother holding her too.*)

MARIA: I'm sorry.

JESUSITA: It's okay. I'm still here. (*Beat.*) After my mother dies, we go back to the ranch in Trujillo, and mi abuela takes care of us. My daddy came, too. We were all together.

MARIA: No mother. Half a family. You and your dad and your abuela.

JESUSITA: Yes, just him and mi abuela. They treat me different. (*Beat.*) My troubles start when I'm twenty-three. I get pregnant with my boyfriend. He says, "I don't care. I don't care if you are. I don't want to get married with you." I say, "Okay, then, okay. I do it by myself. I won't bother you." (*Beat.*) So I never talk to him again. Never. Never. And I don't like him. I hate him.

MARIA: Men are shits.

WOMAN IN THE SAND: María.

MARIA: Well, they are. (MARIA *stops, realizes something.*) And that is the second time you felt like dying. (JESUSITA *nods.*)

JESUSITA: I was getting bigger and bigger, so that my daddy went one night to my abuela's house, and he said, "Who is the father of that baby?" And I say, "I don't know." (*Beat.*) I say that 'cause I didn't want to tell them. It's hard on me 'cause everybody treats me . . . I don't know how to say. They treat me different. They get mad with me, everybody, everybody in the house. And there's nothing I can do.

MARIA: Nowhere to go.

JESUSITA: Yes.

MARIA: Trapped inside yourself. Like your skull is holding your mind hostage. Like your body's a cage, and your soul is an animal.

JESUSITA: I tried to run away once. Like you. But I didn't know where I was going. I was just trying to go to the mountains, I think. It was night, and my sisters feel me get up out of our bed. (*Two* SISTERS *appear.*) They wake up, too, and say:

SISTER: What are you going to do?

JESUSITA: I'm running away.

SISTER: We don't want you to run away.

OTHER SISTER: We want you here with us.

JESUSITA: So, I decide to stay. (JESUSITA *kneels. She cries aloud.*) I don't run away, but I pray in the woods where I was taking care of the sheep, crying in the woods, and ask my Lord to take me with Him, 'cause I want to die, I was so ashamed. I was praying and praying for him to take me with Him. (*Beat.*) Take me, God. Just take me. Take me, God. Just take me.

MARIA: (*Hypnotically.*) Take me, God. Just take me. (JESUSITA *places her hand on* MARIA*'s shoulder.* MARIA *rocks back and forth. Red light on* MARIA. MARIA *lies stretched out on the ground, holding her arm. The light spills out on her arm, creating the image of blood pouring out.*)

JESUSITA: (*Simultaneously.*) And, I was praying. Take me, God. Just take me.

MARIA: Take me, God. Just take me.

JESUSITA: Praying for him to take me. Day and night. But He didn't.

MARIA: Just let me die.

JESUSITA: I'm still here. Thanks to Him.

MARIA: Please.

JESUSITA: He didn't want me that time.

MARIA: Let me die.

JESUSITA: He wants me in this world. (MARIA *begins to cry. Looking up at* JESUSITA.)

WOMAN IN THE SAND: Tell her, María. Tell her what really happened.

MARIA: Nothing.

WOMAN IN THE SAND: Something always happens, or we'd have no stories. Walk back. (WOMAN IN THE SAND *touches* MARIA. MARIA *wears a stunned expression.* MARIA *holds her arm.*)

MARIA: Blood on my arms, spilling out. I can't catch all the blood. I can't stop it. From spurting. Out of my arm. It turns into a man and he laughs at me.

WOMAN IN THE SAND: Who is it?

MARIA: I don't know him.

WOMAN IN THE SAND: Who is he?

MARIA: I'm not sure.

WOMAN IN THE SAND: What does he look like?

MARIA: He is so huge—the hugest man in the world. (*The* MAN *appears. He is laughing.* WOMAN IN THE SAND *removes her hand from* MARIA*'s shoulder. The laughing ceases.*)

WOMAN IN THE SAND: What happened last night?

MARIA: (*Gulping.*) Last night. Last night, I tried to take my life.

WOMAN IN THE SAND: Come here.

MARIA: No.

WOMAN IN THE SAND: Look. You will see what I see—yourself suspended in the moment before death.

MARIA: I'm alive. (MARIA *reluctantly crosses to* WOMAN IN THE SAND, *but she does not look.* WOMAN IN THE SAND *points out.*)

WOMAN IN THE SAND: A body without a spirit lies in the surf. Your body. The ocean slaps against your blood-drained arms. Your body waits. For your decision.

MARIA: (*Covering her ears.*) Arms with sand in the grooves. A world of people without ears. Mutants. Aliens. I know.

WOMAN IN THE SAND: Take a look. (MARIA *resists, but then looks in with* WOMAN IN THE SAND. *She sees a* MAN *standing beside her body on the beach.*)

MARIA: What's Raúl doing there standing next to me?

WOMAN IN THE SAND: He's not Raúl. Who is he?

MARIA: I've never seen him in my life.

WOMAN IN THE SAND: You've never seen the world without him. (MARIA *turns her back.*) Why do you turn?

MARIA: You promise me all this magic and then you show me him. (*Beat.*) You've got nothing new. Nothing. Nothing that I even want.

WOMAN IN THE SAND: (*Beat.*) I read your blood. When blood spills a certain way, it leaves a story. (JESUSITA *moans.* MARIA *cries out as she did last night.*)

JESUSITA: I had a hard labor 'cause I was scared. (JESUSITA *writhes with labor pains.* JESUSITA *cries out in a final push for the birth of a baby.* WOMAN IN THE SAND *motions to stop the crying. It stops dead.*)

BLACKOUT

Evangeline Blanco   First Prize: Novel

Caribe (excerpt)

CHAPTER I
DR. RAFAEL RODRÍGUEZ

When he began his 1890s excursions, heart-stopping blackness covered the mountains of the Central Cordillera on crescent moon nights. To carry out his master plan of helping his downtrodden compatriots, Dr. Rodríguez made an annual three-month trip throughout Puerto Rico giving free treatment to the poor. His travels also allowed him to keep track of the growing legion of his offspring and to look for children with particular attributes to lead an army of revolutionaries. At night his pupils dilated in his widened eyes to no avail. Blinded, he felt unanchored, as if he floated without direction in an inky limbo of threatening sounds and earthy scents. The cool, dark void disoriented his mind and confused his senses so that wind rushing through coconut palms sounded like drops of fanciful rain. He attached cowbells to mules loaded down with his medical supplies, rode slowly through narrow mountain passes, and held a lantern high in his black right hand. It shed light only a few feet in front of his donkey, and many times his uncanny instincts alone—inherited from some unknown ancestor—tingled with fear and danger, and made him halt to save himself and his animals from plummeting down dark ravines that bordered dirt roads. Giant ferns, bamboo trees, and other luxuriant foliage grew up the sides of steep inclines and gave bottomless drop-offs the treacherous illusion of gradual down slopes.

In the dark, buzzing flies sounded like mosquitoes, squawking parrots like dangerous birds ready to swoop and attack. In the croaking of tree frogs he imagined that bandits signaled each other, and in the gurgle of streams he heard footsteps. Calming his heartbeat with his own voice and fearful the Spanish militia might shoot him with their rifles for the revolutionary he was, the black doctor shouted his mission.

"Free treatment for the poor! Medicine for the sick!"

Gradually he relied on his lantern, the clang of the cowbells, and the clop, clop of his donkey to identify and protect him from attack by bandits, grateful that the sting of iodine on an open cut might save their fingers or hands, but mainly to attract the peasants who awaited his care and who called to him.

"Over here, Dr. Rodríguez. Watch your left side. Rainfall has swollen the stream."

His lip curled at the lisp of their Spanish accents as it did at his inability to segregate the various noises of the mountains. When he could discern the direction of the caller, Rodríguez drove his tired, stumbling animals toward the voice and asked, "What's the problem here?"

"My child has a fever," some answered.

Children were his favorite patients. Redeeming an otherwise unproductive trip was the saving of a child's life, or the grateful smile that rewarded his soothing the hot itch of chicken pox with camphor. The comfort shining through their feverish eyes filled him with a joy that lifted his usual gloom.

One or two of his patients yelled, "My wife bleeds too much." In some of those cases he looked around the small, shabby dwelling with its central dining table, which had held food for meager meals, fabric for sewing dresses, patterns cut from plain brown paper, as well as, on sad occasions, the overripe corpse of a beloved child, skin turned magenta in death. Parents, loathe to bury the lost child, often waited too long, until the tiny body burst forth its internal liquids. Then, fearing unsanitary surfaces, Rodríguez had little choice except to set up a makeshift clinic with tent poles and sheets outside in the open air, pray it would not rain, operate to remove tumors or cancerous intestines, and pray again that he have no further use for his now bloody and contaminated surgical instruments until his next trip. Sometimes he arrived too late after the woman, anxious for the well-being of her needy family, continued to work without complaining, and lost so much blood that she was beyond saving. On those occasions his tongue tasted the rotted fruit of defeat, which soured his entire rounds.

Often, some of his patients hung their heads in shame for troubling him with mundane matters and said, "My chickens are dying." When this happened, he treated those too without protest or judgment because he knew it meant the difference between life and slow starvation.

This night he heard a squeaky, apologetic voice.

"My hand hurts."

In the paltry arc of his lantern, Dr. Rodríguez stared at a short, stick-thin peasant wearing ragged pants shrunken to mid-shin, looked at the straw-covered roof of his single-room hut resting on stilts, and glanced around for one of the barefoot children of the household.

While he led his mules to the front of the home, dismounted, and climbed the steps to enter, the family lit candles so he could see to examine them. Inside the hut, he spoke only to the husband without glancing at his wife, a woman Rodríguez knew too well.

"Was this an accident or a knife fight?" he asked the peasant, Miguel, who unwrapped a ragged, blood-stained cloth from his left hand.

"Accident. Cutting coconuts with my machete."

"Had you been drinking?"

Miguel hesitated as his eyes flew to those of his wife. "Just a little," he replied.

"I'll teach *that* child," he said, pointing to this household's mulatto.

Rubbing his eyes, this particular sleepy boy, with skin a deeply burnished copper and hair standing upright, approached haltingly.

"Here I am," he said, standing barefoot.

"Pay attention," the doctor commanded. "We have to help your father become well."

"What needs to be done?" the wife asked, smiling. She walked toward him in her nightgown without an effort to cover herself and brushed her fingers on his arm.

Rodríguez stared stonily at her brazen behavior in front of her husband for a half-minute without replying until her mouth opened in mystification over his rudeness. Then he turned to her injured husband who had been watching the exchange so intently he sat as if forgetting his pain.

"Have your son bring me boiled water if he knows how."

Year after year his tactics quieted the families, protected unfaithful wives, as their mates—confused by the formal manners of the black doctor—doubted the truth of nasty rumors and regretted any suspicions they harbored against their wives and against Rodríguez.

Between the boy's running trips to gather wood, start a fire, and fill a pot with stream water, Rodríguez barked orders at him.

"Faster! You're too slow and sloppy. Bring me some moonshine. Here, bring it closer. Stop your laziness."

Close to tears, the harried boy watched Rodríguez as he poured mountain-made white lightning on a red, open gash splitting his father's left palm.

"I have no iodine left. See what I'm doing?"

"Wasting good moonshine?"

"Wrong!" Both father and son startled at the doctor's forceful voice. "Sterilization is all it's good for. Drink it and you might as well poison yourself and throw yourself off a cliff. This rotgut blinds you and makes you stupid." Rodríguez glanced at Miguel then back at the boy, "Understand?"

"Sí, señor."

"Boy, go wash your filthy hands," Rodríguez said. "Don't you know enough to keep yourself clean?"

Rodríguez knew such comments further confused the men of the house. They reasoned it made sense for the doctor to dote over a child that was his instead of treating the boy or girl like a trained insect. He ventured that those thoughts filled many a humble stepfather with an urge to protect the child who was obviously not his. That, along with their fervent desire to believe in their wives' fidelity, led white men to accept the possibility that a mulatto child could really be theirs.

Supervising, he watched the boy wash his father's injury with soap and rinse thoroughly with boiled water. He took over with another application of moonshine before stitching the wound with a large needle and thick black thread. Miguel whimpered and shook. Then his son applied a salve and a bandage, as he was instructed.

"Now, open your palm and look at these two white powders. See the difference?"

The boy nodded. "One is thinner than the other."

"Show me how much of each you can pinch with your thumb and index finger." The boy did so. "Good. This one is for pain. With boiled water allowed to cool, give some to your father every five hours. This other is quinine for fever. No matter how hungry you feel, you must not eat any or you will become very sick. Understand?"

"Yes, sir."

"Are you in school?"

"My son is a good boy," Miguel said, with an edge creeping into his voice.

"I know he is. But good is not enough. We have to be smart and fast, very fast."

"He is."

Noting the child's obvious surprise at his father's support, Rodríguez smiled and ignored both as he repacked his tools and powders, closed his medical bag, and approached the doorway.

"I'll try to return," he said over his shoulder, "in a couple of days to check on the healing. Let me give your son a few last instructions."

Shaking, the boy followed him into the darkness outside.

Hiding behind his mules from the prying eyes of the child's parents, Rodríguez whispered, "How do your brothers and sisters treat you?"

The boy lowered his head and did not answer.

"I'll return to check if you're learning to read and write. The Spanish will never allow a mulatto like you to enjoy your life if you're ignorant. When Puerto Rico is free of them, you can do whatever you like, as I do, but only if you have an education. Will you do that?"

"Yes, sir."

"Don't tell your family because they're white and will not understand." He paused, heartbroken that his parents did not know how to handle the boy's hair. "Have your mother cut your hair very close to your scalp instead of brushing it up like that."

"Yes, sir."

Rodríguez allowed the boy to go back home, confident that it never occurred to the children's ignorant fathers, not familiar with the intricacies of manipulation, that he did not always scold the children, that in his own way he loved them because he had great plans for them.

Spending blinding, sunny days in the open burned his brown skin to almost charcoal. During chilly nights along the mountain roads he followed, biting winds stung his sensitized face and hands. Dr. Rodríguez ground his teeth in frustration, not finding the children he sought.

Men who labored in fields for twelve-hour days and worried about their livelihood the rest of the time, neglected the niceties women craved, and their wives, starved of nourishment for their emotions as well as their bodies, turned to a solicitous, educated man willing to listen, to pet them, and to feed their inner hunger.

He carefully allowed himself to be approached only by milk-white women for his "little mothers" as he called them. The doctor encountered them everywhere on the island, in the cities among the educated and in the hills among the illiterate, young and old, rich and poor. He thought them all flirtatious and greedy and took advantage of their willingness to claw for attention, affection, and sexual fulfillment to feed their vanity and petty carnal needs at the expense of their hard-working husbands. If not him, he felt sure, it would be some other man, perhaps one of the many Puerto Ricans forced to become migrants in their own country by constantly moving between sugarcane fields and coffee and tobacco plantations in their search for work or food. The women fit his agenda although he hated them because they reminded him of two Spanish sisters, his adoptive "aunts."

In his memory it began with his beloved Tata, the chubby housemaid who took time from her kitchen chores to brush fleshy lips on his forehead and call him *negrito lindo*, an endearment the two "aunts" never used. That, or any other. Tata taught him to play a game called the wheel. He jumped up to grab the waist of her apron while she held it fast and twirled around and around, lifting him off his feet causing him to fly in a circle. Josefa, the eldest of his adoptive "aunts," pursed her thin lips at the laughter in the kitchen, stood in the doorway, and watched, arms crossed, until her disapproval silenced them.

"Go to your aunt now," Tata said, almost whispering. "I have scrubbing to do and will talk to you later."

"No, you will not," Josefa commanded. "And you stay, boy. One is never too young to learn so there will be no further mischief in the future." Josefa placed him in front of herself by holding his shoulders and turning him around to face Tata. "We bought him and he belongs to us, not to you. We told you when he first arrived that you were to teach him to take over your duties if you wanted your freedom. Did you not understand?"

"Doña Pepa, he is still too young to do so much work. The house is so big I can hardly do it all myself."

"That's because you spend too much time playing with him. Do not think we will easily grant you permission to marry."

"I'll help, Tata," he said, worried about the fear demonstrated on his friend's face.

Josefa punched him. The force of the blow on his cheek swiveled his small face and neck so violently to the left he thought himself unable to move his head. Numbed with pain, his eyes watered, but he did not cry. In shock, he stared, open-mouthed.

"Us. You help us, not her. She is our servant."

The unspoken "and so are you" filled him with a sense of otherness, his color.

After that, he and Tata settled into a damaged relationship, quiet and aloof except for a dry explanation about how her job was her livelihood and she could not afford to lose it, and that, in the future, he would make new friends. Although he understood the anxiety his nearness caused her, he still sought her out only to be pushed away. By the year Tata went away, leaving him with the household chores, the boy had accepted and lived with the pain of separation, the loss of kind, loving banter for a long time.

No matter how much he begged, his "aunts" refused to allow him to attend school with other children by saying they did not want him among ruffians and individuals with strange ideas, although they did not say specifically what these strange ideas were. They educated him at home with tutors.

"That way we can watch you ourselves," they said.

The first of the soon-to-be-many contracted teachers looked from the "aunts" to him and asked, "What exactly do you require?"

"We want to know if you can teach him anything," they answered.

In one of his rare impetuous moments the growing child spoke with pride, "I can learn anything."

Like something out of a dream, he felt the blows before his eyes registered long rustling skirts coming at him so quickly that their feet did not seem to touch the floor.

"Speak only when spoken to," Josefa screamed. Shame burned his face as he hung his head in front of the stranger.

"No hitting!" the teacher said, a bit too loud. "I don't teach that way." The indignant young man straightened and stuck out his chin. "Besides, the boy is right. Why shouldn't he be able to learn?"

His other "aunt," Isabel, more controlled and businesslike, answered him, "Thank you for coming, but we will not need your services."

When he recovered from his stunned silence, the tutor said, "My references are impeccable."

THE CHICANO/LATINO LITERARY PRIZE ૎ **241**

As the young scholar kept his eyes locked on Rodríguez, the "aunts" showed him the door without reply and continued to interview.

Although he was present during subsequent exchanges, the boy heard nothing as his thoughts filled with the difference yet similarity between Tata and the teacher. Although white, creole, educated, and outspoken enough to try to defend him, the teacher had been just as powerless to help as his former friend.

Finally after several teachers were hired, Rodríguez—damned if he would let himself fail—toiled through his lessons while the small white women listened, sat side by side, and waved their fans.

"Excellent student," his tutors reported. "He learns everything the first time it is taught to him. You may want to consider an additional, more advanced teacher."

"We will."

"Also, I want to enter one of his essays in a competition."

"No, we don't wish to become a laughingstock in case he wins. We forbid it."

"But he's brilliant!"

Yet, listening behind doors, Rodríguez also heard those same thin, immaculately groomed scholars say, "I would never have thought a Negro could be that intelligent." Often the spinsters reminded him of fat hens fluffing their feathers in front of a rooster as they fanned themselves and cooed through tight, smug smiles.

"It is, no doubt, our influence."

They taught him proper manners and educated him, but he hated their control. Wrapped inside the cloak of adoptive caring maidens, their grasping fingers and greedy hands stroked him intimately when he was long past proper age. If he objected, with "Stop. What are you doing?" he was punished, made to stand in the patio where the midday sun roasted his skin and scalded him until he felt faint.

During those times he stood erect, closed his eyes against the dazzle of sun ghosts dancing in the air. He allowed perspiration to drip down his temples past his lips, soak his chin, and continue all the way to wet his socks and shoes. Rodríguez let the streams trickle without once wiping himself off, every thought focused on not allowing his knees to buckle in a faint before one tutor or another arrived to rescue him.

Sometimes his "aunts" gave in out of fear they might kill him and rushed to him in the patio carrying water, or a *pava*, a straw hat.

"You are very lucky and must respect our affection," they said, "without making improper insinuations." Calmly, they fitted their white lace gloves on each stubby finger. "We consider you our own even though you aren't. Even though you're black, we are very grateful to do so much for you." They flounced away to church fanning themselves.

As he watched their mantilla-clad heads retreat, his hatred for Spanish domination grew strong as did his desire to understand how he could be considered lucky. Inherited lands and money did not come free.

A slave is a slave.

Why had the white spinsters adopted him? If, as they said, he had been born out of wedlock to a poor family from Loíza Aldea, had they started out with good intentions that deteriorated through time and circumstance? Rodríguez thought not, or else his "aunts" would have accepted one of the many white or mixed-race babies offered daily by distressed parents who could not bear to watch their children starve.

Fueled by the conviction that his fate decreed great accomplishments because he believed himself more logical than others, he often promised himself that someday Negroes from Loíza Aldea, including the natural parents who gave him up, would have the same opportunities to make a good living as the ruling class, and would never have to forfeit their children again.

Obsessed with freedom, Rodríguez studied history to find out why the Cuban revolution against the Spanish succeeded, while the Puerto Rican cry of independence organized the same year of 1868 by his exiled idol Betances had been aborted in its infancy. He read pamphlets detailing Puerto Rican lack of armaments, traitorous informers, and about patriots jailed together and abandoned to yellow fever.

"So what?" he thought. No fight for freedom ever lacked these same elements. He found nothing in the records to provide an answer to the question, "Why did the revolution just stop?"

On the eve of his sixteenth birthday, Rodríguez formulated a theory. As he sat in a large metal tub full of heated water, he watched the two women with amusement as they soaped and sponged his penis and testicles. He had gotten too old for this ritual and knew this had to be the last bath they gave him. As determined as they looked to make the most of it, he also determined not to get an erection they could laughingly chide him about. Rodríguez watched their flushed faces concentrate on keeping their composure while they stuttered and stammered.

"Get more water."

"No, you get it. I'll continue scrubbing."

Both refused to leave, and Rodríguez thought, *One, I can strangle. Two, . . .*

"The numbers!" he said, raising a soapy index finger.

"W-what?"

"Nothing."

He found his answer. In contrast to Puerto Rico, Cuba's population had been numerous with many more mistreated slaves motivated to fight for freedom. Less simple-minded in their acceptance of fate and better educated, Cubans even had Negro generals to lead their revolt.

Rodríguez despaired for his fellow Puerto Ricans and began to think of them as Simple Simons.

He did not object to giving his "aunts" a rare, farewell kiss on the hand as he packed his suitcase in preparation for his studies abroad.

"Make us proud," they said. "Keep your attention on your studies and not on inappropriate women."

Pausing from stuffing shirts into his soft leather satchel, he turned to face them.

"Who is inappropriate?"

"Those neither educated nor virtuous."

How many Negro women will have my schooling?

Elated to be rid of the short, square women, Rodríguez looked forward to studying in France, possibly meeting with the exiled patriot Betances. He expected to practice medicine in Spain and obtain freedom in the middle of his enemies.

During his education in Europe, the French and Spanish of the late 1880s greeted Rodríguez with comments like, "Isn't it wonderful that someone from the colonies can also have all the opportunities."

"Someone like you," is what he heard and dove into his textbooks.

Beautiful Spanish women from large cities had many wealthy suitors and no interest in Rodríguez once they satisfied their curiosity about his studies, his travels, and his homeland, marveling over the generosity of his "aunts," so Rodríguez sought the company of the less attractive. He first found the "little mothers" in Spain's countryside, small white women with slivers of lips stretching from one ear to the other and square jaws atop square bodies. They lived for one compliment after another on their "good looks." Loving to be called *guapa*, the women flirted shamelessly to hear it.

He found them all amusingly similar until he met La Mercedes, a younger, more charming woman who did not avert her large, black eyes to speak to him and laughed easily about her gypsy blood, offering to read his palm for a gold coin.

"Aha!" she said. "A very long life line." He laughed. "But my goodness, look at this. No love line, yet many wrinkles at the side where children are supposed to be numbered." He laughed again, more loudly.

"Señorita, children are the furthest thing from my mind. If you plan to make your living from palmistry I fear you will miss a few meals."

"Speaking of which," she said, "dinner is served."

With that, she took his arm and escorted him to the dining room. There he repeated his often-told tales of France and Puerto Rico to her parents and her brother, each of whom invited him to return.

Fooled by their polite hospitality, he thought her family found him intelligent and attractive enough for serious consideration as a marriage mate to Mercedes, especially since the recent death of his "aunts" had made him a wealthy man. But when he returned her attentions in a self-deceptive need for real love, her horrified expression at his overtures for a formal relationship convinced him otherwise. She shunned him politely with an insipid excuse.

"You're an educated man," she said slowly, suddenly averting her entire face, "but I'm already engaged to one of my brother's colleagues and I never thought of you as anything but a friend."

Knowing otherwise, that obvious unsubstantiated lie was a bigger blow to his ego than if she had simply said, "No, I don't love you nor do I want to marry a Negro." He might have understood such an explanation since he had a first-hand understanding of prejudice. He cursed his stupidity over misinterpreting what he meant to Mercedes as real feeling rather than as simple entertainment. *What can be more pathetic than a needy person?*

"Forgive my imprudence," he said, kissing her hand. When he had taken his leave, vowing to sever the friendship, he mourned his situation. Too dark-skinned for educated white women and too educated for dark-skinned women working as domestics, he would have to search far and wide for a soul mate.

After obtaining his second medical degree, he practiced in Spain for almost two years until a poor country couple came to see him.

An elderly farmer who had not bothered to change out of his stable-scented work clothes pushed a thin, very young woman toward him.

"I've buried three wives," Pepe Soto said, without looking at him. "Now this one won't give me sons either."

Milk white, the girl's skin paled further as she kept her eyes on her fingers. His patients fell into two categories. The first came to stare at his dark face and the second, too poor to afford another doctor, averted their eyes.

"How old is your wife?"

"Fifteen."

"Does she menstruate regularly?"

"That's the trouble." Pepe struck a blow on her arm. She lost her balance, almost fell. "She bleeds every month."

"It might be her youth. Suppose I examine you first."

"Not me. There's nothing wrong with my functions."

"What a dumb fool," Rodríguez thought. In spite of four supposedly infertile wives, it had not occurred to the old cretin that it might be his own infertility keeping him from having children. Knowing he could do very little, he put a bottle of tarlike tonic in the hand of each.

"These will take time," he said. "Please return in three months."

After the allotted time, she returned by herself. Assailed by her husband's complaints and distressed by his sexual demands, the unattractive young wife begged Rodríguez for help.

"Look what he did to me," she said, uncovering her back. "Every time I menstruate, he beats me."

As he applied salve to raised red welts on her white skin, Rodríguez, moved to pity, identified with her predicament.

"Ignorance is a terrible enslavement," he said. "In my country, life is so hard that many accept themselves as Juan Bobos, content with a despicable and unexamined existence."

With eyes blank and mouth open, she stared. "Señor Doctor, your words are too difficult for me."

Unconsciously, he reached out and patted her hand, "What I mean . . ." He paused when she squirmed at his touch and withdrew her hand. As he looked straight into her small, close-set eyes, he could hardly believe her presumption that he was trying to make an improper overture. Still in love with Mercedes, he found her with her large nose, ugly by comparison. This had happened once too often and it awoke his sleeping fury of rejection, of being considered inferior. "You're a beautiful woman," he lied, "and your husband is a very stupid man. If this happens again, I will talk to him."

The next time the homely young woman visited him, he gave her a bouquet of flowers and some perfumed soaps he ordered from Madrid.

"Perhaps, aided by your natural beauty, these will help," he said and waited to see if she told her husband. She did not. If she had, he might have reconsidered his resolve to rid his heart of the last vestiges of a Puerto Rican inclination toward sympathy. On hearing of an enemy's downfall, most reacted with *bendito*, poor thing.

On subsequent visits she offered him a whiff of the perfume lingering from her bath and listened to his Simple Simon tales. Then she found excuses to see him for headaches, indigestion, and broken fingernails, laughed that her husband Pepe might be Juan Bobo, and did not withdraw her hand. Squashing any idea of hope that she might be sincere, he hardened himself against feeling sorry for her.

In time he felt confident enough to recite erotic poems and declare his passion until he believed her to be so impressed that he could safely graduate to greater intimacies.

When she began to avoid him, her growing abdomen and her new formality told him what to expect.

"Señor Doctor, your services are not needed. The town midwife will attend to the birth of my husband's child, not you."

Rodríguez found that the old farmer proved not so stupid after all. Pepe did not accept the possibility that he had moorish blood to explain the brown infant whose hair, unlike the dead straight hair of his parents, turned wiry after his third month.

"I'm from León," Pepe said, as if that explained everything. "We killed all the Moors. Watch out for yourself, Moor." Old Pepe shook his rake at Rodríguez and added, "Watch out you're not skewered on a night as dark as your soul and your testicles fed to my pigs."

That incident alone did not chase Rodríguez from Spain, but news from Puerto Rico did. He heard about a growing movement advocating autonomy from Spain and learned of both the establishment of the Puerto Rican Autonomy Party, begun by Román Baldorioty de Castro's "Autonomy Credo," and of a secret organization called The Old Man's Tower, which was to give economic preference to creoles by boycotting Spanish-owned businesses. Given the political upheaval occurring in Spain between monarchists and non-monarchists, he believed in the possibility that Puerto Rico might be freed. Patriotism surfaced in him with the idea that his grand purpose in life ordained his return to the island to take part in the struggle against Spanish colonial rule, and he quickly made plans to return home at once.

Time abroad had dulled his memory of his homeland's tropical beauty. Shortly before his ship sighted land, the air changed. Breezes carried the scent of mangoes, rose apples, and guava. Pineapples mixed with coconut oils and acerola, wet earth with tuberose to form a unique aura, the unmistakable bouquet of Puerto Rico: hot, sweet, and sad. Through flared nostrils and open mouth, he took deep gulping breaths of the scent as if he had been drowning.

His eyes watered at the sight of giant coconut palms towering near white sand beaches bathed by a multicolored Caribbean Sea. Brilliantly hued royal poincianas, *flamboyán*, along with poinsettias, decorated the countryside. *Cucubanos*, large relatives of the common firefly, lit up bread-fruit trees, *guanábanas*, papayas, and sea grapes.

At home, Rodríguez also became reacquainted with ignorance. Illiterate because of the lack of schools, or the necessity to work at a very young age, few among the lower class could read, write, or even reason logically whereas the well-off still lived regally, traveled, and produced a generation of lawyers and journalists, poets and painters. Lack of sanitation, proper housing, and nourishment resulted in short, painful life spans. He felt newly offended at a rigid class system where only appointees of the Spanish court reigned supreme over politics and the economy, perpetuating the unlivable conditions.

He considered Luis Muñoz Rivera, white descendant of Spaniards and leader of the autonomists, totally incompetent, a man who ran his politics on the self-interest of safeguarding his own class power while maintaining the illusion that he was really striving for independence on the sly.

To Rodríguez, the problem remained numbers, education, and cowardice, and he thought about the child in Spain. If he had many children in many different parts of the island and educated them, they could make a difference. As the legal, light-skinned offspring of white parents, the Church could not include the names of those children in the secret documents they kept to record all of mixed heritage, denying them opportunities. Startled, he remembered Mercedes' fortune-telling and began to make himself available to his "little mothers."

When he started his amours in Puerto Rico he found most of the creole parents isolated and ignorant of history, easier to persuade than the old Spanish farmer, Pepe Soto, that no matter how fair skinned, few could argue positively that they had no Indian or black blood unless they were newly arrived from Europe.

Simple Simons!

In a country of people filled with deep-seated bias in favor of good looks, money, intelligence, and above all light skin, Rodríguez believed only those who fit that description had a chance at being accepted or voted into positions of leadership, and he wanted his children to be among those leaders. Remembering a lonely Betances abandoned by former compatriots after the mysterious death of Segundo Ruiz Belvis, Rodríguez decided not just one or two but many generals were needed for the fight. In order to break future generations of their genetic passivity, his task required that he create those generals and teach them to hate a yoke of any kind until that hatred boiled up in them like a bubbling tar pit.

Then what? He weighed the consequences of violent revolution against the possibility of insidious infiltration and takeover. Without being able to choose between the two, he decided on a combination of both to ensure continuity of rebellion. "No matter," he thought. "My sperm, my tar pit will know what to do."

Over the years he rejected many of his children as leaders because he did not see the right combination. Two or three turned out good-looking, either with light skin, his hair, and negroid features, or very dark with straight hair, but in the illumination of his lantern showed the dull eyes of the mentally slow. He did not abandon those he considered his infantry. He visited them whenever possible to speak to them and leave gifts of money and food, but he accelerated his adventures, going so far as to initiate encounters with reluctant women to continue his quest for the leaders he wanted to produce.

1995-96

Mike Padilla **First Prize: Short Story**

Hard Language

They had been living legally in the United States for a year and a half when Antonio announced to his wife in no uncertain terms that they were going to learn English once and for all.

"We know less now than we did when we moved here," he said, pacing the border of the frayed oval rope rug. "There's no way we're going to get ahead if we don't know the language."

On the sofa Pilar thumbed through one of her Mexican movie magazines while *menudo* simmered in the kitchen. "And where am I going to find time to take a class?" she said. "I have this house to take care of and you to cook for and the neighbor's kids to watch in the afternoons."

"Most of my customers are going to speak English," he went on. "There's no way I can grow the business otherwise."

"Fine." She snapped her magazine shut. "Get me my own car so I don't have to walk half an hour to get groceries, and plan on cooking some of your own meals, and get the building manager to finally fix that washing machine. Then I'll take your class."

She went into the kitchen and gave the *menudo* a forceful stir, took it off the stove and turned down the flame. At the table she laid out a bowl and spoon for each of them and a plate of olives from the Greek store downstairs. They sat down. Steam rose up between them, a gauzy curtain.

"There's one more thing," Antonio said, tucking his napkin into his shirt. "If we're going to do this, we have to do it right. No more Mexican movies and Mexican radio and Mexican newspapers. Everything is going to have to be in English from now on."

She ladled out the soup, shaking her head as if listening to a lunatic's ramblings.

"Pilar, look at the Pachecos. They've been here for five years and they still can't say anything. Why? Because they only talk Spanish around the house, they only have Mexican friends."

"So now you want me to give up my friends, too? Maybe I could also bleach my hair and eyebrows. That way I'd look *and* sound like an American."

Antonio cleared his throat. "In the long run, Pilar—"

"How is it you know what's best 'in the long run'?"

"I want us to make progress."

"Leaving Tijuana was supposed to be progress."

"We had nothing in Tijuana."

"We had our own house."

"It was your parent's house."

"At least it wasn't a moldy shoe-box, and at least we had more to eat than watered-down . . ."

"Pilar!" He pounded his fist on the table so his soup splattered. He did not wipe it up.

She pursed her lips. Dark lines radiated out from the corners of her mouth, her eyes. Then she threw her twisted napkin on the table and left the room.

When she came back a few minutes later, she had her hair pulled back into a ponytail. "All right," she said. "I'll sign us up for the class tomorrow. But don't expect more than baloney sandwiches for dinner and don't come griping to me when you find you don't have enough clean shirts for the week."

Antonio's heart swelled with gratitude, but he kept his head lowered, his face somber. From the day they got married, he had asked more of her than it had been fair to expect. Trying to start his own scrap business while working at O'Connor's machine shop meant they hadn't spent a weekend together in six months, and it had been more than a year since they had returned to Tijuana to visit her parents. That night in bed, Antonio slipped his leg between hers. He wanted to make love to her, to show her how much he appreciated her. But she only moved to her edge of the bed with her arms wrapped tightly around a pillow.

In the morning, they rose and showered together without talking. She scrambled his eggs and *chorizo* in the kitchen, working the pan with violent motions, her lips clamped in a bitter smile. He chose to leave her alone. Women were entitled to periods of extreme anger and sadness, and he had learned it was best to indulge them. The inner workings of their hearts were intricate and fine—too delicate to be tampered with by clumsy men.

On Friday of that week, he came home from work to find Pilar chirping happily on the phone with her mother. She waved to Antonio, then got off the phone quickly to greet him with a kiss. He put his arms around her, buried his face in her hair. "Did something good happen to you today?" he said.

"Nothing in particular. Maybe it's just because today is the first day of spring. You know how nice weather affects me."

But Antonio noticed something different about her that night as she started dinner. For a long time he couldn't pinpoint what it was. Not until he asked her if she needed help and she waved him away from the counter did he figure it out. Pilar was smiling in the kitchen. He had never noticed it before, but now he realized Pilar never smiled in the kitchen. She hated to cook, and normally grumbled and clattered and thrashed her way through preparing even the simplest meals. But today she was smiling, like someone on the cover of a homemaking magazine.

She smiled throughout dinner, too, then hummed through the clearing of plates. From the sofa in the living room he watched her carefully, the way she nearly danced to secret music in her head from counter to cupboard. It wasn't until later, when she stepped out to see her friend Monica but did not come back for nearly two hours, that Antonio's thoughts, like iron shavings to a magnet, adhered themselves to the possibility that Pilar was having an affair.

It had happened once before, while they were still living in Tijuana in a brown-faced cottage Pilar's parents had rented for them on the east side of town. Over the side-yard fence Antonio had seen Pilar walking toward the house with a delicate-jawed, sleek-haired young man who owned the grocery store down the street. Their shoulders brushed as they ambled along. What had ensued from Antonio's accusation was a single, unending night of tables pounded and doors slammed, faces contorted in rage and words honed to murderous pitch. Yes, she finally admitted, she had spent the day with him at the movies. But she had come from an active family of seven children, was not accustomed to spending her days alone, and anyway, if Antonio had taken her to the movies the weekend before as he had promised to in the first place . . . No, she said, there was nothing between them, he was just a boy, for God's sake. After hours of argument had exhausted them to the point of gray numbness, they at last sat across from each other in the haggard dawn, and came to an agreement: They would accelerate their plans to move to the United States. And in return, he would never again accuse her of something of which he had no proof.

"Why so serious today, Antonio?" Miguel said. He was standing on a crate at his lathe in the machine shop, being too short to reach it himself. "Problems with the wife, maybe?"

Antonio smiled, but concentrated on his lathe, fitting the shaft into the chuck.

"You should have seen the one I had last night," Miguel said, loud enough for everyone in the warehouse to hear.

"How does anyone so short and pudgy get so many women?" Gómez, one of the other workers, shouted.

"And with dragon breath on top of it," someone else said.

"I have what women want," Miguel said. He held a nine-inch length of shaft up over his head and shook it. There was a burst of laughter. Someone threw a turning at him, but he deflected it with his arm. "And you know what the best thing about her was? She was married. Married women in unhappy relationships are always the wildest."

"What about the poor husbands?" someone said.

"They should thank me," he said. "After all, I'm doing them a service, returning their wives to them satisfied and in a good mood . . . ."

Antonio slammed the off button on his machine and tore off his goggles. The compressor whirred to a stop. He headed toward the rest room. Miguel followed him.

"What is it, *hombre?*" he said. "Something's gotten into you today."

"You shouldn't talk that way," Antonio said.

"I wasn't serious," he said. "I just make these things up. You know, to make the time go faster."

"But you have cheated with married women, haven't you?"

"Well, sure. And Carmela used to cheat on me too. Everybody does it."

Antonio said nothing, only stared at his shoes.

"Listen," Miguel said. "You're my best friend. I don't want to offend you. If it will make you feel better, I'll try to tone things down a little."

Antonio thought for a moment. "Tell me, is there a way to tell if a woman is cheating on you?"

"Ah," Miguel said. "It's in the touch. Like when your chuck isn't tightened right. You can't tell by looking, but you can feel it in your hands."

That night Antonio came up behind Pilar in the bathroom and as carefully as if he were conducting the most delicate of experiments, put his arms around her. The curves of her body yielded into his, like molten metal filling its cast. Surely she couldn't have responded this way if she had recently been with another.

But moments later she was on her way out to the dry cleaners to pick up something that she said she'd forgotten there earlier.

"Do you know where the *TV Guide* is?" he said to get her attention.

She stopped in the door frame, with one foot in the living room, one foot out in the hall. "It probably fell between the cushions," she said, but she did not come back in to help him find it. Instead, she glanced over her shoulder—not at him, but at the clock above his head.

Antonio felt his heart cool to a solid. He could not move, as his suspicions swirled up around him. He imagined a man waiting for her—in a parked car, a hotel room, an office. He pictured him looking at his watch, wondering what was keeping her. Pictured Pilar's nervous, bird-like stride as she hurried to be on time.

Antonio sat for a long time after Pilar was gone, watching his own distorted reflection in the curved TV tube which was not on—the face of an imbecile, a fool. Then he left the house and started to walk. He walked west of the commercial district and under the freeway, then out past the train tracks to where a stale wind was sweeping over barren fields. He walked quickly to keep the images from overtaking him, spiky cattails catching in his pant cuffs. Something painful and watery rose in his throat. He wanted to be where no one would see him should he start to cry. But no sooner was he alone than he felt a desperate need to be among the living. He turned back. Perhaps if he wandered long enough he would find her, catch her coming out of an unknown apartment, see *him* waving goodbye from an unfamiliar doorstep. Is that what he was hoping for? What would he do then? To her? To him?

His mind was beginning to grow numb when he passed the Bal Theater, where Spanish-language movies played along with American films dubbed into Spanish. He had passed it once already. But now fear spilled out of him, leaving him a clear, quivering, embarrassed shell. He knew exactly where she was.

He bought a ticket without looking to see what was playing and went into the theater. The girl in the tubular box office window called out that the next showing was not for another hour, but Antonio kept walking. There was no one in the lobby to take his ticket, so he walked into the theater.

He found Pilar in the back row where she usually liked to sit, her coat drawn over her lap against the theater chill. He sat down next to her, but she did not notice him. The border of the screen trembled unevenly, but at its center a smartly-dressed man and woman held each other firmly. Was that Claudia Beltrán, the star of their teen years that they had gone to see when they'd first been dating? He couldn't remember, but he thought so. Antonio felt his own heart blossom against the inside of his rib cage. Or was it only the orchestra's swelling violins that were making him feel this way?

He touched Pilar's hand and she jumped. "¡Ay! Antonio! Why are you here?" In a rushed whisper she began to explain, but he stopped her by pressing his lips to the back of her hand. His penitent tears dripped onto her wrist. He threaded his fingers through hers, marveling at the fit, a fist in his throat blocking words.

He did not let her talk as they walked home. It was dark by now. In the clear and glittering sky he saw reflected the state of his own heart. "I'll take you to the Spanish movies any time you want," he said. "I don't know what I was thinking. I never meant to be so harsh, Pilar."

That night sweet guilt fueled his lovemaking with her. He did for her all the things she liked, poured favorite words into her ears, the ones that made her arch her back and strain her toes as if trying to touch something just the other side of this world. Maybe it was a mistake to concede so completely, but . . . there was no "but." There was only this, only Pilar, only now.

The English class took place in the gymnasium at the local high school. The teacher, a boy-faced man of about twenty-five with James Dean sideburns, arrived to class in a knitted sweater with the print of a parrot spreading its wings against a sunrise. Immediately Antonio did not like him. He was too young and obviously spent too much time caring for his appearance. He moved about the room too energetically and taught with elaborate gestures that Antonio thought were unnecessary and effeminate. Antonio sat silently through the first class, gnawing his pen cap into a gnarled lump.

"I think the teacher's a fag," he told Pilar afterwards. She was sitting on the living room floor starting their first assignment, legs tucked under the glass coffee table.

"He's a good teacher," she said. She adjusted her black-framed reading glasses, but didn't look up.

"How can you say that? It's only the first class. He hasn't had a chance to teach us anything."

"I can tell, that's all."

"You like him because he's attractive," he said.

"I like him because he's interesting." She took Antonio's hand and pulled him down to the floor with her. "Come sit. We can do the first assignment together."

He scooted close to her, flipped through the first few pages. "Admit you think he's attractive," he said after a few minutes.

"I think *you're* attractive," she said. She took off her glasses and circled her fingers around the back of his neck, but he resisted her kiss. He hated it whenever Pilar condescended to him. With his broad flat nose and pocked moon face, he often wondered what Pilar had ever seen in him. Since his childhood, his father had constantly reminded him that he was both dense and ugly. "Plan on making your living with your hands rather than your brains," he used to advise. "And don't be picky when it comes to choosing a wife. A face like yours is more likely to attract flies than women."

The next week the teacher went up and down the rows asking each student to read a few sentences aloud, stopping each person every few minutes to correct pronunciation. But when he got to Pilar, he did not stop her. He let her read for several minutes. Then he broke out into slow, deliberate applause. "Thank you, Pilar. You pronounce beautifully."

Pilar sucked in her lower lip and blushed behind her curtain of black hair. Antonio thought he had never seen her look so beautiful. Others were look- ing at her as well, and some of the guys continued to gaze at her long after the teacher's attention had turned elsewhere. During the break, Antonio moved his desk flush against hers and held her hand throughout the rest of the class.

But as the hour came to an end, Antonio could tell the class was going to be more difficult for him. Trying to speak English had always been like trying to tie a cherry stem into a knot with his tongue. His mistakes seemed to echo louder and reverberate longer in the huge building than anyone else's. He left class with a burning face, his insides knotted with humiliation.

"Don't you see he's after you?" he said to Pilar later. "The way he looks at you, they way he leans against your desk."

"I thought you said he was a fag," Pilar said.

"Even a fag has to notice someone like you," he said.

She started piling up her books.

"Where are you going?" he said.

"Someplace where I can concentrate. You're being ridiculous, and I'm not listening to you anymore."

He followed her to the bedroom. "He likes you," he said.

"Because I'm a good student," she said.

"What's that supposed to mean?"

"Whatever you want."

"You think I'm stupid."

"I think it wouldn't hurt if you studied a little instead of making up fantasies."

At the bathroom door she laid a hand on his chest and pushed him back, then shut the door and locked it. "I'm not stupid," he said, rattling the doorknob. "And I'm telling you, he is after you."

At the shop, Miguel pulled him aside just as Antonio was breaking for lunch. "There are going to be layoffs soon," he said.

"Everybody knows about that," Antonio said. "Why are you whispering?"

Miguel looked over his shoulder. He waddled over to the far side of the silver food truck, gesturing for Antonio to follow him. "I know you're starting your own business. I want to be a part of it."

Antonio shrugged. "I only have two accounts so far. Anyway, you have nothing to worry about. You've been here longer than anyone else."

"And you think I want to be popping out bolts and nuts for the rest of my life?" He pulled Antonio closer by his sleeve. "When the layoffs come, I want to be first in line. You're going to need someone to drive for you and weld boxes and load scrap. And I may be short, but I'm strong as a horse and I have stamina."

"I wouldn't be able to pay you anything until I got a few more accounts."

"In the long run it will be worth it."

"What about your alimony payments?"

"I can barely pay them now."

Antonio thought for a moment. "Are you willing to take that kind of chance?"

"I've always said you're the only Mexican around here with any vision," he said. "I have a lot of faith in you."

On the last day of class, Antonio hurried through the final test. He did not care how he did on it, just as long as he could get out of that classroom once and for all. He turned in his test without looking at the teacher, then rushed out to the parking lot to smoke a cigarette while he waited for Pilar.

A night breeze rushed over them as they walked to dinner that evening to celebrate. "Thank you for taking the class," he said.

He took her hand and tried to go on. There was much more to tell her, but the words struggled against each other, canceling each other in his throat. At the Italian restaurant near their apartment, the waiter seated them outside at one of the patio tables. Insects buzzed about their heads. Antonio tried again. "You made quite an impression on the class."

Pilar bit thoughtfully into a piece of garlic bread. "I was surprised myself. I wasn't expecting it to be that easy."

"Then you're glad I suggested it?"

"I can admit when I'm wrong."

"Yes," he said, "I appreciate that."

He opened his menu, but Pilar didn't open hers. Instead, she took a course catalogue out of her straw bag. "Should we do Wednesday nights again next semester?" she said.

"I thought we would wait a while before we took another class," he said.

"Why shouldn't we keep going?"

"I don't have time now. The layoffs are coming, and I want to have the business built up."

"I thought you needed it for the business."

"I know enough to get by," he said, fumbling his napkin.

"You'll forget everything if you don't practice."

"We can practice at home. We can practice right now."

Pilar looked up.

"We'll take the class in the summer," he said.

"Never mind. I'll just take it myself."

"I'd rather you didn't take it without me."

"Fine." She took up her menu, glared relentlessly into the fold. Over the top of it, the line in her brow darkened.

Antonio picked at the knobby corners of his napkin. Pilar looked around the restaurant, but not at him. She waved the waiter over.

She was silent on the way home. She went into the building while he walked to the corner for a pack of cigarettes. It was always best to give her time to cool off. But when he came in, she was pacing intensely.

"Pilar, please don't be this way."

She turned to him with arms locked in a fold. "I've put up with a lot since we got married," she said. "I've agreed to give up a lot of my time and rearranged my life to learn this stupid language, and now that you see how much I like it, you want to take it away from me. How much more do I have to give up, Antonio? And when do I get to see something in return?"

"It's just that we're married and I think we should do things together."

As she paced, the very air she walked through seemed to boil up around her.

"Pilar, calm down, you're behaving like a child . . ."

Then she did something that she had never before done in their three years of marriage. She picked up a casserole dish and threw it. It glanced off the counter between the kitchen and the dining area and crashed into the glass coffee table. Glass shards spewed everywhere, dispersing the light into a brief, angry rainbow.

"When a woman starts to act up it means she's getting her own ideas," Miguel told him after work the next day. Antonio hadn't wanted to go home and had convinced Miguel to have a beer with him. "Have you thought about hitting her? I don't believe in hitting women, of course. But wives . . . well, that's something different."

"Did you ever hit your ex-wife?"

"Of course," he said. "Why do you think she's my ex-wife?"

"So what kind of advice is that?"

"You didn't say you wanted advice."

"Now I'm telling you."

"What about cheating on her?"

"What good would that do?"

"It would get your mind off her."

Antonio rotated his glass between his palms. Miguel gave a long sigh. "There's only one option left, then. You're going to have to swallow your pride and make it up to her."

"I can't seem weak," Antonio said.

"You have a point."

"Then what should I do?"

"Buy me another beer."

"I already bought you two."

"I think better after three."

They kept drinking until the bar closed. Antonio found Pilar at home curled on her side of the bed, fast asleep. It felt good to slip into the warm sheets with her. He guided the hair away from her face so he could look at her, hoping not to wake her, and at the same time hoping she would wake, that she would turn to him and embrace him as if nothing had ever been bad between them. She stirred. Antonio mouthed a wordless prayer that she not tear away from him.

She stirred again, murmured—his name, or something else? "Don't be mad at me," he whispered. She backed into the curve of him, and he slipped his arm around her. Into her ear he whispered one of the phrases that he knew excited her. This was one of the things they both loved—the exchange of hot, sweet, nasty words. He felt himself getting hard against her back, lifted himself to move on top of her. He eased her leg up over his shoulder, whispered more words. "Now talk to me," he said, "talk to me." She raised her head off the pillow, pressed her lips against his ear and whispered something he did not understand.

"Spanish," he said. "Say it in Spanish."

"I have to practice my English," she breathed.

"Not now," he said, going into her. "Later. Please. Make love to me in Spanish."

But only English words kept coming. For all he knew she was reciting a lesson she remembered from class. He started to go soft, felt his own heart slowing out of rhythm with what he was trying to do. Pilar was smiling at him.

"I can't do it in that language," he panted, collapsing on his back.

"What difference does it make?"

"I don't know. It just does. I never thought it would make a difference."

She rolled away from him and went back to sleep. She was teaching him a lesson, and though he wanted to get angry about it, his heart was too weighted to muster the fight. More upsetting than the lack of sex was how easily Pilar seemed to go without it. Sex was the only way he had ever been sure he was telling her how much he felt. It was his language for giving her joy. Now he saw that perhaps it had never meant that much to her after all.

On payday Antonio came into the machine shop to find a half-dozen of his co-workers huddled around Miguel's workstation, talking about the upcoming lay-offs.

"That rumor's been going around for a while," Antonio said.

"Today," Miguel said. "We're talking about today. They tried to keep it from us until the end of the day, but I saw the pink slips on Martínez' desk."

"Are you sure?" Gómez said.

"I'm pretty sure."

"Pretty sure?" someone else said. "Either you're sure or you're not. Which is it?"

"Calm down," Antonio said. "Tell me, Miguel, did you see any names?"

"No," he said, "but there was a stack of them."

One of the managers came to the door of the second floor office. Everyone looked up, then started to break apart.

Antonio put on his goggles and went back to his machine. He was losing his wife and now he was losing his job, and he had made no more progress on the business. Everything, everything was slipping away at a rate he couldn't seem to counter.

He turned his lathe back on, letting the hum of the machine calm him. He had always found something soothing about machines. Something about the predictability of them, he supposed.

At lunch he found Miguel out by the lunch truck. "I'm breaking away," he said. "I'm quitting. No one's going to fire me from a job. I've been here the least time, so I'm sure to be the first to go."

"Then we'll quit together," Miguel said.

"Are you sure about this?" Antonio said.

"I told you, I'm behind you completely. Anyway, it might save one of these other poor bastards' jobs. Let's get it over with."

On their way up the steps to the office, Antonio wanted more than anything else to call Pilar. He had never made a decision like this before without talking to her, and now he ached to hear her approving voice. Yes, she would approve, he was sure of it . . . . But just to hear her voice, just to hear her voice . . .

On his first day working for Antonio, Miguel worked all afternoon with him in the hot sun clearing space for scrap piles in the two-acre dirt yard that Antonio had rented for his business. They took Antonio's GMC roll-off unit out for a drive so Miguel could get the feel of it, then came back to the yard to weld the drop-off containers they would need for pick-ups. It felt good to Antonio to work with his whole body, even though the work was tiring. But he still only had two regular customers: small machine shops in the south part of Hayward.

"Stop moping," Miguel said. "You have to have more faith. You're doing the right thing. I can feel it in my bones."

When that failed to cheer him up, Miguel disappeared behind one of the drop-off units, then casually reappeared wearing two aluminum oil funnels taped together like a bra as he went back to work. Antonio stared for a moment, then dropped to his knees in a fit of laughter.

At the lumber yard a few days later Antonio saw Rivera, his old English teacher, loading pine beams into the bed of a Ford pick-up. Antonio spun around to avoid him and went into the building with his head down, pretending not to notice him. But standing in line at the register he felt a hand settle on his shoulder.

"Antonio?" the voice said. "How's everything?"

"Oh, fine, fine," Antonio said. "Just picking up a few things for my new business."

"I didn't know you had your own business."

"I just started it a few months ago."

"That's wonderful. I've always wanted to do something like that."

He gave Antonio a friendly smile. Antonio laughed.

"What's so funny?"

"I thought you were going to test me on my English or something."

Rivera laughed too. "Listen," he said. "You left in such a hurry that last day, I never got a chance to tell you how much I enjoyed having you in my class."

Antonio stared at him. "Really?" he said.

"Yes, of course. I've seen very few students put so much effort into my class. And that wife of yours. What a talent. You're a very lucky man."

He shook Antonio's hand, then left him there, speechless. How wrong he had been to misjudge this man, to have made such an issue out of nothing. Certainly he had looked at Pilar with desire, but what man could have helped doing so? Antonio wished he were a stronger man, more deserving of Pilar. But she was the strong one, he knew, strong for being able to put up with his foolishness. Pilar, the pillar. Pilar, his support.

The dark period between them had gone on long enough. He saw what he had to do, while he had the courage to do it: shake off his jealousy and pride, and cast them away and never let them near him again. He would find a way to make things up to her.

So that night, awkwardly, wordlessly, he held out his hand to her in the manner of a gallant requesting a dance. She was scrubbing the bathroom tub at the time, yellow rubber gloves rising above her elbows.

"Please don't fool with me, Antonio."

"I want to take you out tonight."

"I have work to do."

"I'll do it for you later."

"And leave me with more work than if I'd done it myself? Dinner is almost ready. Go and change out of those overalls."

"Save it for tomorrow."

"It won't be as good tomorrow."

He kept his hand out. She kept scrubbing. Finally, she tossed the sponge down, peeled off the gloves. "There's that movie at the Bal. I guess we could go to that together. After we eat."

It was an opening of a new movie with Olivia Rodríguez that had been playing in Mexico for several months, one that the papers were calling her comeback film after a two-year battle with alcohol. As they waited in line, a woman stopped to ask them something in English. Antonio wasn't sure if she was asking directions or what time the movie started, but Pilar answered her right away, in English. The woman asked something else, and again Pilar answered without hesitating. Soon they were deep in the thread of a conversation of which Antonio understood little.

There should have been nothing surprising about this. Pilar had always been fast to understand and had been practicing English daily with one of the neighbors. Only now did Antonio start to see what his wife's talent might mean for him.

Throughout the movie he could not stop thinking about it. He had always thought of the business as his. He had never thought of including Pilar in it, in part because she had never shown an interest, but really because, well, he had never thought of it. But now he saw that she was the one with the talent to help him make it take off. She was the one who could get him the English-speaking clients.

He didn't bring it up right away. He could only imagine Pilar's reaction. Is that what you were buttering me up for, Antonio? Yet another favor, another sacrifice of my time, to be your secretary?

He said nothing about it on the way home, nothing that night. Not until the next morning, after hours in bed crafting his words to sound as unconcerned as possible did he work his way around to the subject.

"Do you have a lot planned today?" he said.

"Housework. Errands. The usual. Why?"

"I was thinking, I'd like to bring you to see the yard sometime. It looks different since the last time you were there."

"Maybe some weekend," she said. "I have a lot to do."

"It must get tiring for you, the same thing every day."

She shrugged. "What's one to do? I can't complain."

"You could always come work for me." He laughed to make it sound like a joke.

"I can see it: me breaking my back at the scrap piles."

"I meant in the office. The phone, paperwork."

She started folding towels on the bed.

"I just thought it would be better than sitting around here all day."

"Is that what you think I do? Sit around the house all day?"

"No, no, no, that's not what I meant. Never mind, I don't know where that idea came from."

Pilar stacked the towels and carried them out to the bathroom. A couple minutes later she came back. "Who would take care of the housework?"

"We both could, on the weekends."

"And if you're working on the weekend?"

"Then it will have to go undone."

"And the neighbor's kids?"

"You've been doing that long enough."

She left the room again. The house was quiet. When Antonio had finished dressing, he came into the kitchen. Pilar was packing two lunch bags. "Let's get going," she said.

"Are you sure?"

She shrugged. "Anything to get out of scrubbing the floors for a day."

At the yard he showed her into the trailer office at the back. With arms folded she looked over the wood plank desk, the rusted file cabinets. She picked through a tangle of receipts on the desk.

"All you'd have to do is answer the phones and do the scheduling," he said.

She ran her finger along the aluminum window sill. Finally she sat down and spread her hands flat on the desktop. "Well, what are we going to call it?" she said.

He stared at her.

"The business. It has to have a name, doesn't it? Otherwise what am I going to say when I answer the phone? 'Hi, this is Pilar, what the hell do you want?'"

He left her emptying the filing cabinets. "This is no way to organize anything," she said. "Give me an hour and I'll have a system set up for you."

Two hours later, she was on the phone with the yellow pages spread open in front of her. She held out two slips of paper to him. "Two new accounts," she said. "I've been on the phone all day calling all the machine shops. Ace through Zúñiga. I'm almost done. Tomorrow I'll start on welding and steel forming. Then I thought we could do our first mailing at the end of the month as a reminder."

"*Oye, hombre,*" Miguel said, after Antonio had introduced him to Pilar. "I had no idea you had such a good-looking wife. I can't believe how she's pulling things together around here. Forget what I said about cheating on her. This one is too good to risk."

That night Antonio awoke at two to find Pilar gone from bed. He found her sitting on the living room floor with green-and-white receipt pages spread out all around her.

"I couldn't sleep," she said, pushing up her reading glasses. "There's a fifty-dollar error on the books and it's been driving me crazy. I have to find it."

"Please, come to bed," he said. "You're working too hard."

"You want this business to be a success, don't you?"

"I don't want you to start hating it."

"Please, Antonio. This is the first interesting thing I've had to do in years. Can't you see how much I'm enjoying it?" She took off her glasses, entwined an arm around his leg and kissed his kneecap.

"All right," he said. "But please don't overdo it."

They worked together for the next five weeks. It amazed Antonio how smooth her face had become, eased of the lines of daily frustration. Antonio often lingered around the office, pretending to be busy just so he could look at her. She was in love with her work, and for the first time in their marriage, Antonio felt that he had actually given her something she valued. They still had not resumed making love, in any language, but they had at last reached an easy truce at home. And Antonio was not so foolish as to tamper with that.

Just before Thanksgiving, Pilar showed him the account books for the work they had done over the summer. They had made a profit for two out of three months. "We can probably start paying Miguel a little more," she said.

"I was planning on it," Antonio said. "Starting the first of the year." He moved to give her a kiss. "Really, Pilar, thank you. There's no way I could have come this far without you. We should have a real Thanksgiving this year. We have reason to celebrate."

"Be sure to invite Miguel," she said. "We owe a lot to him, too."

"I wouldn't dream of doing this without him," Antonio said.

On Thanksgiving Eve, the three of them walked down the grocery store aisles together, Antonio filling the cart with the most expensive items he came across, and Pilar saying over and over, "No, Antonio, that's far too much food for just three people."

Miguel laughed as the two of them played tug-of-war with a frozen twenty-pound turkey. The apartment started to warm early the next day with the smells of the Thanksgiving meal.

Miguel arrived stuffed into a suit with wide, outdated lapels.

"Be careful you don't bend over," Antonio said. "That thing looks like it's about to rip down the seam."

"Don't laugh at me," Miguel said. "I wanted to add a little class to this gathering. But I think it must have shrunk since I last wore it."

They started with wine before dinner, the three of them finishing a full bottle while standing in the kitchen. Miguel told one joke after another, each a little dirtier than the last. How long had it been since Antonio had heard

Pilar laugh this way, without restraint? Since he had seen her look happy? Maybe things were becoming good between them once again.

After the long meal, Antonio brought desserts out from the kitchen.

"Let's wait," Pilar said, crinkling up her nose. "I couldn't stand another mouthful."

But Antonio insisted that everyone try at least a bite of each kind of pie, since he had helped make them. Pilar tried to get up to start cleaning, but Antonio wouldn't let her. "More wine for everyone," he said, tearing the lead foil off a new bottle.

Miguel started into another story, this time about how he had once been with a woman when her husband came home, and he had had to step out onto the tenth-floor building ledge outside the bedroom to hide. "The neighbors started pointing. They thought I was trying to kill myself, so they called the police. They brought out a net for me to jump into."

The three of them laughed, Pilar hardest of all. She put her hand on Miguel's shoulder as if to keep from falling over. Her hand rested there.

Antonio went quiet, as if all the liquor had just drained out of him. He went to the kitchen for a glass of water. From there he could hear Pilar and Miguel's high-spirited chatter, the playful clinking of glasses, hands drumming the table with hilarity. From the doorway he watched them.

A gray light fell over the apartment toward evening. Antonio took the far end of the couch and turned on the football game, but only stared at the set without really watching it. He had never learned the rules of the game, and the scurried movement of the players around the field only stirred his thoughts into greater disorder.

In the kitchen Pilar began putting away plates. From the dining table, Miguel was staring at her, his red eyes traveling up and down the course of her figure as she reached on tiptoes for the higher shelves. Antonio saw her look over her shoulder from the sink and smile at Miguel.

Miguel came over to the couch. "How's the game?" he said.

Antonio stood up and said he wasn't feeling well and went to lie down. He didn't get up again. He could feel himself slipping under the influence of another dark spell of jealousy, and knew better than to trust his own actions when he'd been drinking. Don't start tipping boats, he told himself, forget about it until morning.

Back at the yard on Monday, Antonio could not help noticing how Miguel kept looking at Pilar when he came into the office to check the schedule and drop off invoices. His gaze lingered over the curve of her frame as she talked on the phone or leaned into the open filing cabinet. How stupid Antonio had been to let this happen. Had he been so busy that he could not have seen it coming? He was dense. How could he have forgotten that Miguel was the biggest abuser of women he had ever known?

Antonio began sticking close to Miguel around the yard, began giving him the pick-ups that were the farthest away and took the longest to get to. Anything that needed to be done in the office, Antonio did himself. He could no longer laugh at Miguel's antics. By the end of the day, Antonio was too brimming with self-disgust to face Pilar.

That night, exhausted from his own thoughts, he lay next to Pilar, desperately wanting to hold her again, to assure himself that she was still his. But it would be a mistake to touch her. Any hint of rejection would balloon in his mind into something he did not want to believe. Throughout the night, jealousy and loneliness alternated their visits to him, keeping him from sleep.

At work the next day, his temper finally flared when Miguel locked his keys in the GMC for the third time that week. "Goddamn you, you idiot, the amount of time we waste because of your stupid mistakes. . ." Acid rose in his throat, hot and bitter. He walked away without finishing his sentence.

For the rest of the day, he avoided Miguel at every turn. Every joke Miguel told seemed to have a double meaning. Every movement was an advance toward Pilar.

The next day, Miguel stood staring at him, with mouth slightly agape as Antonio rambled off his vague list of reasons for letting him go. Pilar had shown signs of a flu and Antonio had insisted she stay home for the day.

"I don't understand," Miguel said. "The business is doing so well."

"That was before we considered taxes," Antonio mumbled. "Sometimes these things happen. I can only say that it's a decision made with the business in mind. I'll be happy to give you two-weeks pay."

Miguel looked at him as though he were peering into a dark, deep closet. Antonio hated his idiotic expression, his sloppy, overgrown shrub of a mustache.

"I wish I could explain in more detail," Antonio said.

"What have I done wrong?"

"Nothing," he said. "Now I've got some phone calls to make." He shuffled some papers, but Miguel did not move. Finally, Antonio had to leave the office. He left Miguel standing there, staring blankly at the place where Antonio had been sitting.

When he got home that night, he did not have time to unhook his overalls before Pilar flew at him.

"How could you, Antonio? What were you thinking? Don't you know he has alimony payments to make?"

He started to give her the same excuses he had given Miguel, but her words tore through his, shredding them to nothing. "Didn't you think to talk to me about this? What in the world were you thinking, Antonio?"

"We don't need him," he said.

"You can barely handle the customers you have."

"We need to think about saving money."

"We have plenty of money."

"It's already done." He tried to control his tone, but it was already slipping out of his control. Pilar blocked the doorway as he tried to leave the room.

"You're going to answer me. Tell me why you fired him. Something happened between the two of you. What was it?"

"It was a business decision."

"It wasn't a business decision."

"Why are you so upset?"

"He was our friend, Antonio."

"He was a dirty-mouthed abuser of women."

"He was with us from the beginning."

"Then maybe you'd like to go to him."

Why was it, he wondered, that words, when he most wanted them, were nowhere at hand. And why, when silence was his wisest option, did words fly recklessly from his lips with a life of their own?

"So that's it," said Pilar calmly. "That's what this is all about. You got some stupid notion in your head about the two of us and you went and fired him. Well, I hope you're satisfied."

"Can't I make a business decision without consulting you? It's *my* business, after all."

She held him with a hard, colorless gaze. Then she went into the bedroom and slammed the door.

The next day she told him she was going back to Tijuana to stay with her parents. "Until I figure out what I want," she said. She was in the bedroom packing her suitcases.

"You're not going anywhere," Antonio said, but his words had no force. It was a half-uttered question, not a statement. "I'm not going to let you divorce me."

"I didn't say I wanted a divorce."

"What do you want?"

"I don't know. I want time to think."

"Just because of this? Pilar, it's nothing we haven't been through before."

She turned to him, stopping everything she was doing. "Yes, Antonio. And how many times should I be expected to go through it again?"

"Things were good between us again," he said.

She shook her head sadly and laughed. "Where have you been, Antonio? Things haven't been good between us for a long time. We haven't slept together in months. The only thing we shared was working on the business—excuse me—*your* business."

Before Pilar was to leave, Antonio went out of the house and started walking again. He did not want to be there when her friend Monica came to pick her up, did not trust his own actions. He walked because walking dispersed his thoughts enough to keep him sane from one moment to the next. He walked because he could think of nothing else to do. How had this happened, he thought. How could he have let it? He was losing her just when he was learning how to love her the way she wanted to be loved. He had been losing her for such a long time, the losing was out of his control, how could he have not seen it? He tried to get angry, if only to feel something different than this cold, spinning hollowness. But fear held him tight, the voice of it hovering close, spitting dark words in his ear. Now is the time to be afraid, it said. Later will be the time for regret.

He decided to go to the yard and work for the rest of the day, even though it was a weekend. It was the only place he could think to go, the only place he might be able to forget for a while. But when he opened up the office to get the keys to start up the crane, Pilar's lingering presence beared down on him.

The room smelled of the flowered air freshener she had brought in. Looking for the keys, he came across the neat stacks of billing statements that Pilar had been preparing on Friday. He sat down and paged through them, but didn't know what needed to be done. A different kind of fear swept over him, wrapped its arms around him. Not the pale, achy fear of losing love, but the sharp, pressing practical fear of losing all he had built. Pilar, the pillar. Pilar, his support. How had he let this happen? How had she become the linch-pin to everything that mattered to him?

He went out into the yard to work the crane. Here, for the last few months at least, he had had some happiness. But because it was Saturday, there was no noise coming from the steel forming company next door, no shouting from the construction site across the street. The silence was a canvas on which his mind could paint terrible pictures, write terrible words. To break the silence he turned on the generator and swung the Ohio magnet out over the scrap iron piles to move them into the containers. The loud crashing of steel against steel helped mash down the panic, broke up the fear.

Toward evening, the flat, gray winter light began slipping from the yard. Antonio climbed down from the crane and switched on the yard lights, flooding the yard in white, bringing up shadows in strange places. The electricity hummed, crackled. He went back to working the crane, the long arm of it sweeping back and forth from pile to container, container to pile. Long into the night the loud crashing went on, the crashing that obliterated thought, that obliterated the words that were going through his head, which was the language of love, which was the language more difficult to learn than any other.

1996-97

Andrés Montoya First Prize: Poetry

The Iceworker Sings

THE ICEWORKER IN LOVE

he is in love.
friday nights before work
he sees his woman.
they are not married
and she doesn't know
that he loves her.

he tells her
her hair is like water
and her skin smells of dew.
and she tells him
it'll still cost the eighty bucks
for the three hours
in the crusty motel
that smells of smoke.

he doesn't know her real name.
he thinks it is sofía.
one day she will tell him the truth,
that her name is alexandra,
that her family calls her alex,
and he will feel a little betrayed.

sometimes they smoke weed or crack,
sometimes they do lines of crank.
always, though, they lie naked
next to each other when they are finished,
sweaty and both feeling a little guilty.
they only do it once. he never asks for a second.
and they are content to listen to each other's breathing.
he likes the way she sounds so alive,
the rise and fall of her breath like pain and pleasure.

the conversation is the same every time.
do you ever think of God? she asks.
sometimes, he says. this is why he loves her:
she reads him stories from the Bible
found in the dresser and he is fascinated.
he likes the one about the people in the desert
following a cloud in the day and a pillar of fire in the night,
and he wishes that he had something to follow,
"something to lead me out of this crapshoot life," he thinks.
sometimes she tells him about a man murdered

forgiving everyone, even his own killers.
this is when she cries, and he feels he too should cry,
that he must cry for the man murdered who forgives,
only he doesn't know how, yet.
he only knows that he likes to hear
her stories, that there is something good in her voice,
he only knows that he can smell life in her breath
behind the stale stench of the room's desire.

LOCURA

> *and where, raza, are our heroes?*
> *the heroes of aztlán?*

> *what became of that great nation we were going to build?*
> *where did all the warriors go with their sharpened knives*
> *and loaded rifles?*

everyday i walk through the cracking streets smelling despair like a rose.
i ride on buses freshly laced with the stench of some borracho's vomit
and there are bones and more bones stacking up around me,
murdered by pipes and cops, knives and guns, or just the evil glare
of some rich gava. and not the viejitos sipping tea, or the lovers loving
behind the bushes in the park can make me smile or laugh or see
some glimmer of hope in this crazy cosa called life
            cause i can't get out, the streets keep returning to me the same,
            always the same
                    like a bad dream, and i have come to the conclusion
that this is how it was meant to be: death in my pocket and insanity
the limp that keeps dragging me down. a tattoo teardrop falling from
            my eyes.
                    i can't sing anymore.
                            no whistle pushes forth

from between my lips.
i'm getting ready to bust out loco, and no one hears when i'm yelling

"i gotta go, gotta get outta here!"

so i   smile now   with a cuete tucked in the back of my baggies
and a .40 in my right hand, imagining myself some kind of chulo
cholo, or some other form of vato loco or just another ciclón
waiting to put some little chump stepping up punk down
and then when i'm doing the tecato shuffle, or the borracho bump,
dying coughing in that cockroach motel they found louie in
i'll cry and i'll cry and i'll   cry later   like the tattoo says,
and no one will be the wiser, not my mom working the graveyard
or my girl who looks like her mother, that little girl with my abuelita's
name, who will probably die younger than me
and it all comes down to the fact
i've lived the life of a coward,
a slave, i never had the guts
to explode, really explode, like cuauhtemoc or zapata,
suicide style so my gente can live like gente with honor.

PART II
BEING BORN

i was born in 1978 from asphalt
and the beat-up bumpers of chevys

on fourth and vine
on sanjo's south side. they keep
telling me it was raining
and the lighting was licking the streets
up and down as if the world was a cheap motel
room with cockroaches propped up on the pillows.

they keep saying it was a sign,
the rain and its lightning,
of my darkness.
they say
i was meant for evil.

they say
what else can come
from a syphilitic john

and his saturday night
        whore.

but it ain't so.
        i keep waiting
for the clouds to bust out
in lights. i keep waiting to hear
a trumpet so fine
that the man miles
will bow his knee.

i keep waiting to hear
the Man say,
        "good goin' tommy
                you all right."

they say i was born
from a witch's womb.

but i'm tellin' ya
        i was born in 1978
bowing broken on a chevy's bumper
        my knees digging into asphalt and glass
and a puddle of gunk
        on fourth and vine
                on sanjo's south side,
        my chest heaving a lifetime into the air,
                the moonless night.

i was born in 1978
        sobbing Christ from my lips.

PART III
A LETTER TO KB

kb: tonight the sky in fresno was different shades
of blue. dusk and clouds splitting into two huge arms
like a man reaching to God through sadness, through the stars,
past the moon, as if lifting his arms in praise and thanksgiving.
i wonder if you saw the same old man floating up there.
i am remembering san francisco. you, me, and your sister sitting
in a cafe. the coffee was bad. do you remember? you pretended
to be a mechanic that day. your catholic cheek is what i see still
and the fear that rested on your forehead like a butterfly waving

its wings ready for flight. san francisco. that city always reminded me
of plastic: shiny and freshly pulled from the mold and painted
with sea salt and sheen. i had no memory in that city. in that city
i had amnesia.

here, the memories rise up like anger, like teeth sharp
and sinister. they rise up like the lover you can't bear to leave:
i found my brother, one day, behind a door, arms spread wide
like Christ on the cross, laid out on the floor over a pile of colorful
clothes ready for wash, the sad slashes at his wrists weeping
into the stench of stale cigarette smoke and poverty that held captive
that room, his eyes deep dark wells wet and begging for the logic of death.
goya would have painted this had he had to live with us
in that crumbling house in fresno, in the flats of melody park.
i don't know why, but i love this image, i love this city. if hope
cannot be found here, then where? hope. frisco was never
like that for me. what memories do your hands hold of that city?
what is it that you find beautiful there? perhaps you could paint
for me an image in glass, colored in truth and hope.

have you heard from roque lately? has he taught you any new words?
you know sometimes i think he is so full of crap that i could
close my ears to him forever. but it is his passion, his love
that has infected me. this must have come from God.
he painted justice on the lips of humanity, and struggle
on the forehead. it was love he sketched on the cheeks
and hope he brushed into the eyes. he didn't know it
but it was a picture he painted of our Christ, alive
and extending a hand of mercy, ready to give justice
to the poor. but isn't it crazy, sister, that we keep thinking
of Christ as a thief? what is it that he would take from us?
the love we have for our own legs? sadness? suicide? self-hate?

when i was a kid, i betrayed, like judas, my own brother. i love him
even now his face smooth and jaw square. his eyes were two
huge apples alive in the sun. he smelled of ditch water
and weeds. he was beautiful, that boy. he wanted us
to be brothers forever, to be beat into song under a starry
starry night. but i was in love with power more than i loved
him and i left him on the ground weeping
more at the sight of my back than the memory
of my fists. and when i saw him on the floor, his wrists split
open at the heart, i was angry. i wanted to beat him. i hated his
powerlessness and i wept not for him or for my mother

who would have to bear all of this, but for myself, for in his blood
i saw my life running away in lies and I couldn't stand him.

i am ashamed. what a fool i was. what a scared little boy
i was. he was Christ that day and i held a hammer
and a handful of nails. this is what i hope Christ takes from me.
why is it that we keep believing the propaganda
that God is in love with injustice, or that he is dead,
or, at the very least disinterested in the pain and fear
and love we feel? Christ is alive, and my cheeks
want to touch his, my pores are waiting for him,
and my nose can't wait to feel the heat and wet
of his breath. does this sound strange to you?

i am wondering what you look like in the valley.
what does your name sound like there? does it still smell
of grass green and wet under a sky of morning?
i pray that in your heart will be found hope as huge
as the sky that waits for the coming of clouds. i pray
that you are smiling. i pray joy will be found singing
from your ocean-like eyes. thinking of you, sister: andrés.

LUCIANA: THIS IS HOW I SEE YOU
how will i remember you, grandma?
will it be your name, luciana, that i recall
on nights when the forgetful remember
everything?
luciana: beautiful
like the wind winding whispers
through the arms of the trees.
luciana: my sister carries your name
and she wears your earrings
and her birth will forever carry
your heart
beating boldly for the truth.
how will i remember you, abuelita?
will it be in the kitchen
tortillas on the comal
eggs frying in the pan
and a song of praise
pouring forth from your lips?
or perhaps
it will be your face, a bruised petal of forgiveness
as you told me your story

on a saturday afternoon
in dixon,
how grandpa came for you
smelling of sheep and whores, how your
grandmother
was old and tired and begging for the cool sheet of a warm bed
to lie down and forget her life, how she sold you or traded you
dragging you away from the dolls
to stand before the priest
and become a woman at
twelve.
or maybe
i will remember you
hobbling into the grocery store,
the nylons gathering at the back of your knees
like wrinkled skin,
like survival.
will i remember your hands, your beautiful hands,
two measures of tender masa
you use to lay on the faces of all your children?
will i remember your prayers prayed,
the powerful breath of your hope
forging a way for us all in this madness?

i tell you, grandma, this is how i see you:
you are dancing, your straight leg is bending and your hair
is waving wild
as beautiful laughter like song strums from your mouth into the sky,
and your eyes, your eyes are catching the shine of the Son,
like two huge apples begging notice on the tree, and you are shouting
with your smile, "hallelujah! hallelujah!" and all the angels
are dancing and
laughing with you, and Jesus is saying, "i love you so much, mija."
and you are saying, "mi amor, mi amor," like a beautiful sigh.

RULY

i would give you a star. a multitude.
perhaps
if I were a romantic
i would say:

from the sky I have stolen stones of fire
and strung them together on a tight
invisible string of fishing line.

i have brought them to lace
the shiny skin of your neck,
your wrists, brought them to wrap
your ankles, plant them one at a time,
carefully, in each of the nails of your toes,
starlight lighting the dirt before you feet.

but this would be a lie.
                        they are already yours. The stars.
                                a lie.
                  your feet never needed their light.

what then?
the sun? the moon?   yours.
                                    maybe that single berry
                                    begging notice on the vine?

but even this has fallen
from your breath.

i can offer you
a piece of flesh
fallen from my bones.
another. and another.
another. rotten and smelling.
the bones.
        a bit yellow,
                too, are yours.

i give you
this image:

if you brought fire
                              at the end of a stick.
or maybe just a hot coal,
                      a burning ember,
and touched my lips
burning away to the gums
                      and gums to the skull
                              and skull to the soul to the spirit,
                i would finally sing you,
truly sing you, on my knees, my forehead leading the way . . . love.

1997-98

Angelo Parra   First Prize: Drama

Song of the Coquí
Play in Two Acts (excerpt)

(In Act II, Scene 1, of Song of the Coquí, *RAY, about 40, the Americanized son of* EDNA *and* RAMÓN *now known as "Raymond"* GUERRERO, *makes an unannounced visit to his parents' home, and unexpectedly encounters* TERESA, *about 30, the Guerrero's new neighbor.)*

> *According to legend,*
> *if you take the coquí,*
> *a small frog native to Puerto Rico, off the island*
> *it will survive, but it will never sing again.*

ACT II, SCENE 1

(Present, in the living room of EDNA *and* RAYMOND's *home, afternoon. The yapping of a small dog is heard.)*

RAY: Shhhhh! Shut up, Zorro. It's me, your brother. Shhhhh! *(Pause.)* Here. Bon appetit. *(The dog quiets down.)* Stupid dog. (RAY *enters nervously, fidgeting with a set of keys.) (Calling.)* Mom? *(Pause.)* Mom. *(Pause.)* Mom! *(Pause.)* MOM! (RAY *exits to another room, and returns in a couple of seconds. He looks at his watch, and sighs. RAY picks up some photos and laughs to himself. He turns on the T.V., switches channels until he finds what sounds like a tennis match. He picks up the newspaper T.V. section, plops into a seat, and thumbs through it. After a few moments, the dog begins yapping again, and* TERESA's *voice is heard.)*

TERESA: *(Off stage.)* Shhhhh! ¡Cállate, hombre! You call that a bark? Embustero. Hello. Hellllo, Edna. Edna!

(RAY *gets up quickly, and turns off the T.V.. TERESA enters carrying flowers tied with a bow, and stops when she sees* RAY. TERESA *is in clothes that show her off.)*

(Very pleased.) Well, hello, Ray.

277

RAY: (*Doubtfully.*) Hello. Who are you?

TERESA: (*Suggestively.*) The girl next door.

(TERESA points to the window.)

RAY: Oh, Joe's old place. Right. Eh, how'd you get in?

TERESA: I guess you left the door open.

RAY: I guess I did. (*Jokingly.*) And I don't guess that's for me.

TERESA: It's for your mother, but you could have it if you want it.

RAY: How do you know who I am?

TERESA: Your mother said she had a handsome son.

RAY: (*Laughs.*) My mother's not here. Probably stopped on the way home to pick up some groceries or something. Maybe you should come back another . . .

(TERESA *steps closer to* RAY.)

TERESA: (*Interrupting.*) That's nice.

RAY: Huh?

TERESA: You smell nice.

RAY: Yeah, well, it's some cologne or other. A gift.

(TERESA *puts the flowers down, takes* RAY*'s hand, leads him to the sofa, and sits next to him.*)

TERESA: Your mom says you're this big shot lawyer.

RAY: No, not really.

TERESA: You do divorce law 'n shit?

RAY: Corporate law actually . . .

TERESA: (*Cutting in.*) Maybe you could help me out with my ex. Pendejo, coño. I gotta keep on his ass for my alimony, you know? Maybe you could fix him good, you know, like for friendship, 'cause I got no money for lawyers.

RAY: I really don't think I can help you because, well, I don't take private cases. Anyway, I don't practice that kind of law.

TERESA: You could practice on my case—(*Snaps her fingers.*)—any time.

RAY: (*Nervously.*) Actually, I'm not practicing any kind of law right at the moment . . .

TERESA: No, no, no, no. That ain't no Aqua Velva I smell. It's kinda sweet, but . . .

RAY: I paint. Maybe it's the oils you're smelling on me. It's almost impossible to entirely get rid of the . . .

TERESA: ¡Ay, Dios mío! A lawyer and a painter. So talented. Do you paint women naked?

RAY: (*Backing away.*) No, I usually keep my pants on.

TERESA: I make you nervous or something?

RAY: Me? No. Why? (*Awkward pause.*) So . . . the flowers. For my mother, you said?

TERESA: She's a saint, your mother.

RAY: If you say so.

TERESA: She babysitted my little girl so I could get a job.

RAY: Thus the flowers—a thank you.

TERESA: (*Impressed.*) "Thus"? That's the first time in my life I ever heard somebody actually use the word "thus" in a sentence.

RAY: There's still a lot of lawyer in me. I'm recovering.

TERESA: Some people got all the luck. Your mom's got this nice house, a reliable man, a good-looking son, a granddaughter. She's got it made, you know what I'm sayin'? I mean, I don't mind working 'n shit, but, once in a while, man, it would be, you know, fair if something worked out for me. (*Pause.*) I'm not complaining. I got my health and my daughter, and I got a new job and a place to sleep, pero coño . . . She's definitely got it made, your mother. Claro. Some people got all the luck. (*Pause.*) So, I hear you're divorced.

RAY: No. I mean yes. What I'm saying is that it was a while ago. It feels like another lifetime. So to speak.

TERESA: I know how lonely it can be. Being divorced and alone. So to speak.

RAY: Well, I'm not exactly . . . (RAY *rises, and moves to the plant.*) So . . . you bought it?

TERESA: Yeah, I bought them. I ain't no farmer.

RAY: Farmer? Oh, no, not the flowers; I was talking about Joe's place. Did you buy . . .

TERESA: (*Laughing.*) ¡Ay, Dios mío! I look like I'm made of money to you? I'm renting. I tole you I got no money.

RAY: (*Awkward pause.*) You know, it doesn't look like my mother's going to be home anytime soon. Why don't you come back . . .

TERESA: Did I say something wrong?

RAY: No, it's just . . .

TERESA: You don't like . . . my company?

RAY: . . . I don't even know your name.

(TERESA *extends her right hand, and they shake hands.*)

TERESA: (*Heavily rolling her R.*) Terrrrrrrresa.

(RAY *awkwardly frees his hand.*)

RAY: (*Hard R, no roll.*) Teresa, I'm sort of just minding my own business, waiting for . . .

TERESA: (*Interrupting, heavily rolling her Rs.*) Terrrrrrrresa. Don't be shy with me. Terrrrrrrresa.

RAY: Sorry, I can't do that. I can't roll my Rs, if you must know. My tongue is too fat or something. I can't even pronounce my own name right. (*Hard Rs, no roll.*) Guerrero.

TERESA: Guerrrrrrrrrerrrrrrrro. I'll teach you how to rrrrrrrroll your RRRRRRRRRs. (TERESA *snaps her fingers.*)

RAY: I appreciate your . . . interest, Teresa . . .

TERESA: Terrrrrrrresa.

RAY: Right, but I don't even know you.

TERESA: Pero, we could fix that, enseguida. You know what? I'll make you dinner. I'm a good cook. My husband was a pain in the you-know-what, but he ate good. To this day he says "but that bitch could coooo-ooook." I'll make something you'll like, arrrrrrrroz y habichuelas con plátanos frrrrrrrritos, sweet, real sweet. Y ensalada, because I can see you're the type that eats salad. Con un poquito de cerveza fría, and for dessert I'll teach you to rrrrrrrroll your RRRRRRRRRs.

RAY: Sounds nice, but no thanks, really. Like I said, I don't mean to be rude, but I'm happily . . . girlfriended, and . . .

(TERESA *picks up a photograph.*)

TERESA: This your baby picture?

RAY: Yes.

TERESA: Coquí?

RAY: (*Surprised.*) What?

TERESA: That's what's written on the picture: "Coquí."

RAY: Oh. That's what they used to call me. When I was a kid.

TERESA: You know what that means?

RAY: Yeah, frog.

TERESA: (*Laughs.*) Sí, pero more than that. A coquí is a tweeny-weeny lit- tle frog that lives in Puerto Rico. At night it whistles, like a cricket or a small bird, pero only prettier. Like this . . . (*Half said, half whistled; cricket-like.*) Ko-KWEE, ko-KWEE, ko-KWEE. Like that. They say if you take a coquí off the island, it will live but it will never sing again.

RAY: Well, that's charming, but I'm not a frog, and I hated it.

TERESA: Hated what?

RAY: "Coquí." It sounded so . . .

TERESA: Puerto Rican?

RAY: (*Pause.*) Listen, Teresa, it was nice meeting you and . . .

TERESA: Your girlfriend, she something special?

RAY: Valerie is . . . is . . . Look, I don't even know why we're having this conversation.

TERESA: Valerie?

RAY: Yes.

TERESA: Valerie what?

RAY: You don't know her.

TERESA: I don't think so either, but what's her name?

RAY: Appleton.

TERESA: Apple-ton?

RAY: Yes.

TERESA: A white girl?

RAY: (*Pause.*) Non-Hispanic, if that's what you mean.

TERESA: (*Mocking.*) Well, excuse me. Valerie Appleton. (*Affecting a gentile, upper-class tone.*) Of the Georgetown Appletons or of the Appletons of Boston? (*Normally.*) And what's your ex-wife's name? No. Let me guess. Veronica? Penelope? Gwendolen? No? Certainly not RRRRRRRRosa or Margarrrrrrrrita or Marrrrrrrría.

RAY: (*Pause.*) I'm sorry, but what exactly do you want from me?

TERESA: Nada. No quiero nada. I saw you come in, so I brought the flowers over now. Just to say hello, pendejo.

RAY: (*Trying to stay calm.*) There's no reason for us to get into an argument—

TERESA: (*Overlapping.*) —"Non-Hispanic" Appleton. The apple of your white eyes. Eres un coco.

RAY: Listen, I don't know you well enough to . . .

TERESA: Estás olvidando tus raíces. Coco. Eres un coco, coño. (*Pause as they glare at each other.*) You got no idea what the fuck I'm saying to you.

RAY: I'm not interested. Actually, now would be a good time for you to . . .

TERESA: You're a *coconut*, that's what I said. A coconut. Brown on the outside, white inside.

RAY: Oh, Christ, take a hike, okay? I don't need this from you too. All right? I'll tell my mother you stopped—

TERESA: (*Interrupting.*) —I know you. You ain't nothing new. You one of those Latinos who likes a white girl near him. Your white turkey meat. Right? You don't speak no Spanish 'cause that ain't gonna get you no blonde pussy around the office. Well, let me tell you, you ain't better than me, you ain't better than nobody, mister asshole lawyer. I bet you only got white girls workin' for you at your white-bread lawyer office. I bet you never even been with a Latina. Right? Am I right? I know I'm right. I can see it in your face. What you got against Latinas, pendejo? Tell me. What's your problem? (*Pause.*) Well? I'm all fuckin' ears.

RAY: (*Coldly.*) You finished?

TERESA: Yeah, I'm finished, shithead.

RAY: You're right, I never dated a Hispanic woman. You know why? I never met a Hispanic woman who attracted me.

TERESA: Fucking prejudiced against your own people.

(*As he speaks,* RAY *starts moving in menacingly, backing* TERESA *up until she falls back onto the sofa.*)

RAY: (*With contained fury.*) That's bullshit. It's just that I find Hispanic women brazen, coarse, vulgar, intemperate, uneducated, unrestrained, amoral, and generally uninteresting. You dress vulgar, and act it!

TERESA: All of us?

RAY: Yes!

TERESA: Including your mama? (*A long angry silence.*)

RAY: (*Through his teeth.*) Please leave.

(TERESA *gets up, straightens her clothes, and heads out.*)

TERESA: (*Imitating a Hispanic street-corner wolf.*) "Mira, mira, nena. Lookin' fine, honey. Wassamadda, mami, you too good for me?" (*Pause.*) You know, maybe we act . . . vulgar because that's what men act like they want from us.

RAY: Not me.

TERESA: Of course not. Coconut. (TERESA *walks out with a victorious smirk and a snap of her fingers.* RAY *sinks into a chair. Lights dim on* RAY.)

1998-99

Patricia Santana   First Prize: Novel

Motorcycle Ride on the Sea of Tranquility (excerpt)

CHAPTER 6

The screech of burning rubber, the inevitable hard crash of metal colliding. The first one on Conifer Street to hear these sounds and make it to the telephone dialed "0" for the operator and shouted: "Crash on 5 North between Palm Avenue and Main Street." Most of the neighbors on Conifer Street were already congregated at the end of the block, standing by the chain-link fence at the embankment, observing the bashed-up cars below. Any passer-by would have thought it was a block party.

"Is anybody hurt? Can you tell?" Carolina asked our neighbor, Marisa.

"No, it doesn't seem so, but I can't tell. The crash is over by the Big Sky Drive-In," she said. Marisa looked past Carolina's shoulder, over toward our house. I was sure she was wondering if our gorgeous brother Octavio, whom she had loved probably her whole life, might come out of the house to see the accident too. I bet she was hoping.

Socorrito, who seemed to live in her fluffy blue mules and Hawaiian-print shift, shuffled over to where Mamá stood. "This is very strange, Dolores," she said in a whisper, but loud enough for my antennae ears to hear. "Have you noticed how many car accidents we've had in just these past months? At least four a week."

Mamá was silent, shielding her eyes from the sun which was slowly falling in the west. Her face was stern, the kind of expression I was used to seeing on her when she was studying the monthly bills or watching Walter Cronkite. Her green eyes were now dark and worried, an entanglement of impenetrable greenery. But I knew what she must have been thinking because I was thinking the same: so many car crashes since Chuy had left.

"What do you make of these plane crashes, too?" Socorrito said. "The one in Venezuela, that Arab one, and then one in Monterey, wasn't it? I have a cousin who lives there. His wife is an *espiritualista*, you know, but just practices on Fridays. She's Catholic the rest of the week."

Mamá turned to Socorrito, now giving her full attention.

"Well, this wife of my cousin says these are signs. All these crashes," Socorrito said. "What do you think, Dolores? Here on the freeway and in the air, what kind of signs?"

The sirens were wailing now, approaching the scene of the accident. A familiar sound—especially lately.

"Mamá," Mónica called out, expertly latched on to the chain-link fence as if she were a graceful spider on her web. "Can we go down to the fields to get a better look? The girls said it was okay with them. They'll watch us."

Distracted by something Socorrito was saying, Mamá nodded her "yes". We hopped off the fence and scurried down the embankment into the field, headed for the Big Sky Drive-In.

"Wait, here comes Octavio," our friend Marisa shouted. "Let's wait for him."

Octavio came sauntering toward us, a proud macho swagger. I could understand why Marisa loved him. Who wouldn't? He had a sexy stride, his abdomen thrust slightly forward. He was confident, knowing perfectly well that Marisa was crazy about him, always had been since they were little kids. I was proud to be his sister.

We bounded out into the brush, the sour grass. Carolina, Ana María, Mónica, Luz, Octavio, Marisa, and an assortment of other kids from Citrus Street. We scattered and whooped with joy, running wild, hopping over sagebrush, some pieces of rusty barbed wire, a dented hubcap, a rotting bike tire. The car crash was the last thing on our minds. We only wanted an excuse to hike down into the field, what had years ago been a dairy farm owned by Swiss immigrants, the Vandebergs.

Ana María had wandered off to pick a bouquet of wild flowers, daydreaming about Tito, no doubt.

Octavio, who had been saying something to poor lovesick Marisa, suddenly turned to us and called over to Carolina, "Hey, let's go into the culvert."

Carolina didn't say anything at first. She looked over to where the giant drainage pipe ran under the freeway. "But what about the kids? We can't take them with us."

"Why not?" Octavio said, walking over to Carolina, Marisa close at his side. "They wouldn't understand the graffiti."

"But Mamá and Papá have said they never want to catch us over there."

"So, ¿y qué? How many hundreds of times have we been there? What's the big deal? I'll take responsibility if they find out." It was obvious to us sisters that Octavio was showing off for Marisa, acting real grown up and in charge. We loved him too much to want to ruin his show.

So we gathered Mónica and Luz, and Ana María, Octavio, Marisa, Carolina and I walked across the field toward the freeway, leaving the other neighborhood kids behind in the field.

I could see the Conifer Street neighbors above and beyond us, all seemingly huddled together. I couldn't hear their words, which were drowned by the whoosh of the cars gliding down the freeway, but for a moment I hesitated, wanting so badly to run back up Conifer Street and be in the secure hubbub of their conversation. Mamá and Socorrito were standing next to each other, talking seriously about something, while Mrs. Wiltheim directed her binoculars toward the Big Sky Drive-In, immersed in the gory vivid details of the accident, no doubt. There were many people congregated at the end of Conifer Street, these car accidents becoming the main reason for our impromptu neighborhood meetings. Once we had determined the gravity of the car crash and had sent the victims speeding on their way in the ambulance—and after the fire engines sprayed clean any spilt gasoline on the road—our neighborhood remained standing at the end of the block, by the chain-link fence. Doña Abundia kept close tabs on the soap operas, never missed an episode. So should Mamá have been too busy on any given day to have watched a segment of "La Cruz de Marisa Cruces," then Doña Abundia, at these spontaneous end-of-the-street meetings, was happy to supply the missing segment.

I turned my gaze from the cozy, familiar scene on Conifer Street and looked toward the culvert. I was trembling, maybe because of the sudden cool gust of wind or, maybe because I was excited and nervous. I had never been inside it.

Octavio led the way. "There's a lot of mud and crap, so watch out," he said. "And remember, you all swore you wouldn't tell Mamá about this."

The drainage pipe looked like a monstrous, concrete hair curler and ran the width—east and west—of the freeway. The traffic just above us seemed to roar and reverberate in our heads. I felt as if I were Jonah entering the bowels of the whale.

Although it was dim in the pipe, I could make out the uneven, angry graffiti: MAKE LOVE, NOT WAR! FUCK YOU. KISS MY DICK. US OUT OF VIET NAM. FUCK THE GOOKS.

The stench was putrid—dank and humid, smelling of urine and vomit and shit. Green slime outlined the stagnant water running the length of culvert.

"Uuuuuuuy," Octavio spookily said, his ghost-call echoing against the concrete walls.

"Let's go home," seven-year-old Luz said, whimpering. "I want to go home."

"Ay, m'ija," Octavio said. "It was only me. I didn't mean to scare you." He picked her up and carried her in his arms. "Come on, we're going to the other end and then back. Then home, okay?" Safe in her brother's arms, Luz nodded her okay.

At the end of the tunnel, the round bit of light seemed years away.

In those moments, I wished I could be Luz, that I could be carried protectively in my brother's or sister's arms. I was feeling frightened, uneasy. There was about the whole place, this cold gray tube of concrete with its angry, defiant graffiti, a sense of doom. I felt imprisoned and lost in the stinking, bloody entrails of a monster.

We walked to the other end of the culvert, the west end, and peered out. Not much could be seen, just the same overgrown brush as on the east end.

"Hey, look," Mónica said, "whose are those?" Lying nearby was a brown, raggedy sweater, a pair of black muddied men's shoes, and grocery bags set out as ground covering amongst the bushes.

"Probably some wetbacks camping out," Octavio said. "They camp out here all the time before going onto L.A. Come on, let's go back."

"What's a 'wetback'?" Luz asked Octavio as we all entered the culvert, heading back.

"It's those people who sneak across the border illegally from Mexico."

"Why do they sneak across?" Now ten-year-old Mónica wanted to know.

"Because they shouldn't be in this country," Octavio explained. "So they sneak in."

"Why are they called 'wetbacks'?" Luz asked.

"God, Octavio, that's a hell of a way to explain it to them," Carolina said. "How insensitive."

"Okay, Miss College Girl, you explain it to them."

"Well, *m'ijas*," she said, "first of all, you've got to understand that there are a lot of poor people in Mexico with no jobs, no money, no food. So they come to the United States to find jobs and get paid for their work. . ."

"So then they sneak in," Luz said, "I know that part. Did Mami and Papi sneak in too when they came from Mexico?"

"Shit, Carolina, now look what you've done," Octavio said, laughing. "You've opened a great can of worms."

"No, they didn't," Carolina said, giving Octavio a look. "I'll explain it to you when we get home. Look at this shit. We've got it all over our shoes. Now how are we going to explain this to Mamá?"

"Don't worry," Octavio said, "I'll handle it."

Making our way back through the stench and the mud, surrounded by rude words and epithets on the hard, thick concrete, the excitement of this adventure had died out. We were quiet, concentrating on avoiding the dank spillage that made a stream in the center walking with legs as spread out as possible, waddling.

There were secrets here I knew nothing about, echoes that reverberated from the cold hard walls and into my soul. The graffiti itself hid messages I read over and over. At some point these messages were impenetrable and yet begged to be understood. Who wrote them and when? In the late night? In broad daylight? The clothing strewn on the ground—who was the owner and why was he living here in the bowels of this subterranean freeway giant? If Lydia were here right now, I was sure we could come up with some good explanation.

"Wait, I want to look at something," Octavio called out to us. "Go ahead, you girls." And to Marisa he said, "Come here, I want to show you something." He put Luz down, and she ran over to me. Holding my hand, we cautiously walked to the east end, trying to avoid stepping in the muck. Everyone was too busy keeping her shoes clean and out of the stream of sewage to take much notice of Octavio and Marisa, who lagged behind.

"Ouch," I said, my ankle twisted. I crouched down to ease the pain and at the same time turned to look back at the other end of the long pipe where we'd just been. Octavio was kissing Marisa, grabbing at the front of her blouse. I quickly looked away, feeling hot in my face. I knew Octavio didn't really care for Marisa. He had other girls who made his heart go wild, but not poor Marisa. I felt sick to my stomach.

Once out of the tube and in the fresh air, my stomach was in convulsions, and I vomited on the field, a few feet away from our busy Interstate 5.

The spring air had grown cold in the twilight, and I shivered all the way home.

"You okay, Yoli?" everybody kept asking me.

I nodded, too confused and hurt to look anyone straight in the eyes, except for Marisa. She was sad. She too knew what Octavio's sexual advances had meant: they meant everything and nothing. Just a quick thrill for him.

Make love, not war, I wanted to shout. I felt dizzy and weak. Fuck you, I wanted to answer.

We slowly climbed up the embankment to our street, all of us exhausted. The informal neighborhood meeting had long dispersed. The street was silent, empty, except for the sound of our slow, shuffling feet.

We paused in front of Marisa's house and waved good-bye. Then past Socorrito's. I imagined her on the phone this very moment, reporting to her *comadres* the strange phenomenon: so many car crashes ever since Chuy Sahagún took off on that noisy motorcycle. The "German Spies" were probably in their neat, organized home commenting on the many accidents since April. Did they also think of Chuy Sahagún? Unnatural phenomenon: shooting stars colliding.

I was certain Mamá was this very moment in the back yard watering her rows of tomatoes and squash, the gladioluses. Carolina need not have worried what Mamá would say about our muddy shoes, what excuse or little lie to think up to explain why we were so late in coming home. No need for explanations, I thought sadly. Mamá would not notice the dirty shoes, or our getting home after dark. Her only preoccupation in those days when Chuy was missing was to make sure her plants and flowers were growing, growing, growing.

Already lights inside the houses had been turned on, enticing us to walk a little faster toward home and warmth and family. Out of the cool spring night, into the smells of tortillas and beans, to quick baths and *Crema Nivea*, a dollop of Dep for our hair about to be set on empty frozen juice cans for the straight-hair look. Into security and love and soft living-room lights we would enter as we sat together watching "The Beverly Hillbillies" and "Gilligan's Island." We were content to know that we were not on a deserted island, even as the freeway cars rushing by sounded like waves and the Santa Fe 8:38 train wailed its lonely call. We families were not alone, not alienated on a no-man's island. We could afford to laugh at poor Gilligan and his friends in their futile attempts to be rescued; we could love Granny who continued to be Granny even as she sat transplanted in a mansion in Beverly Hills—such a sumptuous house. How we would love to be Granny! Each one of us dreamt our own dreams of sudden fortune and mansions, swimming pools and movies stars. Such unattainable wealth, but oh, could we ever dream! Sitting on the floor or on the orange vinyl love seat in front of the T.V. watching the Lawrence Welk Show (though we would rather be watching the Alfred Hitchcock Show), the translucent, shimmering bubbles seemed to float out of the screen toward us, inviting us to enter a Bubble Land of opportunities and wishes granted. Although we knew the fragile, almost-illusory bubbles would pop before our very eyes within seconds, we never stopped feeling secure as a family.

I could now smell the light fragrance of our sweet peas. By the time we waved good-bye to Georgie from Citrus Street, and made our way to our familiar rickety fence, night had set in.

AUTHOR INDEX OF PRIZE-WINNERS

A

Leonard Adame, *Flute Songs, 1981–82*
Marisela Cortez Adams, *Tomorrow Is Only Saturday, 1976–77*
Manuel R. Aguilera, *María, 1980–81*
Francisco X. Alarcón, *Tattoos, 1983–84*
José Alfaro, No title available, *1977–78*
Andrés Álvarez, *A Solitary Migration: Baja California, 1981–82*
Roberto Álvarez, Poems, *1980–81*
Gabriel de Anda, Poems, *1982–83*
Andrea Teresa Arenas, Poems, *1983–84*
Ron Arias, *The Wetback, 1974–75*
Alfred Arteaga, Poems, *1980-81*; *Cantos, 1986–87*
Fausto Avendaño, *Los buenos indicios, 1984–85*
Víctor Ávila, Poems, *1983–84*
Carlos López Azur, No title available, *1985–86*

B

Deborah Fernández Badillo, Poems, *1984–85*
Patricia Santana Bejar, No title available, *1991–92*
Juan Manuel Bernal, *Confesiones de un seudopoeta . . . , 1980–81*
Charles Ramírez Berg, No title available, *1986–87*
Evangeline Blanco, *Caribe, 1994–95*
Arnold Bojórquez, *El rey, 1979–80*
María Dolores Bolívar, *La palabra (H)era, 1989–90*
Barbara Brinson-Pineda, *Litanía peregrina, 1981–82*
Elaine Brooks, *Poems, 1979–80*
William Busic, *The Grey Dogs, 1974–75*

C

Rosemary Susan Cadena, Poems, *1979–80*
Rita M. Canales, *The Awakening, 1977–78*
Frank Canino, Yanira Contreras and Beatriz Pizano, No title available, *1997–98*

Jo Ann Y. Hernández, No title available, *1994–95;* No title available, *1995–96*
Rosalinda Hernández, Poems, *1984–85*
Juan Felipe Herrera, *Antiteatro y poemas, 1978–79; Memoir: Checker-Piece, 1984–85*

K

Gary D. Keller, *The Raza Who Scored Big in Anáhuac, 1983–84*
María-Christina Keller, *At the Top of the Stairs, 1980–81*

L

Alberto Ledesma, *Poetry for Homeboys on the Foul Line, 1988–89*
Graciela Limón, *Concha's Husband, 1989–90; Voice in Ramah, 1990–91*
Carlos Lombrana, *I Only Came Here to Grease, 1976–77*
Jack López, *The Boy Who Swam With Dolphins, 1982–83*
Phyllis Victoria López, Poems, *1980–81*
María Josefina López, *Simply María, or America's Dream, 1988–89*
Frank Lostanau, Poems, *1974–75*
Richard Alexander Lou, *Works, 1982–83*
Yolanda Luera, Poems, *1975–76,* No title available, *1986–87*
Tom Lugo, *Mexican Ascent of the Academic Shreckhorn, 1988–89*

M

Amalio Madueño, *Rancho de la nación, 1974–75*
Rey Madueño, *A Pure and Simple Fantasy, 1976–77*
Martha Manqueros, *Claudia, 1980–81*
Arturo Mantecón, No title available, *1987–88*
Patricia Preciado Martín, *María de las trenzas, 1985–86; Songs My Mother Sang to Me, 1988–89*
Cheta Martínez, *Vida loca: Cheta Martínez's Underground Chronicles, 1989–90*
Demetria Martínez, *Chimayó, México, 1987–88*
Rubén Benjamín Martínez, *Plaza mayor, 1989–90*
David Maturino, *California, fragmento de México, 1975–76*
Cathy Medina, Poems, *1981–82*
Rubén Medina, Poems, *1979–80*
David Meléndez, *No Flag, 1989–90*
Jesús Mena, *El risueño, 1979–80*
Héctor Menez, No title available, *1985–86*
Rita Mendoza, *Thoughts of a Chicana Woman, 1974–75*
David Nava Monreal, *A Pastoral Tale, 1979–80; Variations Between Worlds, 1983–84; Cellmates, 1986–87*
Andrés Montoya, *The Iceworker Sings and Other Poems, 1996–97*
Cherrie Moraga, Poems, *1987–88*

Mario Rodríguez, *The Summer Collection, 1974–75*
Roberto Rodríguez, *Mystery Forgotten: The Disappearance of the Maya People, 1976–77*
Salvador Rodríguez del Pino, Poems, *1974–75*
Nydia Rojas, No title available, *1995–96*
Elaine Romero, *Walking Home, 1993–94*
Jesús Rosales, *Parte del proceso, 1980–81*
Silvia Rosales, *El puente de los esclavos, 1975–76*
Samuel Royball, No title available, *1977–78*
Catriona Rueda, No title available, *1997–98*
Nedra Ruíz, Poems, *1977–78*

S

Benjamín Alire Sáenz, *Alligator Park, 1988–89*
Ana María Salazar, *La última despedida, 1983–84*
Clyde Salazar, Poems, *1979–80*
Arturo Salcedo-Martínez, No title available, *1988–89*
Antonio Salinas, No title available, *1996–97*
Elba Rosario Sánchez, *Tunas a la luna, 1989–90*
Rosaura Sánchez, *Transparencias, 1975–76*
Jesús Santana, *Revoltijo poético, 1975–76*
Patricia Santana, *Motorcycle Ride on the Sea of Tranquility, 1998–99*
Lorenza Calvillo Schmidt, *Palabras contigo, 1974–75*
Gustavo Segade, Poems, *1985–86*
Frank Sifuentes, *Mi padrino Apolinar, 1981–82*
Gary Soto, Poems, *1975–76*
Elizabeth Noriega Stein, *Chilpancingo and the Need to Know, 1982–83*
Francisco X. Stork, No title available, *1998–99*

T

Carmen Tafolla, *Hot Line, 1986–87*
Kathleen J. Torres, *The Lantern of her Caves, 1982–83*

V

Gloria Velásquez, *Sunland, 1984–85*
Arthur Valenzuela, Poems, *1981–82*
Liliana Valenzuela, *Zurcidos invisibles, 1988–89*
Raquel Valle, *Alcanzando un sueño, 1989–90*
Victor Manuel Valle, *Ilegal, 1976–77*
Rafael del Valle, No title available, *1987–88*
Armando Vallejo, Poems, *1981–82*
José Luis Vargas, *El ojo del agua, 1975–76*
Patricio F. Vargas, *Payback: Dirty for Dirty, 1983–84*

CHRONOLOGICAL INDEX OF PRIZE-WINNERS

1974-75

Ron Arias, *The Wetback*

William Busic, *The Grey Dogs*

César A. González, *A ver, hijo*

Ana María Hernández, *Grandma*

Frank Lostanau, Poems

Amalio Madueño, *Rancho de la nación*

Rita Mendoza, *Thoughts of a Chicana Woman*

Alejandro Murguía, Poems

Juan Luciano Ortiz, Poems

Ramón Ortiz, *Cecilia*

Mario Rodríguez, *The Summer Collection*

Salvador Rodríguez del Pino, Poems

Lorenza Calvillo Schmidt, *Palabras contigo*

George Verdugo, *F and Independence*

1975-76

Rosa M. Carillo, *Amor y libertad; Calor*

Ana Castillo, Poems

Noé Magaña Chávez, *Más mezcla maistro*

Saúl Cuevas, *El tren*

R. A. Díaz, *Mini-poemas*

Máximo Espinoza, Poems

Arturo Gálvez, *Historia de dragones; Detrás*

Anna Hernández, *Seven Poems*

Barbara Hernández, *Bautizo; Mazmorra*

Yolanda Luera, Poems

David Maturino, *California, fragmento de México*

M. V. Noreña, *A tres bandas*

Héctor González Padilla, *El crimen*

Laura O. Parra, Poems
Anna Pérez, Poems
Guillermo A. Prieto, *Poemas*
Tony Pryzblo, Poems
Silvia Rosales, *El puente de los esclavos*
Rosaura Sánchez, *Transparencias*
Jesús Santana, *Revoltijo poético*
Gary Soto, Poems
José Luis Vargas, *El ojo del agua*
Pedro Ortiz Vásquez, Poems

1976-77

Marisela Cortez Adams, *Tomorrow is Only Saturday*
Carlos Lombrana, *I Only Came Here to Grease*
Rey Madueño, *A Pure and Simple Fantasy*
Roberto Rodríguez, *Mystery Forgotten: The Disappearance of the Maya People*
Victor Manuel Valle, *Ilegal*
Alma Villanueva, Poems

1977-78

José Alfaro, No title available
Rita M. Canales, *The Awakening*
Javier Pacheco, No title available
Dolores Ramos, No title available
Samuel Royball, No title available
Nedra Ruíz, Poems

1978-79

Reymundo Gamboa, *Your Disdain*
Art Godorniz, Poems
Juan Felipe Herrera, *Antiteatro y poemas*
M. C. Peralta, *One Performance Only*
Orlando Ramírez, *Speedway*
Helena María Viramontes, *Birthday*

1979-80

Arnold Bojórquez, *El rey*
Elaine Brooks, Poems
Rosemary Susan Cadena, Poems

Rubén Medina, Poems
Jesús Mena, *El risueño*
David Nava Monreal, *A Pastoral Tale*
Benito Pastoriza, Poems
Clyde Salazar, Poems

1980-81

Manuel R. Aguilera, *María*
Roberto Álvarez, Poems
Alfred Arteaga, Poems
Juan Manuel Bernal, *Confesiones de un seudo-poeta: digresiones de un
        demente*
Zamora Damación, *Orchards*
Pedro Gutiérrez, Poems
María-Christina Keller, *At the Top of the Stairs*
Phyllis Victoria López, Poems
Martha Manqueros, *Claudia*
Michael Nava, *Sixteen Poems*
Jesús Rosales, *Parte del proceso*
Henry Andrew Wade-Varela, *Dulce et decorum*

1981-82

Leonard Adame, *Flute Songs*
Andrés Álvarez, *A Solitary Migration: Baja California*
Barbara Brinson-Pineda, *Litanía peregrina*
Adam Gettinger-Brizuela, *Awakening*
Cathy Medina, Poems
Alfonso Niño, *Mingo's Bar*
Mary Helen Ponce, *Recuerdo: When Rito Died*
José Luis Quintero, *El manuscrito de Heinz Steiner*
Diego Rodríguez, *Un baile sin música*
Frank Sifuentes, *Mi padrino Apolinar*
Arthur Valenzuela, Poems
Armando Vallejo, Poems

1982-83

Gabriel de Anda, Poems
Luis Morones Careaga, *The Goddess within Subterranean Women*
Wilfredo Q. Castaño, *Bone Games*
Gustavo Chavando, *Agustín, el bueno*

Jack López, *The Boy Who Swam With Dolphins*
Richard Alexander Lou, *Works*
Luis J. Rodríguez, *Sometimes You Dance With a Watermelon*
Elizabeth Noriega Stein, *Chilpancingo and the Need to Know*
Kathleen J. Torres, *The Lantern of her Caves*

1983-84

Francisco X. Alarcón, *Tattoos*
Andrea Teresa Arenas, Poems
Víctor Ávila, Poems
Lucha Corpi, *Shadows on Ebbing Water*
Juan Delgado, *Landscapes*
Gary D. Keller, El Huitlacoche, *The Raza Who Scored Big in Anáhuac*
David Nava Monreal, *Variations Between Worlds*
Michael Ricardo, *Grus Xicanus*
Ana María Salazar, *La última despedida*
Patricio F. Vargas, *Payback: Dirty for Dirty*

1984-85

Fausto Avendaño, *Los buenos indicios*
Deborah Fernández Badillo, Poems
Rosalinda Hernández, Poems
Juan Felipe Herrera, *Memoir: Checker-Piece*
Margarita Luna Robles, *Urbano: Letters of the Horseshoe Murder*
Gloria Velásquez Treviño, *Sunland*

1985-86

Carlos López Azur, No title available
Patricia Preciado Martín, *María de las trenzas*
Héctor Menez, No title available
Javier Barrales Pacheco, No title available
Terri de la Peña, No title available
Gustavo Segade, Poems

1986-87

Alfred Arteaga, *Cantos*
Charles Ramírez Berg, No title available
Victor Carrillo, No title available
Olivia Dávila Flores, *Qué, cómo y cuándo*
Reymundo Gamboa, *50/50 Chance*

César A. González-T., No title available
Jerry L. Gurule, No title available
Yolanda Luera, No title available
David Nava Monreal, *Cellmates*
Carlos Morton, *Johnny Tenorio*
Jorge Antonio Renaud, *No title avalaible*
Carmen Tafolla, *Hot Line*

1987-88
Olivia Dávila Flores, No title available
Ignacio García, No title available
Arturo Mantecón, No title available
Demetria Martínez, *Chimayó, Mexico*
Cherríe Moraga, Poems
Alfonso Peña Ramos, *Matachín Dancer*
Rafael del Valle, No title available
Silviana Wood, *And where Was Pancho Villa when You Really Need Him?*

1988-89
Alberto Ledesma, *Poetry for Homeboys on the Foul Line*
María Josefina López, *Simply María, or America's Dream*
Tom Lugo, *Mexican Ascent of the Academic Shreckhorn*
Patricia Preciado Martín, *Songs My Mother Sang to Me*
Arturo Salcedo-Martínez, No title available
José Rendón, Poems
Benjamín Alire Sáenz, *Alligator Park*
Liliana Valenzuela, *Zurcidos invisibles*
Silviana Wood, *Una vez, en un barrio de sueños*

1989-90
María Dolores Bolívar, *La palabra (H)era*
Carlos Nicolás Flores, *La cantina del gusanito*
José Manuel Galván, *Las tandas de San Cuilmas*
Atila Guerrero, *The Crystal Chandelier*
Graciela Limón, *Concha's Husband*
Cheta Martínez, *Vida loca: Cheta Martínez's Underground Chronicles*
Rubén Benjamín Martínez, *Plaza mayor*
David Meléndez, *No Flag*
Elba Rosario Sánchez, *Tunas a la luna*
Raquel Valle, *Alcanzando un sueño*

1990-91

Ignacio M. García, No title available

Graciela Limón, *Voice in the Ramah*

Manuel Ramos, *The Ballad of Rocky Ruíz*

1991-92

Terri de la Peña, *Ventanas*

Mary Helen Ponce, No title available

Patricia Santana Bejar, No title available

1992-93

Laura Fargas, Poems

1993-94

Elaine Romero, *Walking Home*

1994-95

Evangeline Blanco, *Caribe*

Jo Ann Yolanda Hernández, No title available

Alberto A. Ríos, No title available

1995-96

Jo Ann Yolanda Hernández, No title available

Nydia Rojas, No title available

Mike Padilla, *Hard Language*

1996-97

Andrés Montoya, *The Iceworker Sings and Other Songs*

Antonio Salinas, No title available

Norman Antonio Zelaya, No title available

1997-98

Frank Canino, Yanira Contreras and Beatriz Pizano, No title available

Angelo Parra, *Song of the Coquí*

Catriona Rueda, No title available

1998-99

Verónica González, No title available

Patricia Santana, *Motorcycle Ride on the Sea of Tranquility*

Francisco X. Stork, No title available

AUTHOR BIOGRAPHIES

Francisco X. Alarcón was born in Wilmington, California, and was raised in Guadalajara, Mexico. He is the author of ten books of poetry including *Tattoos* (1985), *Ya vas, Carnal* (1985), *Quake Poems* (1989), *Body in Flames / Cuerpo en llamas* (1990), *Loma Prieta* (1990), *De amor oscuro / Of Dark Love* (1991), *Snake Poems: An Aztec Invocation* (1992), *Poemas zurdos* (1992), and *No Golden Gate for Us* (1993). Two of his books have been translated into Gaelic and one into Swedish. Alarcón has been the recipient of the Danworth and Fulbright fellowships. He won the 1998 Carlos Pellicer-Robert Frost Poetry Honor Award (Third Bi-National Border Poetry Contest) and the 1993 American Book Award. He currently teaches at the University of California, Davis, where he directs the Spanish for Native Speakers Program.

Alfred Arteaga is Associate Professor at the University of California, Berkeley. He is the author of numerous books of poetry and theoretical essays. He is the recipient of a Rockefeller Fellowship (1993), the National Endowment for the Arts Fellowship (1995), and the PEN Oakland Josephine Miles Award for Literary Excellence for *House with the Blue Bed* (1997). Additional publications include *Cantos* (1991), *Red* (2000), and *Frozen Accident* (2006).

Ron Arias was born in Los Angeles and has lived in the United States, Germany, Spain, Argentina, Peru, and Mexico. Arias taught literature and journalism at the college level for thirteen years and worked as a magazine journalist for eighteen years. Arias also served two years in the Peace Corps. His short novel *The Road to Tamazunchale*, was nominated for the National Book Award in 1978, and in 2002, it was translated into Spanish by Basarai Bilingual Press. His current project is a novel entitled *Ibarra*, a fictional account of the teenage, mid-16th century explorer of northwest Mexico. Arias is a Correspondent for *People* Magazine, AOL-Time Warner.

Deborah Fernández Badillo lives in California and has worked with La Calaca Review.

Juan Manuel Bernal lives and teaches in San Diego, California. He is the author of *La Cocina en huelga de hambre* (1986), *La Ventana del ojo rojo* (1986), and *Diaridad* (1988). His most recent publication is entitled *Para llevar amorizando* by Editorial Algo (2001).

Evangeline Blanco is a native of Puerto Rico. Her current occupation is Payroll Examiner for the state of New York. She currently resides in Queens, New York. Her winning novel *Caribe* was published by Doubleday Press in 1998.

Wilfredo Q. Castaño is the author of *Small Stones Cast Upon Tender Earth* (1981). He is active at the Poetry Center at San Francisco State University and has had his work reviewed in the *American Poetry Review, The Greenfield Review, Tin-Tan Cósmico Magazine, Kosmos Anthology*, and *City of San Francisco Magazine*. He has translated the work of Otto René Castillo in *Volcán* (1984). He teaches writing and photography at the college level.

Lucha Corpi, née Luz del Carmen Corpi Constantino, was born in Jáltipan, Veracruz, Mexico. In 2005, she retired after thirty-one years of teaching in OUSD's Neighborhood Centers Adult School. Corpi is the recipient of the National Endowment for the Arts in poetry, the PEN-Oakland Josephine Miles Literary Award, and the Multicultural Publishers Exchange Award for her fiction. She is the author of two collections of poetry, a children's book, and five novels. Three of her novels feature Gloria Damasco, a Chicana private detective. Her new bilingual children's book, *The Triple Banana Split Boy/Diente Dulce*, is to be published by Piñata Books in 2008. She is currently working on her fourth Gloria Damasco mystery, *Death at Solstice*, and a collection of personal essays, *The Orphan and the Bookburner*. Corpi lives in Oakland, California.

Carlos Nicolás Flores was born in El Paso, Texas. Flores was awarded the National Endowment for the Humanities Fellowship at Dartmouth College. He currently teaches English at Laredo Community College. Flores's most recent publication is a young adult novel entitled *Our House on Hueco*, published by Texas Tech University Press (2007).

Reymundo Gamboa was born in Anthony, New Mexico, and raised in Lamont, California. He was the 1990 winner of the Silver Poet Award and served as Chair of English at Ernest Righetti High School, Santa Maria, California. His poetry has been published in the *American Anthology of Contemporary Poetry* and *New Voices in American Poetry*. Gamboa was a resident of Santa Maria, California, until his passing in 2001.

Juan Felipe Herrera was born in Fowler, California. Herrera enjoys writing in collectives and for magazines and tabloids. He has served as editor and co-editor for over ten journals and he has founded various performance troupes such as Teatro Tolteca (1971), Poetashumanos (1978), Troka (1983), Teatro Zapata (1990), and Manikrudo (1994). Herrera has received numerous awards such as the National Endowment for the Arts, the California Arts Council, Chicano Award and has been inducted into the Latino Literary Hall of Fame. His most recent publication is *187 Reasons Mexicanos Can't Cross the Border: Undocuments, 1971-2007* (2007). Herrera teaches at California State University at Fresno.

Gary D. Keller is Regents' Professor and Director of the Hispanic Research Center at Arizona State University. He most recently co-authored *Chicano Art for Our Millennium: Collected Works from the Arizona State University Community*. Keller is the General Editor and Director of Bilingual Review Press/Editorial Bilingüe.

Alberto Ledesma was born in Huisquilco, Jalisco, Mexico, but he was raised in East Oakland, California. Currently, Ledesma works as the Writing Program Coordinator for UC Berkley's Student Learning Center. In addition to academic essays on Mexican immigrant literature, Ledesma has published poetry and prose in *Berkeley Poetry Review, Con/Safos,* and in Gary Soto's *Chicano Chapbook Series*. He is currently working on a manuscript tentatively titled, *Secrets of a Wetback Warrior*. Ledesma resides in Castro Valley, California.

Graciela Limón is a native of Los Angeles, California. She is the recipient of the Before Columbus American Book Award (1994) and the Myers Book Away Award (2002). Currently, she teaches as a Visiting Professor at UCLA and UCSB. Her winning entry was published under the title *In Search of Bernabé* (1993). Her most recent book projects include *Erased Faces* (2001), *El Día de la Luna* (2004), *Left Alive* (2005), and she is currently working on *Despiérten, Hermanos!* Limón resides in Simi Valley, California.

Jack López was born in Lynwood, California. He received First Place Winner for Best Literary Short Stories from the Chicano Literary Hall of Fame as well as Special Mention by the Pushcart Prize. López was also the recipient of the National Hispanic Scholar Award. He is Professor of English at CSU Northridge. He has authored *Snapping Lines* (2001). His winning story was part of his autobiography, *Cholos: A Latino Family Album* (1998). López resides in Redlands, California.

Josefina López was born in San Luis Potosí, Mexico, but she has lived in Los Angeles County, California since the age of five. Her plays have been produced over one hundred times and include *Real Women Have Curves* (1996), *Unconquered Spirits* (1997), *Simply María, or America's Dream* (2004), *Confessions of Women from East L.A.* (2004), and *Food for the Dead* (2004). She has written screenplays including *Lotería for Juárez, Add Me to the Party,* and *No Place Like Home.* López won the Gabriel García Márquez Award, and the Humanitas Award for Screenwriting. She was also awarded a Screenwriting Fellowship by the California Arts Council in 2001. In 2007, López completed her first novel *Hungry Woman in Paris.* López teaches writing to local youth at her CASA 0101 space in Boyle Heights, California.

Demetria Martínez was raised in Albuquerque, New Mexico. She graduated from Princeton University after which she decided to dedicate her life to social activism, journalism, and the writing of fiction. She is the author of *Border Wars* (1985), *Turning* (1987), *Three Times a Woman: Chicana Poetry* (1989), *Breathing Between the Lines* (1997), *The Devil's Workshop* (2002), *Confessions of a Berlitz-tape Chicana* (2005), and the award-winning novel *Mother Tongue* (1994).

Rubén Benjamín Martínez lives in Los Angeles, California, and has worked as a writer and editor for *LA Weekly Magazine,* where he became the first Latino on staff. He has since worked as an essayist for National Public Radio and as TV-host for *Life and Times* for which he won an Emmy award. He co-authored *Flesh Life: Sex in Mexico* (2006) and *East Side Stories* (1998). His book *The Other Side: Notes from the New L.A., Mexico City and Beyond* was published in 1993. Currently, Martínez holds the Fletcher Jones Chair in Literature and Writing at Loyola Marymount University. He is also an accomplished musician and has recorded with Los Illegals, Concrete Blonde, and The Roches.

Rubén Medina was born in Mexico City in 1955 and came to the United States in 1978. He has lived in California, Minnesota, and Wisconsin, where he has worked as a gardener, bus boy, cook, laborer, construction worker, Spanish instructor and professor of literature. Currently, he is Associate Professor in the Department of Spanish and Portuguese and Director of the Chicana/o Studies Program at the University of Wisconsin, Madison, where he teaches and researches on modern Mexican and Chicana/o literature. He is the author of *Amor de Lejos . . . : Fools' Love* (1986), which was a finalist in the 1984 Casa de las Américas Literary Prize held in Cuba. He is completing a book of poetry entitled, *Nomadic Nation: Nación nómada.* His research publications include

Autor, autoridad y autorización: Escritura y poética de Octavio Paz (1999) and several articles on Mexican and Chicano literature and film.

David Meléndez. No information available.

David Nava Monreal is a three-time winner of the CLLP Contest. His short stories have appeared in numerous journals, including *Saguaro, Bilingual Review, The Americas Review, Q-Vo,* and *Firme,* among others. He wrote two books of short stories, *The New Neighbor and Other Stories* (1987) and *A Season's Harvest* (1998). He is also a novelist and a writer of non-fiction and published *Cinco de Mayo: An Epic Novel* (1993). Monreal lives in Lake Forest, California.

Andrés Montoya's work has appeared in various literary journals, including *The Santa Clara Review, In the Grove, Bilingual Review/Revista Bilingüe,* and *Flies, Cockroaches, and Poets.* His various occupations included field hand, ditch digger, canner, ice plant worker, and writing teacher. His *The Iceworker Sings and Other Poems* (Bilingual Press, 1999) won the Before Columbus Foundation American Book Award in 2000. He was born on May 18, 1968, and died on May 26, 1999, at the age of 31.

Carlos Morton was born in Chicago, Illinois. Morton taught as a Distinguished Fulbright Lecturer at the Universidad Nacional Autónoma de México, 1989-90, and again, at the Marie Curie-Sklodowskiej University in Poland, 2006-2007. He was inducted into the Writers of the Pass in El Paso, Texas, in 1999. Morton was the First Prize Winner of the National Hispanic Playwriting Contest for the Arizona Theater Company in 1995. His most recent publications include *Dreaming On a Sunday in the Alameda* (2004) and *Children of the Sun: Scenes and Monologues for Latino Youth* to be published in 2008. Morton is Professor of Theater at the University of California, Santa Barbara. He resides in Santa Barbara, California.

Michael Nava was born in Stockton, California, and raised in Sacramento. Nava is a gay-rights activist as well as a novelist. His books include *The Little Death* (1985), *Goldenboy* (1988), *Finale* (1989), *How Town* (1990), *The Hidden Law* (1992), *Created Equal: Why Gay Rights Matter to America* (1994), and *The Death of Friends* (1996). He currently lives in San Francisco, California, where he practices law.

Angelo Parra, a New Yorker, is an award-winning playwright with production credits in New York, Los Angeles, Chicago, Washington, D.C., Florida, and at the Edinburgh International Festival. The critically acclaimed *The Devil's Music: The Life and Blues of Bessie Smith* won him the New York

Foundation for the Arts Playwriting Fellowship and was named Best Solo Show in South Florida in 2001. In addition to the CLLP Prize, *Song of the Coquí* won the 1998 American Dream Prize. Parra also wrote the award-winning *Casino* and *Journey of the Heart*. He was selected a Tennessee Williams Scholar for the prestigious Sewanee Writers Conference in 2000. Parra teaches playwriting and theater at Ramapo College of New Jersey and is the Founder/Director of the Hudson Valley Professional Playwrights Lab.

Mike Padilla was born in Oakland, California, and currently lives in Los Angeles, California. His novel *Hard Language* was published by Arte Público Press (2000). Padilla works as a Writer for Campaign Operations at UCLA.

Terri de la Peña was born in Santa Monica, California. Her current occupation is Senior Administrative Analyst at UCLA, where she has worked since 1986. In 1999, she wrote *Faults: A Novel*, published by Alyson Books, and a children's alphabet book *A is for the Americas* co-authored with Cynthia Chin-Lee. "A Saturday in August," one of her stories for which she won first prize in the CLLP was published in *Finding Courage* edited by Irene Zahava (1989). De la Peña resides in Santa Monica, California.

Mary Helen Ponce was born in Pacoima, California. She earned advanced degrees at California State University, Northridge, and at the University of New Mexico. She works currently as a Freelance Writer and Consultant and lives in Sunland, California.

Manuel Ramos was born in Florence, Colorado. He holds degrees from Colorado State University and a law degree from the University of Colorado. He won the Colorado Book Award (1993), the Law Alumni Award for Distinguished Achievement (1996), the Jacob V. Schaetzel Award (1998), and the Chris Miranda Award (2004). He continues to practice law and is the Director of Advocacy for Colorado Legal Services. His recent publications include *Moony's Road to Hell* (2002), *Brown-on-Brown* (2003), and a short story "The 405 Is Locked Down" to be published in *Latinos in Lotusland* (2008). Ramos's winning novel *The Ballad of Rocky Ruíz* was published by St. Martin's Press in 1993, and a new edition was reprinted in 2004 by Northwestern University Press. Ramos resides in Denver, Colorado.

Luis J. Rodríguez is the author of several award-winning books, poetry, children's literature, memoir, nonfiction, and fiction. He is a columnist for *The Progressive Magazine* and editor of Tía Chucha Press and *Xispas*, an online Chicano magazine. He currently lives in San Fernando, California.

Elaine Romero was born in Santa Rosa, California, and raised in Orange County, California. Romero won a play commission from the Kennedy Center for the Performing Arts/White Historical Association for *Xochi: Jaguar Princess* and a second commission from the Alley Theater for *Something Rare and Wonderful* (Houston, Texas). She was also named TCG/Pew National Theater Artist in Residence for the Arizona Theater Company, where she wrote *Before Death Comes for the Archbishop* and *Secret Things.* She wrote *Barrio Hollywood* during her tenure at NEA/TCG Theater Residency Program for Playwrights at the San Diego Repertory Theater. Her most recent publications include *Secret Things* (2007), *A Simple Snow* in *The Best 10-Minute Plays for 2 Actors* (2007), and *Voices in First Person: Reflections on Latino Identity* (2008). *Walking Home* was published in *Ollantay Theater Magazine* (1996). Romero lives in Los Angeles and Arizona.

Margarita Luna Robles resides in San Francisco, California, where she is a well-known poet and activist.

Jesús Rosales was born in Durango, Mexico, but was raised in Santa Barbara, California. Rosales works as Professor of Spanish at Texas A&M University in Corpus Christi. He published academic writings including a book-length study on Alejandro Morales (1999), and has recently published several academic articles including "Fictional Testimony: Mr. Hank Tavera: el sembrador de palabras" in *Puentes: Revista méxico-chicana de literatura, cultura y arte* and "La frontera como falso refugio chicano, el caso de Oscar Zeta Acosta: The Brown Buffalo" in *Confluencia: Revista Hispánica de Cultura y Literatura.* Rosales resides in Corpus Christi, Texas.

Nedra Ruíz lives in San Francisco, California. She has worked as a Criminal Law Attorney for twenty-five years.

Benjamín Alire Sáenz was born in a small village on the outskirts of Las Cruces, New Mexico. He has published several novels including *The House of Forgetting* (1997), *Elegies in Blue* (2002), and children's titles, *A Gift from Papa Diego* (1998) and *Grandma Fina and Her Wonderful Umbrellas* (1999). His first young adult novel, *Sammy and Juliana in Hollywood* (2004) won numerous citations and awards including The Americas Book Award, the Patterson Book Prize, and the J. Hunt Award. His most recent publications are entitled *In Perfect Light* (2005) and *Dreaming of the End of War* (2006), a book of poetry. He teaches in the Creative Writing Department at the University of Texas at El Paso.

Rosaura Sánchez is Professor of Latin American Literature and Chicano Literature at the University of California, San Diego. She is the author of

Chicano Discourse: A Socio-Historic Perspective (1983) and *Telling Identities: the Californio Testimonios* (1995). Sánchez is known for her work in Critical Theory, Gender Studies, and Third World Studies as well.

Patricia Santana was born in San Diego, California. Santana's novel *Motorcycle Ride on the Sea of Tranquility* was listed in the 2003 Best Books by the American Library Services Award, the 2003 California Readers Collection, and the San Diego Magazine Best Fiction Award 2003. She currently works as a college Spanish instructor. Santana's recent work entitled *Ghosts of El Grullo* (2008) will be published by University of New Mexico Press. Santana resides in San Diego, California.

Gustavo Segade is Professor of Spanish at San Diego State University. He is involved with the Border Institute for Advanced Nonlinear Studies, and has worked extensively as a translator. Recently, he translated *Permanent Works: Poems 1981-92* (1993) and *Woman on the Road* (1994) in conjunction with the Baja Literature Project.

Carmen Tafolla travels throughout the United States, Mexico, Canada, and Europe performing a dramatic medley based on excerpts from her poems and short stories. She is the author of five books of poetry, television screenplays, numerous children's stories, and a non-fiction work on racism, sexism, and Chicana women. Tafolla was awarded the Art of Peace Award in 1999 from St. Mary's University for writing that furthers peace, justice, and human understanding. Alex Halley, author of *Roots*, described Tafolla as "a world-class writer." Tafolla's recent books include *Baby Coyote and the Old Woman* (2000) and *Sonnets and Salsa* (2001).

Gloria Velásquez was born in Johnstown, Colorado, but grew up in San Luis Obispo, California. She is Professor of Chicano Literature at California Polytechnic State University. Her publications include *I Used to Be a Superwoman* (1994), *Xicana on the Run* (2005), and *Tyrone's Betrayal* (2006)— the seventh novel in The Roosevelt High School Series. Her selection herewith will be part of her upcoming publication *Toy Soldiers and Dolls/ Soldaditos y muñecas*. In 2001, Velásquez was honored by the Texas House of Representatives for her achievements as an author of *Voces Latinas: Hispanic Reading Series for Young Adults* in Dallas. Velásquez resides in San Luis Obispo, California.

Alma Luz Villanueva was born in Lompoc, California, and was raised in the San Francisco area. She has held Writer-In-Residence positions at Cabrillo College, the University of California at Irvine, Stanford University, San Francisco State College, and the University of California at Santa Cruz. She currently lives in San Miguel de Allende, Mexico, and teaches Creative Writing at Antioch University, Los Angeles. Her books of fiction include *Ultraviolet Sky*, winner of the 1989 American Book Award, *Naked Ladies* (1994), and *Weeping Women: La llorona and Other Stories* (1994). Her poetry titles include *Planet, with Mother May I* (1993), *Mother, May I?* (1978), *Blood Root* (1977), *La Chingada* (1985), *Life Span* (1984), *Desire* (1998), *Luna's California Poppies* (2002), and *Vida* (2002).

Liliana Valenzuela was born and raised in Mexico City, Mexico. She is the poet of the collections *Bocas palabras* and *Mujer frontera, mujer malinche*. Valenzuela is the translator of *Caramelo* by Sandra Cisneros, *La conquista* by Yxta Maya Murray, *Latin Jazz* by Raúl Fernández, and *La yagüita del pastor* by Isaías Orozco-Lango.

Helena María Viramontes was born in East Los Angeles, California. Recipient of a National Endowment for the Arts Fellowship, Viramontes has collaborated with María Herrera-Sobek on two anthologies, *Chicana Creativity and Criticism: Creative Frontiers in American Literature* (1988) and *Chicana Writers: On Word and Film* (1995). She wrote a screenplay *Paris Rats in E.L.A.* that has been produced by the American Film Institute. Viramontes wrote *The Moths and Other Stories* (1985), *Under the Feet of Jesus* (1995) and her latest novel, *Their Dogs Came with Them* (2007). Viramontes is Professor of English at Cornell University.

Silviana Wood lives in Tucson, Arizona. She is the author of the winning play *And Where Was Pancho Villa When You Really Needed Him?* which was published in the anthology *Puro Teatro: A Latina Anthology* in 2000. She currently works as a bilingual actor, director, storyteller, and playwright.

About
The Chicano/Latino Literary Prize

THE CHICANO/LATINO LITERARY PRIZE was first awarded by the Department of Spanish and Portuguese at the University of California, Irvine during the 1974-1975 academic year. In the quarter-century that has followed, this annual competition has clearly demonstrated the wealth and vibrancy of Hispanic creative writing to be found in the United States. Among the prize winners have been —to name a few among many—such accomplished authors as Lucha Corpi, Graciela Limón, Cherríe L. Moraga, Carlos Morton, Gary Soto, and Helena María Viramontes. Specific literary forms are singled out for attention each year on a rotating basis, including the novel, the short-story collection, drama, and poetry; and first-, second-, and third-place prizes are awarded. For more information on the Chicano/Latino Literary Prize, please contact:

Contest Coordinator
Chicano/Latino Literary Contest
Department of Spanish and Portugese
University of California, Irvine
Irvine, California 92697